the mystery of the cache creek murders

Roberta Sheldon

[signature]

Published by Talkeetna Editions
in association with

PO Box 221974 Anchorage, Alaska 99522-1974

ISBN 1-888125-82-9

-

Library of Congress Catalog Card Number: 2001088467

Front cover photograph © Irene Owsley Spector
Maps by Talkeetna artist, Rob Holt

Manufactured in the United States of America.

dedication

to justice

table of contents

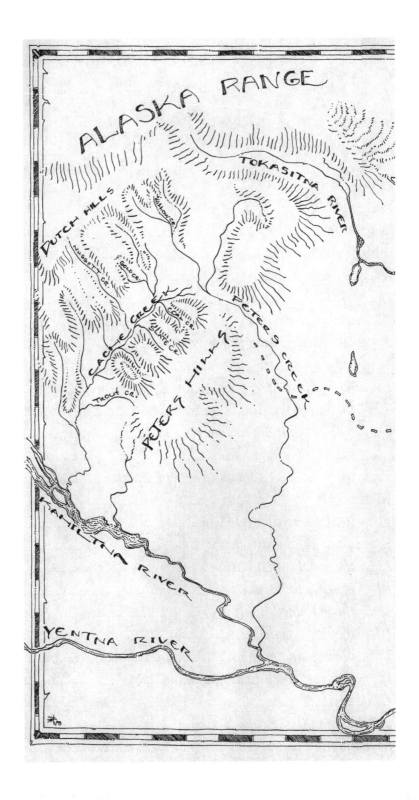

6

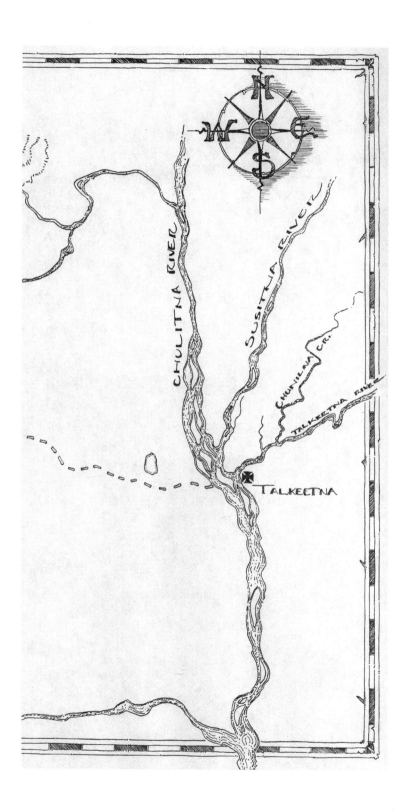

remarks and acknowledgements

The Cache Creek murders occurred long, long ago. Though the passage of time has all but erased these vicious acts and the furor that surrounded them from the collective memory, the evil of the deeds is not diminished. There is no statute of limitations on murder, and the same could be said for justice.

In late 1995 I published a book, *The Heritage of Talkeetna,* in which I recorded what little information was then available to me about the murders. As I moved through the lengthy research for this manuscript, it became clear to me that the earlier account contained certain flaws and, as a result, a degree of misinterpretation. I am glad to say that these have been corrected in this book.

I am deeply grateful to Dennis Garrett and Ron Wendt, without whom the scope of this book would simply not exist. Dennis served as my excellent guide in the Dutch Hills mining country and shared his lively story, contained in this book, about his experiences there. Of huge importance to the reader is his role in helping me access the investigative reports about the murders. Though I was initially informed that no records could be found, Dennis was able to provide me with proof that they existed. Although it took two long years to actually obtain these reports (a small story in itself), the documents were so vital to the integrity of an account of the Cache Creek murders, that perseverance was the order of my day.

Ron Wendt, a generous and gracious lifelong Alaskan, author, prospector, and the publisher of Goldstream Publications, patiently educated me about early-day placer mining in Alaska and cheerfully answered my many requests for detail. It was also my very good fortune that Ron should lead me to Maxine Brittell and Frank Sandstrom, other valuable sources for this book. Thank you so much, Ron.

I am equally grateful to Maxine Brittell, a remarkable Alaskan who provided me with her important memories of the summer of

1939 in the Dutch Hills, thereby contributing further integrity to this account. She also shared several important photographs found in these pages, and letters of special value to the story. My heartfelt thanks go to Maxine for her kindness and patient assistance.

My sincere thanks go to Frank Sandstrom, who also shared his important memories of the summer of 1939.

Were it not for June Berg, Dick Francis' niece, no photos of Francis would appear in this book. I am truly grateful to June for disturbing her private scrapbook to make them available to me. Her kindness will not be forgotten, and I deeply regret that she did not live long enough to read this book.

My grateful thanks also go to my kind friend Gale Weatherell, who shared his mother's memoirs with me. These give us insight into the times and provide a valuable first hand account following the murders. I am very appreciative of this contribution and of the great support Gale has shown me.

Ernie Bull's colorful first-person account of his employment at the Jenkins' mining operation adds even more substance to this story. Ernie was a wonderful correspondent, and it was with true sadness that I learned of his passing in 1997.

Special thanks to my wonderful editor, the dynamic Sondra Porter, who spent fall, winter, and spring days going over my manuscript with me, providing insights and a valuable perspective.

More special thanks go to John Carlson of Talkeetna, who was infinitely and cheerfully patient with my questions about various firearms and their intricacies. Also to Dave Johnston, who kindly provided me with a detailed distance log of the Petersville and Dutch Hills area.

Thanks to H. Willard Nagley II for contributing photos of his father. And to June Scheele for locating a photo of Ben Mayfield and other photographs.

And thanks to Evan Swensen for going that extra mile for me.

I also thank Dan Cuddy, The Mt. Shasta Herald, Phil Brandl, Eleanor Martin, Robert Sheldon, Mary McCrum and Anna Lou Levinson of the Talkeetna Public Library, Helen Dolenc, Doug Geeting, Frank O'Brien, Michelle Stevens, Lance Jordan, Special FBI Agent Brett Bray, Carol Young, Allan Dahl, Don Warden and Don Hanson of the Anchorage Memorial Park Cemetery, Bob Young, Penny Bloodhart, David Roberts, Kim Rich, Marthy Johnson, and Wayne Sivertson.

One name has been changed in this book to protect the privacy of that individual. This story is a reconstruction of events and representations wholly derived from public records, FBI investigative reports (a Freedom of Information Act release), court records, newspaper accounts, and interviews with individuals who knew the victims and certain people connected to the investigation. For the sake of narrative, some modest liberties have been taken by the author to enhance certain scenes, with great care taken to reflect probable and plausible conditions and circumstances. Certain statements depicted in a conversational format in the text are drawn from language contained in investigative reports; since this is data recorded by law enforcement officers in an unquoted form, these statements do not appear in quotation marks.

Depictions of weather and temperatures were drawn from actual records of the time. Portrayals of seasonal changes are based on my own knowledge and observations made during many years of residency in the Susitna River Valley.

It is my hope that the publication of this book might provide an important perspective unavailable until now, and touch on the ethereal nature of justice.

est fee for the comfort the place had afforded them. A code of trust and honor was well ingrained in the scattered mining community.

Certainly, every one of the six people in the large, dimly lighted room was worn out. Since May, each had worked ten-hour days for seven days each week. But each day had been important in the short Alaska mining season—better to work steadily through the season and catch up on rest and sleep in the winter.

Perhaps coincidentally, Christ Hansen happened to be at the road-house on the night that Frank and Helen Jenkins were there. Almost three years earlier, the trio had clashed in an Anchorage courtroom over Hansen's complaint that rock tailings and debris from the Jenkins' mining operation had washed down onto his claims, aggravating his efforts to work his ground. Though a judge eventually dismissed Hansen's complaint, the resentment between the miners had not dissipated, though it may have eased a bit during the ensuing years.

Christ Hansen, called Chris by everyone who knew him, was an amiable and soft-spoken sort of man, while Frank Jenkins was volatile and driven. Helen, Frank's wife, was petite, darkhaired, and known for her sharp tongue and excitability. Many people considered her to be eccentric, and some even thought her quite mad. Though each had appeared to tolerate the other's presence in the roadhouse this particular evening, tension seemed to hang in the air while the large stove whuffed and hissed with its load of split spruce, the wood occasionally crackling, spitting, and popping with heat.

A sturdy counter of rough-cut lumber ran along one side of the big room, with a string of stools along its length, but most of those present sat on crude chairs at or near a long table in the middle of the room. Jenkins and Bob McClanahan, a young worker he had employed that summer, sat there along with Frank Lee and another miner named Nick Balabanoff.

A big man, Balabanoff was Russian and had worked his claims on Nugget Creek in Cache Creek country for several years now. He was a naturalized American citizen, who still spoke with a heavy accent and was known along the creeks as The Galloping Russian. An inveterate walker, Balabanoff thought nothing of walking the 45 miles to Talkeetna when he ran out of snuff. Once he'd made his purchase, Balabanoff pocketed the little cans, turned around and walked back to his camp.

The table conversation had been agreeable enough until around nine o'clock when Frank Jenkins began to talk about Dick Francis. He bitterly complained to Frank Lee that Francis was "staking the whole country up around Willow Creek." Worse, he said, the miner's rock tailings were interfering with his own adjacent operations.

"There's no law that will allow a man to dump tailings on my ground like Francis is doing," Jenkins groused.

This was too much for Chris Hansen who, seated farther down the room, rose and walked to the end of the table and told Frank Jenkins, "You have been dumping tailings on my ground for the past four years and you think that's all right. But nobody can dump on your ground."

Frank Jenkins was out of his chair like a shot and leaped towards Hansen. With the agility of a kick boxer, he swung his foot in a high, wide arc at the miner's stomach but didn't quite reach him. "You liar!" he shouted.

Frank Lee saw Jenkins' leg go up in the air beside him and jumped to his feet to move between the men. .

"Boys, cut this out!" Lee yelled. "No fighting here, boys! If any fighting's to be done here, I will take a hand in it myself!" Lee grabbed Jenkins and held him tight.

Curses and shouts filled the room. Balabanoff would later testify that Jenkins called Hansen "a lot of vile names."

"They were all calling back and forth so many bad names, like 'son-of-a-bitch' and 'stinking skunk'—almost every kind of a name," Balabanoff said later.

But the most enraged person in the room was Helen Jenkins, and when she entered the fray the scene became chaotic. Screaming curses along with her husband, Helen ran from one side of the room to the other in an attempt to get close to Chris Hansen. Finally, she grabbed a stick of stove wood and started swinging it wildly at the miner. Both Frank Jenkins and Frank Lee shouted at her to put the wood down, but she kept at it until Bob McClanahan yanked it away and threw it on the floor. He took hold of Helen and told her, "Keep out of it. Keep still."

But Helen was incensed and broke free. This time she grabbed an empty quart bottle and tried to strike Chris Hansen.

"Let me get him! Let me get a lick at him!" Helen screamed. She began cursing again.

Once again Helen was subdued, and the bottle wrenched from her hand. At that point Frank Lee told Chris Hansen to follow him out of the building, and the two men left. Nick Balabanoff, who had stood almost motionless throughout the melee, followed them into the cold night air.

That night Lee, Hansen, and Balabanoff slept in the horse barn, and the Jenkinses and their employee remained in the roadhouse. Peters Creek whispered in the distance.

Everyone was up early the next morning. Muddy puddles of water around the roadhouse were plated with ice now, as were swampy areas nearby. A few dry, golden leaves still clung to big cottonwood trees near the trail, gleaming dully in the predawn light and rattling softly in a cold breeze. More brittle leaves fluttered in thick willow stands and alder bushes, stubbornly clinging to life. The intermittent and erratic rustle of dying vegetation was a lonely sound that spoke of the loss of summer.

"We all got our breakfast in the roadhouse, each cooking his own," Frank Lee would say later, "and then we all left. Not another word was said about the little argument the night before, which didn't amount to anything nohow."

Another mining season in Cache Creek country had ended.

————

The erosion of time, like wind and weather on a mountain gradient, has consigned the terrible, unresolved events to an almost forgotten past. If mention is made at all, the brutal killings are referred to as the "Cache Creek murders." Only certain elderly Alaskans, or someone interested in exploring the history of a small mountain group along the western boundary of the Susitna River Valley at the base of the great Alaska Range, can speak to the subject with any kind of familiarity.

Sixty years ago four gold miners lost their lives by diabolical means in the eastern part of the Dutch Hills, roughly four miles north and slightly east of Cache Creek, at three separate locations within a couple of miles of each other. The Dutch Hills lie amidst dramatic beauty, surrounded by relentlessly wild rivers and immense glaciers to the east and west, and the raw, rugged mountains of the Alaska Range to the north. Only a gifted wordsmith might do any sort of justice to a portrayal of this place which dates its origins to many millions of years ago, when the Pacific Plate forced itself into a series of violent encounters with the North American Plate. A close neighbor to the north is the massively regal Denali (Mt. McKinley), 55 million years old and the tallest mountain on the North American continent at 20,320 feet.

To the west of the Dutch Hills sprawls the monumental Kahiltna Glacier which empties into the braided, silt-laden river of the same name, and to the east lies the rough, rotting terminus of the vast Tokositna Glacier, which drains into its own wild and tangled Tokositna River. Both derive their names from indigenous Dena'Ina Indian designations, Kagheltna and Tuqashitnu. Framed by this powerful panorama, the Dutch Hills appear to be almost gentle and rolling, with elevations to around 4,000 feet. Situated in a roughly southwest to northeast direction, the mountains bear numerous small creeks along their southern flanks that eventually join one of two larger tributaries. One of these, Cache Creek, travels about twenty miles through a valley to empty into the Kahiltna River while the other, Peters Creek, moves southeasterly through the Peters Hills, another modest mountain group to the south of the Dutch Hills.

About equal in dimensions, both the Dutch and Peters Hills cradle Cache Creek, which flows between them in the valley that eventually acquired the informal name "Cache Creek country," probably because more active gold claims proliferated along this creek than anywhere else in that region. This characterization assumed such frequent use that when an Anchorage newspaper initially ran articles about the Dutch Hills murders in September, 1939, it identified the acts as having occurred in "the lonely mountains of Cache Creek country."

Mankind has always been willing, even eager, to trade loneliness for gold. And it was the search for gold that brought the first white Americans to the Susitna River Valley in Southcentral Alaska in the 1890s. Many years before, a few Russian expeditions had made brief explorations of the area but none lingered, probably because they lacked the means to finance any committed presence there. One of these Russians, a historian named Petroff, described the Susitna Valley at that time as a "sealed book." Information about the area was nonexistent and obtained only as the result of occasional encounters with the Dena'Ina Indians then frequenting the country. These native people were seminomadic and moved about the great valley between the Alaska Range to the north and west, and the dense Talkeetna Mountains to the east.

The Susitna is the dominant river of the entire valley, collecting water from all directions for ultimate conveyance to the south and to Cook Inlet. It was this watercourse the first prospectors used to travel north from the inlet to look for gold. Even prior to the Klondike gold rush, several adventurous groups were in the Susitna River Valley without maps or data of the region. All were shocked at the vicious assaults by dense swarms of mosquitoes. A prospector named William Dickey encountered one individual driven to his limit who told him he refused to look for gold in a country "where he was obliged to tie up his head in a gunnysack every night in order to escape the mosquitoes."

When the big news about the Klondike strike drew worldwide attention in 1897, the idea to research an all-American railroad route to the Yukon goldfields began to emerge. Three government-sponsored expeditions explored and mapped the Susitna Valley in 1898 and 1899. As their information about the region was made available, more and more prospectors traveled there to undertake a tough search for an elusive metal. They encountered raw wilderness with silty rivers as cold as the

site. A Dena'Ina hunter, Nakeet, lamented the decrease in the number of moose and caribou in the area, and attributed the scarcity to the presence of the work crews.

The A.E.C. activity quickly became an incentive for enterprising people to travel to Talkeetna, where they set up a variety of small businesses; a bunkhouse, bakery, and sawmill were established, and H.W. Nagley completed a large general store heavily stocked with his supplies. The Woodland Inn, Birch Roadhouse, and Imperial Cigar Store opened for business in crude log structures. Ambitious residents petitioned the Alaska Road Commission to construct a wagon road along Henry Bahrenburg's trail from Talkeetna to the Cache Creek diggings, and the agency responded by putting crews to work on several miles of rudimentary road.

The people at Talkeetna were a durable lot. Alaska was then a wild frontier country, and character and grit were essential. Most of those making up the A.E.C. work crews perceived their work as little more than a job and a paycheck, and left when the work was completed. But other individuals toughed it out and worked hard to establish an economic niche for themselves. Among these were two brothers named Frank and Ed Lee who arrived in Talkeetna in 1916. Strong and capable men in their late thirties and early forties, they had spent most of their lives in logging work, and some time in the Yukon freighting with dogs. When they learned that a new road would give access to the Cache Creek gold claims, the brothers spent what money they had on the purchase of some freighting horses, harnesses, and sleds, and went to work to haul food and supplies to the gold country.

In the late spring, when river levels were low and currents moderate, the men made the horses swim across to the trailhead on the west side of the Susitna River, where they would be staged for the summer months. Here the horses were hitched to sleds loaded with supplies, and the long, rugged trip to Cache Creek country began. The journey took five days, sometimes six if they visited all the claims; when the horses had been given a rest they headed back. Sometimes miners would pay to go along on the back-haul in order to conduct business and errands in Talkeetna, and Ed and Frank always returned to the settlement with more supply lists to be filled by Talkeetna merchants.

In the fall, when freeze-up threatened and the miners left their claims, the freight horses were made to swim back across to Talkeetna where the Lee brothers kept a log barn for them. There the horses enjoyed a good rest until late December or early January when the Susitna River froze solid. Then these tough and durable animals were hitched to supply-laden winter sledges and driven across the frozen river and on to the many trapper cabins in the area. In this way, the Lees were able to generate both summer and winter income. It was a tough way to make a living, but then, everything about this country was tough: the bitter cold, primitive living conditions, nasty insects, and wild, unforgiving terrain.

In 1917, a woman named Belle Grindrod arrived in Talkeetna, an unusual occurrence given the dominantly male environment there. Belle, in her late thirties, had abandoned an unhappy marriage in the states and spent a year in Alaska surviving on odd jobs. She had enough money to purchase a small log cabin on the banks of the Talkeetna River, and she did laundry and cooked meals for transients. She became acquainted with the Lee brothers and they spent time together discussing the needs of the miners at Cache Creek and the benefits of providing them with services.

Within a year, Belle and Ed Lee developed a serious relationship and married. Eventually these two would open the Talkeetna Trading Post where supplies were stocked and sold, and Belle cooked meals. For now, Belle did what work she could while Ed and Frank freighted the

Ed and Belle Lee, 1918. Belle operated the Talkeetna Trading Post for many years and once put up bail money for miner Frank Jenkins when he broke the law.

supplies to the miners and trappers throughout the year. They were hard workers and, along with merchant H.W. Nagley, probably the most committed business owners in the little village of Talkeetna.

Talkeetna was the image of the raw frontier town depicted throughout American history, the more so for its additional northern hardships. Despite these, those who cast their lot here developed a deep attachment to the north country.

In time, many others would come for the gold.

jenkins and francis

Among the men who entered the Susitna River Valley to search for gold in the early 1900s were two from California who traveled up the Susitna River in 1911 and 1914.

The first was Frank W. Jenkins, who was born on August 27, 1879, and appears to have spent his early years in southern California, probably at Monrovia, near Pasadena. Jenkins had two brothers and three sisters, but little is known about his parents. At age 19 or 20, almost certainly drawn by the fantastic stories of gold in the Klondike, an adventurous Jenkins journeyed to Alaska, far from the security of his home turf. But, like so many others who struggled that far north only to find virtually all of the good claims taken—along with a sea of disillusioned and unemployed humanity—he knew he had to change his plans.

In 1900, Frank Jenkins decided to hunt for gold in South America. For two years he explored and prospected in Columbia and near the reaches of the Amazon River, but finally gave up this venture too. We do not know if he departed with any gold, but he did leave with vivid memories of the Amazon.

In 1902, he returned to Alaska for good, this time to Nome, the new gold rush settlement that had all but emptied the Klondike town of Dawson in 1899. When Jenkins arrived, frontier lawlessness plagued the town. We don't know how long he remained there, or whether he found any gold, but by 1906, when production declined, Nome became another deserted gold rush town. Just when Jenkins left this area is unknown.

Jenkins most likely entered the Susitna River Valley in the spring or summer of 1911 and did some prospecting in Cache Creek country at that time. At the end of the year he purchased a cabin at Susitna Station, along the mouth of the Yentna River, and probably spent the remainder of the winter trapping for fur. A year later there is evidence that Frank Jenkins had made a connection of sorts with the ardent gold hunter named Al Stinson, who had been testing creek gravels in the area since 1905. A dozen years older than Jenkins, Stinson must have liked and trusted him because at the end of December, 1912, he recorded a Special Power of Attorney granting Jenkins the authority to "locate, stake, and record lode claims and placer mining ground in the Territory of Alaska" in Stinson's behalf.

This special legal power was widely used among prospectors who trusted and respected each other. Should one of the men discover good gold bearing gravels, he could stake claims near his own for those whom he trusted. This practice was most likely reciprocal, giving each man more chances to be in on a good discovery in the short span of time that the Alaskan summer allowed for the search. The document also allowed claim-related certificates to be signed, conveyed, and even sold if necessary. During an era when expeditious communications and transportation were nonexistent in remote Alaska, this special power of attorney provided an important tool for the serious prospector who was "out in the hills" for weeks at a time, unable to have contact with others when important mining business might need attention.

That Frank Jenkins had joined the ranks of committed prospectors like Stinson illustrates that he was definitely on the move, looking for gold.

He must have liked the country, or perhaps he found enough gold to sense that it held promise for him, because he didn't leave. In his early thirties now, Jenkins weighed about 135 pounds, was a slim and wiry 5 feet, 7 inches tall, and exuded strength, vitality, and drive. His healthy, light brown hair framed purposeful blue eyes in a disciplined face. Like most of the other men around Susitna Station, he trapped in the winter and spent frequent evenings listening to the others talk about the areas they had prospected. When spring arrived, he was among the first to get his outfit together—a heavy wood-framed pack, bedroll, frugal food supplies, miners' tools—and head to the Dutch and Peters Hills. Amazed at the virulent swarms of mosquitoes he encountered, he learned to attach a net to his hat that hung to his shoulders to spare his face, and to keep a smoke smudge kindled when he stopped to eat or spend the night.

Jenkins surely visited the extensive Cache Creek Mining Company operation which held active title to so many miles of claims along the creek. Here was a sawmill that furnished lumber for buildings, sluice boxes, flumes, and other needs, and rugged horses to drag in the logs for the mill from more heavily timbered country. Here were bunkhouses and cookshacks and storehouses and outbuildings. Low-grade lignite coal, abundant in the area, was arranged in piles for fuel for the equipment. Jenkins probably saw the miles of ditches that had been channeled into the hillsides to divert creek waters to a more desirable location; sixteen-inch and even 34-inch pipes, freighted in during the winter by horse-drawn sledges, were used to convey the water more precisely. It is entirely possible that he not only visited this big operation, but even worked there for a couple of seasons, observing and learning the essentials of the mining trade in Alaska.

When railroad construction activity began at Talkeetna in 1916 and it became certain that a source for food and mining supplies would be situated closer to the mining claims, Frank Jenkins prudently made the decision to shift his base to the new settlement. Many others from Susitna would join him, including Al Stinson, and these men became a part of the hustle and bustle of Talkeetna.

By 1918, Jenkins had become a member of the Talkeetna Commercial Club, an organization formed primarily to promote Talkeetna as the "supply headquarters for miners and prospectors from the Cache Creek, Iron Creek, and Broad Pass Districts." The ambitious group petitioned the federal government to improve the condition of the Cache Creek trail, to construct three shelter cabins along the trail's length, to provide mail service to the mines, and to install a telephone cable across the Susitna River and on to the mining area. These people were all business, even to the extent that they imposed a fine of twenty-five cents on any member who arrived late at one of the club's meetings.

While the Talkeetna group worked to gain government sanction for mining support services, it focused most heavily on a crusade to persuade federal authorities to place the newly platted Talkeetna townsite lots on the market. A petition to that effect, signed by fifty residents—including Frank, Ed, and Belle Lee, and merchant H.W. Nagley—also bore the name of F.W. Jenkins. Then, in early 1919, railway construction was completed to Talkeetna and the frontier town was solidly linked to transportation and supplies. In October of that year, the land sale was approved and the Alaska Engineering Commission auctioned off eighty lots in the new town. While Nagley bought fourteen lots and Frank Lee two, Jenkins' name did not appear on the list of purchasers. He possibly had already found a place to live in the little townsite or needed what money he had to finance his prospecting ventures.

Records show that Jenkins was probing the Dutch Hills. In December of that year he filed a mining declaration that signified his interest in certain placer claims located along the hills' eastern slopes. He recorded two claims on Little Willow Creek, and others along Rocky, Snowshoe, Falls, and Slate Gulches. He also declared an interest in five quartz mining claims near Bird Creek that he named Three Star Quartz, Three Bar, Gold Saddle, Blue Bird, and Good Hope.

The following year Jenkins filed the federally required Proof of Labor declaration that reflected each miner's performance on his claims. This recorded statement served to confirm claim ownership each year, and to verify that various improvements had been made to the property, an obligation mandated by the government in exchange for ongoing ownership. Jenkins testified that his work had consisted of "general mining, developing, and the making of repairs necessary in the operation of said claims...." His expenses and labor had amounted to $1,200 in value, he said. This declaration still listed the placer claims at the Willow Creek location, but the quartz mining claims near Bird Creek were absent. As the year 1920 drew to a close, Frank Jenkins, now age 41, seemed well established in the mining environment of "the lonely mountains of Cache Creek country."

Richard Allen Francis was another Californian that ventured north alone. Born on January 23, 1879, in Lumpkin Mills, Butte County, in northern California, he was just seven months older than Frank Jenkins. Francis had two sisters, Margarite and Caroline, and a brother named Isaac. There is some evidence that his father was involved in mining activity in Butte County, but at some point the close-knit family moved to Mount Shasta, where work was available in the lumber mills. After finishing school young Francis, popularly known as Dick, found work where he could. There is evidence that he spent time in Oroville and Siskiyou County, but as he entered his third decade his thoughts must have turned to the north country. He had read about Alaska and thought about adventure and gold, and began to save his money. Finally, in August of 1913, he headed north to Seattle at the age of 34.

Francis was a healthy man who stood 5 feet, 9 inches, on a 150 pound frame. His dark hair encircled an attractive, rather sculptured face that featured an angular nose and clear blue eyes. He was a friendly and congenial man, and one who could unmistakably watch out for himself. In Seattle he boarded a steamship bound for Seward, Alaska, and left the states behind him.

The Territory of Alaska was everything Francis had hoped it to be. No record indicates where he spent that first winter in Alaska, but the following summer he found his way up the Susitna River to where it junctured with the Yentna. At Susitna Station he heard the men talk about the Cache Creek area where men were finding enough gold to make their work worthwhile. He learned that most of the good prospects on Cache Creek itself were already held by the Cache Creek Mining Company and others, but he was assured that there was plenty of unprospected ground in the area for a man who was willing to work. Francis set out to look for himself.

Like all the others, he made the long, tough journey from Susitna Station over the many rugged miles of forest, swamps, creeks, and hills to the mineralized valley where Cache Creek rushed. He probably packed the length of the creek over a period of days, stopping along the way to visit with men on their claims, who likely offered him coffee and a bowl of beans from pots most of them kept simmering on wood stoves. He saw how the simple one-man, pick-and-shovel operation worked, with a home-made sluice box, sometimes constructed from a hollowed-out cottonwood tree trunk, set right in the creek. The men shoveled the gravels into the box, and the stream washed the rocky debris on through, while any gold sank and lodged in the handmade riffles placed in the bottom of the box for that purpose. Francis observed that most of the men lived in crude tents, for they would be here only for the short summer months.

Then Francis came upon the Cache Creek Mining Company operation and saw its ambitious investments that illustrated more tangibly than anything else that gold was in the region. He probably visited a bit with the men and observed the methods employed at the company camps up and down the creek, then shouldered his outfit and moved along.

Francis kept moving to the northeast until he had reached Peters Creek, where more independent claim holders were hard at work. He spent some time watching their operations, shared coffee with them, and then hoisted his heavy pack and continued in his eastern direction. To his left, the Dutch Hills sloped in alluring beauty, and when he stopped to rest, he surely couldn't help but gaze in that direction. But he must have heard about activity at Long Creek, which was still farther east, because that's where he headed. As Francis retraced the path of the original gold seekers in the reverse direction, he occasionally stopped to test various creek waters for traces of gold.

When he finally emerged from the valley at a high elevation, he could gaze over to Long Creek which descended several miles from the eastern limit of the Dutch Hills to join with the great glacier-fed Tokositna River. And, as he moved along, he must have been stunned to see the dramatic scene that emerged to the north. There, the mammoth expanse of Denali dominated a transcendental landscape that extended to the vast Tokositna Glacier and a myriad of rugged peaks in the foreground. It was magnificent, wild country, the like of which he'd never seen in his life.

That season Dick Francis spent the long northern daylight hours prospecting in the Long Creek area, and during this time got to know and like Al Stinson. He learned that the older prospector, along with three other men, held title to several placer claims on the creek that they called the Portland Association Group. That Stinson was involved with ground here must have reinforced Francis' interest in the area, and Francis spent time talking with him about what chance he might have to succeed there.

That Francis gained Stinson's trust and approval became evident that September when Stinson offered him an interest in the Portland Group. One senses that Francis accepted eagerly, because at the end of the month he and Stinson recorded a deed that granted Francis a substantial interest in the ground. Francis paid the men $100 for this investment, and since it was his first real commitment to mining in Alaska, he must have felt some excitement when he held the deed in his hand.

Francis embraced everything Alaskan with great enthusiasm. That first winter in the Susitna River Valley he learned to deal with the bitter cold that could drop to 30 and 40 below zero and to make the best use of just six hours of daylight during most days in December and January—months of darkness that challenged a man's character. He learned to dress well in woolen pants and shirts and to buy boots in sizes too large so that he could wear several pair of wool socks in them. He almost certainly did some trapping and sold his pelts to H.W. Nagley who, besides serving as the primary merchant at Susitna Station, also functioned as a fur buyer for the big fur exchanges in Seattle. And it is quite probable that at some point in time Dick Francis made the acquaintance of Frank Jenkins, either at Susitna Station or on the trail while trapping or prospecting.

For the next couple of years, Francis diligently worked the Long Creek claims, occasionally writing home to Mount Shasta, and even sending along some photographs that illustrated elements of his new life in Alaska. In 1915, he mailed off a picture of three friends posing alongside a cabin, the roof of which is composed of raw, unpeeled, whipsawed lumber. A large grizzly hide, covering almost an entire wall, is nailed to the cabin, providing a brawny backdrop for the men who look self-sufficient and pleased with this moment in their lives. Their rifles are prominently displayed, attesting to their value to the men. On the back of the photograph Francis remarked, "Some of my pals. Man in center is my pardener."

Francis had obviously learned one of the most important lessons of the north country in the early 1900s: regardless of how capable and self-reliant a man was, life in Alaska often imposed unpredictable calamity. A partner doubled one's chance for aid or survival in a remote area in a bad situation. If a man met with trouble out on the

In 1915, Dick Francis sent this photo to his mother in California. On the back he wrote, "Some of my pals. Man in center is my pardener." (courtesy June Francis Berg)

trapline and didn't return as scheduled, his partner went looking for him. A partner shared the back-breaking work on a mining claim and helped with the cooking and other chores; with two at work, more got accomplished in a shorter time. And during the winter on the trapline, when the days were so cold, dark, and short, it was nice to have the company of another human being to temper aloneness.

In 1916, Dick sent a picture of a heavily furred, malamute dog with a friendly face to his mother in Mount Shasta. His handwriting on the back explained the dog's identity: "Old Knik, My favorite, and one of the best dogs in the country." In the same letter, he included a winter photo of himself standing in front of a rough-hewn cabin; snowshoes, a wooden packframe, washtub, and sundry other items are attached to or leaning against the modest structure, which was almost certainly his trapping cabin. Though there is no evidence that he ever joined the Talkeetna Commercial Club or signed any of its petitions, Francis had probably by now shifted his attention to the Talkeetna area, when that location became more convenient for supplies.

In 1917, Francis revealed his bent for adventure. Photos he sent to California included one of a Fort Yukon boat guide standing by a riverbank somewhere along the Yukon River in interior Alaska. Francis' caption explained: "Native pilot at Fort Yukon. Hired him at Stevens Village. He was a dandy too." Francis had apparently been over 450 miles north of Talkeetna, just south of the massive Brooks Range. Absent his letters, it's not clear what he was doing this far north or how long he spent in the area, but it is without question that it had been a rugged challenge for him to make it that far when boat or horseback travel were the sole means of transportation in the Alaska wilderness. Was he looking for gold? Perhaps, but maybe he settled for adventure. Another 1917 photograph surely connected to this trip, shows Dick Francis standing atop a rocky ridge, surrounded by a sweeping complex of mountains. On this one he wrote, "How do I look on top of Range, Some view from here."

But Francis' heart seemed to rest in the Talkeetna area where, at the end of the year, he met his 1917 and 1918 mining obligations by recording declarations for his claims on Long Creek. To these, he added a new claim called Bertha Placer Claim on Canyon Creek. Francis was branching out now and apparently had found promising "colors" on this small tributary that flowed into Long Creek from the eastern end of the Dutch Hills.

At the end of April, 1919, when heavy snows were not yet gone from Cache Creek country, Dick Francis traveled to Anchorage, probably on the new Alaska Railroad. Perhaps he went there to conduct business of some sort, or to locate some piece of mining equipment he needed. Age 40 now, he somehow became involved in an altercation that left him with a broken arm. Angry enough to hire a lawyer, Francis filed charges with the Anchorage District Court against a man named James Wilkinson who, he complained, "wantonly, brutally, and maliciously assaulted" him. Wilkinson had "struck and beat him" with a pair of blacksmith tongs, Francis protested, and had "seriously wounded and bruised" him by breaking his left forearm. As a result, he had been left "sick and sore and unable to attend to his business."

Francis complained that Wilkinson had caused damages to him in the amount of $750. He maintained that his adversary had been "animated solely by malice, hatred, animosity, and ill-will," and had assaulted him "for the purpose of gratifying such malice." Therefore, he contended, he should receive an additional $750 for punitive damages. He and his lawyer asked for $1,500, plus payment of Francis' attorney fees.

Three weeks later, James Wilkinson responded that he had "acted in self-defence (sic), and to prevent bodily injury was compelled to repel an attack contemplated by (Francis)." He went on to say that

Dick Francis, 1917, in a photo he sent to California with the notation, "How do I look on top of range. Some view from here." (courtesy June Francis Berg)

Francis' allegations were "not being founded on facts," and asked the court to dismiss the case.

The case was not dismissed that summer, and when snow was on the ground in November, Wilkinson, now represented by an attorney, filed a new response with the court. He said that he had been employed as a blacksmith for the Alaska Engineering Commission in Anchorage and, while engaged in his duties at his workplace, Francis had "assaulted him and would have struck and knocked him into the fire if he had not defended himself and necessarily committed the act complained of."

The few pages that exist in this aged case file reveal only the story about the dispute. Further research provides no clue as to the ultimate finding of the court.

In April of 1920, Dick Francis joined with a man named Fell to file four new claims on Long Creek which they called Knik placer claims. They also recorded a Notice of Location of Water Rights that allowed them to divert water from Long Creek to the Knik claims by means of a hand-dug ditch.

Water was a critical component of the placer mining conducted in Cache Creek country because it was needed to wash gold-bearing gravels (paydirt) through sluice boxes to entrap the gold. In the earliest days of this mining region, many of the men had simply set their sluice boxes in a creek and shoveled the gravel in by hand, a rugged, laborious process that restricted them to the immediate

Dick Francis lived on his mining claims in the summer and his trapline during winter. He's shown here at his trapping cabin around the early 1920s. Francis vowed that he would never leave Alaska "unless I have a round-trip ticket." (courtesy June Francis Berg)

site. But good prospects weren't always near water, and some way had to be found to deliver the vital flow. Men, like Francis and his associates, dammed nearby creeks and forced the water through hand-dug ditches in the desired direction, often for distances of a mile and more. To ensure the authority to make use of a particular creek, they filed for water rights in much the same way that they filed on mineral claims.

Dick Francis was a "hand miner," engaged in some of the most labor-intensive activity on the creeks. It was all pick-and-shovel work and ditch digging, just as it was for other hand miners who had neither the money nor ambition to invest in more aggressive, labor-saving equipment. But one shift had been made away from the "old days." Instead of devoting a tremendous amount of labor to any spot where some "color" had been found, the prospector became more selective about where his hard work would be invested. Extended prospecting in search of a consistent, high-grade pay streak now took priority and, in the long run, provided for more effective production.

By the time 1920 drew to a close, Dick Francis, like Frank Jenkins, had become well established in the Cache Creek mining country, albeit much farther to the east than most other miners. And in one of his letters to Mount Shasta, he declared that he "would never leave Alaska unless I have a round trip ticket."

searching for the pay streak

In the early 1920s, the Alaska Road Commission worked to improve the trail from Talkeetna to Cache Creek and completed nine miles of "wagon road" and more than thirty miles of "sled road." Talkeetna's railroad link with Anchorage, the expanding town 115 miles to the south, enabled more and more people to access Talkeetna and the adjacent mining district. In 1921 almost two thousand people traveled the primitive road to the Cache Creek area and points beyond. Over one thousand wagons, horse-drawn sleds, and pack horses facilitated the movement of 778 tons of gear, equipment and supplies that year. Prospectors were moving into the Dutch Hills now, even over to Ramsdyke Creek which flowed through some of the wildest country in the area to the Tokositna River. The Ramsdyke Creek Mining Company formed in 1921 and began to work twenty-two placer claims there, spending close to $5,000 to haul supplies and lumber, build flumes and sluice boxes, erect pipeline, clean ditches and trails, and sluice gold bearing gravels. This was an ambitious venture considering the logistical challenges presented by the remote and rugged terrain.

Dick Francis continued to work his claims on Long and Canyon Creeks, and in June of 1922, he filed a Proof of Labor declaration that evidenced his addition of two more claims on Canyon Creek. Heightened interest in the area and the increasing numbers of people entering the district may have been encouraging to men like Francis and Jenkins, who had been around now for several years. Improved services and availability of supplies, stimulated by the growing demand for them, surely eased the toil and exertion connected with their efforts in the rugged country they traveled.

The increased activity also produced a level of intrigue; for where gold and men exist, it is said, so does chicanery. An example of how some gold seekers were capable of behaving was illustrated when the Cache Creek Mining Company decided to move its huge gold dredge machine a considerable distance from one part of Cache Creek to another of its holdings farther north. Originally barged to the area unassembled several years earlier, and then hauled in by forty freight horses, the dredge's massive assembled bulk necessitated some travel over ground that wasn't held by the company. When word of this plan circulated, the wiles of unscrupulous and lazy men began to emerge. Dorothy Wolfe recorded some of these antics after she interviewed miners who had been in Cache Creek country at the time.

"Many are the tales told about how the miners tried to extract money from the (Cache Creek Mining) Company by having a claim staked on the creek and refusing to permit the dredge's passing until the claim was bought at the miner's price. One miner discovered a fraction of a claim that ran out into Cache Creek. Here he erected his tent and set his claim posts. The dredge operator was amazed to see a tent almost in mid-stream. He told the miner to move the tent and his stakes, but the miner was adamant in wanting his price. Angrily, the operator tore out the tent and drove over the posts. Hot words were exchanged but nothing else."

Wolfe related another incident that occurred during this time: "At another place near the mouth of Nugget (Creek) a bonafide claim was left by the owner in care of a friend who was to (act as caretaker) for the owner. Knowing that if left alone the diggings would go back to open ground, the friend let the (improvement work) slide. Then he and another miner staked the claim at midnight for themselves. The two men were bought off with $1,000 so the dredge could pass. Back came the outraged owner who saw to it he received the money that his dishonest pal had tried to cheat him out of."

Intrigue was not confined to the mining district, but extended to Talkeetna as well. Frontier isolation and tough living conditions have historically created a market for alcohol, and the new village showed no sign of deviating from the pattern. But the Alaska Dry Law, which prohibited the sale of liquor at this time, was actively enforced by the law in Talkeetna. When a U.S. deputy marshal named Young asked for a search warrant to inspect the property of a local resident suspected of violating the law, the local U.S. commissioner issued the authority to investigate. Young's target was Belle Lee.

Belle and Ed Lee, both in their early forties, had been married for five years now. Ed, with chiseled, movie star looks, wavy brown hair, and a dark mustache, presented a dashing appearance. He was almost exclusively involved with the freighting of supplies to Cache Creek country and encountered his share of experiences along the trail. Once, while leading a string of heavily laden pack horses to the various camps along Cache Creek, he was startled by the behavior of his lead mare who began to act in a disturbed and erratic manner. Amid the dense swarms of mosquitoes and flies that continually tracked the horses, the mare stamped and snorted in alarm, and the effect began to spread. Dorothy Wolfe describes the incident:

"The rest of his pack train were catching the near panic fever, but their heavy packs and trail-weary legs kept them from stampeding, although they did trot grotesquely from the trail. Ed's main thought was for his pack train. Seeing that the lead mare had stopped and had turned facing the camp, and thinking a bear had spooked her, Ed snaked his trail gun forward for a quick shot. Then he saw the huddled form lying near the cabin. Stepping as quickly from his saddle as his stiff muscles would respond, Lee straddled to the prone figure. Gently, Lee turned the face upward. Billy Peterson's dead eyes started unseeingly up into Ed Lee's startled ones. As near as he could figure, Billy had been dead several days."

Lee was aware that Peterson had been among the group that had first discovered the gold along Cache Creek in 1905, and that he was well respected in the mining district. Now, he guessed, the old miner's life had finally run its course. He covered the lifeless man with a blanket, calmed his nervous pack horses, and continued along the creek to spread the word of Billy's death. Everyone stopped their work and proceeded to Peterson's camp where they built a coffin from his sluice boxes, placed Billy in it, and buried him on a hill overlooking his discovery claim. A sense of community, based on need, trust and respect, was emerging in the mining district.

Belle Lee was hard-working and industrious, with light brown hair pulled away from her face and secured in a chignon at the back. Her features were full and fair and her eyes direct and alert, and one could sometimes sense in them a quality that spoke of hard times overcome. For herself, Belle seemed to sense that people succeeded by work and deed alone, and her activities in Talkeetna revealed the presence of a sage entrepreneur. At the west end of town near the river, Belle and Ed had acquired a log structure that Belle turned into a modest roadhouse that provided meals and bunk space. Nearby, she kept chickens and geese for meat and eggs and worked a large, productive garden in the summertime. In close proximity to these were the stable and work-shops that Frank and Ed Lee maintained for the freighting business. Belle was fond of the horses, and one woman claimed that she had a different name for each chicken in her large flock. Belle was always busy, and now, in 1922, was suspected of involvement in a side venture to supplement a meager frontier income.

Deputy Marshal Young's search warrant declared that information had been received "under oath" that Belle had "intoxicating liquor" in her possession, and was selling it from her premises. The warrant noted that this was in violation of the Alaska Dry Law which had been approved by Congress in 1917, and that Young had cause to search "a certain log house, tent, and cache ... known as Belle Lee pool room and restaurant and lodging house..." at the west limit of the new town-site, near the Talkeetna River. When he had finished there, the warrant advised, he was to search the Lees' own residence and an adjacent cache that were located just south of the first set of structures.

"You are therefore commanded to make immediate search of said log house and tents and buildings adjoining and appurtenant, also make search of the Lee residence as described above, and if you find any intoxicating liquor or things used in the manufacture of the same to bring them to me," the commissioner ordered.

It's not clear if Young's search yielded anything of value, or if charges were ever filed against Belle. The outcome of the deputy marshal's investigation is relegated to the past because, like many other old papers from the territorial days of the early 1900s, documents pertaining to cases like Belle's were either destroyed as time passed or disposed of in a manner that thwarts research or recovery. The old, handwritten pages of this particular search warrant are singular and water stained, the result of lying for decades in an old shed with a leaky roof in Talkeetna where they were found. They are but another clue to the rugged, early days of Talkeetna.

———

In August of 1923, Dick Francis branched out again. On the first day of the month he filed a Notice of Location for a claim on Quartz Creek, another small tributary of Long Creek. Francis spent twenty-three days prospecting here, digging water-collection ditches, and sluicing gravel on the 330-foot by 1,320-foot tract that he named the Hazel mining claim. When he returned to Talkeetna he filed the required Proof of Labor form, attesting to the work and improvements he had completed. This was acknowledged and recorded by the merchant H.W. Nagley, who had attained the position of U.S. commissioner at Talkeetna in 1921; among other official duties the commissioner acted as the recording agent for all the mining activity in the area.

Hard working and efficient, Nagley was well respected in the village of Talkeetna. His family, wife Jessamine and baby son, H. Willard II, were now well established and lived near the Talkeetna River in an attractive log home. Mr. Nagley, as most everyone called him, played many roles in the area. In addition to his function as a government official, he was a leading merchant that sold food and supplies, traded fur, and frequently grubstaked gold seekers to a summer's worth of supplies and gear. Such an advance was made with the hope that the prospector would locate good gold-bearing gravels and assign a part of the value of the claim to the grubstaker. Nagley (and eventually, Belle Lee) often counted it luck if the prospector just found enough gold dust to pay for the food and supplies; if poor judgement had been exercised in gauging a man's character or knowledge of prospecting, the value of the stake became a loss. Mr. Nagley was a man who chose carefully.

In October, a few months after Francis had worked Quartz Creek, Frank Jenkins signed an agreement with two brothers named Hatch and another man named Rice. The arrangement allowed Jenkins to work their claim called No. 1 on Gopher Gulch (which held a tributary of Willow Creek) beginning the next spring. Gopher Gulch was in the same area that Jenkins had staked

H.W. Nagley, leading Talkeetna merchant and fur buyer, also served as U.S. Commissioner and the village's postmaster. Shown here at a Cache Creek gold clean-up in 1929, with miner Jim Murray. (Courtesy H. Willard Nagley II)

his other claims several years earlier along Willow Creek, so this section of the Dutch Hills continued to hold his attention. The men agreed that Jenkins would pay them a royalty of 10 percent on any gold he found if the total value extracted was under $10,000; should the value exceed that, Jenkins would pay a royalty of 15 percent. According to the agreement Jenkins could mine portions of the claim by hydraulic methods, an indication that he was growing more sophisticated and efficient about his mining procedures.

Jenkins was tired of being a hand miner. He knew that the faster more quantities of paydirt could be moved, the more gold could be recovered. The hydraulic method of mining yielded this result when water was moved down through a series of size-graduated pipe casings that caused the water pressure to build up and finally emerge with great force through a hose and hydraulic nozzle called a "giant." The giant then directed the pressurized water to wash away vast amounts of overburden (earth and small rocks) to expose the gold-bearing gravels and bedrock beneath, where the gold was most concentrated. Eventually the giant washed the gravels on through sluice boxes where the gold was trapped and unwanted gravels, called tailings, were discarded. The system also blasted the tailings out of the way to permit more material to pass.

Tremendous amounts of gravel could be processed in this manner, and Jenkins obviously felt ready to advance to this level of gold production. The hydraulic miner, however, shared the same vital need as the hand miner. Without water a man could not mine, and for those at a higher altitude, as Jenkins now was, the opportunity to trap water was more reduced than at the lower elevations. But Jenkins started work on an extended network of water-collection ditches, and rose to the challenge.

Something else about Jenkins' new agreement was significant to his life but had nothing to do with mining. The document included the signature of a woman named Helen Jenkins who acted as a witness to the signing. Now married to Frank, Helen was in her early thirties, some ten years younger than her husband. She was a slender, almost petite woman, 100 pounds in weight, and 5 feet, 3 inches in stature. She wore her light brown hair cut short and parted in the middle, allowing it to fall in a line about her face which carried features that one observer described as "plain looking." But Helen's demeanor was anything but commonplace; she harboured a strong personality, an excitable disposition, and tended to be scrappy when she felt it necessary. Other personality traits caused various people to view her as "different." Some even thought her quite odd.

No records reveal just where or when Frank got to know Helen, whose given name was Zella Helena. Possibly they met in Anchorage, or Jenkins, after several years in Alaska, traveled Outside (stateside) at some time and became acquainted with her there. In any case, he and Helen had recently married and begun an intensely loyal partnership. Two months after Jenkins signed the Gopher Gulch agreement, the two appeared in Seattle where Frank visited an attorney's office and drew up a will, naming Helen as the sole beneficiary of his estate and the executrix of his will upon his death. Maybe this trip filled a multiple purpose; perhaps the two were journeying to meet with relatives, or Jenkins was inspecting specialized mining equipment and arranging for its shipment to Alaska. A combination of these, together with a honeymoon of sorts, is not implausible.

Sometime during this period Dick Francis again found time for adventure. This time he teamed up with the freighter, Frank Lee, and two other men. Later, a young Talkeetna Trading Post freighting assistant named Wes Harriman would listen to Frank Lee reminisce about this trip with Francis.

"I guess nothing seemed impossible to him," Harriman said. "He told me about taking a trip to the Arctic in the early twenties. He bought a boat with a motor and loaded in on the Alaska Railroad to Nenana. He told me that Dick Francis, a fellow named McKinnon and a fellow named McGregor went with him. They put in at the Nenana River and went from there to the Yukon, and then up the Porcupine (River). Then they walked over the Endicott Range and clear down to the Arctic Ocean. I remember Frank telling about Dick Francis shooting a caribou when they was coming back over the Endicott Range. He told how big that herd was; it went on for hours and hours and hours across this river. Dick Francis had shot a caribou for meat for the camp, and to carry with them before they got (back) to the boat. I guess they were looking for something that was outstanding, or gold, or something besides adventure. That was quite a trip for them, but I guess it was a hurried trip because the season isn't very long above the Endicott Range.

"Dick Francis always looked the part of the prospector," Harriman said. "He always wore side arms, always carried a gun in his holster. I never knew for what reason; perhaps he had reasons of his own. I think a lot of prospectors that were alone and way out carried a six-gun for their own protection against bears, and perhaps against injuries they might have where it might become a hopeless situation. They'd have that side arm with them to take care of themselves. But Dick was a very congenial sort of fellow ... and likable. Everybody liked him."

In the spring of 1924 Jenkins was back in Alaska and prepared to mine in earnest in the Dutch Hills. Gopher Gulch was situated at about the 2,700 foot elevation along a southeastern slope of the hills in a pure, alpine environment. Here, above tree line, visibility was unhindered and sounds carried for miles. Frank and Helen most likely traveled to their site early, sometime in April, as extensive preparatory work had to be done before the snows completely left in early June. Snow needed to be cleared at strategic locations to hasten ground thawing, and mechanical equipment had to be set up in working condition, ready to perform. Sluice boxes needed to be inspected, repaired, or replaced, and the entire camp put in working order. Frank and Helen probably made do with modest living quarters, most likely a canvas wall tent with a wood frame and plank floor. The untimbered elevation also required that they haul in some firewood to supplement the low-grade coal found in the area, to take the edge off the cool spring nights and to fuel the wood cookstove.

When June arrived, the surrounding country burst into the early stages of verdant growth, accompanied by vibrant sound. The haunting call of the golden-crowned sparrow began to mingle with the cheery song of its white-crowned cousin as they searched out nesting sites in the dense alder patches farther down from Gopher Gulch. Parka squirrels, having already emerged from their long hibernation in early May, chirped and scampered among the heavy new grasses that began to blanket the hills. Along the creeks ferns unfurled among shoots of sedge, glacier flower, and leafing scrub willow. Both Willow and Little Willow Creeks, now released from winter dominance, descended from the Dutch Hills near the Gopher Gulch mining site, producing a stirring murmur that lent background to the insistent sounds of new life that arose everywhere—not the least of which was the ubiquitous mosquito.

Approximately five wilderness miles to the east, Dick Francis worked the many claims he had an interest in on Long, Canyon, and Quartz Creeks. Because some mining records were lost to fire in Talkeetna in the 1920s, it is not possible to identify which claims he focused on this summer of 1924. But he was certainly involved in "sluicing, ditching and general prospecting for the pay streak," language he favored and had included in his most recent Proof of Labor records. Here, at the somewhat lower elevations, Francis contended with thick concentrations of alder and willow, and a denser tangle of vegetation. While breezes at the higher elevations helped to check mosquito swarms to a modest degree, here at the lower levels the insects massed inexorably. Smoke smudges and mosquito nets were still the favored means of resistance, and Francis used them. Whether Francis worked alone or was aided by a partner is not known, but he was on-site and continuing his quest for gold.

In late 1925, an article appeared in an Anchorage newspaper called *The Alaska Weekly*. Its title, "Cache Creek District Enjoyed The Banner Year In Production Of Gold," was eye-catching, and led to columns that offered more good news:

> The Cache Creek mining district will this season produce not less than $225,000, according to a care-

ful estimate of a well-informed operator of that camp, making the biggest production in the history of that placer field since its discovery.... And what is more, according to this same authority, the next season will show a still greater increase in the production of raw gold, and the time is not far distant when Cache Creek will be one of the major placer producers, for individual miners, in the Northland. This belief is predicated on the discovery of other and deeper paystreaks, and also to the fact that the Alaska Railroad and the Alaska Road Commission have greatly lessened the heretofore heavy transportation costs. The heaviest gold producer in the district is the Cache Creek Mining company's dredge, operating on Cache Creek, with a total yield this season of $150,000.

The article went on to identify eleven individuals in the mining district that had done particularly well, and among these it was noted: "Frank Jenkins had a good season on Gopher Creek, a tributary of Willow Creek."

That same year a U.S. Bureau of Mines engineer filed a detailed placer mining report that included these remarks: "Cast and Mack had a good season hydraulicking on Poorman Creek, as did Frank Jenkins on Willow Creek just above the canyon, where he mined light gravel averaging five feet in depth.... The operations on Poorman and Willow Creeks have used only the local water, which is usually a very small supply necessitating impounding and using it in short, intermittent splashes...."

These public indicators that Frank Jenkins was enjoying some success for his hard work may have pleased him but might have perturbed him too. He and Helen were private people and, like most miners, not particularly eager to advertise the value of their holdings. Through the coming years, they would gain an identity that cast them as distrustful, somewhat cynical, and not very social. Both seemed quite content to rely on the self-contained existence they were fashioning for themselves, and together they conveyed an attitude that emphasized the stamina and strength of character to sustain it. According to more than one source Helen was so devoted to their alliance that she would get down in the mining pits alongside Frank and work like a man.

Life was not good for one Talkeetna resident, the freighter Ed Lee. In June of 1928 he shot himself at The Landing, the name people had attached to the Cache Creek trailhead, across the Susitna River from Talkeetna. Some said Lee had taken his life because he drank too much, but others said he had a terminal illness, possibly throat cancer. Regardless, his death was unsettling to many and a shock to his wife, Belle, and his brother, Frank Lee. Just a couple of years earlier Ed and Belle had opened the Talkeetna Trading Post which stocked all the fundamental supplies needed by miners and trappers, a logical complement to the freighting operation the Lee brothers had engaged in. The responsibility now fell to Belle to carry the business burden, and Frank Lee responded with as much help and support as he could give her, primarily by continuing with the freighting to Cache Creek country.

Talkeetna in the 1920s. Postmaster H.W. Nagley, the man in the middle, speaks with a customer who has just loaded his dog team sled with supplies from Nagley's store (left), which also housed the village post office. Tom Weatherell, store clerk, is on the left. (Courtesy H. Willard Nagley II)

In early 1929, one of Frank Jenkins' brothers joined him at Talkeetna. This event suggests that Frank was doing so well that he needed some help, and may have written to Ray Jenkins in California, asking him to work at the mine. Slight in stature like his brother, Ray had also grown up in California and knew machinery and work. In late March, in anticipation of the approaching season, Frank, Helen, and Ray drew up a contract agreement that identified each as a partner with the others in mining five claims on Willow Creek, one on Ruby Creek, the claim on Gopher Creek, and another on Puzzle Gulch. It was agreed that Frank and Helen would advance the money for the equipment and claim costs, and that Ray would work off his share. Frank Jenkins retained full authority to manage all the business of the mining venture, and to retrieve the project's initial costs before any gold was divided among the trio. That season the three worked together for the first time in the Willow Creek area.

As the decade of the twenties drew to a close, the effort to make a living in the Susitna River Valley continued valiantly, with the focus on gold. Now and then though, someone came through the country for other reasons. One of these was the well-known Alaskan artist, Sydney Laurence, who had once prospected the Cache Creek country himself until he discovered that his talent as a painter paid more than any gold he had ever found. He had once partnered with Henry Peters, one of the original discoverers of Cache Creek gold, who was fond of saying

Belle Lee's Talkeetna Trading Post and freighting operation, 1932. Belle once employed Antone Stander, one of the legendary Klondike gold rush "Eldorado Kings," who had moved from spectacular wealth to hard times before he arrived in Talkeetna. (courtesy Eleanor Trepte Martin)

about his prospecting, "You can't see it—you've got to find it." These two had prospected the Ramsdyke Creek area together, and during this time Laurence had made some sketches of the great mountain, Denali, and other features of the Alaska Range. The artist had apparently also established a good friendship with Dick Francis during those days, evidenced by remarks made by Laurence's wife, Jeanne, in a memoir she wrote after her husband's death.

In the spring of 1929, Laurence and his wife traveled to Talkeetna by train, and headed out for Cache Creek country with a packhorse and wagon train laden with food and supplies for an entire summer. Laurence wanted to return to the Ramsdyke Creek area to make sketches, and it took several days of slow travel over the rugged roads to reach the Dutch Hills. The expedition stopped for one of its overnight rests at Dick Francis' camp, where Jeanne Laurence was moved to remark on Francis' hospitable nature.

"... we reached our next stop which was Dick Francis' cabin. (Sydney said,) 'Here is where we are going to eat. One always finds a pot of beans cooking on the stove for all who pass by and are hungry. Dick expects them to go in and help themselves.' Sure enough, on entering we found a pot of beans cooked and ready to eat.

"We were all very hungry and I can say I do not think I ever ate better beans in my life. Dick was not there when we arrived but came soon after we had finished dinner. It was heart warming to see the greetings of the two old friends who had not seen each other for a number of years.

"Early next morning we got underway. Dick and his seven huskies joined our group. He wanted to come along and help find Sydney's old camp and to give a hand in putting up the tents. Poor Man's Creek was our next stop, Sydney's old mining camp, which was (several) miles from Dick's place."

Dick Francis had now entered his fifth decade and seemed to enjoy widely-held respect and friendship. Essentially a loner, he had apparently never married, but there is evidence that he had a fondness for the ladies. On Christmas Day, 1929, he penned a letter to Belle Lee's sister, who divided her time between Washington state and Talkeetna where she had gotten to know Francis, probably at Belle's trading post during one of his visits there. Daisy, who loved parties, pretty clothes, and a good time, was well-known and very popular among the miners and trappers who wintered in or visited Talkeetna. They bought her drinks, danced with her, and generally enjoyed the exposure to a woman who wore lots of powder, lipstick, and pretty jewelry, and who paid them a lot of attention and laughed at their jokes. Francis, who spent so much time alone, was not immune, and perhaps on this special day he was feeling a bit lonely as he sat in his trapper cabin and wrote to Daisy in Washington.

> Your very welcome letter and Xmas card just received. And I was sure tickled pink to hear from you. Had sort of a sneaking idea that you would probably forget all about me. As you did not, will apologize for entertaining any such ideas.... You were sure lucky getting out when you did as this month has been one continual cold spell. Last few days has been better than 20 below. However it clouded up this morning and has got considerable warmer. My old pard Jack came up today to visit me. Was expecting him so layed in and proceeded to get him up a little

dinner. Which consisted of new light bread. Ginger bread. Fat juicy moose roast with outside spuds. Cheese, apples, nuts, coffee and some of that which Belle gave me. The recipe made a batch and it turned out all o.k. And that is good enough for any old trappers. Had bad luck early in Nov. Chunk of frozen wood landed in my left eye and almost put it out of commission. It is improving right along but is only about half an eye at that. Was my shooting eye at that. Trapping has been very poor. So far the whole bunch in this section has only caught enough to make a seasons catch for one man.

There is a new freighting outfit on road. Two of them just came up to my camp this evening. They must be hitting Belle pretty hard as they have all of Dollar (mine) freight and Carlsons outfit. All told about 18 tons. Belle and Nagley must have had quite a falling out of some sort.

Francis went on to describe the travails of a trapper friend named Johnny Kimball, who had been recently stranded in a remote area with few supplies, and remarked, "I'll bet the end of a rabbit trail looks good to him about breakfast time." Following a few personal remarks he closed the letter noting,

"I am like you are, not so much talking on paper as first hand which is better. So will close for this time trusting this finds you all o.k. and that you have had an enjoyable Xmas and a very Happy New Year. Thank you very much for (the) card and write soon to your friend Dick."

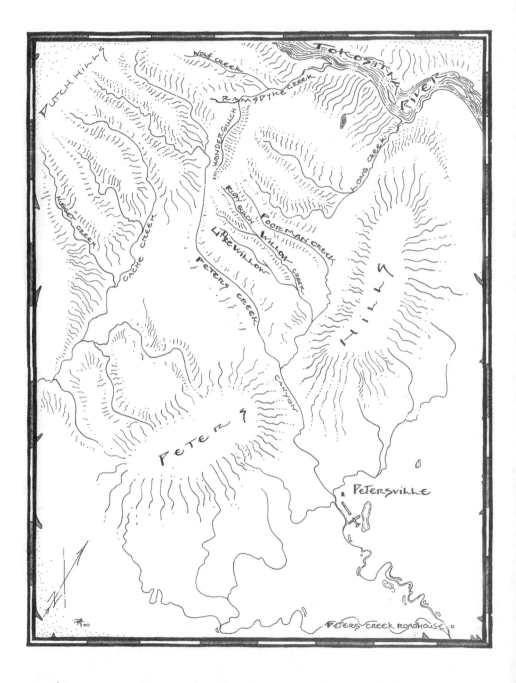

As the decade of the thirties dawned with sub-zero temperatures and transitory daylight, Frank Jenkins went to Commissioner Nagley's office and filed a Proof of Labor record that described $800 worth of labor and improvements he had performed on eight claims along Willow Creek in the Dutch Hills —including the Gopher Gulch claim he had leased from the Hatch brothers. What he did next indicates that he had, at some point, entered a joint venture with these men on all eight claims. On January 24, 1930, Jenkins filed a Notice of Forfeiture in two Anchorage newspapers that announced his expenditure on the claims and notified the Hatch brothers that,

> ... if within ninety days from the last publication of this notice you fail or refuse to contribute your proportion of such expenditure as co-owners, your interest in said claims will become the property of the undersigned, your co-owner, who has made the required expenditure. Your proportion of the said expenditure is the sum of $400.00

Jenkins, after almost twenty hard years spent prospecting and mining in the area, obviously expected a serious level of commitment from his associates. If they couldn't rise to the scale of Jenkins' ambition, he was not averse to turning them out.

In late April, the Jenkinses returned to Willow Creek in the Dutch Hills to open camp for the season. Sometime in late May, when the snow had receded enough to allow such work, Jenkins filed on two more claims that he called One and Two Association on Little Willow Creek. These were just west of his other claims on Willow Creek, which miners sometimes called Big Willow. That summer he performed $200 worth of labor and improvements on the ground which consisted of digging ditches for water collection and diversion, sinking shafts to bedrock, building sluice boxes, making riffles, and general repair work. Ray, his brother, continued to work with him.

Several claims held by an old-timer named Christ N. Hansen were situated to the south of Jenkins' mining area. Called Chris by everybody who knew him—and just about everybody did—Hansen had been in the area since 1909, two years before Jenkins' arrival at Susitna Station. As the summer progressed and the Dutch Hills exploded with thick vegetation and bustling wildlife, Jenkins' activities began to disturb Hansen farther downstream. Though no problems had previously existed between the two men, it seemed that the growing magnitude of Jenkins' operations might now bear some consequence. The problem centered on rock tailing cast-offs from Jenkins' sluicing operations; the debris, once it was separated from the gold, was washed on downstream to Hansen's area.

During the summer, Hansen said later, he had communicated his concerns to Jenkins but had been ignored. As the end of the season approached, Hansen grew angry enough to travel to Anchorage and file a complaint in the court system against both the Jenkins brothers.

Now, wild blueberries, cranberries, and currants began to ripen in Cache Creek country, and any remaining songbird species began their migration south. Thick alder and willow stands assumed a tired, dark-green color, as though the urgent summer growth had finally drained them of spirit. In Anchorage, birch, cottonwood, and aspen trees displayed the same wearied green, with a dull blotch of yellow and gold here and there. Chris Hansen found an attorney named Price, who prepared a complaint and filed it in the District Court on August 22.

The document gave an overview of Hansen's co-ownership of two large sets of claims called the Snowshoe Group and Squirrel Group, which he said he had operated for almost twenty years. He went on to contend that the Jenkins brothers were conducting placer mining opeations on Willow Creek just above Hansen's claims and had "made no provision for the empounding of tailings ... but permits them to deposit on the claims operated by plaintiff." Hansen further alleged that the men's actions had left large portions of his ground unworkable, and that if they continued to operate in this manner, they would destroy his property. In fact, he said, a great amount of damage had already occurred, but the exact value of the damage was difficult to determine because part of his property still remained to be properly developed by him.

Hansen went on to explain how he had notified the Jenkins brothers of the problem, but with no result. "They have entirely disregarded the rights of plaintiff, and threaten to continue the same attitude," he charged. He asked the court to prohibit the miners from depositing more tailings on his ground and requested that a temporary restraining order be issued against any further activity above his claims. Hansen also asked to be compensated for his legal fees.

On September 6, while the birch and cottonwoods grew golden in Talkeetna, U.S. Commissioner H.W. Nagley hired a local man named Jeff Nations to deliver a summons to Frank and Ray Jenkins at their Dutch Hills claims. Nations was a good-natured, longtime Talkeetna resident, and freighter Harriman remembered this about him:

"He'd shoe horses for the (Talkeetna) Trading Post a lot, and for the Road Commission crews. Jeff was well-liked, very witty and entertaining. He married an Indian girl and had several children. One time Jeff wanted some beer late at night when everything was closed. Well, late at night Belle wouldn't open the door for anybody. So Nations asked Nagley to open up his store so he could get some milk for his crying baby. Then, after he got the milk he said, 'While I'm here, give me two cases of beer too.'"

On September 15, Nations made his way across the Susitna River and traveled the long miles back into the Dutch Hills where he delivered the complaint, along with a summons that informed the Jenkins brothers they were required to appear in Anchorage within thirty days to answer to Hansen's charges. The summons went on to warn them that if they didn't appear, Hansen could take judgement against them "for the relief demanded."

Frank and his brother were probably fully involved with producing the final "clean-ups" of gold for the season, but the thirty-day provision allowed them the time to wrap up the summer's mining and to prepare for closing the camp for the year. Then, on October 9, an attorney hired by Jenkins filed a motion to strike Hansen's complaint, on the grounds that it was "sham, frivolous, and irrelevant," and that the alleged damage to Hansen's property could not be determined by a court of law.

This action was followed by another "Motion To Make Complaint More Deffinite (sic) and Certain." Among the items Jenkins wanted clarified were a more specific description of the claims that were affected; a description of the acts that made Hansen's claims unworkable; more detail about which property would be destroyed; and an explicit account of when the Jenkinses were allegedly notified of damage to the miner's property.

Now, colder nights, light snowfalls, and frozen ground called a halt to the mining season. Frank and Ray Jenkins had winterized the equipment, stored sluice boxes, lumber, tools, and supplies, and secured sheds and buildings against the bitter winds and weather of imminent winter. Then, together with Helen, they headed in to Talkeetna. By now, Frank and Helen were well-established in the settlement and owned a small complex of structures in the middle of town, just down the street from the Fairview Hotel. Besides their primary living quarters, Frank had constructed a number of buildings to house firewood and coal, and for the storage of tools, supplies, and equipment. He had produced these after building his own small sawmill on his property, which generated rough-cut lumber for both his personal and mining needs. Occasionally, if he liked someone, Frank would cut lumber for others for a fee. Jenkins had also constructed an extra small cabin for living quarters, which he and Helen made available to Ray, who continued to stay on with his brother.

In mid-October, snow fell in Talkeetna and the Jenkinses had to give full attention to the legal aspects of their lives. Frank's request that Hansen's complaint be dismissed had yet to be resolved. Then, on October 29, the Anchorage court held a hearing with the miners' attorneys, heard their arguments, and issued a decision: Jenkins' motion to dismiss Hansen's complaint was denied, as were other minor requests. But the court did grant his motion to compel Hansen to clarify his complaint even further.

The legal process was likely growing expensive. Now, Chris Hansen brought all of his mining partners into the conflict; two men named Johnson, another named Hansen, and a woman named Thompson joined him as plaintiffs and filed an amended complaint on November 11. They described the Snowshoe Group of claims that contained eighty acres of placer mining ground, and the Squirrel Group that consisted of another forty acres. They explained that Jenkins' claims were above and immediately adjoining theirs, and that the brothers "have deposited large quantities of waste material, or tailings, consisting of rock, earth, sand and stone on the lower portion of their mining claims adjoining and above the Squirrel Group of claims...."

The amendment went on to contend that:

> ... annually, during the spring season of every year, the waters of Willow Creek, by reason of freshets occuring at such times of the year, overflow, and that by the natural flow of said Willow Creek ... all such waste materials and tailings ... deposited by defendants, without impounding ... is being washed, carried and deposited into Willow Creek and ... due to high water from the spring freshets (are) carried and deposited over and across the placer mining claims belonging to (plaintiffs) making it impossible ... to mine and operate their said placer mining claims.

In a flash, Jenkins challenged the amendment. He was in Anchorage now, working with his lawyer, and on November 12 the two filed an objection that questioned the ownership and "community of interest" in the Hansen claims, and asserted that the complaint didn't produce enough facts to warrant any action by the court. This triggered a hearing set for November 17, at which time the court upheld the Jenkins objection, while granting the Hansen group yet another week to further amend its complaint.

For the third time, Hansen's complaint was amended but, curiously, the revisions contained little of additional significance. The document was filed with the court on November 26, and that same day the Jenkins brothers filed a flat denial of all the allegations.

In another document, Jenkins contended that Hansen's claims "have been so little prospected and are of such uncertain value that plaintiffs cannot determine the amount of damage claimed to have been done...." He also said that the Hansen group had "done little more than assessment work upon said claims ... and that said claims have not been operated as a placer mine ... during the mining season for many years." Jenkins went on to claim that Hansen was "a trapper and hunter, and is not engaged in placer mining upon said claims during the mining season."

Jenkins even asserted that he believed that Hansen "is seeking delay in the trial ... for the purpose of working a hardship upon defendants and compelling defendants to buy the claims alleged to be owned by plaintiffs and which (Jenkins) believes are without value as a placer mine...."

Next, Frank Jenkins began to complain about the expense he, his wife, and brother were incurring by remaining in Anchorage. He asked that the inevitable trial take place soon, because any more delays might interfere with his preparation for the 1931 mining season at a great financial cost to him.

Finally, on December 4, the court informed all parties that the trial would be held sometime in March or April of 1931. With that, the miners collected their things and headed for Talkeetna on the Alaska Railroad. The December days were short, cold, and snowy, and all the participants in the legal conflict were probably relieved to leave the more heavily populated town of Anchorage behind them.

As the year drew to a close, Dick Francis was out on his trapping line somewhere in the Peters Creek area. Around the time that the Jenkinses arrived back in Talkeetna, Francis sent in an order for supplies to Belle Lee at the Talkeetna Trading Post. He ordered white and whole wheat flour, lima beans, (canned) peaches, prunes, apples, spuds, onions, lard, carrots, baking powder, coffee, bacon, butter, gasoline, eggs, honey, matches, cigarette papers, velvet tobacco, three plugs

Star, soap, Kellogg's bran, cheese, tea, and "one cheap watch." Just before he sent the list out with Frank Lee he added, "six No. 4 Victor jump traps with teeth," and asked that the items be sent out on the trading post's next freight trip.

———

The Jenkinses settled in for the cold days of January. They kept to themselves, seeing few people except Ray Jenkins, who lived in the cabin nearby. Then, in early February, 1931, Frank Jenkins followed up on his warning to the Hatch brothers, against whom he had filed the notice of forfeiture the previous year. He went to Commissioner Nagley's office and filed an "Affidavit of Non-Payment," declaring that the Hatches had not complied with his demand and had failed to pay their share of the costs incurred in the development of the Willow Creek ground. Through this act, Jenkins became eligible to take full ownership of the pertinent claims.

As February progressed, the days grew longer by six minutes each day. A sense that the toughest part of winter was behind them lifted the spirits of everyone in Talkeetna, and the cold was somehow easier to deal with as the lengthening sun flashed off the snow. The sun had grown even higher and stronger by March when both Jenkins and Chris Hansen learned that the court had selected March 18 as the day for the trial that would address their dispute.

All involved traveled to Anchorage again, and this time Frank Jenkins was accompanied by five people who had been subpoenaed to testify in his behalf. Hansen brought a supporter too, and he was Dick Francis. The trial was held without a jury, and the judge listened as Hansen spoke in his own behalf on the morning of the eighteenth. Following this testimony, Jenkins' attorney asked for a dismissal of the case, which the judge denied. After a lunch recess Dick Francis was called to testify for Hansen, but details of his testimony do not survive in the court record. When Hansen's lawyer concluded his case, the attorney representing the Jenkinses again moved for a dismissal of the case on "grounds of insufficient proof." Now the judge paused and seemed to give the motion serious consideration. In the end the judge granted the dismissal, which surely must have been a cause for elation in the Jenkins camp.

Four days later the Jenkinses boarded the train in Anchorage and traveled to Talkeetna, arriving there at 11:30 at night. And, in a little more than a week, Frank Jenkins found himself in a lot of trouble.

On March 31, Frank and Ray Jenkins and a man named Ross Joyner walked into the Talkeetna game warden's office with thirty beaver pelts. Each filled out the standard affidavit form that attested to the legality of the skins, noting that the animals had been trapped some-time during the open season from January 1 to March 31. Each man registered ten beaver, and identified the area where they had trapped the animals as "on Moose Creek and around Bunco Lake." They said they'd taken the beaver during the last week of March. Then the three left the warden's office, and the Jenkins brothers walked down to the Talkeetna Trading Post where they sold the pelts to Belle Lee.

The warden, George Nelson, apparently questioned the validity of the affidavits. The next day he called the men back to his office to give more detailed statements. Frank Jenkins did so, declaring,

> That I, in company with Ross Joyner and Ray Jenkins left Tal-keetna at about 9:00 A.M. the 23rd of March, 1931, and arrived at Moose Creek Cabin at about noon, set 5 traps, left next morning and arrived at Rodgers Cabin and staid there all night. We left next morning and arrived at our camp (at) Willow Creek, staid there at our cabin that night and left next morning for Rodgers cabin, got there before noon, set traps in afternoon and staid at that cabin that night. The morning of the 27th I caught four beaver, the 28th I caught three beaver and the 29th I caught three beaver.

Ray Jenkins gave a similar statement, with only the number of beaver taken at certain locations varying from those of his brother.

The early April days were brilliant now, with the sun climbing higher and daily temperatures hovering in the high twenties. Winter had passed for the most part, and it remained only for the snow to disappear before that could truly be said. Warden Nelson sat in his office and pondered the affidavit information. He wasn't buying it. Ross Joyner had not yet filled out a more detailed statement, and Nelson most likely spent more time talking with the man and questioning him at length. Finally, on April 6, Joyner did make a long statement.

> That on the 23rd day of March, 1931, I left Anchorage, Alaska, in company with F.W. Jenkins, and Raymond H. Jenkins, bound for Talkeetna, Alaska, presumably for the purpose of joining them in trapping beaver, that we arrived at Talkeetna about eleven thirty o'clock on the night of March 22, that on the morning of March 23, 1931, we started on a trip and went from Talkeetna to Moose Creek, where we stayed alnight at a Road Commission cabin; on the 24th day of March we continued our journey to Peters Creek, and stayed alnight at the cabin of Henry Rogers; on the 25th day of March, 1931, we continued our trip to the mines owned by Jenkins Brothers on Cottonwood Creek, stayed there the night of

March 25, 1931. That on the 26th day of March we returned to the cabin of Henry Rogers, thirty three miles out from Talkeetna, stayed there alday the 27th of March, and the night of the 27th also, on account of the sickness of Raymond Jenkins. On the 28th day of March we returned to Moose Creek and stayed alnight at the Road Commission cabin. That on the 29th day of March we returned to Talkeetna, and stopped at Jenkin's house that night, that during the entire trip I did not trap any beaver and I did not see either F.W. Jenkins, or Raymond Jenkins trap any beaver, and I did not see either of the Jenkins bring any beaver pelts back to Talkeetna with them. That the first beaver pelts I saw was at the cabin used by Ray Jenkins at Talkeetna, Alaska. This was on the night of March 30, 1931. That on the 31st day of March, at the request of both F.W. Jenkins and Raymond Jenkins, I signed an affidavit that I had taken ten beaver pelts, and the beaver were sealed by George B. Nelson, Notary Public, that the pelts were then sold to Mrs. Lee of Talkeetna, by the Jenkins brothers, or one of them, that the entire lot sold was for the sum of $216.00, that I was paid by Raymond Jenkins the sum of $72 as my share, that on or about the 1st of April, 1931, I returned to Anchorage, Alaska.

What had prompted Jenkins to commit such an act? Was he flush with his recent success in a court of law? Was he badly in need of the money to pay his legal bills? Whatever his reason, he now found himself right back in the province of the law. On April 11, Warden Nelson drew up formal complaints, citing each of the Jenkins brothers for the crime of perjury in connection with the violation of Alaska game laws. On the same day Commissioner H.W. Nagley issued an arrest warrant for both men. Another game warden, Homer Jewell, carried out the arrest and brought the brothers before Nagley, where Frank Jenkins asked for a two-day delay "for the purpose of consulting counsel."

The game laws were heavily enforced in order to combat rampant hunting and trapping abuses taking place all over Alaska at this time. Trapping fur was one of the few ways a man could make any winter money, and many attempted to evade certain laws. Commissioner Nagley imposed bail on Frank Jenkins in the amount of $2,000, but granted him until the thirteenth "to make arrangements." Bail was fixed in the sum of $1,000 for Ray Jenkins.

H.W. Nagley's official role in penalizing the brothers did not endear him to Frank Jenkins, who viewed his actions with deep resentment and animosity. From that day forward Frank and Helen would take great pains to avoid any contact with Mr. Nagley, even crossing the road when they saw him, to avert an encounter. Since Nagley had also been appointed as the town's postmaster in 1926, it became difficult to always avoid him. But the Jenkinses worked around that too, by taking their mail to the train and asking the conductor to post it for them in Anchorage. Helen even sent away for some red sealing wax to secure her letters, in anticipation of the mining season when their mail would travel by freighter from the Dutch Hills to Talkeetna, where it would pass through Postmaster Nagley's hands for processing.

On April 13, Belle Lee walked over to the commissioner's office and signed an affidavit as a surety for Frank Jenkins' bail. But another whole week passed before Ray Jenkins' bail was pledged by both Helen Jenkins and (perhaps a financially reluctant) Belle Lee. Frank must have been relieved because he and his brother would soon need to be in the Dutch Hills to prepare for the mining season.

In late May, when the song sparrows had returned to the alder and willow bushes at the lower reaches of the Dutch Hills, the Jenkinses were just about ready to start some serious mining. They had cleaned the water ditches of winter debris, cleared away most of the snow in the area, and had the equipment running. While thus occupied, a criminal indictment against Frank Jenkins was filed with the District Court in Anchorage; a grand jury for the Territory of Alaska had found Jenkins responsible for "the crime of unlawful possession of the raw skins of land fur bearing animals."

Christ N. Hansen must have smiled. That fall, at the end of August, he made sure to visit Commissioner Nagley's office and record the labor he had performed on his claims that summer. He had put in $200 worth on the Squirrel Association Group from late May to July, and $300 worth on the Snowshoe Group in July and August. His work, he said, had consisted of "cutting brush, ditching, building dams, and turning the creek for about 800 feet."

How actively the court was proceeding with the charges against Frank Jenkins during the mining season is unclear, but it does appear that no indictment was ever brought against his brother, Ray. Frank was still busy in September. Frost had already nipped the mountain flora, and bold swathes of red, gold, and burnt orange splashed through the tired greenery that still managed to withstand the cold. The brothers had probably made their last serious gold clean-up for the season when Frank turned his attention to more new claims. On September 20, he went farther south and posted claim notices on Cottonwood Creek, above and below the point where the stream junctured with Willow Creek. He staked six claims, and Ray and Helen Jenkins acted as witnesses for the recorded declarations.

Then, in mid-October, Jenkins was called to Anchorage to appear before the court on the beaver pelt charges. Records show that he "stated

to the court that he wished to enter a plea of 'guilty' to the charges...."
This done, he headed back to Talkeetna on the train to await the court's
disposition of his case and to prepare for the winter ahead.

———

In early February, 1932, Frank Jenkins finally received the judgement of the court. He was informed that he would be "fined in the
sum of One Hundred and Fifty Dollars ($150.00), and be imprisoned
in the Federal jail at Valdez, Alaska, not to exceed one day for each
two dollars of said fine."

On June 10, while Jenkins was surely at work on his claims in the
hills, Alaska United States Attorney Warren Cuddy issued a bench warrant for the arrest of Jenkins "for the reason that said defendant has

Dick Francis mined on Ruby Creek, which flows at an angle from top to
bottom through the center of this photo. Ruby junctures with Willow Creek,
which flows from left to right at the bottom of photo.

failed to satisfy the judgement of this court rendered February 8, 1932."
On September 20, the court issued yet another warrant: "(Jenkins) was
fined the sum of $150.00 and in default thereof was to be imprisoned
in the Federal Jail at Valdez, Alaska, not to exceed one day for each
Two Dollars of said fine, and whereas said fine has not been paid this
is to command you forthwith to arrest the defendant ... and commit
him in default of his failure to pay said fine."

And there the case file ends. No records indicate whether Jenkins
ever paid the fine or actually traveled over 200 train miles to Seward,

Alaska, to board a boat for the 100-plus miles of travel to Valdez and the federal jail there. In October, however, an order was issued to destroy all the seized beaver skins because "said skins are no longer needed as evidence in this case, and they are so badly eaten by moth that they have no value." The skins were burned in the fire box of the jail boiler at Valdez.

Earlier that fall, while Jenkins was conducting his affairs in the shadow of the judicial process, Dick Francis had made a shift in his search for gold. One might call it a significant shift, considering his many years spent mining in the Long Creek area. In September, he had spent some time prospecting in the Dutch Hills with another longtime prospector named Clarence Sullens. The men must have panned out some "promising color," because on September 8 they staked two large claims at Ruby Gulch where a modest creek by the same name flowed into Willow Creek. They recorded the claims, which were located about a thousand feet up from

A part of Willow Creek in the Dutch Hills, a stream Frank Jenkins' thought of as "Jenkins territory."

the mouth of Ruby Creek, as "Shurething No. 1 and Shurething No.2."

Each claim was 1,320 feet long and 660 feet wide, and together they reached a long way up Ruby Creek, which had derived its name from the proliferation of tiny low-grade, muddy-red garnets that turned up in the gravel there. The men recorded their claims at H.W. Nagley's office on October 11, and the man who witnessed their documents was Henry Peters, who had been mining in Cache Creek country now for twenty-seven years.

These Ruby Gulch claims were located just above one of Frank Jenkins' important ditch systems, and some of his active and productive mining tracts.

no fighting here, boys

In early 1933 Frank Jenkins made a deal with three young men who were new to the area, all of whom were eager to mine for gold. A handwritten agreement outlined the terms:

This contract agreement (is) entered into this April the 11th day, 1933, by F.W. Jenkins, party of the first part, and Robert McClanahan and Ed Smith and Charles Smith parties of the second part. It is desirous of second parties to placer mine on Lucky Gulch for the season of 1933 beginning June 1933—ending first of October 1933. It is agreed by second parties that they will build up Ruby ditch and make any repairs necessary on Ruby Gulch or Lucky Gulch for the purpose of mining, and therefore will leave it in good condition at the expiration of this agreement—to the satisfaction of first party. And they will replace all mining tools or equipment they may use in mining, in fact everything they are using belongs to first party and the owner of this property. It is understood by second parties that Ruby and Lucky Gulch property will not be holding for any debts incured by second parties. And it is therefore agreed that second parties will help to protect any damage done to water right or ditch on Ruby Claim or the dumping of tailings on property rights by some men by the name of Clarence Sullen and Dick Francis, who is starting to mine up above Ruby ditch on Ruby Gulch, and any information or claim they can give for their own protection or for the protection of first party they will gladly give. And will be awake to any damage done to Ruby ditch by these men. It is agreed that first party is to be informed of all cleanups so he will be present at each cleanup. It is further understood this contract agreement is not transferable. Clarence Sullen and Dick Francis is forbidden on the works of any and all of this property.

Rock and gravel tailings might be washed onto Jenkins' ground! Even more aggravating, the ditch system that provided so much of Jenkins' crucial water requirements might be affected. Worse yet, just three days after the men signed the agreement, Francis and Sullens made their way down Ruby Gulch and staked another smaller claim to the south of Shurething No. 1, *even closer* to Jenkins' ditch. The staking couldn't have been an easy task for the men in April, as several feet of dense, compacted snow still remained in Ruby Gulch to impede their efforts. The new claim was only 200 feet long, and the two men named it "Wolverine placer mining claim." They identified it as "a fraction lying between the Shurething group, and No. 1 on Ruby Gulch" (the latter a claim owned by Jenkins).

It's not hard to speculate that Frank Jenkins had entered his agreement with the Smith brothers and McClanahan so that they could keep an eye on Francis and Sullens, while Frank worked farther to the south on Willow Creek. The idea most likely began to form when the three men, all strong and in their early twenties, had appeared at Jenkins' camp that spring and told him they were looking for a "mining opportunity." Jenkins took time to talk to the eager young men and show them around his ground. He pointed out some claims he had on Lucky Gulch, immediately adjacent to Ruby Creek, and offered them the deal that was later contained in their formal agreement. Jenkins would let them use his equipment on the claims and, in return, the trio could keep half the gold they recovered.

More important to Jenkins was their usefulness as watchdogs. He didn't trust Dick Francis. For that matter, Frank didn't trust anyone who ventured too close to his mining operations. Just a year earlier another prospector named Larry "Rocky" Cummins had moved too close for his blood. Rocky was tall and skinny and rumored to have been a bootlegger in Southeast Alaska in years past. He had been around for some time, prospecting the Dutch Hills and finding just enough gold to get by. He had once staked ground right next to some of Jenkins' claims, and Frank had immediately contested his recorded boundaries. An unpleasant dispute ensued, and Rocky had been intimidated enough to pull up stakes and move two or three miles to the west, toward Bird Creek. Frank Jenkins was becoming known for many such conflicts.

Helen was an eager accomplice. She was even more suspicious than Frank, and threats seemed to compound in her mind. Too, she wanted to be sure that these Smith boys and their partner were trustworthy enough to be allowed in "Jenkins territory." While Frank drew up the agreement, she wrote a letter, bypassing Nagley, to law enforcement officials in Anchorage that inquired about any disreputable history the men might have. She carefully sealed it with her red wax and included it with their outgoing mail.

Around this time, Helen was writing other wax-sealed letters to post office officials in Anchorage. She told them that she was convinced that Postmaster Nagley was opening her mail when it passed through Talkeetna. In one letter, she insisted that Nagley had read her mail, and she wanted to report that to his supervisors. She reportedly also complained that Nagley held too many positions of authority in Talkeetna and that something needed to be done to correct the imbalance.

During the time that Bob McClanahan and the Smith brothers were working in Lucky Gulch, the Smiths somehow became acquainted with Dick Francis. One night they told McClanahan that Francis had encouraged them to "jump" the Jenkins' claims. McClanahan, who got on well with both Frank and Helen, reported the incident, believing it to be just the sort of thing they wanted to know about Francis' activities. Jenkins, furious that the brothers had been friendly with Francis, terminated their agreement and told them to get off his property. Eventually, the Smiths found work at the large Peters Creek mine, several miles to the south, where the two men openly complained that Jenkins had "beat them out of their earnings."

McClanahan stayed on and worked as a laborer for Jenkins the rest of the season. Frank liked him, and he apparently also met with Helen's approval. At mealtimes Frank would sometimes tell his new employee about the problems he'd had with people in the area. Some years ago, he said, he had had a dispute with another miner named Al Wolf, and Wolf still "had it in for him." Another was Robert Dahl, who had worked for him but did not fulfill his verbal contract. He had refused to pay Dahl what he said he had coming, Jenkins said, and Dahl was still angry about it.

Sometimes the conversation would turn to gold or banks, and Frank would frequently insist that gold was "safer buried in a sandhill than any commercial bank." He seemed embittered about banks and alluded to a substantial loss he had taken as the result of a "closed bank" somewhere in the states. The Great Depression was reaching its height at this time; if Jenkins had positioned his money in a bank somewhere on the West Coast, it is possible that he had indeed been damaged.

As spring progressed to full summer, Dick Francis must have liked what he saw in Ruby Gulch because on July 1 he sent Clarence Sullens to Talkeetna to record yet another placer claim at Nagley's office. This was Shurething No. 3, and it added another 1,320 feet to the Ruby Creek tracts. But this claim was recorded in Francis' name only, while Sullens and Henry Peters acted as witnesses to the document. Possibly, Sullens may not have wanted to assume the burden of the additional assessment work and its attendant costs.

Frank Jenkins was busy mining, but took time out in late August to file on some new claims at Little Willow Creek, adding these to others he had previously staked there. Curiously, there is no evidence that Ray Jenkins was around to help this summer, and his absence may have been a factor that contributed to Bob McClanahan's continued employment with Frank and Helen.

McClanahan helped the Jenkinses close down their operation that fall and was still with them in early October when they made their way to the Peters Creek Roadhouse with the horse freighter,

Belle Lee's Peters Creek Roadhouse. The structure, located midway between Talkeetna and Cache Creek country, was a welcome respite for weary miners and prospectors. (photographer unknown)

Frank Lee. The big roadhouse, located about halfway between Talkeetna and the mining country, had been constructed fairly recently by Belle Lee as a complement to her trading post activity in Talkeetna. The place had immediately become popular as a way station that provided groceries, supplies, and a place to eat and sleep for weary travelers.

Freighter Wes Harriman's description of the place in the early thirties is a testament to the code of honor that was now in place in Cache Creek country.

"The roadhouse was built at ... what they call 'the forks' in the road where it continues on up towards Peters Creek Canyon from the Cache Creek trail," Harriman said. "Frank Lee hewed all the timbers for that, and Big John, Black John, and George Blair helped build it. It was built for the trading post because there was more prospecting. The Peters Creek Roadhouse was active in summer, not in winter. In winter, Belle left a stock of groceries there. Anyone who wanted anything would take what they needed and write down what they took. In the spring, Belle would pick up the pad and send them bills for what they got."

When the small group reached the roadhouse early that evening, Frank and Helen must have been unhappy to see Christ Hansen in the building. Though the three miners managed to tolerate each other for a couple of hours, the tension finally snapped around nine o'clock when Jenkins and Hansen had an angry exchange. The ensuing fracas, involving just about everyone in the room, infuriated the Jenkinses so much that Frank filed a complaint with U.S. Commissioner H.W. Nagley:

> I, Frank W. Jenkins, of Talkeetna, Alaska, being first duly sworn according to law, depose and say: That on or about the 6th or 7th day of October, 1933, at Peters Creek Bridge Road House, some 23 miles from the town of Talkeetna, on the Cache Creek Highway, one Christ N. Hansen did make threats against my life by saying and doing the following:
>
> He, the said Christ Hansen rushed across the room at me and struck at me, saying you son of a bitch, I will kill you. You are dumping tailings on my ground. I'll get you yet. This all without provocation on my part.
>
> At a previous date, about March 7th, 1932, he, Christ Hansen, accosted me at Talkeetna on the street and called me all kinds of vile names and made threats that he would get me.

Helen, never one to sit on the sidelines, filed a similar affidavit.

Later, following the legal procedure required of his position, Commissioner Nagley took formal depositions of two witnesses to the episode. The first man summoned to his office was Nick Balabanoff, The Galloping Russian. In occasionally halting English, the miner responded to Nagley's questions.

> Q. What is your name?
> A. N.R. Balabanoff
> Q. Where do you reside?
> A. At Yentna in the summer time, and at Talkeetna in winter.
> Q. Are you a citizen of the U.S.?
> A. Yes, by naturalization.
> Q. What is your occupation?
> A. I am a placer miner, I mine at Nugget Creek, in Cache Creek.

Q. Were you, on or about the 6th or 7th day of October, 1933, on the road from or to Cache Creek?

A. Yes.

Q. Where did you stop over night on the trip?

A. At Peters Creek.

Q. Who were there besides yourself?

A. Frank Lee, Mr. and Mrs. Jenkins, Bob McClanahan and Christ Hansen.

Q. Did you hear or see any argument there that time, if so state just what it was and all the circumstances concerning it.

A. Well, I there sitting in the room, and Frank Lee and Frank Jenkins were on the other side of the table out in the room more, and they were talking, and Jenkins said that there was no law that would allow a man to dump tailings on his ground like Dick Francis was doing on him. Then Christ Hansen arose from his chair and stepped to the end of the table and said, You have been dumping tailings on my ground for several years and you think that all right—but nobody can dump on your ground. Jenkins then rushed and jumped towards Hansen and kicked at him and called him a lot of vile names. He, Jenkins, did not quite reach Hansen with his foot, but I saw his foot reach up close to Hansen's stomach.

Q. What took place then?

A. Well, Frank Lee jumped up and said, Boys, cut this out, and No fighting like that, and What do you mean, cut it out. Frank Lee grabbed Jenkins and was holding him tight. Mrs. Jenkins picked up a stick of stove wood and was trying to get a lick at Chris Hansen, and McClanahan and Jenkins told her to put down the wood and keep out of it, and they got the stick of wood out of her hand and threw it down. Mrs. Jenkins rushed about and grabbed an empty quart bottle and was trying to strike Chris Hansen with it, and was saying, Let me get him, let me get a lick at him, and calling him all kinds of vile names.

Q. What were the names, some of them.

A. Well, I heard almost every kind of a name, son of a bitch, stinking skunk, and everything. They were all calling back and forth so many bad names. I could not remember every one.

Q. What took place then, what did Jenkins and Hansen do, did they fight or hit one another, and did Hansen call any names to the Jenkins?

A. They did not strike one another. Just then Frank Lee told Hansen to get out towards the door and go on over to the barn and they would all go to bed, and we did. Myself, Hansen and

Frank Lee slept in the barn and left the house for Mr. and Mrs. Jenkins. There was not anymore said nor done. I did not hear Chris Hansen call any names, nor make any threats of any kind. He only said what I said before, about you been dumping on my ground for many years. You know Chris, he says one word and take him half hour to say another. He did not seem very mad, and he did not rush towards Jenkins at all. He only stood up and he was long way from Jenkins, and he stood right there.

Q. Did you hear anybody in this crowd say anything about kill or killing?

A. No, I did not.

Q. Did you hear Chris Hansen say that he would kill?

A. No.

Q. How far away from these people, the Jenkins, were you, and could you have heard all that was said and seen all that was done?

A. Only a few feet.

Q. Did you hear Chris Hansen say to Jenkins, I will kill you, you son of a bitch, I'll get you yet, or anything like that?

A. No, I never heard such a thing and I was sitting right there.

Q. Did Chris Hansen strike at Jenkins or anybody, at any time, during this time?

A. No, he did not strike, never raised a hand, but just stood there talking, now and again.

Q. What did he say, you say he was talking?

A. Well, I said that he spoke about Jenkins dumping on him, and he was saying few words low. I could hear so many bad names and swearing from all of them—Hansen, Jenkins and Mrs. Jenkins —that was all, and Mrs. Jenkins was running around hollering, Let me get a lick at Chris, and she finally did grab Chris by the shirt sleeve and there was such a confusion and noise for a little while, you could not remember every word and who was saying it. But I never heard Chris or any one say he would kill Jenkins or anybody.

Q. Is that all you saw and heard said that evening and at that trip on the road at Peters Creek at the Road House with the people above named?

A. Yes. That is all and everything that I can remember.

Q. At about what time of the day or night was this that you were all in the Road House, and that this argument and trouble took place?

A. I should say about eight and nine o'clock in the evening on the sixth of October, 1933, to be exact.

About a week later, Commissioner Nagley called the trading post freighter, Frank Lee, to his office to give his account of the conflict.

I, Frank Lee, being first duly sworn, according to law, on his oath, deposes and says: That on or about October 7th, 1933, he, the Frank E. Lee, the deponant, was at the Peters Creek Bridge Road House and spent the evening and nite there; that at about eight o'clock p.m. he and one Frank Jenkins were sitting about the middle of the room talking, and that Jenkins said that one Dick Francis was staking the whole country up around Willow Creek and that he would never be allowed to dump his tailings down on his ground, etc. That Chris Hansen, who was sitting behind the table which was between he and Jenkins, arose and stepped to the end of the table and said that you, directing his words to Jenkins, have been dumping tailings on my ground for the past four years and that makes no difference to you. Where-upon Jenkins jumped up and said that you are a liar and he, Jenkins, kicked at Chris Hansen. But I don't think he reached him with his foot, which I saw come up in the air beside me.

I quickly jumped up and in between them, Hansen and Jenkins, and declared, No fighting here, boys, cut that out. If any fighting to be done here, I will take a hand in it myself. I told Chris Hansen to keep still and also Jenkins, and not to be scrapping like that. I stood right between them or I guess there would have been a fight. They were calling all kinds of names back and forth and every-body was talking. Mrs. Jenkins, who was also present, was run-ning from one side of the room to the other and talking and trying to get in to it. I told her, as did Frank Jenkins, to put that down, whatever she had, and keep out of it. Bob McClanahan, who was also present, took hold of Mrs. Jenkins and told her to keep out of it and keep still. Nick Balabanoff, also present, was sitting behind the table and he did not get up, but set there taking it all in, only getting up to try and take Mrs. Jenkins off of Chris.

I did not hear Chris Hansen make any threats of any kind nor say but very little of anything, nor did he raise his hand or foot, but just stood there on the floor until it was all over, and then I told Chris to come on with me, and we men went to the barn to sleep for the nite and left the Jenkins there in the Road House. The next morning we all got our breakfast in the Road House, each cooking his own, and then we all left. Not another word was said about the little argument the nite before, which didn't amount to anything nohow, and there was nothing to it.

I did not hear Chris Hansen say that he would kill Jenkins and call him a son of a bitch or anything of the kind, and I was right there between them and in the midst of them all and did not hear such a word spoken, and don't think that Chris said it and don't think that Chris Hansen is that kind of a man, he wouldn't shoot anybody or say so. This one page has been read to me and I have read the same and swear that the same is true as I believe to the best of my knowledge.

———

Following the episode at the roadhouse, another winter drew near. Vast forests of birch and cottonwood, now leafless, massed in skeletal repose, awaiting the first snow. Nights grew gradually colder, and words huffed out in visible vapor when people talked outside. Dick Francis had finished his work at Ruby Gulch and began to prepare for the trapping season. In Talkeetna on October 28, he went to Belle's trading post and asked her to put up an order for him and transport it over to the Peters Creek area where his trapping cabin was located. Items Francis would need included "salt, lard, lima beans, pinto beans, honey, eggs, spuds, onions, beets, carrots, (canned) peaches, figs, and apricots, canned milk, assorted vegetables, candles, cookies, cocoa, baking powder, apples, lemons, olive oil, K. bran, pepper, files, sacks, dog chain, and a bucket."

Francis spent some time in Talkeetna, sleeping on a cot upstairs at the trading post and sitting around the big barrel stove downstairs during the day, catching up on all the news with the other miners who were in town. He also talked at length with Belle, who must have listened intently. After nineteen years spent mining in the Long Creek area, Francis was apparently ready for a change. He had taken the first step when he filed on the claims at Ruby Gulch, but now the combined assessment work for all the claims he held had probably become an unrealistic burden for one man. As a hand miner, he had persuaded enough gold from the ground along Long Creek to suit his needs, but to achieve optimal production now probably required a more aggressive financial investment and powerful equipment. The ground was good for someone with the ambition to take it on. The camps were established, and stocked with tools and equipment he'd managed to acquire over the years. A permanent tent-cabin frame was probably on site, and a network of the critical water ditches, which he'd labored so hard to create, was in place. Francis seemed to want to remain what he had always been, a loner and a hand miner with modest needs. As he approached his fifty-fifth birthday, the Ruby Gulch claims seemed to suit him fine.

Belle Lee was an astute businesswoman and, after dealing with gold miners for so many years, knew good ground. She probably knew she could lease out the Long Creek claims for a good annual sum and recover her investment on a timely basis.

The two old friends struck a deal and signed an agreement of sale on the third of November. Francis received $1,500 at the execution of the agreement, along with a pledge for an additional thousand dollars to be paid him within the next year. The money would help him to get established on the new claims.

Francis headed out to his trapping camp and settled in for the season. On November 20, he sent another supply order to Belle, asking for "one 10 x 12 tarp, 1 quart apple vinegar, 3 cartons Chesterfield cigarettes, 2 mantels and generator, 1 doz. #1 victor traps, 4 No. 13 jump traps, 6 bars ivory soap, 1 towel, 2 leather shoestrings, 50 cts. matches, 1 bottle Sloan liniment, 1 pkge whole cloves, and 6 mouse traps."

After the holidays and the arrival of the new year, litigation continued to be a relentless component of the Jenkinses' lives. On January 9, Christ Hansen, who had lost his case over mining tailings to Jenkins in the spring of 1931, objected to being penalized for the travel expenses and other costs of Jenkins' many witnesses. But, while Hansen's lawyer filed formal papers to this effect, Frank Jenkins' attention was focused on Dick Francis. On January 13, 1934, Jenkins had his lawyer file the following complaint against the hand miner on Ruby Creek:

> That during the mining season of 1933 in the months of June, July, August and the early part of September ... Dick Francis, in the prospecting and development of his said placer mining claims Sure Thing No. 1 and Sure Thing No. 2 so conducted such operations as to fill with gravel and rock the ditch of the plaintiff ... so that the supply of water through said ditch was reduced and diminished in flow and volume, and further in such operations (Francis) caused debris in the shape of rock and gravel to fill the pen stock and clogged the head gate, in said ditch, in such a manner that the same could not be operated until cleared away, all at the expense, cost and damage of (Jenkins).

In an accompanying affidavit Jenkins went into more detail. He identified one of his important claims as Discovery No. 1 on Ruby Creek. It was here that he had tapped into Ruby Creek, and here that the outset of his ditch was located. The ditch moved several hundred feet through this claim, he explained, and then meandered in a southerly direction for a total length of about 3,000 feet, to a point where it finally emptied into Lucky Creek. "The ditch is about $2^1/_2$ feet wide at the bottom, flows down through a very steep gradient, carries about 12 inches of water in depth and is wholly necessary and required by (Jenkins) in his mining operations," he testified.

Jenkins went on to complain that he had "often requested (Francis) to desist," but that the miner had not paid attention and had continued with his operations. He also asserted that such conduct would "practically destroy and render useless said ditch and render valueless (Jenkins') placer mining claims...."

Jenkins maintained that Francis was "insolvent" and didn't have the means to pay for what he alleged were damages already done to him in the amount of one thousand dollars. He argued that unless Francis was restrained by an injunction during the upcoming mining season, the damage to Jenkins would be irreparable. In a separate document prepared by his lawyer, Jenkins formally petitioned the court for a temporary injunction against Francis.

When, in late January, Dick Francis responded through his Anchorage attorney, Warren Cuddy, the conflict began to take on the dimensions of the Hansen-Jenkins dispute. Francis said he didn't have "sufficient information" to evaluate some of the charges. He denied that the water conveyed in the ditch was essential to Jenkins' mining operations. He denied that the head gate of Jenkins' ditch was located on a claim belonging to Jenkins and asserted that the gate was instead located on his own claim, "Wolverine Fraction." Francis denied all the other allegations made by Jenkins.

The court set a hearing date for the case to be heard in Seward on February 14. Cuddy immediately petitioned the court to hold the hearing in Anchorage in May, citing "a severe financial loss" to his client should he have to leave his trapping line and go to the expense of traveling over 200 miles to Seward.

Frank Jenkins protested the idea of a hearing during the month of May, when he needed to be out at his claims getting everything ready for mining in June. Spring breakup (when the river ice broke loose) also occurred in May, Jenkins argued, and during this time rapidly melting snows transformed the trails from Willow Creek to Talkeetna into mires of nightmarish travel. Attempts at passage at such times became unsafe and, in some instances, even impossible. Besides being hazardous, the time-consuming trips required to reach Anchorage could jeopardize his ability to start sluicing gold by June first. He needed the entire month of May, he insisted, to prepare for the mining season.

This argument triggered the affidavit of a man named Charles Cooper, who said,

"That he is now a resident of Seward, Alaska, and engaged in the retail grocery business. That for four years he was engaged in mining on Willow Creek and its tributaries. That during said four years he freighted his supplies from Talkeetna to Willow Creek and is familiar with trail conditions between said points. That travel between Willow Creek and Talkeetna during the month of May is not unsafe or impossible. That he has made the trip during the month of May many times. That he recalls on one occasion early in May leaving Willow Creek at five P.M. with two dogs and having his dinner that evening at Talkeetna at eleven."

Many local miners would probably have questioned Cooper's assertion. The court also seemed to grant Jenkins' argument some credibility, because it moved quickly to set the court date for March 5, in Seward.

It's not clear whether Dick Francis couldn't or wouldn't leave his trapping camp, but he did not travel to Seward for the hearing, relying instead upon his attorney to represent his interests. But Frank and Helen Jenkins did take the train to the little town on Resurrection Bay, the port of call for most of the steamships from Seattle. Seward was warmer, and the coastal trees were thicker and more attractive than the tough "swamp spruce" around Talkeetna. The sea air was bracing, and the lengthening March sun glanced pleasantly off the bay and snow. Maybe the couple even saw some old friends there, getting on or off the big boats. But Frank Jenkins probably spent little time at anything but consulting with his attorney, who lived and practiced in Seward.

On March 5, the court gave Jenkins a temporary injunction. Francis was ordered to "absolutely desist and refrain from in any manner depositing or causing to be deposited, debris, rock or gravel upon the mining claims of plaintiff situate (sic) on Willow Creek and on Ruby Creek or gulch and on Lucky Creek or gulch ... or in any ditch, flume or pen-stock of the said plaintiff used in connection with the mining of said placer mining claims."

Later that month, when the Jenkinses were back in Talkeetna, they learned that the travel expenses and other witness costs they had petitioned for in the Hansen case, had been approved for reimbursement by an Anchorage court clerk. Hansen's plea to deny these had been unsuccessful, and the old miner was ordered to pay up. There is no evidence that Jenkins ever did anything further to pursue his more recent assault complaint against Hansen. Perhaps Jenkins had second thoughts about the accusations he had made against the miner, or he felt sufficiently avenged by his continued success in the courts. Regardless, Jenkins had his hands full with the Francis conflict.

That year big news swept through Alaska. The value of gold had risen from $20.67 an ounce to $35.00 an ounce! Activity in Cache Creek country responded accordingly, with more prospectors moving into the area, more claims being filed on, and additional investment put into existing mines. Dick Francis, reacting in kind, did some more claim locating of his own. But this time he acted alone, because on March 30 he and Clarence Sullens had dissolved their partnership. The reason for this is not evident, but Sullens may have been alarmed by the brewing legal battle with Jenkins. At any rate, Sullens was soon to experience bad luck with his health. Freighter Wes Harriman remembered, "He had been grubstaked by Belle McDonald over the years. He hadn't been real successful. He had a blood disorder, so he was going Outside. When he went Outside, Belle and a small group took up a collection for him for his expenses, and to see a doctor so he could get reestablished in the states. Everybody contributed one day's pay, which was then $5. And he did go Outside."

Francis moved just south of his Wolverine Fraction and filed on a full-sized claim he called the Wolverine Pup. The next day, May 5, he filed on yet another large claim that took in the mouths of both Ruby Creek and Gopher Creek. Willow Creek ran right down the middle of this claim, which Francis named the Hungry Dog.

Perhaps unaware of the location notice Francis had filed in May, Frank Jenkins filed a blanket Proof of Labor record for the sixteen claims he held on June 18. Among these were his Discovery Claim on Ruby Creek, and Number One Above Discovery on Willow Creek— tracts that encompassed the mouths of both Ruby Creek and Gopher Creek. He declared that the labor and improvements on all the claims consisted of "repairing ditches, building houses, building dams, building flumes, building roads, and prospecting."

In early July, for reasons that would emerge later, Jenkins took the precaution of filing a Certificate of Location of Placer Claim that reaffirmed his ownership of Discovery Claim on Ruby Creek—the tract that encompassed the onset of his ditch, including an important dam he had installed there to regulate creek water. The young man who served as witness to this document was named Ken Brittell.

A new face in Jenkins' camp, Brittell was 25 years old and trained as a teacher. He had heard about Cache Creek country from his friend and fellow Nebraskan, Bob McClanahan, and it is possibly through this connection that he obtained work with Jenkins. Frank grew to like and trust Brittell and even helped him to file on some claims near his own; he also served as a witness when Brittell recorded the claims in Talkeetna.

In July, Dick Francis sent in an order to the Talkeetna Trading Post for lemons, one plug Star tobacco, onions, one carton Velvet tobacco, and six books cigarette papers. Belle, now remarried to a road worker named Mac McDonald, extended credit to just about all the miners while they were out at their claims, and the men paid her periodically or at the end of the season. In late July, Francis made a trip into Talkeetna and gave Belle three ounces of gold as payment on his account. And, in October, he sent in a note to Belle and asked her to pay Frank Lee $80, probably for freighting services.

In late October, Ken Brittell filed on two claims in the wild Ramsdyke Creek area, where the now-defunct Ramsdyke Creek Mining Company had invested so heavily over a decade earlier. Located a rugged two and a half miles over the ridge from Jenkins' operation, the claims were staked just above the mouth of Wolf Creek, a tributary of Ramsdyke Creek. Frank and Helen Jenkins signed as witnesses when Brittell recorded the claims with the new U.S. Commissioner in Talkeetna, Ben Mayfield.

Mayfield had done some mining in the area and was familiar to local residents. He had applied for the commissioner job, perhaps as the result of dissatisfaction among some that H.W. Nagley held such a bounty of paid positions, and possibly because his mining efforts had not panned out to his expectations. The position was tacitly filled by political appointment, and officials were assured that Mayfield belonged to the party then in power. Jobs were extremely hard to come by during these years in Alaska, and a decision was apparently made to approve the wider dissemination of opportunity. Though H.W. Nagley would retain his position as postmaster of Talkeetna for many years, Helen Jenkins became convinced that she had single-handedly caused him to lose the commissioner position.

Now temperatures plummeted, snows fell, and winter embraced the area once more. In Anchorage, lawyer Warren Cuddy, representing Dick Francis, petitioned the court to move the Jenkins-Francis case from the Seward venue to the Anchorage docket. He said that the expense would be burdensome for all concerned should the case be tried in Seward, and the court kindly agreed.

In 1935 about forty or fifty people lived in Talkeetna, many of whom were miners that spent half the year at their claims, and lived in the village during the winter. Though the Jenkinses lived in this manner, there is no evidence that Dick Francis ever took up residence in Talkeetna. Instead, he seems to have spent most of the winter residing at his trapping camp, returning in summer to live and work on his mining claims. But he visited Talkeetna frequently throughout the year and, as he grew older, even took to spending a month and sometimes more in Anchorage during the winter, probably to escape the bitter January temperatures. He usually stayed at the Inlet Hotel in Anchorage, where he developed a close friendship with Ed Carlson, who had operated the hotel for many years. The two talked about gold and mining and sometimes discussed forming a partnership on claims in the Dutch Hills. Occasionally Francis would borrow money from Carlson when he'd had a bad year and pay it back when he got the fur or gold.

In Talkeetna the two major sources for supplies were still Belle Lee McDonald's trading post and H.W. Nagley's store. Accommodations were available at both the trading post and the larger and more sophisticated Fairview Hotel, a two-story building that offered rooms, a small dining area, and a large bar and card room. Wes Harriman, who had arrived in 1934 at the age of twenty, said of Belle McDonald and her business activities at this time: "She was generous, had good sound judgement, and good advice. Her trading post was the last log building down near the river, and that's where I lived. There was a blacksmith shop where they had their own blacksmith equipment to take care of the horses and anything that needed to be repaired. Then there was a big log barn farther down. The trading post was well-managed and well-equipped; and Belle served meals, had kind of a hotel there. It was not very fancy; there were no rooms. Anybody that stayed there stayed upstairs, which was all open. There were canvas cots, quite a few, because it was a good-sized building. That was their room, a cot in the open part of the trading post. The chimney from the stove downstairs went up through the second floor, so it was comfortable even in the winter. She didn't have a dining room. There was just a counter with a lot of stools, used as a bar as well as for serving meals.

"It was fancy enough for most people. The people that wanted to go 'first class,' or with more luxury than what the trading post could offer, would stay at the Fairview Hotel. It seemed to be a different group that was around the trading post, different than there was at the Fairview. The people that stayed at the trading post, you could kind of judge them. They always did their own sewing; they had patches on the elbow and knees, and a patched shirt. Frank (Lee) and I smelled like a horse or a sweaty harness because we were handling horses all the time, but that was never objectionable to anybody that was there. The old-timers generally stayed there; they knew Belle and Mac, and was aware of the accommodations. Food was always served at the counter or bar where we sat on a stool."

Often, in the late evenings when his work was finished, young Harriman would sit on a stool at the trading post and listen to the old-timers talk. One night one of the elderly men told him, "This freighting will never put you in a high place in society. But remember, you're in good company."

Harriman had a great deal of respect for his boss, Frank Lee, the chief freighter for the trading post.

"Frank was a quick, wiry man and a rough fellow. A trusting and honest man. He had had a hard life, but an interesting life to listen to. He had sharp, curly hair ... and was very healthy. He would always do his share of the work, and he expected a fellow to do a day's work and do it willingly. We had an awful lot of experiences and a lot of hard days, long days, cold days. But Frank was the nicest guy I ever worked for; he was considerate, would always do his share ... and was reasonably even tempered. He certainly knew the freighting and the packing business. Frank never carried a time piece with him. No matter how late we stopped (along the Cache Creek trail), he'd be up and ready to go at five o'clock in the morning. Every time. But whenever I asked Frank, 'When are we going to start out in the morning?' he'd say, 'Any time from now on.'"

Of the general activity taking place, Harriman said, "Most of the trappers would trap to get a grubstake to go mining in the summer. And then mine in the summer to get a grubstake to trap in the winter." The cabins kept to support these endeavors were available to anyone who might pass by in the owner's absence. "Cabins had a supply of kindling wood. Anyone who passed by the cabin and used it, always replaced the wood before they left," Harriman recalled. Further, he said, "Every creek between Talkeetna and Cache Creek had a trapper's cabin on it. There were no locked doors. And every trapper had a dog team." To keep track of time, "Every prospector or trapper had a calendar and they crossed off each day."

Harriman came into contact with most of the people in Talkeetna and the nearby mining country and found them to be interesting and rugged individuals. He met Antone Stander, who had been in the Klondike gold rush where he was fortunate enough to strike it so rich that he became one of the legendary "Eldorado Kings." But Stander went on to squander his wealth on drink, women, dubious business investments, and exotic jewelry. Now, Harriman said, he lived at the Talkeetna Trading Post and worked for Belle McDonald, "taking care of the fires and cutting up wood and working in the garden. Belle said that he was a tremendous worker."

Among the men who were trapping in the Yentna area to the west was an Irishman named Pat Patterson, who would occasionally walk seventy-five miles to Talkeetna from his cabin near the Yentna River. Harriman said he guessed that Patterson "came to stay in touch with the world." On the other hand, a prospector named Dassell stuck close to his mining ground at Cache Creek year-round, because he had a history of heavy drinking and knew that if he went to Talkeetna he would squander his savings on the liquor that was available there. At one time, Dassell worked long and hard to save all his money to get his ailing teeth fixed. When the right amount had been collected, he traveled to Talkeetna to catch the train for Anchorage where dental care was available. "He came to Talkeetna, and he got to drinking, and he spent every cent he had and had to go back to Cache Creek," Harriman said.

The elderly Henry Peters, ("You can't see it—you've got to find it"), had always wintered in Talkeetna. Another old-timer lived near the Fairview Hotel and, Harriman observed, "used to talk to himself. A lot of times you'd go by his house and you'd think he had several visitors there, but it was just him." One other old-timer named Rabideux went to Anchorage to be fitted for false teeth, but returned to Talkeetna on the train in an angry mood. He informed Harriman that the dentist's price for false teeth was outrageous—but he had fixed him, he had purchased a meat grinder. There were other men who had been in the Klondike during the gold rush and told about earning money by packing supplies and equipment over the Chilkoot Trail for other gold seekers. Yet another old-timer, Lymer Cox, had been prospecting in Alaska even prior to the Klondike and was highly respected for his ingenuity, resourcefulness, and integrity.

"There were very interesting people in Talkeetna," Harriman said. "Everybody knew everybody else. You didn't know everything about anybody, because people didn't pry into people's past. They just listened to what they had to say and didn't ask questions. The people were so friendly and generous. They all had down-to-earth feelings. Every time I'd see or talk to them their parting words were often, 'I'll see ya farther on up the trail.' It was always a friendly parting, friendly words. It was a whole different life than in the Northeast where I came from. People seemed more sincere. It was a good experience."

Wes liked the new U.S. Commissioner in Talkeetna, Ben Mayfield. "He was a friendly fellow with a good sense of humor. He was graduated from Washington State." Mayfield also played the cello. A visitor to Talkeetna, named Frances Thompson, observed that he was "good natured, had a close-cropped mustache, and a precise way of speaking that sounded a little British."

Harriman also noted the importance of the weekly arrival of the train in Talkeetna. Indeed, meeting the train was a major social event, and since it generally came in at night, people would gather at the Talkeetna Trading Post or the Fairview Hotel in the evening to await its appearance. Here, Harriman said, they would listen to the news broadcast from an Anchorage radio station, play cards, and "hope for music."

"Besides the news, there was Dick McLaughlin that played the organ," he said. "(People) would always come in every night for that part." Harriman also observed that the approach of the train was announced by the local dogs. "You could always tell when the trains were coming because the dogs would start to howl. And it seemed when they was howling that everybody in Talkeetna owned a bunch of dogs. They would get on top of their dog houses and howl and howl and howl."

"People were always interested in who came on the train, whether they were new people, or strangers, or whether they were people they might know that was coming back from Outside, or a trip to Anchorage," Harriman said. But most important was the mail that came off the train. Mr. Nagley, the postmaster, would meet the train with everybody else, take delivery of the mail, and transport it to the small post office located at the back of his store. "He would sort the mail out that very night," Harriman said. "Even if the train arrived after midnight."

Visitor Frances Thompson became intrigued with this weekly event and observed, "It took Mr. Nagley quite awhile to sort the mail it seemed. He was in no hurry, nor was anybody else, so people sat around and visited, some talking quite a lot, others saying only a few words. But to sit and listen, one got the idea it was as good as a town newspaper. Some people came in for their mail, got it, and went right out. Others lingered and sat and chatted, while others waited until Nagley was through with his post office work, (then) bought groceries before leaving. Everybody seemed friendly with each other and there did not seem to be any 'protocol.' I was to learn later, of course, that this classless system prevailed all over Alaska."

But there were differences of opinion among people, and Frances witnessed one argument in a local roadhouse that she recorded in her memoirs years later.

"One of the white women was complaining about the native women not having any morals as far as sex was concerned, and this man exploded," Frances relates. She describes the exchange:

"Godalmighty woman, do you realize we have some 2,000 years of rules and regulations we are governed by and we call it "civilization," while these poor people have just come out of the brush and do not even have one generation behind them to teach them our rules? How long would you last if you had to live by their rules?"

"Well," the woman snorted indignantly, "apparently they haven't any "rules" as you call it."

"Oh yes," the man said, "they have rules, much harder and stiffer than our so-called rules."

"What kind of rules do you mean?"

"The rules of a country that's under snow two-thirds of the time, (with) rain and bugs, (rough) rivers and swamps, and problems of finding enough food to eat, madam. They are called survival rules!"

Life could be tough for a lot of people in the area. A miner's wife named Margueritte Trepte recorded one story about a trapper and his wife who had some bad luck. The woman already bore a long scar on her arm, acquired when she shot at a bull moose for winter meat and was trampled by the injured and enraged animal. Trepte tells us more about the couple:

"Last winter her husband was taken ill with appendicitis while on the trap line, miles from everyone (in) soft snow, and no trail to speak of. She lashed him into the sledge and, taking the gee pole, drove the dog team to the trading post. From there a native took a message to the railroad.... It was a brave fight, but in vain, for her husband did not survive."

Enterprising hydraulic miners faced their own set of difficulties in Cache Creek country. Most kept a daily journal of their activities, and brief excerpts from one of these, recorded in 1935, provide a glimpse of some of the aggravations connected with the trade.

> June 5 - Snow about gone in pit. Hope to be washing by June 12th. Intake dam in creek in bad shape.

> June 11 - Sluices are in horrible shape but have no lumber here yet, + will wash in old ones + old long riffles. Bad setup.

> June 16 - Muck moves slow, gravity piping leaves all the rock back in pit + retards movement. 1800 inches water.

> June 18 - Two 2-men shifts piping. Ground moving slow. Lots of frozen ground in virgin face of bank. Hard to work.

> June 19 - Had top gun piping pay streak on top + soaking up blue bank. Undercut with big gun + had a big 3,000 yd. cave down. But it has to lay and thaw out. Most of it is frozen.

> June 24 - Gravity hydraulicing no good, too slow, cannot move the rock to dump + get 90 per cent of the gold in riffles.

But life would begin to grow more convenient in 1935, when a small gasoline-powered tractor, or "cat", ordered by the Alaska Road Commission, showed up in Talkeetna. Hitched to a crude sled called a "go-devil," the machine could haul supplies and equipment from Talkeetna to Cache Creek country in a more timely and serviceable manner. Now, Frank Lee began to think about switching to a tractor, and his young assistant, Wes Harriman, remarked later, "It's a good thing tractors replaced horses, because it was a helluva life for the horses, and the men too."

Even more remarkable was the appearance of an airplane now and then. Though prohibitively expensive for most miners to hire, these fast machines caught everyone's attention when they landed or took off on any of the suitable river gravelbars in the area.

January of 1935 lay heavily on the land when Frank Jenkins and Dick Francis traveled to Anchorage to appear in court. Numbing cold temperatures, heavy snows, and cheerless days prevailed during this most wintry month of the year. Jenkins and his lawyer were well prepared and, on January 21, introduced forty exhibits to the court, consisting of mining deeds, proof of labor affidavits, contracts, and photographs. Ken Brittell, Helen Jenkins, and Al Stinson were registered as witnesses for Jenkins.

A brief filed by Jenkins' lawyer, L.V. Ray, outlined the problem. Despite the temporary injunction granted to Jenkins earlier, Francis continued to aggravate the miner's operation. "Three or four times a week it was necessary to watch the intake dam and clear out the ditch to extend operations, at a loss of time and with a loss of water which cannot be estimated in money." Ray added that an adequate supply of water was "as essential to placer mining as gasoline is to an automobile."

The attorney agreed that there was some contention over claim boundaries, but he insisted that Jenkins held rightful possession of the claim that contained the important dam. He also maintained that Francis' mining claims did not contain enough gold value to warrant the disruption of Jenkins' important water network. After he remarked that Frank and Helen worked twelve to eighteen hours a day during the season and "interfere with no one," Ray continued with his argument that a permanent injunction against Francis was in order.

A formal portrait of Dick Francis, taken in Anchorage sometime in the 1930s—possibly during a time when his bitter legal conflicts with Frank Jenkins were full-blown. (courtesy June Francis Berg)

Francis' lawyer, Warren Cuddy, asserted that "the only real point at issue is the mining ditch between Ruby Creek and Lucky Gulch." He said his client had constructed "brush dams, and that they securely and firmly held all the tailings from his mining operations." He went on to note that Al Stinson, who had now testified for both sides in the dispute, had "stated that he had been on the ground several times during the mining season of 1934, and saw no evidence of tailings either at the head gate or in the ditch." And, he added, everyone knew how many years of experience Al Stinson had.

Cuddy argued that it had not been proven that Francis' work would produce irreparable injury to Jenkins. And the reason little gold had been recovered on Francis' claims thus far, was that he had not yet had the time to fully develop them. He argued that case law directed that an injunction be denied if important facts were in dispute; too many facts were indeed contradictory between the plaintiff and defendant in this case. The injunction should be denied, he said.

When the arguments were completed and the court took the case under advisement, Dick Francis probably headed right out to his trapline. Jenkins may have spent time working with his little sawmill in Talkeetna to produce lumber for ongoing construction projects at his claims. Jenkins was always busy.

February, with its longer days and higher sun, came and went, and the winter turned the corner to March. Still cold, sometimes windy, but with even longer, brighter days, mid-March found Dick Francis in Talkeetna, probably with some furs, getting together a $184.79 order of food and supplies at Belle's trading post.

He needed flour, corn flakes, salt, coffee, butter, onions, garlic, ham, cheese, crisco, milk, canned peaches, apricots, pineapple, plums, raspberries, strawberries, blackberries, grapefruit, and pumpkin. Also sweet potatoes, spinach, corn, oysters, honey, baking powder, olive oil, lemons, pilot bread, eggs, rutabagas, carrots, beets, cookies, and Velvet and Star tobacco. Also one long-handled shovel, one pick handle, one mattock, copper rivets, rope, knives, forks, spoons, nails, one 8 x 10 tent, one pair Ball Brand boots, regular socks, siwash socks, ivory soap, one pair khaki pants, and one dog chain.

The inclusion of the large tent ($18.75) among his purchases suggests a resolve to endure, no matter what the outcome of his legal struggle with the Jenkinses. When the judge issued his decision on March 28, Francis had his food and equipment staged in the Dutch Hills, ready to transition from trapping to mining.

Judge Simon Hellenthal seemed to want to accommodate both parties, and his official decision reflected a strong effort to do so. The first part of his judgement recognized that Jenkins had a water right to the ditch that ran laterally from Ruby Creek to Lucky Gulch. He went on to acknowledge that Francis' activity at his Sure Thing claims caused "a certain amount of" gravel and debris to travel down Ruby Creek and be deposited in front of Jenkins' dam—causing interference with the ditch that carried the water to Lucky Gulch. While no major damage had been done, he observed, these occurrences "did cause damage to the operation of (Jenkins') ditch and interfered with the use of his water right...." If allowed to continue, he said, this could result in serious damage to Jenkins' operation.

But if Dick Francis would take certain preventative measures, the situation might be salvaged, the judge said. If he built suitable barriers on his claims, and took proper precautions, he could develop and work his claims without interfering or obstructing Jenkins' water right.

Hellenthal became specific: "The court is of the opinion further, that a sand box of the usual construction, placed in (Jenkins') dam, cleaned at regular intervals ... so as to prevent and keep said sand box from filling up, said sand box to be so constructed as to catch all sand and debris before the same enters (Jenkins') ditch line ... will prevent interference with (Jenkins') water right and the use of the water of Ruby Creek by (Jenkins)."

The judge said that Jenkins should allow Francis to build this sandbox in his dam, and to clean it out regularly. If Francis failed to meet the court's criteria, he would be enjoined from performing any more work on his Sure Thing claims. Hellenthal added that the court should continue to monitor the situation and be ready to give further orders "should the need arise."

Before the judge's decision could be formally affected, trouble was brewing at Ruby Gulch.

Despite the intensity and warmth of the high April sun, heavy snows still lingered in the Dutch Hills when Frank and Helen arrived at Willow Creek to begin preparations for the 1935 mining season. Always there early, the two arrived at their claims on April 27. On that same day Frank had an encounter with Dick Francis that set him so on edge that he immediately wrote to his attorney, L.V. Ray, in Seward.

> Dear Sir:
>
> On arriving here at the mine today we find that Dick Francis has moved down from No. 1 and 2 Sure Thing on Ruby, to No. 1 Above Discovery on Willow Creek. He has with him another man named Larry Cummings (sic). He has definitely stated that he will not move from this claim without a court order signed by Judge Hellenthal to the effect that the property belongs to F.W. Jenkins and that he, Dick Francis, must move. It seem to me this is a direct trespass on

my property and a deliberate baiting to prevent my operations on this ground this summer. What procedure do I follow in getting this man off of my ground and preventing his operation there this summer. Please get the necessary papers ready immediately and since you are my attorney proceed as you think best in this matter but do so immediately. I am very anxious to clear this matter up in order that I may clear my obligations with you as soon as possible.
Yours truly, F.W. Jenkins

There is no evidence of any action taken by L.V. Ray with regard to Jenkins' angry request. Francis' alleged exploit might have been an isolated act, because no record exists of any aftermath related to this incident.

While both men continued to prepare for the mining season, Judge Hellenthal issued a more detailed decree that ordered Jenkins to provide a permit allowing Francis to place a sandbox in his dam, and to file a copy of the permit with the court. At the same time, he issued another decree that emphsized his warning that Francis' activities should in no way interfere with Jenkins' water right.

One senses that Jenkins was loathe to grant Francis any kind of access to his ground, but on May 24 Frank filed the required permit with the court:

Permission in writing is hereby given to the defendent above named, Dick Francis, to build a suitable sand-box as the same are generally constructed, in the plaintiff's diverting dam and intake located on Discovery or Number One on Ruby Creek or Gulch ... and further permission is given to said defendant, by this writing, to clean by shoveling, and not by sluicing down creek, said sand-box from time to time from any debris, sand or gravel which may settle therein, but said supply of water flowing into dam and ditch must not be reduced in volume at any time.

Another confrontation occurred in June. Though neither man filed a complaint about it until after the mining season was over, their documents describe what happened during a tense two-day period. Dick Francis told the court that he

... started to install the sand-box on the 18th day of June, 1935. That (he) further constructed barriers on ... Sure Thing No. 1 and Sure Thing No. 2 to further prevent the sand, gravel, and debris from damaging, and in every way attempted to comply with the order of this court.

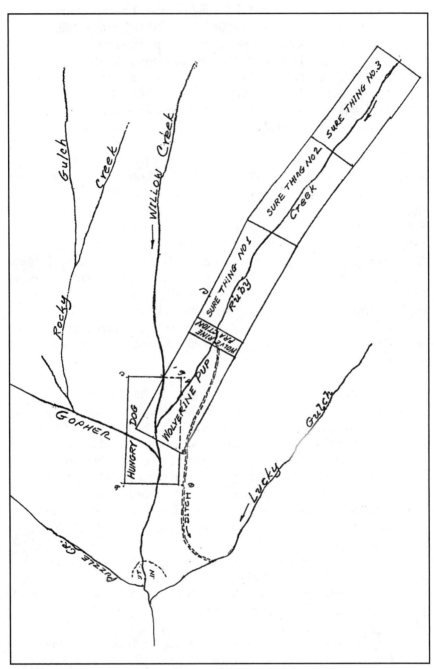

A claims diagram submitted by Dick Francis as a court exhibit in his case against Frank Jenkins. (National Archives-Pacific Alaska Region, Anchorage, Alaska)

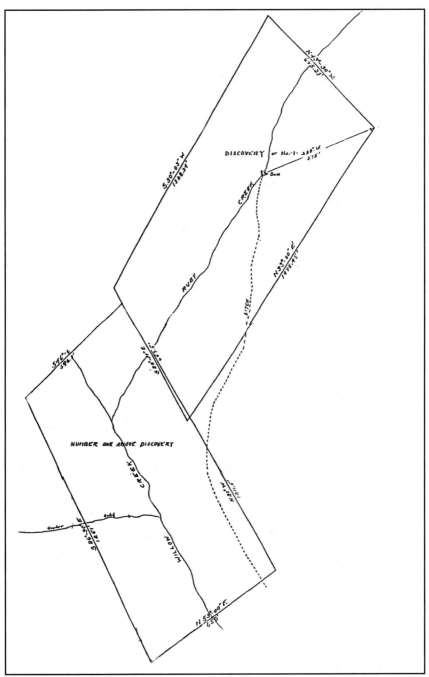

Frank Jenkins submitted this diagram of his claims that contained his water ditch as a court exhibit during his legal battle with Dick Francis. (National Archives-Pacific Alaska Region, Anchorage, Alaska)

> That (Jenkins) and his agent, Mrs. Helena Jenkins, came to the said dam on the 19th day of June, 1935, and interfered with the further construction of the sandbox. That (Jenkins) and his agent ordered (Francis), and his employees, away from said dam and that the said agent then and there placed her hands upon the sand-box to prevent the employees of defendant from further construction. That (Jenkins) and his agent then and there refused to permit (Francis) from further constructing the same.
>
> That on the 20th day of June, 1935, (Jenkins) and his agent, Mrs. Helena Jenkins, again visited the dam and (Francis') claims, above mentioned, and they then and there filled the said sand-box with rocks and gravel and tore out the barriers (Francis) had constructed. That (Jenkins) then and there posted a notice on the dam notifying (Francis) that he would not allow him ... to construct the said sand-box.

Frank Jenkins' version of the confrontation differed significantly from that given by Francis. He said,

> That on the 19th day of June, 1935, (Jenkins) discovered (Francis), with two men, attempting to install a sluice box, with a sluice gate, in the diversion dam in such a manner as to seriously impair the flow of water in the ditch and causing the dam to leak badly with danger of it being carried out entirely during a flood. Thereupon (Jenkins) told (Francis) to either constuct the sand-box and install it according to the decision of the court or to cease work on said sand-box immediately, and (Jenkins) then caused the following notice to be posted on the diversion dam at the head of the ditch:
>
> "Notice is hereby given to R.A. Francis that a sand-box was to be constructed in the usual way in the dam so as to prevent sand and tailings from entering the dam or ditch; the sand-box was to be constructed as to prevent said debris from going down the creek; said supply of water flowing into the dam and ditch must not be reduced in volume at anytime. A settling dam is not to be made of the dam or in anyway interfere with the water in use of by (Jenkins). The barriers to be constructed on Sure Thing No. 1, and Sure Thing No. 2, and not on No. 1 on Ruby."

It is not clear if this particular conflict continued past June. Both men seemed wholly unwilling to allow legal problems to interrupt their work during the short summer season, and they appear to have steered clear of another serious confrontation.

Both men had been packing guns when the tense encounters had occurred.

Sometime in the past year, Christ N. Hansen had passed away. The administrator of the old prospector's estate hired Dick Francis to perform the important annual labor on Hansen's placer claims, so in the spring Francis moved on down to Willow Creek, south of Jenkins' operation. According to a Proof of Labor record that Francis filed on July 9, he and three other men worked for forty-two days "digging ditches, clearing brush, and general mining." It is not unreasonable to speculate that Francis and Hansen had been good friends, particularly with the knowledge that Francis had been the old-timer's lone witness during the Hansen-Jenkins legal dispute. It therefore may have been a cheerless task for Francis to tend to Hansen's ground while the Dutch Hills burst into wild, green growth, and the birds reappeared with their lively summer melodies. The rush of Willow Creek and the winsome whistles of the parka squirrels would never be heard again by Hansen.

When Francis, now 56 years old, had finished the estate work, he returned to his camp, got his gear together, and went prospecting. Was he uncertain about the long-range value of the Ruby Creek claims? Was he a bit edgy that Jenkins might be as successful with the currently pending case as he'd been with Hansen? Or was Francis simply the quintessential prospector, always searching for the big pay streak? After he'd made his way up through the willows and alders along Ruby Creek, he left the upper reaches of Ruby Gulch and emerged onto a plateau that extended for about a half mile in a northeast direction. An imposing ridge, also trending north and east, rose to his immediate right as he covered the relatively flat terrain of this open section. Off in the distance, to the northwest, loomed the dramatic and weather-lashed crest of the great Denali, its immense lower mass cut off from Francis' view by the Dutch Hills and other peaks in the Alaska Range.

Leaving the plateau, Francis approached the first rugged features of Wonder Gulch, a ravine that paralleled the ridge on his right for eight-tenths of a mile, then dropped in a rough, steep descent to the wild country of Ramsdyke Creek. The modest creek that flowed through Wonder Gulch interested him, and it was here, along its higher reaches, that Francis spent his time prodding and picking and panning for some "color." We don't know how long he spent here, but it was long enough to convince himself that the ground was worth filing on. On July 9, when he was in Recorder Mayfield's Talkeetna office filing the paperwork for Hansen's estate, he also filed on two parcels he called Little Wonder Nos. 1 and 2 placer claims.

While Francis had been occupied to the north, Frank Jenkins was hard at work producing gold at his ever-expanding, labor-intensive operation along Willow Creek. In his mid-fifties like Francis, Jenkins had now achieved a level of production that required more and more help. Gone was the time when he had employed an occasional worker; this spring he had hired three for the whole season. Ken Brittell was back, along with his 21-year-old brother, Joy, from Nebraska. Jenkins

Wonder Gulch in the Dutch Hills, a place of drama during a volatile snow-storm in 1939.

must have needed more help badly, because he had even placed an ad in a Seattle newspaper looking for labor. He chose an adventurous 17-year-old named Ernie Bull.

"I saw an ad in a Seattle paper asking for a young man to work in a placer mine in Alaska," Bull remembered. "I figured, that's for me. I wrote to the Jenkins and they told me to be up by the middle of May. With my folks' permission, I sold my saddle horse and left for Alaska.

Aboard the *S.S. YUKON*, just out of Seattle in heavy fog, we had a collision with the *S.S. RUTH ALEXANDER*, arriving from the Orient. Four crew members were killed on our ship. The Coast Guard towed us back to Seattle. Two days later we boarded the *S.S. DENALI*."

The teenager docked in Seward, rode the Alaska Railroad to Talkeetna, and made his way over to the Dutch Hills, arriving there on May 10, 1935. By now the Jenkinses had established a substantial and permanent camp at Little Willow Creek, about a quarter mile up from its juncture with the larger Willow Creek. The complex, which consisted of Frank and Helen's cabin, sheds, and a cache, now included a bunkhouse for hired help. Though Frank excavated mine "pits" throughout his claims, often working several different locations in a season, the camp on Little Willow was his base. Bull's observations provide interesting detail about the Jenkinses and their operation when he worked there.

> We were always up by 6 a.m. (and) had breakfast in the Jenkins' cabin. Jenkins did feed well. Breakfast was always a hearty meal that started with oatmeal, along with pancakes, often accompanied by eggs. The eggs were stored in pottery crocks which is probably the way they were shipped. Bacon was also served regularly, and there was coffee and canned milk. Mrs. Jenkins baked a lot of bread and pies, and made a very good apple pie from dried fruit. Sometimes we would shoot ptarmigan and Mrs. Jenkins would fix them for dinner. All the cooking was done on her wood stove, which was fired mostly with low grade coal from an open vein nearby.
>
> We were on the job at 7 a.m., had an hour off at noon, then back to work at 1 p.m. We worked ten hours every day. Only one day off all season, and that was the Fourth of July, which happened to be my birthday.

Bull and the two Brittell brothers bunked together, he said, in

> ... a large tent over a wood frame, with a wood floor and sides (which had) a 50-gallon oil drum wood stove in the center, and two bunks on each side. We had electric light, as there was a wind generator that furnished juice for that and the radio. We sometimes cut small willow trees for wood to heat the tent, but mostly used the coal that was there.

At the end of the day, when the men had finished with their meal, Bull said that they "sometimes sat around after dinner to listen to news on the battery radio." While the men caught up on the news, Helen Jenkins would usually eat her dinner.

The Jenkinses' Little Willow Creek mining camp in 1939. The hill in the background held the onset of the northbound trail that Frank Jenkins and Joy Brittell traveled to retrieve a radio and battery at Ramsdyke Creek. (courtesy Maxine Brittell)

The young Ernie Bull formed certain impressions of the Jenkinses. "They were an odd couple. Didn't seem to have many friends, if any. Frank Jenkins was a good miner and a hard worker, (and) not very sociable. He was of small stature, about 5 feet, 6 inches, but very wiry. Always wore a moustache. If you have seen the movie "Lonesome Dove," the actor (who played the character) Gus was a dead ringer for Jenkins in looks and also voice. Frank was a Welshman. He told me a little of his life, said he used to make whiskey and sell it to the Indians."

Jenkins told Bull that he had a brother living in California, but that he and Helen "didn't get along with him." This comment might have been made with regard to Ray Jenkins, who appears to have left Alaska after the illegal beaver pelt episode.

Though Frank and Helen seemed distrustful of most people, Ernie Bull observed that the Brittell brothers "seemed to get along quite well with the Jenkinses—especially Joy."

There had been help in the past, however, that hadn't met Jenkins' standards. Bull learned that Frank was firm about one camp rule among his employees that involved alcohol. It wasn't allowed in the camp. This was reinforced by a remark Jenkins made to Bull about a man who had worked for him a part of one season. "He didn't want him back because he sneaked booze with him out to the mine," Bull said.

As the summer months progressed and Bull became accustomed to the hard work and routines of Jenkins' mining operation, he also became aware of the conflict with Dick Francis.

"Whenever we had work to do near the boundary of the mine, Jenkins always carried his gun, always expecting a shoot-out with Francis," Bull said. Helen Jenkins was more graphic about her animosity toward Francis and even made a dramatic proposal to Bull.

> Mrs. Jenkins said to me one evening after dinner, "You and I should take a can of gas each and go over to Dick Francis' and set his cabin on fire while he's asleep." I told her, no way, I wouldn't have anything to do with it. She always spoke of Francis as 'that animal.' She was very hyper and very "bushy." I always thought that she should have been in the nut house. Whenever we washed a pit down to bedrock, Helen would come out and turn over rocks, which usually had a few nuggets under them. She would pick them out, jump up and down, and holler, 'Praise God—Praise God.' She claimed to be quite religious (and) read the bible often—when she wasn't cussing out Dick Francis. I don't remember ever seeing her smile.

In a bold move, the curious young mine worker decided to conduct an investigation of his own. "One evening I sneaked off and hiked over to see this man, Dick Francis, that I heard so much about." Bull covered the two miles or so between the two camps, and reached Francis' tent-cabin where the miner's two malamute dogs, Amos and Andy, were tethered nearby. "He seemed to be a mild-mannered man, and was very nice to me. He talked about his problem with Jenkins, and the fact that they were accusing him of mining on their property."

His daring curiosity satisfied, Ernie Bull finished out the mining season at the Jenkins' camp. He liked Alaska, and instead of returning to Washington, he decided to spend the winter in Talkeetna, with plans to resume work at the Jenkins operation the following year.

As mining wound down in September, Ken Brittell hiked over the ridge that paralleled Wonder Gulch and made his way down its rugged face to Ramsdyke Creek. Then he moved downstream a short distance to the mouth of Wolf Creek and staked four more claims adjoining those he had filed on the previous year.

Later that month, he went to Mayfield's office and recorded the new claims. Dick Francis was there that day too, recording his Notice of Annual Assessment Work for his Ruby Gulch claims. At the same time, Francis filed on another claim in Wonder Gulch, which he described as "a valuable mineral bearing vein of rock," located near the head of the gulch. He called it the Dream Girl claim.

Now the country began to shut down with cold nights and barren trees. Another mining season was over. Another winter loomed.

7   matters that are axiomatic

A pattern had formed in the lives of the two min-
ers. April through October were months they devoted to mining, and
winter was the time for their legal battles. In December Jenkins and
Francis resumed communication with their lawyers, and Dick Francis
filed the next complaint. On the fourteenth he signed papers that
described his attempt to comply with the court-ordered sandbox place-
ment in June, and how the Jenkinses had obstructed those efforts.
He said that their interference had prevented him from mining on his
claims because, without the sandbox in place, the court would consider such mining in violation of the court order. For that reason, he
asserted, he did not work the property.

Further, if he had been able to work his Sure Thing claims, he
"could have made a profit of $5,000 during the season of 1935." He
was damaged in that amount, Francis said, and Jenkins should pay it,
along with $50 for damage to the sandbox Francis had constructed
and $500 in attorney fees. Finally, he appealed to the court for "an
order restraining (Jenkins) and his agents or assigns from any further
interference with the construction of the sand box and barriers so
that (Francis) may comply with the orders of this court."

On the day after Christmas, Jenkins signed a document that described his frustration with Francis' actions the previous June. He
said Francis hadn't met the court's sandbox requirements and had
even damaged his dam. He also complained that Francis hadn't constructed the court-ordered barriers on his Sure Thing claims and had
only placed "a few armsful of brush" in Ruby Creek. He contested
Francis' statement that he hadn't been able to work his claims that
summer. Instead, he said, "(Francis) carried on mining operations in
defiance of the injunction, on his claim Sure Thing No. 2, by making
three or four open cuts ten to twelve feet in width, by thirty to one
hundred feet in length. The tailings from these open cuts were caught

in a reservoir built two years ago on the upper end of Sure Thing No. 1 claim. When the reservoir was full of tailings and there was a sufficient head of water, the said tailings were released through a gate in the reservoir, thereby clogging the dam, ditch, and penstock with tailings, thereby causing (Jenkins) untold labor and expense."

The court should order Francis "to show cause as to why he has failed to comply with the terms of the injunction, and why he should not be punished accordingly," Jenkins declared.

Now the winter eased into 1936. A remote northern sun made a wan appearance as heat columns rose from smokestacks over Anchorage, where the continuance of the mining case, *Jenkins vs Francis*, would be heard at the courthouse. The case had apparently reached complex proportions because each man now had two legal representatives.

This time Dick Francis was well prepared. His primary attorney, Warren Cuddy, introduced a drawing of Francis' Ruby Creek mining claims, the sandbox permit that Jenkins had granted, along with the warning notice that Jenkins had posted at his dam in June. Fifteen photographs of the sandbox, brush barriers, and other pertinent items were also introduced, and two witnesses were registered for Francis.

The witnesses were Wes Harriman, the trading post freighter, and Larry "Rocky" Cummins, the miner who had experienced his own problems with Jenkins. The previous summer young Harriman had spent some time working a claim on upper Willow Creek, above both Francis and Jenkins. "While I was mining there I'd walk over to Ruby Creek and visit with Dick. So I knew him pretty well as a neighbor," he recalled.

> Rocky and I went to Anchorage with Dick, and we were witnesses," Harriman said. "The courthouse at that time was just about opposite the Anchorage Hotel; it was an all wooden structure, painted gray, and looked like a station. That was kind of an interesting thing; I had never been in a courtroom in my life. So Rocky and I were waiting to be witnesses, and every now and then they would have a short recess and Rocky would give me a short yank and say, 'Listen, let's get out of here, and let's go get a drink.' So we would do that. That's when they used to sell sample liquor in small bottles. So we'd hurry and buy one of them and get back. And we was sitting right behind this great big iron stove out in the middle of this courtroom. And Rocky dozed off. So they called for Lawrence Cummins. Well, Rocky didn't hardly know his real name, he'd always been called Rocky. I said, 'Hey, that's you.' Well, Rocky got up, but instead of walk-

ing out to the aisle, he walked down past the stove, and he kicked the stove poker right out in the middle of the big room. It didn't disturb Rocky very much. He got up and answered questions, and then they called me. We were glad to do it for Dick."

The men's testimony most likely centered on Francis' efforts to comply with the court order. But Jenkins wasn't having any of it. He repeated his denials that Francis attempted to install a sandbox in his dam, or constructed the required tailing barriers on his claims. A few armloads of brush placed within one hundred feet of his dam was "inconsequential and inadequate," he said. Jenkins denied that anyone had interfered with Francis; instead, he had "warned (Francis) not to erect a sluice box and gate in said dam, contrary to the order of the court." A sluice box was not a sandbox, he declared.

Jenkins denied that he had posted a notice on the dam that prevented Francis from installing a sandbox there. He said that Francis had not been damaged in the amount of $5,000; instead, he, Jenkins, had incurred $1,000 worth of damage from Francis' tailings, and another $1,000 in legal costs. He asked the court that Francis "be further restrained from installing a sand box or any other kind of a box or device in the dam ... and from in any way interfering with said dam or with the water impounded within said dam." And he wanted Francis to pay the $2,000 worth of damages he had suffered.

On January 23, Jenkins' new attorney, Arthur Thompson, filed a detailed brief with the District Court. He suggested that the court-ordered sandbox in Jenkins' dam was doomed for failure from the start. He cited the "unfriendly relations between plaintiff and defendant" as reason enough for this. When Jenkins needed a free flow of water in his ditch, Francis might choose that time to clean out the dam, thus impeding Jenkins' work, he argued. Thompson told the court that "factors controlled by nature" were also of consideration, because those forces "introduce elements of uncertainty which are inconsistent with the certainty required in judgements of the courts." The lawyer offered an example of this:

"In view of the mining conditions here, it is to be noted that the time when water would be plentiful and (Jenkins) could least afford to be delayed, would be the very time when delays could be expected, if (Francis') mining operations could also be going full blast."

Then Thompson made some bold statements.

"In view of the animosity between plaintiff and defendant it is respectfully suggested to the court that friendly relations cannot be established by judicial decree anymore than a lack of friendly relations can be penalized by the court," he said.

"There can be no joint use of plaintiff's dam. The purposes for which plaintiff and defendant use the dam are wholly incompatible. When the dam is full of sand it cannot be full of water, and when it is full of water it cannot be full of sand, and the degree of conflict is accurately measured by the amount of the filling," Thompson added.

He also, rather grandly, informed the judge,

"It does not require judicial decision to determine matters that are axiomatic, and the uniform teachings of human experiences remove from the field of discussion matters that are commonly accepted."

Thompson continued to attack the sandbox problems, especially Francis' substitution of a sluice gate for the box. Jenkins had been justified, he said, "in placing his own interpretation on the order of the court, and he was justified in providing such limitations in the written permission he gave as he thought necessary to protect his interest."

He said there was ample evidence that Jenkins had been damaged, citing "indisputable testimony that (Jenkins') dam was filled full of rock, sand, muck, and debris ... and that the character of the debris clearly showed that it came from the placer operations of the defendant...."

Now the attorneys for both sides put their cases to rest. Now it was up to the court to administer justice. Everybody hoped that the court would issue an expeditious decision, before spring arrived and the miners were called back to the search for gold in the Dutch Hills.

But as the weeks passed and the winter grew old, and as the sun rose higher and glanced sharply off the snow as the days lengthened, Dick Francis became angry. So angry that he went back to Anchorage and filed his own suit against Jenkins.

————

While the quest for justice moved forward in Anchorage, young Ernie Bull was experiencing his first winter in Alaska. Ken Brittell, his co-worker at Jenkins' mine, offered to let Ernie winter in a cabin he now owned in Talkeetna, one that had been constructed from lumber that Jenkins had processed at his mill. But the place was equipped with such a small wood stove that it proved almost impossible to heat that cold winter. So Ernie made a deal with Jack Devault, another roadhouse owner, to stay in an old cabin he owned; in exchange, Bull would dig up a large garden spot for him.

Bull remembered that winter.

The snow was about two and a half feet deep, and it was very cold. Thirty below was pretty normal, but we had a few days that fell to 35 below, and I remember one day down to 40 below.

On one of these cold days I was hunting ptarmigan on snow-shoes. When I took my mukluks off, my big toe on the right foot was black. I had Mrs. Mayfield look at it as she had been a nurse. She said I'd better get the morning train for Anchorage and see a doctor. The doctor I contacted said, 'You go get a bowl of soup for lunch, and at one o'clock I'll amputate your toe.' This scared hell out of me. I told my problem to a druggist, and he got ahold of Dr. Romig, the old "dogsled doctor." He treated the toe and had me stay for eight hours to see if gangrene would set in. All went fine; I still have the toe.

Ernie liked Talkeetna: "I always thought of it as a beautiful little frontier village, especially in winter, with its snow-covered cabins and icicles hanging from the roofs. The people were very friendly," he said. Bull visited often with one couple that taught at the school, and another family named Sherwood, with whom he played cards through the long winter evenings. He also enjoyed "sitting around the potbelly stove at Belle's, listening to some of the stories of the old-timers."

Bull also got to know and like Commissioner Mayfield. "I played a lot of pool with Ben Mayfield. He was a very nice fellow. He was rather heavyset, a big man. He was a heavy smoker, but always used a cigarette holder. He always wore breeches and high, lace-up boots."

But there was one person that the 17-year-old could not abide. He was a man named Clark, who was living in Talkeetna when Ernie arrived there in the fall. The same Clark, he learned, that Jenkins had dismissed after he'd brought alcohol to his mine.

Clark was living in a log cabin when I arrived in Talkeetna," Bull recalled. "I would guess him to be about 35 years old. I don't remember seeing him sober all winter. I never had an intelligent conversation with Clark as he was always drunk. I never heard him called by a first name, just Clark. A few other names given to him I don't dare to repeat.

One day, while Ben Mayfield and I were playing pool (at the Fairview Hotel), Clark came in, went behind the counter a minute, and then left. Shortly after, Mr. Nauman (the owner) went to the cash box and the money was missing. He asked if we had seen anyone come in. We told him Clark had come in for a minute and left. No doubt he took the money.

Clark was a no-good S.O.B., always a trouble maker. I knew that he was dangerous. I had a fight with him one day in Devault's place. He didn't put up much of a fight, but I hit him in the jaw and he fell over the hot stove. I told him if he ever bothered me again that I would kill him. He never did.

He seemed to enjoy looking for trouble. The only fellows that I ever saw him hang around with were the two half-breed Larson boys, who he drank with. That winter Clark had taken in a prostitute to live with him. She was a heroin addict, and they both stayed drunk or drugged. They ran out of firewood and burned up the table and chairs; only a bed and an empty nail keg was left, and a lot of empty whiskey bottles on the floor. He had shot holes through his stove pipe, and the pots and pans that were hanging by nails on the wall.

According to Bull, the presence of heroin in Alaska was rare at this time, but the woman had recently traveled from the Hawaiian Islands where it was readily available.

"At this time Ben Mayfield was instrumental in getting the woman out of town. To get rid of her the Mayfields got enough people to contribute for a railroad fare, and gave her a 'blue ticket' (a one-way fare) to get out of town. Ben also told storekeepers not to sell any more whiskey to Clark. He was found to be using what heroin the woman had left hidden in the cabin, as he was out of whiskey," Bull said.

Sometime in the early spring of 1936, Bull remembered, Clark left Talkeetna. "I never saw him again," he said.

————

Dick Francis was a frugal man. Records of his purchases at the trading post attest to this, as did the simple life he lived. No evidence suggests that he ever invested in a home in Talkeetna, and he may have chosen to live on his trapline and his mining claims because it was financially prudent. Shouldering the burden of the legal bills he was accumulating can't have been easy.

Though Jenkins had charged in legal documents that he could not hope to recover damages from Francis because he was "insolvent," it is interesting to note that Warren Cuddy, a prominent and respected attorney in Anchorage, continued to represent Francis despite the miner's mounting legal costs. Francis must have somehow shown good faith, and Cuddy was obviously giving him the benefit of the doubt.

Whatever his financial circumstances, Dick Francis filed suit against Jenkins on February 28. The judge had still not issued a decision on Jenkins' suit, but that didn't deter Francis. This time he focused on claim boundaries. He gave legal descriptions of his Wolverine Fraction, Wolverine Pup, and Hungry Dog claims, and maintained that

Jenkins claimed rights to the same ground. Jenkins' claims were "without legal and equitable foundation and void," and this placed a cloud on his title, he said.

Francis' complaint went on to say that Jenkins had entered upon these claims in 1934 and 1935 and mined gold dust and gold nuggets in the amount of $5,000. Unless the court stopped such trespass, Jenkins would continue to remove the gold and financially injure Francis. The court should determine the true ownership of the claims in Francis' favor, he said, and stop Jenkins from future trespass. Francis should be paid $5,000 for the gold extracted thus far, $500 in attorney fees, and any other relief the court might consider fair.

On March 4, legal notice was served on Jenkins, and on March 19 Warren Cuddy filed a motion for a temporary restraining order that would prohibit Jenkins from trespassing on Francis' claims. That same day Judge Hellenthal issued an order that required Jenkins to appear in court on March 25 to show why he should not be restrained from entering the claims.

Just four days later, the judge issued his long-awaited decision on Jenkins' case. The focus of the court's consideration was the permitted sandbox. The judge acknowledged that Jenkins had given written permission for the installation of the sandbox, but said that the permission was flawed.

The judge went on to decree:

> That the defendant attempted to install the sand box, but that he was prevented from so doing by the plaintiff.
>
> That the permission to construct the sand box did not comply with the decree of the court, and was therefore defective.
>
> That by reason of the defectiveness of the permission to construct the sand box, the injunction was inoperative and the defendant was therefore not prevented from operating his mining claims ... Sure Thing No. 1 and Sure Thing No. 2.

Judge Hellenthal ended his decision with the conclusion that Francis' petition for $5,050 should be dismissed, but that he could recover the sum of $100 in attorney fees from Jenkins.

Thompson, Jenkins' lawyer, immediately protested the judge's decision. He took strong exception to the ruling that the sandbox permit was defective. He protested the judge's finding that Jenkins had prevented the installation of a sandbox. Francis' contrivance bore no resemblance to a sandbox, he said, and instead had damaged a wall of Jenkins' dam! He took exception to the award of $100 to

Francis, and to the judge's conclusion about the injunction. A review of the document containing these protests engenders a sense of profound indignation on the part of Thompson.

A few days later, as the high March sun again graced the snow covered land, Thompson filed a motion for a new trial. He cited several "errors of law" and the insufficiency of evidence to support the court's conclusions. He and Jenkins weren't taking this sitting down.

Meanwhile, Francis' own suit moved forward. On March 25 the miners met again in court.

Dick Francis (right) at Ruby creek, in a photo submitted as a court exhibit during his acrimonious legal disputes with Jenkins. The man with him is probably Francis' partner, Ed Carlson. (National Archives-Pacific Alaska Region, Anchorage, Alaska)

Frank Jenkins filed an affidavit in which he swore that he had no interest whatsoever in Francis' Wolverine, Wolverine Pup, and Hungry Dog claims. But he was the owner of two claims called No. 1 Above Discovery on Willow Creek, and Discovery Claim on Ruby Creek, he said, and in 1934 and 1935 had taken less than $100 worth of gold from these claims. Jenkins said he held a water right on Ruby Creek, and had exercised that right for over six years. Furthermore, he had acquired these claims long before Francis had filed on his.

Helen Jenkins filed an affidavit that emphasized that her husband had been "in actual possession of said Discovery claim on Ruby Creek ... when (Francis) located his pretended Wolverine, Wolverine Pup and Hungry Dog claims in May, 1934...."

Jenkins also filed an answer to Francis' complaint. He said that the chain of ownership of his claims dated to 1906, and that this was a well-known fact in the area. He believed that Francis' claims conflicted with his own, and if this was so, Francis' claim was absolutely inferior to his own. The court should validate this, rule in his favor, and award him all his legal fees and costs.

Dick Francis testified that the claim Jenkins called his Discovery Claim on Ruby Creek was the same ground as Francis' Wolverine and Wolverine Pup claims, which he had filed on in April, 1933. Jenkins, he contended, had not filed on his Ruby Creek claim until July, 1934. Francis submitted copies of recorded certificates to substantiate this.

As March ended, Francis' second attorney, Clyde Ellis, filed another motion in District Court. It identified much of Jenkins' response as "sham, frivolous and irrelevant," and challenged Jenkins to produce a chain of title to prove his ownership of the pertinent claims.

As the season to move to the Dutch Hills approached, a sense of urgency prevailed. On April 6 two last briefs were filed. Arthur Thompson imparted more of his wisdom in Jenkins' behalf.

> (Jenkins) has ... stated in his sworn affidavit that he claims no interest in (Francis') Wolverine, Wolverine Pup, and Hungry Dog claims. The question presented for the determination of the court by (Francis') complaint thereby becomes moot—there is nothing for the court to try. It is like a case of a man coming into court claiming a horse and asking the court to declare him to be the owner thereof, when nobody is claiming the horse.
>
> If (Francis) can find some way of getting the judgement of the court that he is the owner of the Wolverine, Wolverine Pup and Hungry Dog claims and that (Jenkins) has no interest therein, we have no objection. However, we do object to the court awarding to (Francis) any of the ground claimed in our answer by reason of our Discovery Claim on Ruby Creek and our No. 1 Above Discovery on Willow Creek.

Thompson said that Jenkins had worked his own ground, not Francis' ground. He owed Francis nothing. And there were no issues raised by Francis that could support an injunction against Jenkins.

Now, Clyde Ellis rose to represent Francis. Referring to his brief he argued,

> The affidavits of (Jenkins) and his wife in one paragraph deny that they claim any right, title or interest in the Wolverine or the Wolverine Pup.... If this be true, no harm would result to (Jenkins) from an injunction restraining them from trespassing on this property. However, the affidavits do contain allegations which would indicate that Discovery on Ruby does conflict with (Francis') claim.

Ellis continued to challenge Jenkins' ownership of the pertinent claims. If Jenkins purported to own Discovery on Ruby since 1906, why did he file a location notice on the claim after Francis had filed his? Jenkins' location notice seemed nothing more than "pretended rights" to the property, he said. Ellis concluded with the statement that "This court should issue an order restraining (Jenkins) from further working this property until the title to the same is finally determined."

Aware that time was of the essence, Judge Hellenthal issued his decision immediately. He acknowledged the conflict over the men's claims and focused on that fact. Rightful title to the ground needed to be established, he said. For now, he issued an interim decision: "The attorney for (Jenkins) may prepare and present an order denying the injunction pending the final determination of this cause."

On April 27, after deleting six lines of the order that Thompson had submitted to him (which seemed to attempt to establish Jenkins as the rightful owner of the disputed claims), Judge Hellenthal signed the document.

Dick Francis was feeling pretty good. Not only had the judge dissolved Jenkins' injunction in March, he seemed now to question Jenkins' ownership of the ground involved in the dispute. Around this time Francis wrote a letter to his mother in Mt. Shasta, the only relative he still maintained occasional contact with. He told her about the ongoing difficulty he was having with his "neighbors," and his view of recent events. "I beat that outfit good and plenty," he wrote. "And I am the only one who has stood up and made them go. How they do hate me."

Now it was time to mine for gold.

———

During the spring of 1936, Talkeetna U.S. Commissioner Ben Mayfield wrote an article for a Seward newspaper entitled, "Development in the Talkeetna Mining and Recording District." Excerpts from this composition provide a comprehensive picture of activity at both Talkeetna and Cache Creek country at this time.

Talkeetna, Alaska, is the headquarters for the Talkeetna Mining and Recording District.... With the advance in the price of gold, great activity is seen in all parts of the area; many new prospectors are roaming the hills; new discoveries are being made; old operations are being worked on a larger scale; and business over the whole district shows a decided upward trend.

The U.S. Commissioner's office for this district ... is located at Talkeetna on the Alaska Railroad.... The Peters Creek, Cache Creek, Clear Creek, and Fairview areas are supplied from this point. The Talkeetna Trading Post ... includes general merchandise, restaurant, teams for freighting at Talkeetna, and a road house at the Peters Creek bridge, 24 miles from Talkeetna. Jack Devault has a road house, operates the ferry across the Susitna River at Talkeetna, carries the mail twice a month to Cache and Peters Creeks, and does general freighting with a tractor. Frank Lee has just purchased a new tractor and is engaged in general freighting to the various camps. B. Nauman operates the Fairview Hotel in Talkeetna, the only hotel in town. H.W. Nagley is the postmaster and does a general merchandising business.

The Peters Creek Mining Co ... is the largest operator in the district to date.... This company has already moved over 300 tons of freight from Talkeetna to the scene of operations on Peters Creek, 35 miles from Talkeetna. Now they are setting up a saw mill and will soon begin sawing 100,000 feet of lumber for their own use at the plant.

On Willow Creek, a tributary of Peters Creek, F.W. Jenkins, one of the most successful small operators, will be going full blast as he has been doing for the past fifteen years.

Over the divide west from Peters Creek and about 40 miles from Talkeetna lies the Cache Creek area, owned largely by J.C. Murray and H.W. Nagley.

F.J. Englehorn is busy dismantling the old dredge and power house on Cache Creek and freighting the 300 tons of machinery to Talkeetna from whence it will be shipped to the Kenai region ...

the dredging ground on Cache Creek having been worked out. Frank Lee, with his new tractor, is helping with the freighting of the machinery.

Nick Balabanoff has purchased a new hydraulic plant which he will operate on his claims on Nugget Creek this season.

Five new tractors have been landed here this spring, bringing the number of tractors freighting out of Talkeetna to eight. The Peters Creek Mining Co. and the Kenai Gold Dredging Co. each purchased new 40 h.p. diesels, while Frank Lee and Jack Devault each bought a 20 h.p. Caterpillar. The freighting has been going on continuously night and day.

A school was established at Talkeetna last year, and this summer a new $6,000 school building will be erected. Several new log houses have been built during the last year, and more are contemplated.

We now need a larger depot, a station agent, and better facilities for handling the increased tonnage coming to Talkeetna from the Alaska Railroad; and, from the Alaska Road Commission, the necessary help and machinery to maintain the present road of 27 miles, which is badly in need of surfacing to make it passable during the summer, and a continuation of construction to the more remote areas.

Cache Creek country was astir with the hunt for gold, and the Jenkinses and Dick Francis must have felt good to be released from winter and the courts. The miners were back in the hills where a sense of freedom and independence prevailed; where the air was crisp and crystal clear, and one could see for miles from the slopes of the Dutch Hills; where spring enabled everything to snap to action once more. Excited v-shaped lines of migrating geese and other waterfowl filled the air in early May, and the haunting, primitive call of the sandhill crane echoed from high overhead as the graceful birds headed north to their nesting grounds.

In June, sparrows and warblers returned to fuss about the alders and willows, singing continually and adding to the life force of the wilderness mining country. Wild geranium, salmonberry plant, bluebell, fern, and glacier flower joined the urgent growth of wild cotton, laborador tea, devil club, wild daisy, burnet, and other plant life. New, slim stalks of false hellebore snaked through the tangle of vegetation, aggressively insistent upon gaining their share of space. In late June, when these plants reached heights up to six and seven feet, they acquired an imposing presence that lent an exotic aura to the hills. Deeply ribbed and fan-like leaves endowed the hellebore with a unique, twisted appearance, while the plant's attractive white-flowered spikes, with pale green overtones, belied its deeply poisonous nature.

The ubiquitous willow and alder at the lower reaches leafed out fully, while fragile lowbush blueberry and blackberry shoots wound their way through the mossy tangle higher on the hills. Willow Creek rushed tirelessly, fed by melting snows at Ruby Creek and other modest tributaries. Mining was damnably hard work, and the mosquitoes could be wretched, but somehow the compensations of nature took an edge off the strain.

Ernie Bull, now nearing his eighteenth birthday, resumed his employment with the Jenkinses in the early spring of 1936. But he finally confided to Ken and Joy Brittell that he felt uneasy working for the couple. "I never had a problem getting along with people, but the Jenkinses were different, not the type of people that I felt comfortable with. I had a feeling that some day something was going to happen at the mine, but I didn't want to be there when it did," he said.

Bull hauled freight from Talkeetna to the Dutch Hills for Jenkins for a month or so, and "did some sanding of the pit which causes earlier snow-melt for the mining." But when he heard that a mine at Bird Creek was looking for help, he made the decision to leave the Willow Creek operation, knowing that the Brittell brothers were available to Jenkins. He did acquire employment with the Bird Creek mine and remained there for the rest of the season.

That summer seems to have passed with no direct confrontation between Francis and Jenkins. Perhaps both parties made an effort toward this end, to gain relief from the tense legal struggle. Whether Francis' mine tailings aggravated Jenkins' water ditch this season is not evident. But one notable event occurred on July 20, when Judge Hellenthal issued his ruling on the motion for a new trial that Jenkins' attorney had filed in March. The request was succinctly denied in one brief paragraph. There would be no new trial, the judge ordered.

In July and August Ken and Joy Brittell filed on three more claims at Wolf Creek. In the same period, Frank Jenkins filed on claims at Willow and Cottonwood Creeks, and Helen recorded claims at Willow Creek, Gopher Gulch, and Lucky Gulch.

At the end of the season everyone, including Dick Francis, filed affidavits attesting to the labor they had done on the claims they held.

At this time Francis wrote another letter to his mother in which he complained that some of his mail was being lost. He blamed this on his "bitter and dirty enemies," adding that "they would not hesitate at anything." About this time one of Francis' acquaintances in Anchorage, a police officer, said he noticed a slight change in Dick. The hardships of the miner's austere and physically demanding lifestyle seemed finally to be taking a toll, he thought. During one of Francis' trips to Anchorage the two had met on the street and stopped to visit a bit. During the conversation Francis remarked that his right eye was going bad—to such an extent, that he had had to change his rifle over from one shoulder to the other when hunting. Since Francis enjoyed a reputation as an excellent marksman, this circumstance was probably more disheartening to him than he let on.

Another story in modest circulation at this time portrayed Francis as so paranoid about the Jenkinses that one winter night he had become convinced that Frank Jenkins was outside his cabin stalking him. He grabbed his gun, ran outside, and began shooting into the night to scare Jenkins off, it was said. Longtime prospector and friend, Cliff Hall, was believed to have witnessed this episode and to have subsequently expressed some concern about Francis' well-being.

Snow was on the ground in Anchorage when Dick Francis' case resumed in December. On the ninth, Arthur Thompson filed an answer to Francis' allegation that Jenkins could not show proof of ownership for the claims that contained the water ditch. The document, ten pages long, outlined in impressive detail the chain of ownership of the claims dating to May of 1906. The chain led to the Hatch and Rice ownership that had fallen into forfeiture in 1930, when that group failed to contribute its share of the costs that Jenkins had paid for claim improvements. This established, Jenkins asked the judge to dismiss him from the suit, and award him his costs and lawyer fees in the amount of $750.

After the holidays and the arrival of 1937, Dick Francis' response, in which he continued to deny the legitimacy of Jenkins' "professed ownership," was filed in District Court on January 4. He did concede, however, that Jenkins owned "certain water rights on Ruby Creek," because the court had apparently established that in the previous case. But the actual claims remained in conflict, he said, and this needed to be resolved.

Both men were at the courthouse on January 6. Both submitted legal exhibits in the form of mining claim documents and maps, and Helen Jenkins and Ken Brittell were registered to testify for Jenkins. Few court records document this hearing, but one reflects that Arthur Thompson again asked the court to dismiss the case. The judge replied that he would "reserve his decision." The next evidence in the case file does not appear until March, when Thompson filed a weighty twenty-seven-page brief in Jenkins' defense.

Jenkins' claim ownership was established long before Francis' filing, the brief said. And the dams and ditches that Jenkins had constructed were "the best kind of possession." Even Francis had conceded that Jenkins had water rights there, Thompson noted, yet he had brazenly located his claims over those long held by Frank Jenkins. The old claim stakes installed by Jenkins were even in place when Francis filed on his claims, the lawyer contended. "Perhaps his search for the stakes was as thorough as his search for the (mining claim) record," he added sarcastically.

Thompson attacked Francis' allegation that Jenkins hadn't filed on the claims until after Francis had filed. The reason Jenkins had filed another certificate of location for the claims in 1934, Thompson said, was due to the fact that in preceding years a fire in Talkeetna had destroyed some of the mining records in the recorder's office. "He thought the record of his ... (original) location was among them," he said. Regardless, Jenkins' chain of title to the claims should speak for itself, he insisted.

Then a detail surfaced in the brief, the nature of which is not surprising when one considers that Frank Jenkins had been entangled in legal cases since 1930: the Christ Hansen suit, the illegal beaver pelt fiasco, the Hansen assault complaint, Jenkins' own two-year suit against Dick Francis, and Francis' current suit against Jenkins. The many years of court battles and legal fees appeared to have finally taken a toll on Jenkins, because Thompson's brief now stated,

> It is to be noted that defendant has not sought this litigation. He is only here upon the summons of the plaintiff. When the prior suit with plaintiff was concluded, the hope of defendant was that litigation with plaintiff had come to an end. He was anxious to enjoy the fruits of that litigation in peace and quiet. He wanted to make beneficial use of his water right, and his dams and ditches on Ruby Creek, and to continue his mining on Discovery and on No. 1 Above Willow claims. In this he has been encouraged by the hope that plaintiff would accept the judgement of the court and be satisfied.
>
> This suit is of plaintiff's seeking, and he has embarked upon this litigation with his eyes wide open. He knew that the water right and the dams and ditches had been awarded to defendant, and that No. 1 Above Willow had been decreed to belong to defendant.... He was hopeful that he could secure in this suit an injunction against defendant which would deprive defendant of the use of the very necessary water in Ruby Creek, and other-wise interfere with his mining operation: Not that he wanted to use this water himself, or mine upon these claims —he had no such intention. If he should not succeed in this action he has no one to blame but himself; and he should suffer the penalties of those who bring vexatious law suits without foundation.

These statements were followed by a few remarks about case law, and there the brief ended. There is nothing in the file to indicate that Francis and his attorneys filed anything further. The disposition of this case was now with the judge.

On April 12, Dick Francis was out at Ruby Gulch. Heavy snows remained in the area, but Francis was setting up camp. He'd had a large order of supplies freighted to his place from the Talkeetna Trading Post, and now he carefully unpacked the shipment to be sure everything was there. When he had completed the task he sat down and wrote a letter to Belle McDonald.

Dear Belle:
Landed all O.K. but found that my coffee had not been shipped. Also no matches. So please send me as soon as possible, 20 lbs. H.B. coffee, 5 lbs. royal baking powder, $7.00 matches, small boxes. Erickson also found himself short of certain articles."

Then Francis told Belle some disturbing news that indicated the code of honor recognized by the great majority of miners on the creeks had not been wholly observed. It had to do with a mining camp that Belle and her husband owned on upper Willow Creek, much higher on the sloping hill, overlooking Ruby Creek:

Your cache had been raided this winter and ladder left up. Lucky wolverines did not get in. Do not know what was taken. Only bunks had been torn out of camp and lumber taken. I know that was all done since Oct. 12th as I (last) passed there on that date. (Someone) cleaned Cliff Hall out completely. Not enough wood left to start fire. Please send stuff at once as we need it badly.
Yours truly,
Dick.

On the same day that Francis sent his letter with the freighter to Belle, Judge Hellenthal issued his verdict on Francis' suit against Jenkins (though it would be some time until Francis received the news in the Dutch Hills). The length of the judge's decision (fourteen pages) reflected the degree of complexity and significance that the legal struggle had attained in the judge's estimation. First, he reviewed all the facts of the case to do with claim staking, water rights, and mining location notices. In doing so he lent significance to the reason Jenkins had filed for his claims in 1934:

The purpose of making locations of said claims in 1934 was to make a new record of said claims for the reason that he believed the original location notices filed with the Precinct Recorder at Talkeetna had been destroyed...." (The judge noted that Jenkins had later learned they were still on record.)

The judge stated that Jenkins' claim appeared to be covered by Francis' claims. He said that if the ground had been "unappropriated public domain" when Francis had done his staking, Francis' legal action would have merit. It was, therefore, the court's responsibility to determine the validity of Jenkins' locations. And the judge did this now.

> As to No. 1 Above Discovery on Willow, the Court is of the opinion that the ownership of said claim was determined in a prior action between the parties, in which (Jenkins) was adjudged to be the owner of said claim, and that said claim was a valid and subsisting claim at the time (Francis) located or attempted to locate the Hungry Dog on May 5, 1934, and that therefore, the Hungry Dog was never a valid location....

With regard to Jenkins' disputed Discovery on Ruby claim, the judge devoted six pages to complex case law that helped him to sort out the maze of evidence that had accumulated during the course of the trial. His conclusion was brief and clear:

> We, therefore, conclude that at the time the Wolverine was located, April 14, 1934, the Discovery on Ruby was a valid location ... and that therefore (Francis) has no right of possession under said locations ... and therefore cannot maintain this action; that (Francis') complaint should be dismissed; that two hundred dollars ($200) is a reasonable attorney's fee to be allowed (Jenkins) as costs for defending this action and that in addition thereto (Jenkins) should be allowed his costs herein incurred.

Once again it was early spring, when geese and sandhill cranes would soon return to the northland, calling from the sky in graceful, shifting groups. Swans and other waterfowl began to appear in the high, brilliant sunlight, but it was still too early for songbirds or any hint of greenery to show in the snow-locked hills. Dick Francis was now 58 years old, and the news about the judge's decision was surely a blow to him. He must have spent long hours pondering about what to do. His Hungry Dog and Wolverine claims no longer existed, but he still had his Sure Thing ground on Ruby Creek. But these claims still harboured the potential for mine tailing conflicts—though it seemed that Jenkins had had enough of legal strife.

Dick Francis was a man who seemed always to be grounded in reality, and one who accepted his lot in life. Now, as the end of April drew near, he made a decision. He gathered up his gear and headed for Long Creek, his old stomping grounds. This time he inspected the ground on lower Long Creek, nearer to the creek's approach to the vast Tokositna River drainage. After some days spent testing, he drove in stakes on six claims that he called Discovery and 1-5 Above Discovery.

Five days later Arthur Thompson filed a Memorandum of Costs and Disbursements with the District Court in Anchorage. It itemized Frank Jenkins' expenses for witness transportation and fees, and for court clerk, court reporter, and attorneys' costs. The total came to $436, and Dick Francis was soon notified of his obligation to pay it. As the weeks moved through May and on to summer, one senses that the drama of the preceding years had exacted a price in personal vitality on the part of both miners. Records show little evidence of any new claim staking or other activity that might appear in the public register, but Dick Francis did file on one more mining claim in July of 1937. He traveled from lower Long Creek back over to Wonder Gulch and staked a section next to his Dream Girl claim, calling it Dream Girl No. 2.

The mining season appears to have passed quietly enough, and when freezing temperatures arrived to interfere with the smooth movement of water needed for gold production, everyone closed up their camps for another winter. The winter was quiet too, and Frank Jenkins must have appreciated that fact. But he was eager to recover what he could of the expenses he had incurred with Francis, and in late January of 1938, the attorneys for both men appeared before Judge Hellenthal again. The result was a "Set-Off of Judgements." Jenkins, it seems, had never paid Francis the $100 the judge had awarded him in 1936, so now the judge deducted it from the $436 Jenkins had been granted. Francis owed Jenkins the remainder, the judge decreed.

By mid-March the debt had not been paid, and Jenkins must have complained about it, because the judge now signed an order authorizing the seizure of Francis' personal property. On March 19, in the glare of the new spring sun, a notice was posted at the court house in Anchorage declaring that mining claims Sure Thing Nos. 1, 2, 3, 4, and Little Wonder Nos. 1 and 2 were to be auctioned.

Dick Francis must have appealed to his old friend, Ed Carlson, who no longer operated the Inlet Hotel but kept in close touch with Dick. On auction day Carlson made a bid that was accepted, and on April 20 Francis signed a deed for his Sure Thing and Little Wonder

111

claims over to Carlson. The sale of the ground realized $100, which was presumably transferred to Jenkins. On the same day Francis signed a separate deed that transferred his Dream Girl Nos. 1 and 2 claims to Carlson for another $100.00, which probably went to Jenkins as well.

Francis then borrowed about $350 from Carlson, probably to satisfy the balance of the court judgement and to pay something on his legal bills. Eventually the two men reached an agreement that included Francis' continued work on the Sure Thing, Wonder, and Dream Girl claims. Though no documentation exists to detail what was probably an oral agreement, one senses that Ed Carlson was doing what he could for his friend, and Francis was intent on defraying his indebtedness.

––––––

Frances Thompson, who had spent some time in Talkeetna in 1935, had been so captivated with the town and the mining culture that she had returned in 1937 to look for work. Her memoirs, written years later, provide a glimpse at the people and the trade in the Talkeetna-Cache Creek area at this time:

> The town had no water system, no electricity, and oil or propane heat was unknown. Coal was shipped down from the coal mines at Healy on the Alaska Railroad, but people had to get together and order it by the carload. We used gas pressure lamps to light the darkness, and sometimes (in winter) they burned almost all day.
>
> For these people who had lived in Alaska for many years, each had a pattern of their own in attitude, lifestyle, clothing and habits. As I became acquainted with (them) I knew what subjects we would talk about ... and their attitude toward their life. They had one thing in common for the most part, and that seemed to be (their) belief in themselves to take care of themselves without any outside help. And there was hardly any subject they could not talk about.
>
> If you had to build a new privy, or drive a point down in the gravel for a new well, or fix the roof on your house, you could look out the window and see people coming from all directions. Word was passed around, and soon half the town would drop what they were doing to see if they could help.
>
> I think one of the greatest benefits to me was (that) I was constantly learning. Once I was griping about some old guy who was obnoxious when he was drunk. He wasn't any too clean, and always had something sarcastic to say. One of the older men, whom I considered a friend, listened to me and then said,

'Frances, it just might be possible that some time you will be near that old man's cabin and you will be cold and wet and hungry and half frozen to death, and him and his cabin, even if it's filthy, will look like heaven to you.'

Each person had his or her own character, and I could say truthfully that very few people agreed with each other. Everybody had their own opinion, so the success of getting along with one's neighbor or friend was (achieved) by a required tolerance.... You did not need to love your neighbor or even try to understand him.... We saw that basically everyone had the right to be an individual and we respected that.

In a way, life itself was a gamble; you weren't so concerned on being friends as you were concerned on not being enemies. So frequently, if you disagreed with your fellow man, you just shut up and walked off.

We were all ages and all types and, for the most part, all different nationalities. Here we had freedom (which) was our most valued asset. I might even venture to say this was the reason most of us were here.

But the yen for freedom and independence couldn't sidestep the demanding realities of life in Alaska. The toughness of the country often took a heavy toll on the independent minded, and Frances observed how the men reconciled themselves to this fact.

Men were partners in mining (and) trapping because it was easier for two. There were some singles of course, but I could see how they could make far more money if there were two of them; they could work in shifts in the brief summer of mining. On the trapline they could guard each other against the hazards of freezing (or) getting lost. And loneliness was the worst byproduct of the wilderness.

But there was also the problem of people getting along with each other. Sometimes the whole misery of ... monotony and hardship got on mens' nerves, and they would come off the trapline not speaking to each other; or quarrel over the way the (gold) "clean-up" was handled. One famous story was about the way you cooked the coffee.

Now, coffee was the one thing you wanted when you came in tired at night. Especially if you were on the cold-weather trapline. It was the first thing you made on the hot stove in the morning, and the way you made the coffee was something down to a fine point with some people. You put the water in the pot, got the water boiling, and then you stirred the coffee into it until it was done. Some would pull the pot (to) the back of the stove and dump the coffee in and wait until it slowly boiled again. This was called "side-boil," because the coffee pot's side nearest to the stove pipe got hot first. Some claimed this slow boil made the coffee bitter.

(One day) a passing trapper stopped to see a couple of his friends and found one of them laying dead on the floor beside the stove. Shot. He said to the partner, 'Did you shoot him?'

And the partner exploded: 'Sure I shoot the S.O.B., he side-boiled the coffee!"

Frances observed that the self-sufficient Belle Lee McDonald remained the indefatigable, driving force at the Talkeetna Trading Post.

Belle, now married to an old-timer we all called Mac, had a couple of great big percheron horses who roamed the town in search of grass and clover. They were wonderful animals, tame and friendly. She still had her restaurant, a counter with about six stools, and mostly she had stewed chicken. If you wanted chicken stew she set the pot on the counter and you helped yourself. Fishing around in it with a spoon, one fellow told me he came up with a leg and foot of a chicken, the claws opened in a leisurely way, while he just sat and stared at it!

She ran her store, and it was so dark inside you could hardly see the goods. The windows might have given more light, but years of dirt didn't help. But Belle was a fixture in town (and) had been there from the first days it started up. And now, in that old store, with her room upstairs, she felt she had all the luxury she needed. (She was) a short, stumpy woman with white hair she wore pinned in a bun.... She never drank or smoked. But she could swear! She had spirit and I think that's what I admired in her most; a glint of humor, even if it was pretty raw. But then, she had lived a raw life and accepted it.

In 1937, Frances had obtained work at Belle's roadhouse at the entrance to the Cache Creek and Peters Creek mining country.

So I went out to run the roadhouse. The building was log and two story, with a big shed on the back that kept the buckets, axes, shovels, tires—you name it. The setting of the roadhouse was a beautiful thing. (Just) down the road was Peters Creek, and near it was the headquarters camp of the Alaska Road Commission. About twelve miles up the creek was a large placer mine (the Peters Creek mine at Petersville) where at least fifteen men were working to take out the gold. The roadhouse sat at the forks of the road. One road, graveled, went on up the hills, down through canyons, across swamps, and finally ended up going through a deep canyon and on into the mining area of Cache Creek. The other road crossed a big iron bridge and became a "cat road" which went on up behind the Peters Hills.

I really enjoyed it when the people came. There was always a lot of good conversation, and, if it rained, the comfort of the road-house—to get warm and dry out—was enough to put people in a happy mood. It seemed each time people came I learned something more about the country and the people in it. Mail came (along with) magazines and newspapers, so I did not feel so out of touch. If I needed supplies the Road Commission truck went to the river landing every week and would bring back a case or two for me. Everybody cooperated with each other as a matter of course.

The next year, 1938, Frances took a job working as a camp cook at a small mine in the Cache Creek area. Prior to her travel there she watched the village of Talkeetna gear up for another mining season.

While the river was still frozen and snow (covered), there had been those who departed with dog teams to get to their claims early (to) do the "deadwork"—setting up mining equipment, (clearing) ditches, and getting the camps ready for the season.

After the ice on the rivers broke free and the water ran steadily, Frances watched as the activity along the riverbanks increased. Among the men hauling freight across the Susitna River and on to the mining country were George Weatherell, Jack Devault, and Frank Lee.

Jack Devault ran the "ferry," as it was called, and was hauling freight across the river. (It was) an outboard motor-powered, flat-bottomed boat that looked pretty frail in that vast expanse of water. (In) the swift current the motor chugged along, and sometimes it seemed he didn't gain an inch. The boat was piled high with boxes and sacks, and the water seemed to be going over the sides, as there was very little freeboard. But no, it didn't, and he would come spinning back to take more freight across. Jack had a truck on the other side of the river and would take (miners) as far as the road allowed. Then, he had a little gas "cat" (that pulled) a load on a wagon, or go-devil, or sled, depending on the amount of snow there was. (He) hauled them on out to the hills and eventually Cache Creek, where they had their claims.

When it came time for Frances to set out for her job along Cache Creek, she traveled with George Weatherell.

> (It was) a long grinding haul with a "cat" and wagon, at three-and-a-half miles an hour for about 50 (sic) miles. We went by the way of Petersville (the name now attached to the Peters Creek mine complex) ... as the Road Commission had roughed in a pretty good road. You rode awhile and then walked, to relieve the jarring, jolting ride on the wagon; but it was hard to keep up with the consistent three-miles-an-hour speed of the cat. I had my first ride through Peters Creek Canyon, and it was hair-raising, as the road was roughed out on the side of the canyon wall. And there, far below, ran Peters Creek. You looked over the edge and almost straight down; in fact the canyon over-hung the creek in so many places you wondered where the creek was. That road seemed to cling, with just enough room to (move), and no place to pass if you met somebody coming the other way.

When Francis and Weatherell emerged from the canyon they moved to above timberline where Frances could view the pretty valley between the Dutch and Peters Hills. Eventually they made it to Cache Creek, and finally to a small tributary where her employers, Cal Reeve and his father, had established their mining camp.

> It consisted of a bunkhouse and a cookhouse, both small; but then, we were far from timber and everything had to be freighted in. I had a small cookstove, some groceries, and a bunk in the cookhouse. There was Cal Reeve and his dad to cook for. In front of the cookhouse was a sort of shed, and there hung a great big quarter of moose. So I had meat to cook.
> This was my first experience at cooking in a "rough" camp. I know I must have produced edible meals, but I was a novice at sourdough (baking), working a little, stubborn stove, and dreaming up some kind of a variety of things when I had only the bare essentials of flour, sugar, canned milk, eggs, and meat. But Cal and his dad were good-natured, hard working, and very pleasant people to be around, and I enjoyed them.

When she could, Frances observed the Reeves' mining methods and the effort they put into finding the gold. Frances said:

116

It was hard work, there was never any doubt about that. You got wet and muddy, and your hands wore raw in spite of wearing gloves. The weather could be raw and rainy ... (and) when it rained you had lots of water to use. But when the sun shone the creek went down, and then the water power slacked off. So you shoveled by hand and did the best you could.

Was it worth that struggle to get it? All that back-breaking labor in the wet, cold, and rain? Wet clothes, hands raw and bleeding, back aching from moving rocks and boulders, all the "deadwork" involved in setting up a pit? What was it then, that meant so much? Well, it was freedom, an independence, a way of

Frances Weatherell (left) the feisty mining camp cook who held a gun on the man she and others believed to be a suspect in the Cache Creek country murders. With friend Carl Peterson. (courtesy Gale Weatherell)

life you could choose, and it had dignity. You were your own boss and you were making money. But it was more. When you got that gold out of the ground, it was *yours*. It had never been anybody's, and now it belonged to you! It had lain there for ages just so you could find it. In a way it was a spiritual experience. Nothing on this earth could be more yours than that glittering gold in the pan as you washed the sand and gravel away from it. This is *mine*.

The summer moved by quickly and then it was fall, when the

nights grew cooler and darkness fell a bit earlier. Leaves on the cotton-wood trees at lower elevations turned slowly to gold, and Frances watched blueberries and cranberries grow ripe.

It was getting toward the end of the season, and soon the water would diminish higher in the hills and the creek would go down. A time when everybody ... worked like crazy to get the last of the season's gold. Finally one fine night it cleared and froze, and that marked the end of the season. It thawed enough to clean up the (sluice) box, but there was no use starting another pit. And here came George (Weatherell) again, with his cat and wagon, to pick up the miners who wanted to leave and go to town. He gathered them up from along the creek, and soon there were thirteen or more of us to start the long trek to town. We piled our gear on the wagon and, for the most part, walked beside it.

In Alaska there are no strangers, so we all knew each other before we had walked a mile. Each had some story to tell of the season's adventures, so we were like a group of friends travel-ing together. If some had not mined much gold (this) season, there were no gripes; there was always another season coming next year.... There was a feeling of comradeship, for everybody knew hard work, discouragement, and bad seasons. And those who had struck a good paystreak knew enough not to brag.

I will never forget one of the fun things that happened on that trip. We had finally slogged through rain, cold, and even hints of snow that seemed to follow us along the trail. We had alternately ridden and walked, to keep warm and to avoid the jolting of the wagon. When we reached Moose Creek and the big log cabin there, the vote was to stop and stay all night. It was getting dark, and raining, and the dry camp looked good. There was a big barrel stove there, and we soon got a fire going and coffee made. We all had sandwiches and food from our camps, so we ate and prepared to bed down in our sleeping bags on the floor. There was a sort of alcove, and here a man and his wife put their bags down in semi-privacy. But I had to lay mine down with the men, which didn't bother me. We all stretched out there on the floor and soon were sound asleep.

It was just breaking daylight when Cal, who was sleeping next to me, started stirring. I squinted to see what Cal was do-ing; he seemed to be fumbling in his pants pocket, his clothes laying beside him. He looked over at me and saw the gleam of my eyes in the early morning dim light. (He) put his finger to his lips. Ssshhh. He had a handful of something. (He) slipped out of his bag and quietly opened up the big stove door. I saw him toss this handful in on the coals. Quickly he got back in his bag and pretended to be asleep. And all hell broke loose!

He had (thrown) a handful of .22 short cartridges and ash in on the coals (where) they scattered and then exploded! It was like the Fourth of July in that big barrel. Men rolled away from the stove in their bags; some sprang up and got tangled getting out of their bags. I could not very well pretend I didn't hear or see them, but I stuck in my bag because I was so helpless laughing I couldn't have got out anyhow! There was a mixture of laughing, swearing, and consternation, for nobody could figure out what happened in that stove.

It was too funny to keep when I finally got around to solving the mystery for them. The other woman was pretty upset. What if some of the shots had come on through the stove and hurt someone? I tried to tell her that ... the jacket blew off the lead, not vice versa.

I was to recall this episode years later when I heard about one of the trappers who took his new wife to the trapline. He chewed snuff, and she fussed at him about it. So when he was out tending his traps, she went through the cabin looking for his extra snuff cans to destroy them. He also mined in the summertime (when) it was standard practice to put your dynamite caps— used to set off sticks of dynamite—in a snuff box (because) you did not want them to strike against anything or they would go off. They are lethal to say the least.

So, sure enough, she found this extra snuff box, and as she was disposing of the snuff by throwing the little cardboard boxes in the cookstove, this one went in too. She nearly blew the cabin up. The stove came apart at the seams and the blast must have knocked her to the floor. I never saw a snuff box after that that I did not open with delicate care before I did anything with it!

Finally, Frances' group made its way to the river landing, across the Susitna from Talkeetna. There, while waiting to board Weatherell's boat, Frances saw the method people used on this side of the river to alert George—when he was on the Talkeetna side—that they needed transportation.

The way they notified him that they wanted to come across ... was to fire off a stick of dynamite, left there for that purpose. The dynamite and caps were kept in a bear-proof place, fused and ready to set off. So even someone not familiar with the use of dynamite could "call the ferry."

There was always drama when crossing the river; it was seldom a safe and easy crossing," Frances said. "Late in the fall the slush ice would start to run (and) the shelf ice would freeze along the river bank. There was ... danger of people falling in the water. It was cold and swift, and an ugly way to die.

————

Certain mining traditions were still observed at this time. For instance, the "grubstake contract" was alive and well. While Frances had been cooking at the Reeve camp near Cache Creek, Belle McDonald had agreed to finance the food, supplies, and gear needed to search for gold along a tributary of Chunilna Creek, to the northeast of Talkeetna. The man she grubstaked was none other than Antone Stander, one of the original "Klondike Kings." Though he was now over 70 years old and in reduced circumstances, the gold was out there, waiting for him to discover it. The contract laid out the particulars of their agreement:

> This contract, made and entered into this 20th day of July, 1938, by and between A.F. Stander ... and Mrs. J.M. McDonald: That for and in consideration of the necessary provisions, camp equipment, transportation, and the help of one man, (Stander) hereby agrees to proceed immediately to the vicinity of Bacon Creek, tributary of Clear Creek and the Talkeetna River, for the purpose of prospecting for, and locating lode claims. (Stander) further agrees that he will deed to (McDonald) an undivided one half ($^{1}/_{2}$) interest in and to any and all claims located and recorded by him, for a term of one year from the date of this contract.

The power of attorney was another authority still in use that summer, in one instance by the Brittell brothers. While Joy remained at the Jenkins' camp to work, Ken Brittell took time to travel over to Wolf Creek, where he had staked claims previously. This time he staked No. 1 Above Discovery on the creek, and then traveled into Talkeetna with his brother's power of attorney to record the claim in both their names.

Sometime that season, Frank Jenkins needed some specialized mining machinery or equipment that was available only in Seattle. Not willing to leave his mining operation, he asked Ken to travel there to conduct his business for him. Brittell agreed, and left shortly thereafter for Seward, where he would board an ocean steamer for Seattle.

The summer of 1938 was not a very good one for Dick Francis. Debt-ridden and dispirited, he seemed to age visibly and to become increasingly bitter. Ed Carlson spent a considerable amount of time at the Ruby Creek claims where he had installed a new canvas tent-cabin with a plank floor along the Ruby Gulch hillside, about 400 yards above the mining site that he and Francis worked. He also spent a lot of time listening to Dick curse Frank and Helen Jenkins. "He talked continually about them," he would later remark. The couple seemed to prey on Francis' mind, and sometimes he got so worked up that he would lace his invective with threats. But Carlson would take this with a grain of salt. Dick was angry and bitter, just blowing off steam.

Late that fall, as the mining season wound down, Francis made a trip to Anchorage. He was now staying more often at the Northern Hotel when in the city, and it was here and on the streets of Anchorage that he would run into mining acquaintances from all over the Territory of Alaska. One of these, "Prospector Charlie," got in a conversation with Francis and left it with the feeling that Dick was "slipping." But another, named Charlie Harper, observed that though Francis "appeared a little more worn than he had in the past," he had certainly seemed rational. In the course of their discussion, which invariably turned to the subject of Francis' legal problems, Francis told Harper that he was "afraid Mrs. Jenkins might come to his cabin and poison his food in order to get rid of him," Harper said.

In September Helen traveled to Talkeetna to file a proof of labor declaration for all of the twenty-seven claims then owned by the Jenkinses. Most of these were on Willow Creek, but others were on Ruby Creek and on several gulches that adjoined the streams. Helen signed as co-owner of the ground.

In October the snow began to fall. In November the days grew short and dark and cold, and true winter imposed its will upon the Susitna River Valley once again.

9   this gold was a shock to behold

Nineteen thirty-nine seemed to herald great promise for anyone involved in mining endeavors in Alaska. The previous year gold production had exceeded that of any year in the history of gold mining in the Territory of Alaska. In fact, the total gold value realized in 1938 was three times the purchase price ($7,200,000) that the United States had paid for the Territory. Alaska quickly became an object of focus in many circles, not excluding the federal government.

The new year had barely arrived when the *Anchorage Daily Times* printed a large headline informing Alaskans that the Department of the Interior recommended that an 8 percent tax be placed on gold in Alaska. The secretary of the interior had asked the governor of Alaska to submit this proposal to the territorial legislature, the newspaper said. The article triggered an immediate reaction from prominent Alaskans. The Pioneers of Alaska, a proud group of individuals who had persevered despite substantial hardships during their years in the north, declared that the already existing 3 percent tax on gold was sufficient and that a higher tax would be "very injurious to mining in Alaska." The Anchorage Chamber of Commerce weighed in against the tax too, saying it would jeopardize the mining industry. The Juneau Chamber of Commerce said, "... we all know it would be a death blow to most of the mining industry if a tax of this kind ever went into effect."

The controversy over the proposal raged on into February, until the territorial legislature, at the request of the secretary of the interior, had to address it. On the tenth, the *Anchorage Times* said, "Secretary Harold Ickes' proposed tax on Alaska gold was introduced in the territorial Senate today and lived only 12 minutes before it was killed. The bill was introduced at 12:20 p.m. and was killed at 12:32 p.m."

Just two weeks later, another mining issue arose when the federal Wage and Hour Administration ordained a nationwide 44-

hour work week. Miners all over Alaska protested to Alaska's delegate to congress, Tony Dimond, who moved quickly to request exemption for placer miners. An *Anchorage Times* article quoted Dimond's argument: "The placer season in many regions of Alaska is limited to two or three months in the summer. Miners depend upon steady employment with six or seven days a week for work, to earn enough to carry them through the winter." Dimond went on to say that "Most placer miners in Alaska are opposed to a short work week from both the social and economic view points. In most camps they have little else to do but work and it is no advantage to have leisure time."

In mid-March another newspaper headline proclaimed that a raise in the price of gold had been proposed in a bill submitted to Congress. At the same time a prominent Anchorage fur buyer ran a large advertisement in a newspaper notifying trappers of his need for more furs:

BEAVER SKINS WANTED BY KOSLOSKY
During the past week I purchased 502 more beaver skins, making the total for this season 2,651 skins. But I still need 439 Beaver Skins to fill my orders from New York and Paris for 3,000 skins.

Though the ad's math is a bit murky, clearly the markets for gold and fur were not only healthy, but flourishing, and this reality surely drew more people north. People like Dick Francis, Frank and Helen Jenkins, and miners along Cache Creek must have felt some gratification to see their many years of commitment finally witness more market demand than they'd ever experienced.

Frances Thompson was happy this year because she had obtained summer-long employment as a cook at a major Cache Creek mine. While everyone else was beginning to prepare for the long trip to their claims, Frances concentrated on the creation of a huge grocery list that her employer, Cap "One Egg" Morgan, had asked her to prepare. Though Frances wasn't needed on the job until the first of May, plenty of time was required to arrange for the assembly and delivery of all the needed supplies. One evening she and Cap sat down to go over the list to be sure it met with his approval.

"He was known to be stingy with his groceries and supplies of food for the crew," Frances said. "In fact, he became infamous for it, and was called "One Egg Morgan," because it was said that he would stand behind the crews as they sat at the table, and tell the cook, 'Give them all the eggs they want.' And he would hold up one finger for the cook to see."

Now, as they went over the list Frances had drawn up, she was pleased to hear Morgan say, "Well, that's not bad at all." But Frances was mystified when he went on to remark, "You don't have any lemon extract ordered on this."

"I said, 'Cap, I don't use lemon extract. If I need the flavor I use lemons. I don't like lemon extract.'

"'Well,' he said, 'The last cook ordered two cases of it.'

"'Cap,' I said, 'he ordered it to drink!'

"'You mean to tell me he drank it?'

"'He sure did. The whole crew said he was squirrely half the time!'

"'Well,' said Cap, 'He told me the country and the isolation was driving him nuts.'

"Lemon extract has alcohol in it, but also gives people hallucinations," Francis told him.

When the list was finally approved, Frances turned to other matters. More and more people were showing up in town, and the atmosphere there became one of collective anticipation. New arrivals seemed to emerge from the train every night, and Frances, like everyone else, met the train to see who would be on it.

> I was up at the train when it came in from Anchorage and I saw a man get off, a stranger. I had nothing against strangers, in fact I felt we needed new kinds of people, as most of the old-timers really were old and set in their ways. If you ever got off a train in a small community, with only a few other people getting off with you, there is always this little group of curious people sizing you up as "a stranger to these parts," and you suffer a little even if you're not shy. I thought afterward, maybe that's why his eyes looked so cold.
>
> As this man came down the steps of the train I saw his eyes looking, not exactly at me, but through me. It was like he saw, but didn't see anybody. Once he looked at me because all of us were looking at him, and his eyes registered nothing. They were just cold, (with) no flicker of life in them; a sort of grey-blue, like a washed-out blue denim shirt. His face was a pasty color, and he had a great welt of a scar around his neck just under his chin. Even a high collar would not have covered it up. Later on he told some people it was a rope burn he got when playing as a child and running into a clothesline he couldn't see. But I never could believe that. The flesh was rolled over so it looked ... like a knife cut that hadn't been sewed up very good.
>
> He had a peculiar name, Xan Clarke. It sounded phony to me, but then I told myself, it takes all kinds of people in this world.

Later, Frances would hear someone mention that the man was planning to stake some claims of his own in Cache Creek country.

Finally, the time came for Frances to leave Talkeetna for her new job. George Weatherell liked Frances, and it was he that she traveled with on the trail to Nugget Creek, a tributary of Cache Creek. Spring conditions were such that Weatherell took his dog team, and in this way, the two made their way to Nugget Creek mine.

"We finally arrived at Nugget camp and I was almost overwhelmed by the size of my cookhouse, a framed-up tent of heavy canvas," Frances said. "(It held) a big stove to cook on, lots of cupboard room, a nice big kitchen table and big dining table and sink; for a mining camp it was a deluxe set-up. I had a nice little snug cabin off the cookhouse, and even a little stove in that."

"We will have running water in here soon,' Cap said. 'Of course it will be cold, but you won't have to carry it in buckets."

Frances was delighted with both the facilities and the fact that she would receive the same wage as the mine workers. Cap Morgan told her she would be working as many hours as the men, providing four meals a day, including an extra meal for the night crew. There were thirteen men working at the camp, most of them young and with big appetites. Frances said:

> A camp cook absolutely must know how to bake bread, cakes, pies, cookies, doughnuts, you name it. And these young men ate hearty and worked hard and wanted good food above all. It was all they had to look forward to when they came in tired and dirty from their work. It's unbelievable the amount of food men can eat when they are working hard, long hours, and in weather conditions (that are) cold and wet....
>
> They were washing the gravel down from walls of a pit. The mine looked like a big gravel pit, getting deeper and deeper as they mined it, sluicing it with water down to bedrock.... The men had to wear rain gear to keep dry in the blast of water that came from the "giants," as the water spewed back from the banks. And there was, of course, blasting to do and much moving of boulders. The tailings, or washed gravel, ran down through the (sluice) boxes and fell into the canyon below with a roar I could hear in the cookhouse.
>
> If they were having battles with crashing gravel, moving boulders, and ... water, I was having my own battles in the cookhouse. The stove was old as the hills, and temperamental.... I had to ... get the bread to rise in that cold kitchen, get it baked, (and) at the same time prepare meals as tasty as I could

make them.... It took thirteen loaves of bread—big ones—every three days, to say nothing of rolls, cakes, pies, hot cakes, cookies and doughnuts.

When Cap Morgan's wife arrived to spend the summer months, Frances found that she had another challenge to deal with. Tense from the beginning, the relationship between the two women began to deteriorate as the weeks passed.

> I began to have some static from Cap's wife. First off, she came and had nothing to do but sit in their little wanigan. So she would come to the cookhouse and, as she seemed to feel she must be the "boss's wife" all the way, this didn't set well with me. I was cooking for a crew, and her hints as to how to cook things and serve them didn't set too well. Several times she would go to the stove and stir things, taste them, and have suggestions about seasoning, and so on. But when we got the halibut, I blew up.
> I had sliced it, and nice fresh halibut is food for kings.... I put off frying it until almost time to serve it, as I wanted it hot and moist and brown on the outside, and not setting in a pan, getting cold. So here she came while I was fixing it, and objected to the way I was frying it. 'I like my halibut well done!' she said. I handed her the spatula and watched her. She took over the frying of the fish, and I took off my apron and went into my quarters and stayed there. *She wants to cook, let her cook.*

Later that evening, Cap Morgan knocked on Frances' door. Frances liked Cap, and described him as "one of the nicest and most sincere men I ever knew; fair, mild, and pleasant." But she told him there wasn't enough room in the kitchen for two cooks. This conflict was eventually resolved when Frances threatened to quit.

As the weeks passed and George Weatherell made frequent stops at Nugget mine on his freighting runs, he and Frances developed a mutual attraction. Weatherell had apparently given the future a lot of thought, because toward the end of August he proposed marriage.

Frances said, "As soon as I consented to marry him, he wanted this right away and said, 'Leave it to me, I'll be out the first day I can catch Chris (a pilot), and will bring Ben Mayfield along to do the job!' I assured Cap, when I told him, that I would go on cooking until the end of the season, but that George did not want to wait.

> It was very romantic! The plane flew over and buzzed camp, and a pair of shoes came hurling down from the plane, land-

ing in front of the cookhouse! This startled everybody in camp, but George explained afterwards that from where the plane landed, to get to camp, he had to wear his hip boots to wade the creek, and he was damned if he would get married with hip boots on. By the time George and Ben Mayfield walked up ... the wedding party was ready. The crew came down from the pit, and as the news had flashed up and down the creek, there were others there, so it was quite a wedding party! George stayed the night and caught a plane out the next day, because he had to get on with his freighting and run the ferry across the river from Talkeetna.

———

Airplanes were now a familiar sight in Cache Creek country, and the most well-known of the aviators was Haakon Christensen who operated out of Cantwell, a small village to the northeast. He was a popular, jovial, and easygoing man of Danish descent, and when the Anchorage newspapers listed the passengers he transported in and out of Anchorage, they often identified him as "The Flying Dane." But most everybody called him Chris, and the pilot and his double-winged Waco aircraft came to frequent Cache Creek country as more and more of the profitable mining operations could afford the air charter rates. Chris was a daring, but safe pilot who hauled increasing amounts of freight, food, and gear to the mines. If he couldn't land at a particular mine, he airdropped the load from his aircraft. He was also adept at securing ungainly pieces of mining machinery onto the struts of his plane and, in some cases, to the underside of the fuselage.

Christensen won another convert to flying during the summer of 1939 when he transported Cap Morgan and his wife to Anchorage. The *Anchorage Times* ran a small article about the trip:

> The airplane had a new friend today in Mrs. C.P. Morgan after her first airplane ride which took her in a few minutes over the trail which has required two to three days for her to follow on foot.... Mrs. Morgan has announced her intention of "never walking over that trail again." Mrs. Morgan has walked the 35-mile trail from Talkeetna to the mining camp for several years to avoid riding in an airplane. Pilot Christensen brought Mr. and Mrs. Morgan, with two others, to Anchorage direct from the mining camp in only 50 minutes.

Another individual that was intrigued with Chris's flying was a young mine worker at Frank Jenkins' operation in the Dutch Hills. His name was Don Sheldon, and, like Ernie Bull before him, he was just 17 years old. He was from Wyoming, and had traveled to the Territory of Alaska on a steamer out of Seattle shortly after graduating from high school in 1938. With a new friend he had met on the boat, he traveled to Talkeetna, where everything he had imagined about Alaska became reality.

> We arrived in Talkeetna, and it was a sight to behold. At this point the miners were coming in from the mines (where) there was great activity at Cache Creek.... There was a considerable number of native families in Talkeetna, and they lived along the old Talkeetna River as it intercepts the Susitna. This native settlement was complete with dog teams, smoked moose meat, and salmon drying in the sun. The smoke of the wood fires wafting across the town, mingled with the booze fumes of those making home brew, and the raucousness of the several booze joints in town, made for a very colorful village. And the continual howling of the many dogs ... was an ideal setting and exactly what I had featured Alaska to be all about.
>
> We had circulated around this active village of Talkeetna to see if there was a possible chance that we might find some type of employment. Sure enough, they was short of wood. Now, the way you cut wood was by hand. You sharpened your axe, and sharpened the saw, and went into the woods and cut wood the hard way. It was a very slow process, but we cut about thirty cords of wood all-told in the next three months, and as the days grew shorter it was more of a project to cut the tree down, and to buck up the tree into stove-sized wood. The wood cutting continued, the moose chops sizzled in the iron skillet, the storms raged, and the cords of wood stacked up, and we sold as much as we could cut.

After wintering on money they had earned selling firewood, Sheldon and his friend trapped for beaver in March. When April arrived, almost everyone in Talkeetna was gearing up for the mining season. Sheldon was approached by Frank Jenkins, who offered him a job working at his many claims in the Willow and Cottonwood Creek areas. Sheldon's account of his work at the mine provides a close look at the Jenkins' operation that summer of 1939.

> The agreement was to work ten hours a day, every day, all week, all summer, at the rate of $5 a day. My first season, beginning

from May 15, was on location on Cottonwood Creek.... This was in the style of a placer mine. There was a large ditch cut around the side of the mountain which Mr. Jenkins had painstakingly cut by hand for a distance of five miles, and this was to gather water. The water, after the snow is removed from the ditches ... is piped into a huge four-foot pipe (that) graduates down finally into six-inch-diameter sections, and develops a considerable amount of pressure in the process.... Furthermore, the hydraulic nozzles of the unit, called a giant, cause a further reduction down to about a four-inch stream. So there's tremendous pressure that will result from this water dropping 500 feet vertically....

It is with this system that the earth and the smaller rocks are washed away ... and the concentrated pay dirt ... is left near bed-rock. This, in turn, was washed with the hydraulic pressure towards big flume boxes. The boxes contained riffles which stop the gold as (the pay dirt) flows over the riffles and through the boxes.

There was a considerable amount of hard labor involved in moving the pieces of machinery that constitute the hydraulic mining operation. Mr. Jenkins had an old caterpillar which aided considerably in pulling the heavier pieces of pipe into position. Each new location of each pit, which was about 300-foot square, involved moving a complete set-up of the hydraulic giants to wash the gravel into the sluice boxes, and ... another hydraulic unit to blast the heavy rocks and overburden material from the tail end of the box, which was located about forty or sixty feet farther downstream. Needless to say, the work was rugged.

We had a total of four clean-ups. That is, during the process of the summer we cleaned up the sluice boxes (and) recovered the gold from four different pit locations. Now, this gold was a shock to behold—extremely bright gold, nearly absolutely pure, and it was in very coarse nuggets. Often the bedrock, where the gold was recovered, would be blue clay, which was a tremendous contrast with the gold and the glitter of the gold itself. There's other types of bedrock too, but the greatest contrast was when the blue clay bedrock would be in the area of the gold clean-up, and the gold resting on the blue clay was a very striking sight.

In early June, Jenkins hired another young hand named Ira Diess. As time passed, he and Sheldon became friends and talked about doing some trapping together when winter came. Both men seemed to meet with the Jenkins' approval, because Helen relaxed enough to talk candidly about gold. On one occasion she told Diess that the only safe place for gold was "underground." That Helen worried about the security of the Jenkinses' gold became clear when she told him about the ruse she had employed to safeguard their gold at the end of the previous season. She had concealed most of their gold pokes in a large coffee pot for the trip from the mine to Talkeetna, she told him. It was a good blind, she said, no one would ever think of looking in a coffee pot.

On another occasion Helen remarked that she and Frank intended to prosecute Dick Francis. They continued to have problems with rock tailings in their dam and ditch from the Ruby Creek claims worked by Francis and Carlson, she said. Though no public record documents any legal action taken by the Jenkinses at this point, there is some evidence that they had finally been successful in obtaining an injunction against Francis.

Such evidence was contained in letters Helen and Frank received from both Judge Simon Hellenthal in Valdez, and their attorney, Arthur Thompson, in Anchorage. As early as March Thompson had written to the Jenkinses to acknowledge their recent complaints and to assure them that there would "be no difficulty in stopping Francis and Carlson." Judge Hellenthal, in response to letters he had received from the couple, advised them there was little he could do "unless Francis has violated the injunction." If such was the case, he said, Francis could be held in contempt.

Helen had raised another issue in her correspondence with Hellenthal that had to do with Francis' mental condition. He was not sane, she had informed the judge. To this issue Hellenthal counseled that "if Francis has gone entirely wrong," the Jenkinses could request a hearing to test his sanity.

As the weeks passed, Diess and Sheldon became more familiar with the feud between their employer and Francis. And a story then in circulation only added more fuel to the fire. The previous year, it was said, a local prospector had met up with Dick Francis somewhere along a creek in the Dutch Hills. After an exchange of greetings, Francis was said to have announced in a loud, angry voice: "Say, you tell that rat-faced Jenkins that if I had seen him and old she-hen five minutes sooner yesterday I would have got them both." The prospector noted that Francis was carrying his rifle at this encounter.

At some point Frank Jenkins told Diess that he didn't like Rocky Cummins. The young mining hand probably wondered if the Jenkinses liked anyone; they seemed to have very few friends and to be distrustful of just about everyone. Later, Diess would hear the couple described as miserly, antagonistic, and not well liked.

There were significant reasons that Ken Brittell wasn't a part of the crew at Frank Jenkins' mine that summer. He had married and was entering his first season as a full-fledged miner in his own right. A teacher by profession, Brittell had spent the past couple of winters working at schools in the Aleutian Islands, but his summers were devoted to mining. He was now 30 years old and eager to develop his several placer claims along Wolf Creek. Frank Jenkins, who had given him advice on mining procedure and technique, was very supportive and wished him well in his venture. And when Jenkins had asked Ken to travel to Seattle the previous summer to conduct some business for him, little did he know that it would be there that Brittell would meet his future wife.

A rare photo of Helen Jenkins, at the Jenkinses' Little Willow Creek cabin. Strong-willed, excitable, and suspicious of people, Helen sealed her letters with red wax and was good at hiding gold. (photographer unknown)

Tay Craig was a Seattle businessman and a master machinist who produced high quality work and had gained a favorable reputation among veteran Alaskan miners, including Jenkins. It was he who introduced Ken Brittell to his daughter, Maxine, during the time that Brittell spent in Seattle. The two became serious about each other, decided to marry, and traveled together to Alaska on the steamer *BARANOF*, arriving at

Seward in August, 1938. Arrangements had been made for their wedding at a church in Anchorage that night, so the couple boarded a small plane in Seward and took off.

Maxine, in her early twenties, had never been in an airplane before, and this flight was not an ideal introduction to flying. The turbulent ride through the Kenai Mountains was okay, but when the little aircraft reached Turnagain Arm it ran out of gas and its engine quit. The pilot managed to land on the beach, but there the plane flipped over. No one was hurt, and the men thought they were near a railroad work crew camp, so the three set out in that direction. Ken and Maxine finally managed to get to Anchorage on a hand-pumped railroad cart, and were married on schedule.

The Brittell Wolf Creek camp in spring, 1939. Note camp tents in lower left corner. Ramsdyke Creek lies between the tents and the bluff in the background—an extension of the same bluff everyone ascended to Wonder Gulch. (courtesy Maxine Brittell)

They spent the winter on remote Sanak Island in the Aleutians, where Ken taught at a small village school. In the early spring of 1939 they traveled on a government mail boat to Seward, then continued on to Anchorage where they got on a plane piloted by Haakon Christensen, who flew them to Wolf Creek. Chris's aircraft was equipped with skis and took off on the Cook Inlet mud flats, which did not enhance Maxine's already sketchy conception of flight. Nor did the arrival near Wolf Creek, where they landed on the side of a mountain on heavy snowdrifts that still lingered in the wild, remote terrain of the Dutch Hills. Maxine was glad to get out of the plane. Finally, the two snowshoed down to their camp location, where Wolf Creek flowed into the more prominent Ramsdyke Creek.

Sometime prior to Ken and Maxine's arrival, Joy Brittell and Frank Jenkins had traveled from the Willow Creek operation over to Wolf Creek with Frank's small tractor. They cleared the snow for a camp-

Left to right: Joy, Maxine, and Ken Brittell at their Wolf Creek camp in the spring of 1939. During the mining season they would have to deal with a mysterious fire in their tent and a pushy prospector who staked claims close to theirs. (courtesy Maxine Brittell)

site there, and erected three simple canvas tents, supported with tree pole frames. It is clear that Jenkins was doing all he could to help the younger miners along. Joy was now his brother's partner and intended to spend most of the summer developing gold prospects with him at Wolf Creek. Later, Maxine's brother, Tim Craig, arrived from college in Washington and became the fourth member of the Wolf Creek work crew. Craig liked to take pictures, and photographs he made this summer show a happy and enthusiastic bunch.

The Brittell venture was a simple hand and shovel operation, and

Left to right: Ken Brittell, Joy Brittell, and Tim Craig at Wolf Creek, spring, 1939. Having learned the basics of placer mining from Frank Jenkins, the Brittell brothers were eager to mine their own claims. (courtesy Maxine Brittell)

everything to be accomplished required dogged physical labor. The plan for this first season was to install sluice boxes at the lower limits of their claims, which started just above the mouth of Wolf Creek, and then work their way up the creek. Maxine remembers that "they (Ken and Joy) had prospected it pretty thoroughly, and their findings were certainly positive, especially up toward the top of Wolf Creek where there was more gold." As the summer progressed, they managed to prepare their ground farther and farther up the creek.

At some point the group made its way over the ridge to the Jenkins camp. Wearing rugged knee-high rubber boots everyone called "mud packs," the four waded Ramsdyke Creek and moved up the ridgeface that led to Wonder Gulch. The trek up and along the gulch and on over to the Jenkinses' operation was a long one, taking anywhere from two to three hours, depending on how encumbered a traveler was with weight in a pack, and how many rest stops were taken. On this occasion an important part of the visit might have been to introduce Maxine to the Jenkinses. While the men talked mining, Maxine spent time with Helen, who welcomed her and gave her the benefit of many years of experience in dealing with gold.

Maxine described the Jenkinses as "very friendly, very helpful." At one point Helen opened a large, black purse and pulled out six pokes of gold, which she showed to Maxine. The gold had been sorted according to size, and most of the bags held extra large nuggets. Then Helen spoke frankly about the fine points of safeguarding one's gold, and told her, "Maxine, be sure you hide the gold before you go out with it (at the end of the season). Don't even keep a list of the places you hide it, because someone might find the list." Good places to hide gold, she counseled, were "under the woodpile," and "in your flour bag."

On subsequent visits that summer, Maxine would listen to Helen grouse angrily about Dick Francis and declare that she and Frank were "going to run him out of the country." Maxine eventually gained the impression that Helen was more bitter about Francis than her husband was.

———

While the Brittell group settled into their camp and work on Wolf Creek, another gold seeker appeared in the area. After arriving in Talkeetna on the train in early March, Xan John Clarke had settled in at the more affordable Talkeetna Trading Post. Clarke was close to 36 years old, having been born in New Brunswick, Canada, in 1903. At the age of 25, he had entered the United States at Buffalo, New York, and in early 1929 had joined the U.S. Army and been stationed in Hawaii for about six years. He had then requested and received a transfer to Spokane, Washington, where he continued to serve in the Army until May of 1938. Just before he left the service he had applied for naturalization as an American citizen.

Clarke spent several weeks at Belle's trading post, accumulating needed items and talking to the old-timers and miners who were gearing up for the season. He was a fairly sociable sort, and in the course of conversation said that he'd first come to Alaska during the summer of 1938 and, with two other men, had done a little prospecting in the Nelchina area, on the other side of the Talkeetna Mountains. He had stayed on in the country, he said, and then gotten work

Ramsdyke Creek flows through some of the most wild and rugged country in the Dutch Hills.

with the Evan Jones Coal Company in the Matanuska Valley, until an injury at that mine had hospitalized him for several weeks.

Clarke likely asked a lot of questions about the prospects in the Cache Creek area, and just about everyone who moved in and out of the trading post was friendly and helpful. The unwritten "code of the creeks" held that life was tough enough in Alaska without a helping hand; one never knew when one might need the help in return. Clarke probably listened to the men trade news and stories and almost certainly heard them talk about the Jenkins-Francis feud in the Dutch Hills, an ongoing topic among all the miners. Such talk also included the rampant speculation that Frank and Helen were hiding their gold on their property because they didn't trust banks. Frank had lost a considerable sum of his money in a Seattle bank that had failed during the Great Depression, they said. Frank was bitter and hated banks, they said. Frank Jenkins was one of the most successful miners in Cache Creek country, they agreed.

Clarke was going out prospecting in April, an ambitious project because the hills and valleys were still blanketed with snow. In addition to staying at the trading post, he probably also purchased most of his food and supplies at Belle's. In apparent return, Belle made a friendly offer of the use of one of her mining camps for a day or so, if trail or weather conditions should become a problem to him.

Then Clarke made his way to Cache Creek country. It's not clear how or where he initially spent his time in the area, but at some point he broke into an old cabin in the Dutch Hills that belonged to Frank Jenkins. Though Jenkins had built the structure during his early mining years at what was now an older camp, the place remained a modest component of his operations. Later, Clarke would explain to Jenkins that he had forced entry to "get in out of the weather," during a snowstorm. At this time Clarke probably first made the acquaintance of Jenkins, who apparently told him that he would inspect the cabin to see if everything was in order. If all was intact, he said, and Clarke replaced the broken lock, he would not pursue the matter. (Helen was not so lenient; she told Ira Diess that she intended to prosecute Clarke.)

Clarke remained in the Dutch Hills and seemed to be interested in Ramsdyke Creek, because he spent a good deal of time scrutinizing the area. Finally, on April 30, he staked two placer claims that he called Norma Discovery and One Above Norma. The discovery claim was located on Ramsdyke Creek, approximately 100 feet below the mouth of Wolf Creek. The next day he drove in stakes and posted location notices for two more claims—Two and Three Above Norma—which, together with One Above, were directed up Ramsdyke Creek. He sent formal notice of his claims with one of the freighters to the recorder's office in Talkeetna, where Ben Mayfield entered them into the record on the twentieth of May.

An old, abandoned cabin was located along Ramsdyke, a short distance west of the mouth of Wolf Creek, and Clarke moved into it. Now the snows began to rapidly recede under the pressure of the high spring sun, and sparrows and warblers arrived for nest building activity in the thick brush that lined Ramsdyke. An occasional grizzly bear appeared along the creek, but kept moving in an ongoing search for food. On the first of June, Clarke located two more claims, one downstream from his discovery claim that he called One Below Norma, and the other upstream that he called Four Above Norma.

At some point he wrote a letter to Belle McDonald and sent it in to Talkeetna.

> Dear Bell:
>   You know you told me I can stay a few days at your camp but I didn't as I got a ride from Joe.... Thanks just the same. In return I may as well tell you that Jenkins staked your ground. I saw the stakes myself. But don't mention my name will you, as I try to keep out of squabbles here. If you want to save your ground I think you can if you get someone on it before 1st of July.
> Yours truly, Xan J. Clarke
> C/O Pilot Christensen

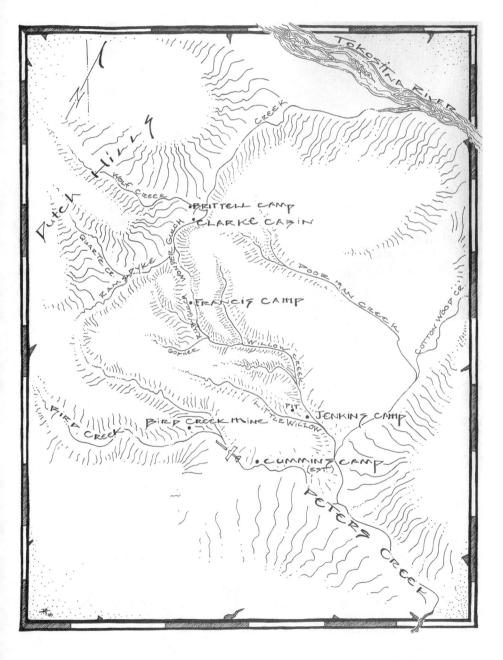

it is beautiful today

Xan John Clarke seemed to be a loner, but he was sociable as well. A tall man, he carried 185 pounds on an erect, 6-foot, 1-inch frame. Brown-haired and blue-eyed, his ruddy face bore dual 4-inch scars that traveled along both left and right jaw lines, from his ears to his chin. He gave his name as John Clarke and appeared interested in becoming familiar with the miners and their social network.

He was able to cultivate amicable relations with most people, an achievement in large part attributable to the generous standard of hospitality that prevailed along the creeks. Newcomers were common to Cache Creek country, and virtually everyone honored a welcoming atmosphere—unless there was a powerful reason not to—when anyone stopped by. If a visit happened to coincide with a mealtime, the caller was usually invited to share. While this attitude had its roots in mutual respect and consideration, it was heavily reinforced by the belief that no one could afford to have enemies in the remote Cache Creek country. Hence, a policy of tolerance (the same that had so impressed Frances Weatherell) was widely observed. Too, everyone on the creeks had experienced hardship, and turning anyone away from a camp was unthinkable.

So it was that Clarke gained ready access to any camp that he approached, even the Jenkinses'. Though Helen might have preferred to view the newcomer as potential legal quarry, even she yielded to the code. But a rumor had surfaced about Clarke since he had come to the area and was now making the rounds. When he had worked for the Evan Jones Coal Company the previous year, it was said, he had feigned the back injury that had hospitalized him. He had filed suit against the company and was successful to the tune of $2,000, an awfully lot of money in 1939. Word circulated that a longtime prospector, who was suffering from frostbite and had shared a hospital ward with Clarke, observed the injured man leave the hospital immediately upon receipt of the money. Others, the story went, had seen him out dancing the next evening, apparently having made a complete recovery.

Still, when Clarke began to visit the Brittell camp now and then, he was treated cordially as was the custom. But Maxine was uneasy when he was there. She said that "he didn't look like a pleasant person." His look and demeanor, she thought, conveyed an "I'm in charge" message. He was muscular and extremely physically fit, she remembered. Mostly Clarke talked mining with the men, but Ken Brittell became irritated with his persistent questions about Frank Jenkins' operation. Clarke wanted to know where Jenkins' claims were located and what gold values had been found there. Did Ken know how much gold they were actually taking out of the ground? He became visibly aggravated when Brittell told him that it would be more appropriate for him to ask Jenkins himself for the information.

On another occasion, Clarke reportedly admitted to Ken that he had swindled the Evan Jones Coal Company by faking an injury. Sometime after that, he apparently told another story about his past in the Nelchina mining district, on the east side of the Talkeetna Mountains. An old prospector there had taken a shot at him and his brother, Clarke said. In return they had "burned out his camp."

One evening in early June, Clarke visited the Brittell camp and talked to the brothers about some concerns he had about his Norma Discovery claim, located just below the mouth of Wolf Creek. The Brittell sluice boxes were situated near the mouth of the creek and that could cause him some problems, he said. Tailings from their sluicing would probably travel down the creek and onto his claim.

Silence must have reigned as images of the Jenkins and Francis feud probably emerged in the minds of those in the tent. Clarke's coal company story probably came to mind too; he had demonstrated that he was no stranger to the courts. Clarke, however, went on to indicate that they might be able to work something out. He suggested that he draw up an agreement that would allow the Brittells to dump their tailings on his ground. Ken said they would look at it.

Clarke soon returned with a proposal that Ken studied carefully. He noticed a clause that granted Clarke half of one of the Brittell claims near the creek mouth. Brittell pointed this out and said, firmly, that they would never agree to that. Clarke immediately grabbed his hat and, without another word, left the tent and headed for his cabin.

The next morning he was back. He asked if they had given any more consideration to the agreement. Now that they'd had time to think about it, didn't they agree that his proposal was the best way to solve the problem? Ken Brittell told him no, that he would put in dams to prevent their tailings from moving on down the creek into Ramsdyke. But, Clarke told him, that would cost quite a lot in money and labor. Then he proposed that the Brittells pay him $500 for the right to dump tailings on his ground. Brittell said they would have to think about it.

After a couple of days, Clarke approached them again. At the time the Brittells and Tim Craig were preparing to head upstream to work on one of their claims, but Clarke began to badger the group about accepting his agreement. Ken Brittell stood his ground and told Clarke they were still thinking about it. The four then gathered their gear and set out on the long hike to the ground they intended to work that day.

"We headed on upstream where we were working on the upper claims," Maxine said. "It usually took us about forty-five minutes to an hour, because it was rough country, uphill, and not cleared. While we followed the creek, we didn't always stick on the trail, but had to probe into the side areas." Along the way the four talked about Clarke's demand for some kind of compensation. "That was sure a rough deal for us at that time, and $500 in those days was a lot of money!" Maxine recalled. Finally, they reached their claim and set to work.

When working that far upstream, the group generally put in a full day and headed back to their camp as dinnertime approached. But on that particular day, as the afternoon progressed, they realized they lacked certain tools and gear to finish the tasks they had set for themselves. "Since we needed more things up there, we decided to return to camp and go up the next day to finish up," Maxine said. So the group set out, earlier than usual, over the rugged country that led back to their camp.

Later in the afternoon, they returned there to discover that their primary tent was on fire. Maxine remembered the "horrible trauma when we saw it full of smoke and some flames as we came back from up-creek. It was severely damaged, especially inside. But the tent was still standing and we were able to clean up and use some of the things. I don't remember what all was lost in the fire; it would have been everything had we not returned when we did, because the fire was obviously well set. I don't mean we knew exactly how it had been done ... but it was a big, well-burning fire when we got there, meant to destroy everything," she said.

The days in June were long and light, and the Brittells worked through the evening to salvage what they could. After some discussion, the group decided that Joy should make the long trek over to Frank Jenkins' operation. "Joy walked over to Jenkins' camp to see if he had extra sleeping bags, and possibly another tent we could store elsewhere...." Maxine said. Maxine soon became concerned that Clarke might have been responsible for the fire, and eventually the others were too. But there was no way they could prove that, and they were long, remote miles from Talkeetna.

In the end, the Brittell group signed an agreement. Ken told the others he didn't want to fight all summer long about the tailing conflict, and that any further harassment from Clarke could seriously hinder the work they had to do. The contract that Ken, Joy, Maxine, and Tim Craig signed ensured the payment of $500 to Xan John Clarke, but made provision for two pay periods. The first $250 would be payable immediately, and the remainder was to be deposited in Clarke's account at the Bank of Alaska in Anchorage by the tenth of September. The security for the latter payment would be the Brittells' claims and mining equipment.

Ken and Joy apparently did not have $250, because they hiked over to the Jenkins' camp and asked to borrow the money. Frank Jenkins listened to their story and wrote out a check for what they needed. That he tacitly sanctioned the agreement perhaps speaks volumes for the circumstantial dominance held by Clarke. And that he gave them the money illustrates the regard Jenkins held for the young men.

On June 12, the money was paid to the prospector who had staked his first claim across the mouth of Wolf Creek.

———

Belle McDonald was over 60 years old now, but still active at her trading post. She had grubstaked many down and out prospectors over the years and, in due course, had received title to various mining claims staked by gold seekers who had been unable to pay her back for the food and supplies she had gambled on them. Six of these were located at the upper reaches of Willow Creek, at a considerable elevation above the Jenkins' operation in the Dutch Hills. This wasn't very desirable ground because it was so high, and because water volume was often insufficient to provide for proper sluicing. But Belle had quite a lot of mining gear and equipment stored there, and there must have been enough "color" in the claims for her to continue to hold them.

Oddly enough, Belle had let the assessment work on these claims slide, and when she received the brief warning letter from Xan Clarke she decided to take the message seriously. She made a lease agreement with a man named John Hill, who had told her he intended to prospect in the Dutch Hills that summer. Belle probably allowed him to work the claims in return for labor and improvements that would satisfy her annual assessment requirements. It's possible too, that she threw in some supplies to help the deal along.

Sometime in early June, Hill and his 18-year-old stepson, Frank

Sandstrom, packed up their outfit, some 400 to 500 pounds of food and gear, and made arrangements with Frank Lee to freight them back into the gold country. Frank took the two men across the Susitna in his riverboat and then loaded the outfit onto an old Model T Ford that he had staged at the river landing. The aged Ford had fifteen gears, Sandstrom said, and an old Chevy truck rear end. They managed to get as far as Moose Creek before it broke down. While the two prospectors waited, the weary but persevering Frank Lee, now in his sixties, made his way back to the landing and fired up his caterpillar tractor, hooked it up to a go-devil, and slowly headed up the Cache Creek Road. At Moose Creek he reloaded the men and their outfit and took them as far as Petersville.

From there, Hill and Sandstrom packed their supplies on their backs the extra miles to the southeast slopes of the Dutch Hills. It took several trips, with the younger Sandstrom doing most of the packing, and finally they got their outfit back into the Willow Creek area. They reached the Jenkins' mine and stopped in to say hello and, as a courtesy, tell them what they were doing in the area. Helen was alone at the cabin when they arrived, and reacted quickly.

"You're going nowhere," she told them. "We've got all that area staked."

Hill and Sandstrom left and camped for the night; they discussed what they should do. Hill finally decided that his stepson should remain with their outfit while he covered the long miles back to the river landing. Hill made it to Talkeetna and went straight to the U.S. commissioner's office where the mining records were kept. He explained his problem to Ben Mayfield, who told him to go ahead with his plans. "The Jenkinses already have too many claims," he reportedly told Hill, who later repeated this encouragement to his stepson.

Hill traveled back to Willow Creek, and he and Sandstrom followed it to its upper limit. There was plenty of equipment at the McDonald camp, Sandstrom said, but Belle's storage cache had collapsed from either heavy snows or disturbance by bears. They rummaged around and managed to recover a canvas tent that they mounted on a wall-tent frame that was installed on the property. "There was quite a bit of grub up there too," Sandstrom recalled. The two men found several cans of corned beef, some of which were badly rusted and they fed to a dog they had with them. The others they ate during the time they were there, along with their own red and white beans that were their standard fare. "A big slab of salt pork and a few spuds and rice" rounded out their meals, Sandstrom said.

The two began their work. Sandstrom said there was some old hydraulic equipment at the claims, and they used a hose with a four-inch nozzle to knock dirt loose where needed. They made some open cuts, one of which was in the middle of the creek bed, "which was easy to do because it was so dry," he said. They also strung out a few lengths of pipe for water transfer. The men worked in this manner for a couple of weeks, until one day they saw a man approach their camp.

Clarke told them who he was and where his camp was located. He watched them work for awhile and chatted about mining. He learned that the McDonald project was just a part of their plans that summer and that the two wanted to prospect elsewhere in the area when they had finished.

"C'mon and prospect over at my place," Clarke invited. He mentioned that he might have some work for them at his claims if they were interested.

When Clarke was gone, the older man and his stepson discussed the proposal over dinner and decided it wouldn't hurt to take the man up on his offer. So, a few days later they packed some food and gear and headed down Willow Creek and up Ruby Gulch. Above Ruby they crossed the plateau to Wonder Gulch, which led on down to Ramsdyke Creek. Rotted snow still lingered in the gulch, and at one point Sandstrom broke through a moldering snow bridge, but emerged unhurt. When they got to Clarke's camp, he was friendly and accommodating, even offering to let them sleep in his cabin while they were there. The two men proceeded to prospect for a couple of days and found a little gold.

On July 2, Clarke had staked two more claims on Ramsdyke, Five and Six Above Norma. On the same day he filed, by mail sent in with a freighter to Talkeetna, a Notice of Location of Water Right on Quartz Creek, a small tributary on the northwest limit of Ramsdyke. Clarke noted that he reserved "the right of diverting any or all water in said creek to work Ramsdyke Creek placer claims." He told Hill and Sandstrom about this and said he needed a ditch from Quartz Creek to his claims. Were they interested in digging the ditch?

He couldn't pay them much, Clarke said, but if they would do the work he would let them have half of the profits from the claim that would be worked with the water from the ditch. The two prospectors agreed. They stayed in Clarke's place, which Frank described as "a pretty small cabin." They cooked together, and Hill slept on the floor at night while Sandstrom slept in his bag on the table. During the evenings they sometimes conversed, and Clarke told them he was of Hungarian descent. He seemed to be well aware of the Francis-Jenkins feud and said he was on speaking terms with them both. Sandstrom got the impression that Clarke was French-Canadian and had a military background.

The two men worked for about two weeks on the ditch and

completed one a mile long. It wasn't a major ditch. "We just turned the sod over to one side and got the water from Quartz Creek to where Clarke wanted it," Sandstrom said.

At one point during the course of the digging, Clarke reportedly asked John Hill, "Do you suppose that the Jenkinses have their gold cached in the old camp?" Hill replied that he didn't think it was any of his (Hill's) business, and the subject was dropped.

When the ditch was completed, the three men talked some more, and Clarke persuaded Hill and his stepson to join him in filing on some claims. Together, on July 10, they staked four claims that Clarke named Norma Side Claims. Three of these adjoined the Brittell claim stakes on Wolf Creek. When young Frank Sandstrom began, as required, to sign his name to the posted notices, Clarke snapped at him, "Don't scribble like that. No funny stuff." Frank didn't like it, but he didn't say anything.

The Brittells were probably startled when they saw the stakes adjoining theirs. The next day, in self defense, Ken, Joy, and Maxine staked two claims in the immediate vicinity in order to secure an area where Ken had long planned to put a water ditch of their own. This rankled Clarke and, shortly thereafter, he paid a visit to the Brittell camp. He told Ken that the men he was working with were very unhappy with the Brittell staking, and they felt that Ken was impeding their work. He was convincing enough that Ken offered to let them work with a portion of one of his new claims. That, or Brittell was just plain weary of the interference that Clarke seemed skilled at and made the concession to appease the aggressive man.

It's not clear just what Clarke told Hill and Sandstrom about the matter, but Hill began to get a bad feeling about the man. So, he asked Clarke to draw up the agreement that granted half the values of the ditch-fed claim to Hill and his stepson. To his consternation, Clarke refused, telling the two that this was not the term of their agreement. Just what had been agreed upon was not made clear, and Hill decided he'd had enough.

"My stepfather was a pretty sharp guy," Sandstrom said. "He was a good judge of men. He didn't trust him. (That's) about the time we got out of there."

When they were alone, Hill told Frank, "Get your gear together. We're pulling out. And don't tell no one we're leaving."

When the time was right, the two men shouldered their packs and departed. But Hill wanted to make a side trip to the Brittell camp first, which they did. There he told Ken Brittell that he and his stepson had had little to do with the staking of the claims abutting theirs. He was earnest, and it seemed important to him that Brittell believe him. This

146

done, Hill and Sandstrom crossed Ramsdyke, ascended the ridge along Wonder Gulch, and packed on over to Ruby Creek. When they reached Willow Creek, they stopped at Jenkins' camp. Frank was glad to see them because he was badly in need of more help. He asked Frank Sandstrom if he would stay and work for him. The teenager, however, had formed some impressions of his own, and he didn't like the Jenkinses. "Jenkins was a mean one," he said, and he declined the request.

After a short rest, Hill and Sandstrom continued on up the creek to Belle's camp on upper Willow. That evening the men were going through their gear when something about his gun, an old 30-40 Craig army rifle, caught Sandstrom's eye. When he examined its barrel he saw that it was packed tight with rocks and mud. An examination of John Hill's old military revolver revealed that it was similarly jammed, and it unnerved the men. Had they taken a shot at small game or anything else during their long trek, the result could have been grievous. "The firing pin might have blew in my face," Sandstrom said. Both men were certain that Clarke had done it. "He rammed rocks and mud in as hard as he could," Sandstrom said.

While Hill and Sandstrom had been at Ramsdyke Creek, Dick Francis was looking over some ground at Poorman Creek, a stream about a mile to the east of Ruby Gulch. Francis was now 60 years old and had been prospecting these creeks for twenty-five years. This summer he and Ed Carlson had apparently concluded that the Ruby Creek claims were just not profitable enough. Though Ed had put in a few long sessions at the claims this season, he had since returned to Anchorage to tend to other business. Now Francis spent some time with their elderly friend, Al Stinson, testing for colors along Poorman. The two savvy miners liked what they found and staked out a claim they called the Francis and Stinson Placer Mining Claim. But the ground they were really interested in was a group of claims, together with a cabin, that the First National Bank of Anchorage held title to, probably as the result of a foreclosure.

By the time August rolled around, Francis had corresponded with the bank and expressed an interest in leasing the claims and cabin. Al Stinson also agreed to participate as a partner in the lease, and Ed Carlson had shown an interest in throwing in with them.

The first part of August is the last of summer in the Susitna Valley. The early days of the month embrace warmth and light, but vegetation senses that its cycle has peaked and, as the days and weeks pass, starts to display a heavy appearance in both hue and texture. Berries of many kinds ripen, and great salmon runs move up the Susitna River and its tributaries to seek spawning grounds. The angle of light is similar to that in May, casting a bit of white glare that glances capriciously in the air. Migrant songbirds are abandoning the north and taking their music with them; black and white birds like the chickadee, magpie, raven, and ptarmigan remain because they are biologically committed for the long term.

As warm summer temperatures decrease, the great glaciers of the Alaska Range cool as well, and the tremendous amount of silt discharged with summer glacial melt diminishes in the wild rivers. Late in the month, the cold rushing water begins to flow a clear green, like pale silk, and, overhead, lines of geese, ducks, swans, and cranes call out their farewells. Knotted clumps of the false hellebore flower mature to seed another generation of unusual, statuesque plants. Though daylight is displaced at the rate of several minutes each day, it is still fairly light out at ten o'clock at night in late August. But the nights grow cooler, and change must begin to take place for everything.

In 1939 the month of August was one of the rainiest ever recorded in Southcentral Alaska. *The Anchorage Times* characterized it as "one of the most miserable months since weather records were started in 1916." At its end, official records would show that only two days had been free of rain or cloudy weather that month. For miners in Cache Creek country the persistent precipitation was a mixed blessing; though cold and miserable to work in, it provided valuable water for sluicing.

———

Ira Diess had injured his foot while working at the Jenkins' operation, and when its condition did not improve, he decided to seek medical treatment in Anchorage. On August 1 he informed Frank Jenkins of his decision, and on August 2 he left. Jenkins had only Don Sheldon for help now and apparently asked Joy Brittell to lend a hand until he could replace Diess. Then, on August 8, a young man walked up to the camp and asked Jenkins for work.

Bob Meade, 23, was dark-haired and from Syracuse, New York. He had been in Alaska for just three months, having arrived on the *SS ALASKA* at Seward in early May. He had obtained work as a section hand with the Alaska Railroad in Anchorage and, at some point, was transferred to Talkeetna, where he worked until August 3 when the railroad laid off several men. Commissioner Mayfield had become acquainted with Meade while he was in Talkeetna and suggested that there might be an opportunity for employment at the Jenkins' mine, due to Diess's departure.

Meade traveled with George Weatherell to a point about three miles from Jenkins' Little Willow Creek operation. From there he began to hike but became confused by the various trails. Somehow he ended up at Dick Francis' camp, where the friendly miner gave him further directions. As the day grew late he found himself at a mine in the Bird Creek area operated by a family named Wagner. They invited him to stay for the night because, they told him, he still had some distance to go. The next morning he set out again, only to end up at Rocky Cummins' camp, a two hour walk to the west of the Jenkins'

A rare photo of Frank Jenkins (left) at his Little Willow mining operation. Next to him is Ken Brittell. Jenkins, an aggressive and successful miner, worked his employees hard and didn't trust banks. (courtesy Maxine Brittell)

mine. When he finally arrived at the Jenkins' property, he first encountered Sheldon and Brittell who pointed out Frank Jenkins in the distance. When Meade told Jenkins that Mayfield had suggested he apply for work there, Frank told him to "go to the cabin and see Mrs. Jenkins about the matter." Meade apparently passed Helen's scrutiny because she hired him and informed him that his wage would be $5 per day.

Meade found Frank Jenkins to be a demanding boss. The day started with breakfast at 6:15 a.m. sharp (an indication that Helen's preparation began much earlier), and work began at seven o'clock. Hard physical labor followed until the lunch break and continued through the work day until it ended at six in the evening. Meade would later remark that Jenkins was a hard man to work for.

Ben Mayfield had briefed Meade about the long-standing conflict between the Jenkinses and Francis, warning him not to take sides in the matter. So when Helen inevitably disparaged Francis at meal times, Meade made no acknowledgment and kept his silence. This wasn't difficult to do as Frank and Helen had little, if anything, to say to Meade. They seemed to make it clear that he was nothing more than a short-term employee. As soon as the evening meal was finished, the young laborer would leave the cabin and go to the bunkhouse for the remainder of the evening.

Frank Jenkins' figure can be seen at the center of this view of his Little Willow operation. Jenkins was outraged when miner Dick Francis staked claims near his important water ditch system. (courtesy Maxine Brittell)

Meade noted that Helen Jenkins was "suspicious of everyone." Though he wasn't aware of it at the time, just the sight of Rocky Cummins' dog in the area was enough to inflame her interest. In a little daily diary kept by Helen, she noted on one August day that "Rocky's dog was down in our pit this morning. Rocky must have been somewhere around."

During the month or so that he worked at the mine, Meade also observed that no one dropped by except a miner named Clarke, who occasionally came by for coffee. The man seemed to annoy Frank Jenkins, who privately expressed his irritation one day as he and the men walked back to the mine pit after finishing their lunch. Along a hill in the distance, the figure of Clarke could be seen approaching the pit by way of a difficult trail that was rarely, if ever, used by anyone. Jenkins paused at the sight and remarked to Brittell that he couldn't see Clarke's reason for choosing that particular route to travel. Joy agreed and added that the obscure trail was not only strenuous but, compared with the regular route, required much more distance to be covered. Jenkins' quizzical tone soon turned to one of displeasure and he remarked that he didn't "like the idea of Clarke snooping around." Finally, he muttered that it seemed the Ramsdyke miner was "always coming around to chisel a free meal."

Around mid-August John Hill and Frank Sandstrom had run out of food and decided to quit the Dutch Hills. It was another rainy day when they closed down Belle's upper Willow Creek camp, packed their gear together, and headed down Willow to its juncture with Ruby Creek. The two then made their way up Ruby to the Francis-Carlson camp, stopping to say goodbye to Dick. During his visit Hill asked Francis if there was anything he could do for him in Talkeetna or Anchorage, and the miner replied that it would be helpful if they could carry a grocery order to a store in Anchorage and arrange for Chris Christensen to deliver the groceries the next time he planned to be in the Willow Creek area. Francis then carefully weighed out three ounces of gold dust to pay the grocer and related costs, and gave them to Hill.

When the conversation turned to Clarke, John Hill told Dick Francis that he did not trust the man. "Be very careful of your dealings with Clarke," he said. Then he packed Dick's grocery order away, shouldered his gear, and he and Sandstrom headed down Willow Creek.

Ken Brittell had received a letter from the territorial school system in July, informing him that his teaching post for the upcoming school year would be at Squaw Harbor on Unga Island along the Alaska Peninsula. Ken and Maxine decided to leave Wolf Creek somewhat earlier than usual, in order to shop and prepare in Anchorage for the long months at the remote island. At first they targeted August 25 as their departure date, and mentioned this casually one evening when John Clarke had dropped by to visit. But later, when Ken learned that Maxine wanted to walk out rather than fly, they decided to leave on August 23. Joy agreed to stay and close up the Wolf Creek camp for the winter. Then, he said, he planned to move over to Little Willow Creek and work for Frank who needed the help.

Ken had wanted to fly out from Wolf Creek, but Maxine had been thinking about her disagreeable flight experiences, and told him she wasn't climbing back into another airplane. Her feelings became unshakeable and they finally agreed to cover the distance to Talkeetna on foot. On August 23, Ken, Maxine, and Tim Craig shouldered their packs and set off down the slope to Ramsdyke Creek. As they moved up the stream toward Wonder Gulch, they passed Clarke's cabin, where Clarke caught sight of them and appeared, Ken thought, to be "greatly surprised" that they were leaving on this particular day.

Because the two men were carrying heavy packs, the three took their time moving up the trail to the ridge along Wonder Gulch. As they neared the top of the bluff, they paused to rest for a time. It was then that they saw someone moving at the foot of the gulch. Thinking it might be Joy, they stayed where they were in case he needed to talk to them. But the person "used precaution to see that he was not observed," Ken noticed, and this seemed odd. The three were now curious and decided to remain long enough to identify the figure. After some time, the person finally came into view, and they saw that it was Clarke. He was still far enough removed so that Ken had to shout an inquiry. Did he have mail he wanted taken in to Talkeetna? No, Clarke replied, he was just going to Dick Francis' camp to borrow some magazines.

While the Brittells moved to continue on their way, Ken took note of the fact that Clarke visited Francis a lot. Earlier that summer, Clarke had told Ken that during these visits he and Francis would discuss activity at the Jenkins' operation, and Clarke would pass along to Francis anything of significance he might have heard somewhere. During one conversation, he said, he told Francis that he had heard the Jenkinses were going to seek a permanent injunction against him. Francis had reacted angrily and made threats against the Jenkinses, Clarke said.

Brittell, his wife, and brother-in-law proceeded on to the Jenkins' camp, where they planned to spend the night. They spent that evening visiting with Frank and Helen, who confided their season's gold recovery at several thousand dollars and remarked that the year had probably been their best one yet. Helen brought out some large nuggets to show everyone and talked about the plans she and Frank had for traveling Outside at the end of the mining season. Both wanted to get some dental work done in Seattle, she said, and then travel on to California to visit with members of Frank's family. The primary reason for the California visit, she added, was to persuade Frank's brother to come to Alaska the next year to act as foreman at their mine.

This decision, to delegate a major share of the workload, indicates that the labor was finally becoming too much for Frank Jenkins, who had toiled so hard for so many years. In three days he would turn sixty. Perhaps it was time to ease some of the load.

The Brittells and Craig spent the better part of the next day with the Jenkinses before moving on down the trail that led to Petersville. When they reached Belle's roadhouse at Peters Creek, they elected to spend the night there. On August 25, they arrived in Talkeetna, spent some time at a roadhouse visiting with people they knew, and remained overnight.

Joy Brittell spent two or three days closing down the Wolf Creek camp. Equipment, gear, and tools needed to be sorted and organized for the season to come. The canvas tents had to be disassembled and stored to prevent their collapse by the heavy snows common to the area. It's likely that Brittell used the tents to cover and protect the equipment he and his brother had accumulated during their first season. There was also a Fairbanks-Morse brand radio that they had listened to all summer, to hear the news broadcast from an Anchorage radio station. It belonged to Ken who hadn't wanted to leave it at camp, but, together with a heavy battery that powered it, the two items had been too bulky and heavy to carry out when he, Maxine, and Tim had departed. With a pack full of other gear to take to Jenkins' camp, Joy couldn't pack it out either. But he had anticipated this and told Ken that he would stage the two items at John Clarke's cabin until the time came when he could return to retrieve them.

On August 26, Ken and Maxine went to Ben Mayfield's office to record their Proof of Labor declaration for their five claims on Wolf Creek. Brittell described the labor and improvements as "construction of 200 feet of ditch; building a camp; installing mining machinery at a cost of $650; prospecting by sinking eight holes to bedrock; and open-cut work and ground sluicing."

On August 27, Frank Jenkins turned 60 years old. Mining records indicate that the next day, at Mayfield's office in Talkeetna, he recorded his own Proof of Labor declaration for his many mining tracts. The claims he identified as having received labor and improvements included one on Ruby Creek; twelve on Willow Creek; four on Lucky Gulch; one each at Joy, Dry, Puzzle, and Slate Gulches; one on Falls Creek; three on Gopher Gulch; two each at Rocky and Snowshoe Gulches; and eight on Cottonwood Creek.

Jenkins described the work he had performed as "labor and improvements on and for the benefit and betterment of each and every claim, including trail building and trail work, digging ditches and sinking of prospect holes, or pits, to bedrock, to determine where the pay is, repairs on cabins and bunk-houses, and general mining to the equivalent of more than one hundred dollars for each and every claim mentioned in this instrument." Jenkins added that "All of the ... claims adjoin and make one contiguous group of claims."

––––

Toward the end of August, Dick Francis apparently received bank approval to enter the Poorman Creek property, because he packed food, supplies, a pick, shovel, and pan from Ruby Creek on over to that location. He set up a camp of sorts and dug two ditches—one about 30 feet in length, the other 100 feet long—and cleared a twenty-foot area of brush. This work took him several days, after which he headed back to Ruby Creek.

At some point Francis walked about eight miles south to Petersville, where the Peters Creek Mining Company was in full operation. The largest mining concern in the entire area at this time, Petersville consisted of an extensive complex of buildings, sophisticated mining equipment, and a good airfield. It also served as an official mail collection point, and miners in the area often walked there to post outgoing mail for faster transfer.

While there, Francis met up with Al Stinson, and the two talked at length. Francis likely told Al about the work he'd done at Poorman and then went on to relate a conversation he had had with the Ramsdyke miner, John Clarke. The man was interested in becoming a partner with them on the Poorman claims, Francis said. He went on to indicate that he thought this was a good idea; the extra financial investment and physical labor would be helpful. But Al hesitated and finally told Francis that he couldn't agree to the proposal. He didn't know Clarke very well, he said, but there was something about him that he didn't trust. In fact, Stinson said, if Clarke was brought in on Poorman, then he would withdraw from the partnership.

––––

After working a ten-hour shift every day for three and a half months, young Don Sheldon was ready to leave the Jenkins' mining operation at the end of August. Earlier, he had heard from Ira Diess.

> I got a letter from him and he said he was improving, and he would like very much to establish some cabins midway between the Cache Creek area and Talkeetna, in the good fur country of the Kroto River. So our arrangement was that the last day of August I was to work full shift at the mine and then stop the season at the thirtieth day of August, and catch an old freighter, a cat-train, back into the village of Talkeetna.

Sheldon observed that it had been a good season for the Jenkinses. "The season was quite lucrative for the mine," he said. "The gold recovery was beyond expectations, and Mr. and Mrs. Jenkins and Joy Brittell implored that I stay at least two more weeks—into September—to take out at least one or two more gold clean-ups."

Don Sheldon, 18, (left) and Bob Meade, 23, at the Jenkinses' Little Willow Creek camp. Sheldon left summer-long employment there just days before the murders. Meade departed on the morning that Frank Jenkins and Joy Brittell left for Ramsdyke Creek to pick up a radio and battery. (courtesy Maxine Brittell)

But Sheldon's commitment to his friend weighed heavily on him, and he had to say no.

The first week of September in the Susitna Valley is in seasonal evolution, with temperatures decreasing to around the low forties at night. While every fall is somewhat different, depending on weather and temperatures, there always exists a distinct aura that summer has gone and only weeks remain before the first appearances of wintry import. Temperatures may advance to the fifties during the day, but there is a sharp character to the air and the angle of light is more pronounced, adding an intensity to the white quality of the atmosphere. Foliage continues to acquire a dullness in texture and color, but here and there grape-like clusters of birch leaves begin to transform to yellow and gold, presenting a striking contrast with the greater mass of the tree that has not yet yielded to change.

Along the slopes of the Dutch Hills, especially above the tree line, the dense carpet of vegetation begins to acquire bold hues of red, orange, yellow, and even purple. Temperatures are even cooler at these levels, and the threat of a freeze becomes imminent; miners hurry to wash out what gold they can with the seasonally-reduced water flow. Occasionally, early, brief snow flurries may occur as a further warning that this is a serious country that caters to no living thing.

As the days pass, the land grows quiet and vegetation gains in colored brilliance. Now, the sun rises later in the morning and descends earlier in the evening as a loss of around five minutes of daylight occurs each day.

The early days of September, 1939, saw little sunlight. The month was proving to be as miserably rainy as August had.

At some point Bob Meade approached Frank Jenkins and asked him how much longer he would be able to work there. Meade's boots were worn out, he said, and wouldn't last much longer. He wondered if there would be enough work for him to justify the purchase of a new pair. Jenkins only answered that Meade could stay "until the last pit is cleaned up," which he estimated would take place several days into September.

Joy Brittell now worked full-time for Frank Jenkins, and on September 2 he wrote a letter to his mother in Nebraska. He told her that he planned to work for Jenkins until the first of October. He said he was saving every penny he earned to put toward next year's mining operation at Wolf Creek. He hoped, too, that some day he could help his parents with his sister's schooling expenses. He also proudly related that Jenkins had told him that he and his brother, Kenny, were the most dependable men he had ever employed.

On September 6, a rain-filled Wednesday, Jenkins, Brittell, and Meade were just finishing lunch when Xan Clarke appeared at the cabin. Though Jenkins had little to say to him, and he and the men left to prepare for Jenkins' last gold clean-up, Helen conformed to the custom of hospitality and offered him lunch. Clarke ate and remained there all day, most likely reading magazines. He was still there when the men returned for dinner, and Clarke shared that meal too. As was his custom following the evening meal, Jenkins tuned in the seven o'clock news on his battery-powered radio while the men sat quietly, intent upon hearing all the news that took place outside the realm of Cache Creek country. Of particular interest at this time was the upheaval in Europe. Germany, France, and Great Britain were convulsed with war and each evening's broadcast documented a terrible progression of bloody conflict.

Following the news, the radio station aired a special program segment for listeners in remote locations. Important as a means of contact in a vast territory with limited means of communication, the scheduled broadcast conveyed messages of importance to anyone within listening distance. That evening there was a message for Joy Brittell in the Dutch Hills, from his brother. Ken and Maxine were leaving Anchorage for Seward the next day to connect with a boat bound for Squaw Harbor, the message said. It requested that Joy ship the Fairbanks-Morse radio to Ken at Squaw Harbor, when it was convenient for Joy to pick it up.

When the news program was over, Clarke put on his raincoat and hat and set out on the two to three-hour trek back to Ramsdyke. Though clouds and rain veiled the hills, evenings were still light in early September, with dusk descending at 9:30 or so. There is some evidence that Clarke stopped by to see Dick Francis along the way, and he probably arrived at his own cabin well after dark.

Joy Brittell had been friendly and considerate toward Bob Meade during his term of employment with Jenkins and had even done a favor or two for him. Later that evening, when they were in the bunkhouse, Meade mentioned this and offered to help him pack the radio and battery from Ramsdyke back over to Willow Creek when the time came to recover it. Brittell thanked him but declined, possibly because he and Jenkins had already decided to make the trip together. Earlier that summer Ken and Joy had asked Frank for his advice on how to mine their claims on Wolf Creek and also for his opinion of certain equipment they thought appropriate for their ground. Besides helping Joy with the burden of the radio and battery, Jenkins probably reasoned that the trip to Ramsdyke would provide him with an opportunity to get a look at the brothers' ground and to see what particular challenges they were dealing with.

Following several days of heavy clouds and rainy weather in the Susitna River Valley, September 7 dawned with fair, almost clear skies.

157

Chris Christensen rushed to take advantage of the good flying conditions and loaded his plane with supply orders that he had accumulated during the inclement weather. He took off for the Cache Creek area and eventually flew over Dick Francis' camp. After the over-fly to gain Francis' attention, he airdropped Dick's Anchorage grocery order to him. Francis was glad to get it, especially the several cans of Velvet smoking tobacco that he had included on his list. The bad weather had hung in the Dutch Hills for so long that Francis had finally run out of tobacco and been forced to borrow some from Clarke.

On September 8, the weather moved back into the valley and dense skies dropped more rain. Frank Jenkins, Brittell, and Meade worked doggedly on at the mining pit, washing more pay dirt through the big sluice boxes and trapping the heavy gold.

The next day the weather improved again and even began to clear. Finally, under partly sunny skies, Jenkins and the two young men worked the last of the gravel through the boxes. When the gold had been separated out at the end of the long day, Jenkins was not disappointed. Now he could look back on an exceptionally good season and know that all the hard work had produced results.

Meade's employment at the mine was finished, and he probably made preparations for departure that night. Frank Jenkins and Joy Brittell undoubtedly discussed the trend toward good weather and apparently concluded that they should take advantage of it and make the trip to get the radio the next day. The men had been rained on enough in the past weeks, and neither wanted to move through the heavy brush around Wolf and Ramsdyke Creeks in dismally wet conditions.

Everybody was up at the usual time on Sunday morning, September 10. Helen had breakfast ready at 6:15, and when dawn began to emerge just before seven o'clock, it was obvious that the day would be exceptional. Clear blue skies held a brilliant rising sun, and the Dutch Hills reposed in soft golden hues, dappled with swathes of more vividly colored foliage.

At the breakfast table no mention was made of Meade's departure, and he finished his meal and went to the bunkhouse to pack up his belongings. He was in need of a piece of rope to secure his pack, so returned to the Jenkins' cabin and asked Joy if he could borrow one of his. Brittell gave him the rope, and when Meade was finished he went back to the cabin and told the Jenkinses that he was ready to leave. Helen silently reached to the window sill, picked up his paycheck, and handed it to him. Though Meade would be traveling on foot for several long hours, he was dismayed to note that Helen made no offer of a packed lunch, nor even a sandwich to tide him over.

Once outside the cabin, Meade realized that he was still unfamiliar with the trail system in the area and felt a vague uncertainty about which direction to take. The Jenkinses seemed reluctant to tender even small courtesies, and since Jenkins and Brittell were now occupied in getting ready for their long hike to Ramsdyke, Meade set out in his bad boots on a trail to the south and west, hoping it was the right choice.

It is not clear just what time Frank and Joy said goodbye to Helen that morning, but the two ascended the steep hill to the north of the mining camp and gained the trail that led farther north to the wild country where Ramsdyke and Wolf Creeks flowed. Because they would be gone for the better part of the day, both men likely carried a lunch, prepared by Helen, in their otherwise empty packboards.

The two walked in the incandescent sunlight, past tangled vegetation touched by moderate seasonal frosts, and along spongy tussocks that nurtured alpine plants and flowers. Though from this vantage the great mass of Denali lay concealed behind other mountains in the Alaska Range, its summit portion loomed enigmatically in the north, like an iced behemoth engaged in clandestine surveillance as the two figures made their way along the ridge that paralleled Wonder Gulch. A few parka squirrels chittered and flicked their tails as the men approached, and darted among dense mosses and scattered highbush blueberry shrubs that still bore fruit, their leaves now marbled with brilliant color.

It is a flawless day, enriched and warmed by the sun as it ascends a radiant arc over the Dutch Hills.

When the men reached the northern terminus of the ridge and descended its steep, rugged face to Ramsdyke Creek, they were prepared to ford the low, rushing stream. Frank Jenkins in his olive-green rubber hip boots and Joy Brittell in his black ones crossed easily. It is reasonable to assume that the two then headed slightly east to the mouth of Wolf Creek, then up that stream to the closed Brittell camp. It is also reasonable to assume that they spent a couple of hours at the Wolf Creek location, especially if Jenkins wanted to see the upper claims (which he almost certainly did) and also if they finally paused to rest and eat their lunch there.

Then the tough, veteran miner and the friendly, young Brittell probably walked down Wolf Creek to its confluence with Ramsdyke, turned right, and headed upstream a short distance to John Clarke's cabin where the radio and battery were stored. It is not known if Clarke was at his cabin when they arrived, but it is known that the two men collected the items they had come for. Jenkins put the radio set in his pack, and Joy packed the heavy battery in his. Then the two crossed Ramsdyke and headed up the ridgeface along Wonder Gulch.

Alone at Little Willow Creek, Helen wrote in her daily journal: "It is beautiful today."

11   `it was a terrible day`

         Often, when a heavy weather system moves into the Susitna River Valley, it doesn't stop until it encounters the great Alaska Range, at which point it packs up heavily against the massive granite mountains and shifts about thickly and contentiously. On Tuesday, September 12, one such system followed this pattern and splayed its lower reaches throughout Cache Creek country and the Talkeetna area. It clung densely to the region, intractable and head-strong, creating conditions impossible for aircraft to negotiate.

         And Commissioner Ben Mayfield needed an airplane.

         The evening before, on Monday the eleventh, Chris Christensen had landed at the Talkeetna Village Airstrip and hastened to the commissioner's office to report that Dick Francis was dead. The pilot told Mayfield that he had been at Petersville to deliver some supplies that day, when Rocky Cummins had arrived there and asked him to report the death to Mayfield. Details were vague, he said, but Cummins had told him that a man named John Clarke had discovered Francis' body about eight o'clock on the morning of the eleventh, and then gone to the Jenkins' camp to report it. But no one was there, so Clarke had informed Rocky, who traveled to Petersville with the news. Christensen went on to say that he'd been told that it looked like a suicide, because the dead Francis had a revolver in his hand.

         Since the day was late and darkness imminent, Mayfield and Christensen agreed that it would be more practical to fly to the Dutch Hills early the next morning. The pilot told Mayfield he needed to continue on to Anchorage that evening, but he would return to Talkeetna at first daylight to pick him up.

         Then the weather had gotten nasty.

         On September 12, as Mayfield watched the cold rain and recalcitrant weather, he placed a call to United States Attorney Joseph Kehoe in Seward. He explained the situation, and Kehoe instructed him to proceed to the Dutch Hills and begin an investigation as soon as the weather permitted. As for himself, Kehoe said, the weather was so thick in Seward that it was impossible to leave, but as soon as conditions improved, he would travel to Talkeetna and assist with the investigation.

In Anchorage, where Christensen was grounded by the same massive weather system, the news of Francis' death traveled rapidly. Later that day the *Anchorage Daily Times* printed a related article:

DICK FRANCIS FOUND SHOT IN HIS CABIN
Prospector Discovers Tragedy When
Francis Failed To Answer Greeting

Dick Francis, oldtime prospector of the Cache Creek country, was found dead in his isolated cabin in the mountains of Ruby Gulch yesterday morning, according to word brought to Anchorage by Pilot Hakon Christensen.

John Clark of Talkeetna reported discovering the body as he passed the cabin. It was lying on the floor with a pool of blood nearby. A revolver was also on the floor. There was a bullet wound in the head. An investigation was believed to be under way today with U.S. Commissioner B.H. Mayfield of Talkeetna in charge. Mr. Clark, also a prospector, told friends he borrowed some tobacco from Francis Sunday afternoon. Yesterday morning when he was passing the cabin he called and got no answer. Opening the door, Clark said he found Francis on the floor. He went to a neighboring prospector by the name of Rockie, and told him of the discovery. Rockie went to Peters Creek and reported it to Pilot Christensen.

Francis had many friends in Anchorage. He lived at one time at the Parsons Hotel here. Friends said he had been in the country since 1905 and was past the age of 60 years. Pilot Christensen dropped food supplies to Francis about a week ago. The prospector's cabin is about three miles from the nearest neighbor.

Though the article contained some factual errors, people focused on the tragedy while Ben Mayfield waited for the unruly weather to improve. The heavy system, however, remained stolidly in place, all day long and into the night.

Mayfield was up early on the morning of the thirteenth, and the weather remained leaden and temperamental. But at midmorning the skies seemed to improve somewhat, and by noon Chris Christensen was able to land at Talkeetna's airstrip. The two men immediately took off beneath ragged skies for the Dutch Hills and passed over Ruby Creek about twenty-five minutes later. No one appeared to be in the vicinity of Francis' tent-cabin, so they continued in a northerly direction over Wonder Gulch and on to Ramsdyke Creek, looking for Clarke. Finally, they saw him high on a trail near the headwaters of Poorman Creek, east of Wonder Gulch. While Chris circled, Mayfield wrote a note to Clarke, directing him to proceed to Dick Francis' camp. Mayfield would land at the Petersville airstrip, he advised, and then walk up to Francis' place and meet Clarke there. The note was airdropped to the man below, who retrieved it and probably waved an acknowledgment.

There are indications that Mayfield paused at the Peters Creek mine to talk with the men there. He learned more details of Rocky Cummins' report, most significantly that Clarke had gone to the Jenkins' camp to report Francis' death and had found it empty. It was now believed that Frank and Helen were missing. As the men talked, there was speculation about the feud.

The afternoon was growing late by the time Mayfield, on foot, had covered the eight or so miles from Petersville to Francis' camp at Ruby. John Clarke was there waiting for him, and together they entered the cabin. The blanket-shrouded body of Dick Francis lay on its back on the floor, between a modest bed cot and a small wood stove. Clarke explained that he had placed the blanket over Francis the previous day but had not otherwise touched the body or disturbed anything in the cabin.

Mayfield removed the covering and observed that Francis' right hand, which held a .38 revolver, was resting on his stomach. His left hand lay across his chest. A large pool of blood lay along the right side of the body, mostly near the head, and a smaller pool had collected to the left. The officer noticed blood spatters on cartons of supplies that were stacked two or three feet to the right of the body.

Mayfield examined Francis' head and observed one wound on the right side and one on the left, which appeared to be single entry and exit wounds that supported the appearance of suicide. Because so much blood covered the head, the commissioner would later remark that it was close to impossible to examine for gunpowder burns. He also noted that more blood covered Francis' right hand and extended up the right wrist and arm, under his shirt sleeve.

A close inspection of Francis' right, work-worn hand disclosed that the revolver was held loosely, with the thumb resting under the left side of the gun's stock; the remaining fingers curled slightly around the other side.

The distant trickle of Ruby Creek drifted through the open door of the cabin, lending a soft background to the funereal moments of Mayfield's examination. Dick's big, friendly malamute dogs, Amos and Andy, stood at the ends of their tethers, alert to the activity in the cabin.

Mayfield next turned his attention to the tent-cabin, which measured about 10-by-12 in dimension and was composed of strong white canvas stretched across a wood frame. A solid plank floor completed the structure. There appeared to be no signs of a struggle, and an examination of the entrance to the cabin, including the area around the cabin door, revealed no blood stains. Mayfield, therefore, concluded that Francis had fallen just where he was shot. A fairly quick examination of the tent and floor, however, showed no sign of bullets or bullet holes.

While the commissioner conducted his inspection, Clarke stood by and explained that he had covered the body on Tuesday, September 12, when he had cooked food in the cabin for Dick's hungry dogs. Mayfield, though, made a mental note that there appeared to be no dirty dishes or dirty cooking utensils in the cabin. When Clarke also said that Mr. and Mrs. Jenkins weren't at their camp when he had gone there to report the discovery of Francis' body, Mayfield began to consider the possibility that Francis had murdered them both and then taken his own life. This theory seemed plausible, he thought, in light of the bitter and longtime feud between the miners.

As the day grew late, Mayfield concluded his investigation and told Clarke to accompany him back to Petersville. He planned to organize a search party for Frank and Helen Jenkins, he said, and Clarke's knowledge of the trails in the area would be of help.

The two set out, and as they neared Little Willow Creek, about a quarter mile north of the Jenkins' camp, Mayfield noticed something in the tangled grass beyond the trail. Approaching the object, he found it to be a homemade packboard fashioned from canvas and wood. Small blood flecks appeared to speckle the canvas, and though the commissioner examined the surrounding area for any sign of a struggle, none was found.

Though there was no proof that the packboard belonged to the Jenkinses, Mayfield believed that it did and carried it with him. When the men reached the Jenkins' camp, the commissioner noted that their cabin was securely locked and there was no evidence of anyone in camp or of anyone having been there for some time. It was here, as the men stood in the silent camp, that Clarke told the law officer that someone —maybe Jenkins—had been to his cabin on

Ramsdyke Creek on Sunday the tenth, because the radio the Brittells had left there was missing. Clarke explained that he had gone over to visit Dick Francis that day, and when he had returned, he noticed the radio was gone. He must have missed seeing Jenkins on the trail that day, he said.

Mayfield and Clarke finally walked into Petersville after dark. While they ate at the cookhouse there, Mayfield talked to the mine's supervisor. Though the Jenkins camp appeared to be securely locked, Mayfield told him, Frank and Helen's ongoing absence was ominous. He went on to outline the need for a search party, and asked that any

Petersville, site of the Peters Creek Mining Company's operation, 1939. News of Dick Francis' death was relayed from here to the U.S. Commissioner in Talkeetna. (courtesy Maxine Brittell)

workers who could be spared from the company's operation be allowed to take part. They should be prepared to leave first thing in the morning, he said. While the manager passed the word to the men, Mayfield made arrangements for himself and Clarke to over-night in one of the bunkhouses. Then he turned in.

That evening U.S. Attorney Joseph Kehoe got off an Alaska Railroad train in Anchorage and checked in at a local hotel. He then contacted Chris Christensen by telephone and made arrangements to be flown to Petersville. The pilot agreed to meet him at the airport at nine o'clock the next morning.

Ben Mayfield was up early on the morning of September 14 and, though darkness still prevailed, he could see that the sky was shrouded in overcast. At breakfast with the Peters Creek mining crew, he learned from some of the men that Joy Brittell had moved over to Little Willow Creek to work for Frank Jenkins. Given the empty camp, the men now reasoned, Brittell might be included among the missing. Mayfield was also informed that the mine had received a message that Kehoe had reached Anchorage and was scheduled to fly to Petersville this morning.

After breakfast, Ben Mayfield sat down with a map to identify the scope of the search area. Since Clarke had remarked about the disappearance of the Brittell radio from his cabin, the lawman decided to search the estimated four-mile area between Little Willow and Ramsdyke Creeks.

Six mine workers had made themselves available that morning, and the commissioner briefed them about the situation, explaining that John Clarke would supervise the search. He warned the men against touching or disturbing anything they might find. Mayfield also advised them that since the U.S. attorney was expected at Petersville that morning, he would remain there to await his arrival and then proceed with Kehoe to the Jenkins' camp to begin the investigation.

Ed Carlson, who had apparently left Anchorage for Talkeetna at the first news of his partner's death, was also at Petersville that morning. When the search crew left at first daylight, he remained behind with Mayfield, who probably watched the weather, hoping it would cooperate with the task before them.

At half past ten Christensen arrived at the Petersville airfield, and Kehoe, Mayfield, and Carlson set out on the six-plus-mile trek to the Jenkins' mine. The day was proving to be chilly, and an hour or so into the journey a cold breeze appeared and light snow began to fall. Almost three hours later, in continually deteriorating weather, the men walked up to the Jenkins' cabin and observed that the door was still secured with a large Corbin-brand padlock. The camp was empty. A quick check was made of other structures—a cache, bunkhouse, and root cellar—which were all found to be padlocked.

Mayfield and Kehoe broke the Corbin lock and entered the cabin. On a shelf just inside the door, Mayfield found a metal ring containing ten keys. Though the cabin seemed to be in order and undisturbed, Kehoe pointed out a partially eaten piece of bread on the table. Also on the table was a box of .35 automatic Remington shells, six shells missing from the carton; four shells lay on the surface nearby. Mayfield tested the keys and found that one fit the cabin's lock, but that similar tests on the other camp structures provided no entry.

It was at this time that Mel Madson, one of the searchers, arrived at the camp and interrupted the lawmen, informing them that the search party had discovered two bodies in Wonder Gulch, both heavily covered with grass and ferns. Madson said they believed the bodies to be those of Frank Jenkins and Joy Brittell. Other searchers soon appeared, and eventually the entire party set out for Ruby Gulch. The men fanned out along the way to look for Mrs. Jenkins, still believed to be missing. The weather worsened, as the wind increased and the snow grew thicker. Kehoe would later report that it was "snowing and blowing hard" at this point in the investigation.

In a little over an hour the group of men finally ascended the slope to Francis' cabin, halfway up Ruby Creek. Upon entering the structure, Kehoe knelt to examine the miner's body, then carefully removed the revolver from the right hand. An inspection of the gun revealed four good cartridges and two exploded cartridge shells in the cylinder. Dick Francis was dressed in his work clothes, described by Kehoe as "a dirty gray shirt open at the neck, dark wool underwear, badly worn khaki pants, badly worn suspenders, wool socks, and old rubber boots which had been cut off at the ankles."

Kehoe carefully examined the head wounds and observed that two bullet wounds appeared to be located on the right side of Francis' head. While those present pondered this remark, Ben Mayfield took a photograph of the body and its position in the tent-cabin. Kehoe wrapped the revolver in cheese cloth. Ed Carlson watched silently as Mayfield turned Francis' body over on a blanket and rolled it up inside.

Back outside, the men moved off into the snowstorm, now driven by increasing winds that intensified the cold. Half a mile later they reached the plateau between Ruby and Wonder Gulches, an area the men called the summit. When they had covered another quarter mile and moved a short distance down and along Wonder Gulch, the searchers pointed out the two bodies they had found, almost entirely concealed by long, heavy grass, ferns, and snow. Both figures lay face down in the dirt, about six feet apart, with packs strapped to their backs.

Kehoe and Mayfield uncovered the men, removed the packs that contained a radio and a battery, and turned the bodies over. An examination of Frank Jenkins revealed that the left side of his head had been crushed, and his throat cut from ear to ear. Mayfield would later ruefully describe Jenkins' head as "half cut off." Kehoe noted that Jenkins grasped a walking stick in his right hand, and that his "left index finger was smashed and hanging loosely from the finger bone." The dirt and grass beneath Jenkins' head was saturated with blood.

Joy Brittell's fatal injuries were similar, but not so severe. His throat was cut in two places and the left side of his head was heavily bruised and cut. Two more cuts appeared on the back of his head. The grisly scene was surely magnified by the drama of the weather at this desolate location in the Dutch Hills. Here, at about 2,850 feet, an angry and merciless wind whipped snow and freezing cold along Wonder Gulch, lashing the men and swirling frenetically about the bodies. Mayfield would later say that "It was a terrible day, snowing and blowing, with about four inches of snow on Ruby and Wonder."

Though the search crew was cold and tired, its grim task was not completed. The lawmen ordered a further inspection of the area, a challenge now exacerbated by the accumulating snow. Despite the conditions, a searcher named Jack Francis (no relation to Dick) pointed out a .30 caliber Winchester rifle in the Wonder Gulch creek, about fifteen feet from where the bodies lay. The stock was nearly broken from the rifle barrel, and the hammer was cocked. One 30.30 Remington cartridge was in the barrel and three loaded shells were found in the breech.

Finally, when no more evidence was forthcoming, Mayfield directed some of the men to return to Francis' camp, harness Dick's dogs to one of his sleds, and return for the bodies. While the men were gone, Mayfield and Kehoe continued to examine the stormy death scene. The commissioner shouted over the wind to Kehoe that the broken Winchester looked like Dick Francis' rifle.

Around six o'clock Amos and Andy emerged in the windblown snow, pulling their master's sled into Wonder Gulch. The bodies were loaded and tied down, and the pensive group of men slowly made their way from the gulch. When the party reached the slope above Francis' cabin, Mayfield directed that Dick's body be added to the terrible cargo. While Amos and Andy waited along the slope, the men made haste to wrap Dick Francis in a canvas tarp, carry him up to the sled, and secure him there with the other two men. This done, and continually buffeted by the wind-driven blizzard, the procession made its way to Little Willow Creek, arriving just after dark.

The group arrived so late at the Jenkins' camp that the worn out men elected to spend the night there rather than battle the weather in the darkness for more long hours to Petersville. The locks on the bunkhouse door and cache were broken, food stores were distributed, and fires hurriedly kindled in the stoves for warmth. Finally, after what was probably a 15-hour day spent in the arduous elements, all the men retired. While the relentless weather continued to plague the camp in the night, the exhausted men slept.

Outside, Frank Jenkins, Joy Brittell, and Dick Francis lay silently in the dark, wind, and snow, all now wrapped in canvas tarps.

———

Everyone was up early Friday morning when Mayfield sent some of the men to Petersville to ask for a tractor and sled to help with the bodies. Then, a plan was developed to search for Helen Jenkins. This time the group focused on a large area in close proximity to the Jenkins' camp and mine. At the first shadowy, predawn light, the men set out on another grim mission. The weather had improved, in that the wind had calmed and the snow had ceased to fall, but several inches of snow remained to veil the terrain and aggravate the foot gear of the men.

Kehoe and Mayfield spent the morning absorbed in a detailed inspection of the Jenkins' cabin. Aside from the sleeping and kitchen areas, they found that a substantial section was given over to storage. A collection of numerous jars, cans, and buckets had accumulated here, and the two men probed among them. It was Kehoe who came upon two glass bottles that were filled with gold. When weighed out, one bottle was shown to contain a little over forty-seven ounces, the other around seven. Mayfield impounded these for protection as well as evidence.

Another item the men appropriated was Helen's diary. Her last entry was dated "September 10 day," and read: "Frank over on Wolf with Joy to get his radio. It is beautiful today." The bulk of the journal contained routine information about the Jenkins' mining operation, and disclosed that Frank had cleaned the gold from five different mining pits that summer. Helen had also kept notes about various employees and the occasional visitor, and in three separate entries she referred to Dick Francis as "the old buzzard."

When the lawmen had finished gathering their evidence, including Jenkins' keys, they again turned their attention to the bodies. Time was spent in transferring and reloading the dead miners onto a small "cat" tractor and large sled that had arrived from the mine at Petersville. It was decided that Kehoe would accompany the procession to the airstrip at Petersville, where Chris Christensen was waiting with his aircraft to transport the dead to Anchorage. The U.S. attorney would also go along on the flight to supervise the loading and unloading of the bodies, and their transfer to a doctor for autopsy.

Around noon the tractor and its load chugged slowly and noisily away through the new snow. This was probably about the time that the search crew returned to the camp for a lunch break. They had searched for several hours, but had no luck in locating Helen Jenkins.

Two miles to the north, at Ruby Gulch, Ed Carlson pondered the suicide of his longtime friend and mining partner. He felt a need to do something, especially to clean up the terrible mess in the cabin. Near the stove were several items of clothing that Francis had hung there to dry. These were so ragged and threadbare that Carlson removed an old suit of long underwear, a pair of coveralls, some old socks and gloves, and took them outside the cabin and burned them in a pile on the ground. Then he hauled several pails of water from Ruby Creek and threw them on the cabin floor. With a broom, he scrubbed for a long time at the stiff pools of blood and then swept the residue, along with layers of dirt left by the repeated footfalls of the search party, out the door. While he worked, he thought about what John Clarke had told him the previous day.

When Carlson had inquired, Clarke told him that the last time he'd seen Dick alive was around noon on September tenth. Clarke said he had visited the miner, had shared cold coffee with him, and then gone with him to his Ruby mining pit and helped him "pile up sluice boxes."

Now, Carlson made his way over to Poorman Creek to take a look around. He found the ditches that Francis had dug, along with the area that he had cleared of brush. Then he came across the pick, shovel, and pan that his partner had stored there, noting that each had the appearance of recent use. For that matter, all of the diggings had the appearance of fresh operations, Carlson thought. Why would Dick be wasting his energy on Ruby sluice boxes when he had so obviously been concentrating on the work at Poorman for the last ten days or so?

As the afternoon grew late, the search crew returned to Jenkins' cabin, reporting no success during the daylong effort to locate Helen Jenkins. About this time, the *Anchorage Daily Times* distributed its September 15 issue, which displayed dramatic front-page headlines, almost three inches tall.

FIND DICK FRANCIS KILLED THREE, SELF
2 BODIES HIDDEN ON TRAIL, HUNT THIRD

Murder of Mr. and Mrs. F.W. Jenkins and Joy Brittell in the lonely mountains of Cache Creek country and suicide of Dick Francis, oldtime prospector, was disclosed by District Attorney J.W. Kehoe upon returning late this afternoon from an investigation of Francis' death.

Bodies of two of the three victims were found concealed under grass and leaves. They were apparently shot dead in their tracks while on the trail, the official said.

Those found were F.W. Jenkins, about 50, longtime bitter enemy of Francis, and Joy Brittell, about

25. Seven men are now combing the mountains in a search for Mrs. Jenkins who disappeared September 10. The search is under the direction of U.S. Commissioner B.H. Mayfield.

District Attorney Kehoe said the coroner's jury is still deliberating over the case and will return a verdict later. Jenkins and Francis were known to have been bitter enemies for many years, and on one occasion took their troubles to court where Jenkins won a verdict. The argument was over mine claims and rights.

U.S. Commissioner Ben Mayfield and wife Jean, in the late 1930s in Talkeetna. Mayfield's duties were just those of a magistrate, but he valiantly faced the challenges of a multiple murder investigation because no other law enforcement was available. (courtesy Allan Dahl)

The article went on to report more details about the journey to get the radio, the rifle found near the bodies, and the legal conflicts among those involved. In truth, Mayfield had not yet formed a coroner's jury; his time was dominated by the search for Helen Jenkins.

While Anchorage residents read about the deaths that evening, Dr. A.S. Walkowski conducted autopsies on the three men. The procedures took him about two and a half hours, after which he hastened to issue his report. At nine o'clock he was finished, and his conclusions were rushed to local radio stations, one of which carried the remote message service that could be heard as far away as Talkeetna and the Cache Creek area.

The report addressed the question then paramount in everyone's mind. Had Dick really killed the men and then committed suicide? Many Anchorage residents who had known Francis for years could not reconcile such acts with the man they'd known so well. But others thought it possible, given the protracted legal dispute that had almost consumed the miners' lives.

No, said Dr. Walkowski. The autopsy on Francis had revealed two gun shots to the head, either one of which could have caused his death. Francis could not have shot himself twice with his revolver, he said. The broadcast reported that it was now conjectured that all three men had been murdered by someone else, or perhaps more than one individual.

Ben Mayfield and many others knew that the report dramatically altered the nature of the investigation. Now it appeared that a murderer was being sought. Though miners felt some apprehension, their dominant reaction was that of anger. A vague sense that the entire mining community had been violated began to settle over the group.

Mayfield must have felt awfully alone. His job requirements were similar to those of a magistrate: to act as a supervisor of government records, to perform marriages and act as a coroner, to administer oaths, and to handle minor offenses. Criminal investigation skills were not a requisite in his position, nor had he received any training in the field. Now, because Joseph Kehoe had returned to the obligations of his own job and no other law enforcement agency was available, the commissioner realized that he was confronted with a demanding and urgent situation. He rose grittily to the occasion.

One matter required immediate attention. The Peters Creek mine workers who comprised the search party had approached him that evening and said they were needed at the mine. They had gone on to request that they be relieved of duty so they could return to work. Mayfield was quick to recognize the legitimacy of the request and released the men. He badly needed a new search party, and knew he would have to go to Talkeetna to arrange for one.

The potential for more snow that might hinder a search effort was very real, and Commissioner Mayfield felt it urgent that another group be quickly dispatched to the Dutch Hills.

The morning of the sixteenth found Mayfield in Talkeetna, where he passed the word that he needed men. The government would pay a daily stipend, he said, and the men would bunk at the Jenkins' camp. Mayfield personally approached Frank Lee, who had been freighting to the Cache Creek area now for more than twenty years. Lee agreed to sign on, as did Pete Alex and Pete Stephan, both native Athabascan residents of Talkeetna. A fourth, Frank Huffman, had been in Talkeetna for only five days when Ben Mayfield asked him to join the search. Amicable and bright, Huffman was a bit of a vagabond who had moved around Alaska for several years, taking work where he could find it. In a short time Mayfield had appointed six men, whom he directed to round up gear and proceed to the Dutch Hills.

Mayfield looked around town for Bob Meade, who had left the Jenkins' camp early on the morning of September 10. A few days earlier, Mayfield had learned from John Clarke that Meade had stopped at Rocky Cummins' mining camp sometime that morning and had mentioned, among other things, that Jenkins and Brittell were preparing to retrieve the radio at Ramsdyke Creek. When Meade was located, he confirmed his stop at the Cummins camp. He explained that he had been confused about the trails in the area and had inadvertently moved west and found himself there; however, he had been able to access a trail from there to Petersville. He had then moved on to the McDonalds' Peters Creek Roadhouse, where he spent the night, Meade said.

Meade also told the commissioner that he, Jenkins, and Brittell had completed the last gold clean-up the day before, at which time Meade's term of employment had ended. He went on to confide that the Jenkinses were "mean and miserly people," and to express his discouragement at not being offered even a sandwich to see him through the long walk that he faced on the morning of the tenth. Nor would Jenkins offer to point out the trail he should take.

Meade said he spent about ten or fifteen minutes at Cummins' place, during which time he and Rocky engaged in general conversation. He told Rocky about activities at the mining camp and about his dislike for the Jenkinses. He also remembered mentioning that Jenkins and Brittell had intended to go to Clarke's cabin that morning to pick up a radio. Finally, Meade told Mayfield that when he had left the Little Willow Creek operation at about eight o'clock that morning, both Mr. and Mrs. Jenkins were still there, as was Joy Brittell, but the men appeared to be just about ready to leave. As for himself, he had arrived at the McDonalds' roadhouse at about three o'clock that afternoon and had not heard about the murders until Christensen had brought the news to Talkeetna.

When Mayfield concluded his interview, he asked Meade to remain in the Talkeetna area in case he was needed for further questioning. But Meade said that it was important that he head north to find employment for the winter. He promised, however, that he would send his new address to Mayfield if and when he was able to find work at Summit or Fairbanks.

After completing other tasks, Mayfield did one more thing before he moved back to the Dutch Hills. He went to the small village post office and mailed two letters that John Clarke had asked him to post. In fact, Clarke had told him, he had been on his way to Petersville to mail these letters when he had dropped off at Francis' cabin along the way and discovered him dead.

While Mayfield was in Talkeetna and the new search party prepared to depart that day, some of the miners in the Dutch Hills talked among themselves. When they had heard the radio report about the autopsy results, it had been hard for them to believe that such heinous acts could occur in their mining community. Then the incredulity had turned to anger. While they did not discount that a transient murderer might be on the loose in the area (and all now carried guns for this reason), some had begun to harbour suspicions about the man who had discovered Dick Francis' body. Especially when they learned that he had also located the bodies of Jenkins and Brittell.

The men talked about Clarke and the fact that very little was known about him except that he was new to the country. Strangers were commonplace in Cache Creek country, they agreed, but most of these frequented the Cache Creek system itself, and most lasted only a season when they discovered how much work it took to get the gold. This one had situated himself at an isolated spot in the district. At a place where a bad feud festered.

The more the miners talked, the more exercised they became, and finally some decided to conduct an investigation of their own. These men trekked over to Dick Francis' cabin where, one said later, they "made a thorough search of the walls of the cabin for bullet holes." One of the men saw a hole in a rafter, he said, but after inserting a blade of his knife there to probe for a bullet, was able to determine that it was not a bullet hole. No one in the party could locate a bullet hole.

Soon, others joined the private investigation, and the group proceeded north past Wonder Gulch and down to Ramsdyke. No record mentions if Clarke's cabin was locked or not, but the men gained entry and commenced to search through his things. They were looking for any kind of evidence that might support their growing suspicions, they said later, but they were unable to find anything of importance. Later, Clarke would complain about this intrusion on his property.

When Mayfield's new search party arrived at the Little Willow

Creek camp, Frank Huffman observed that the Jenkins' cabin was "in complete disorder." Besides the rigorous inspection made by Mayfield and Kehoe, it appeared to him that many others had also been through the place. Huffman eventually described the cabin as showing "the appearance of having been thoroughly ransacked," and later told Mayfield that he had taken it upon himself to put things in order.

The second search party fanned out over the hills, now joined by other miners in the area. They were, however, unable to turn up any trace of Helen Jenkins.

That same day, Attorney Kehoe traveled on the Alaska Railroad from Anchorage to Seward. Sometime after his arrival there, he wrote out a request to his federal supervisors and sent it out by telegraph:

> Request authority to pay for autopsy on bodies Francis, Jenkins, and Brittell. I brought bodies from Peters Creek to Anchorage and ordered autopsy at once by Dr. A.S. Walkowski because of condition which made it dangerous to wait. Cost one hundred fifty dollars. Completed trip to Peters Creek found Francis shot twice in head. Also found Jenkins and Brittell on trail with skull fractures and throats cut. Consider it unlikely that Francis could kill self in manner described. Mrs. F.W. Jenkins wife of F.W. has been absent from home since about date of killings which were done on September tenth. Search party of men with U.S. Commissioner still searching for her. Due to many difficulties encountered in determining responsibility I urgently request the designation of FBI investigator to cover whole case....

And, finally, late that afternoon, the *Anchorage Daily Times* was quick to rectify its headline of the previous day. Another dominant front page headline gave updated information:

HUNT KILLER OF FOUR
FRANCIS HELD VICTIM WITH THREE OTHERS IN CACHE CREEK MASSACRE—AUTOPSY UPSETS THEORY OF MURDER AND SUICIDE—FAIL TO FIND MRS. JENKINS

Proof that Dick Francis, oldtimer in the Cache Creek country, was murdered, was found at an autopsy last night, confounding officials investigating the deaths of three persons and probable death of another. Several theories prevailed while a party of seven men continued efforts to locate the body of Mrs. F.W. Jenkins, believed to be the fourth victim of a massacre in Ruby Gulch, about eight miles beyond the Peters Creek mining camp.

The autopsy, performed by Dr. A.S. Walkowski, on the bodies of Dick Francis, Joy Brittell, and F.W. Jenkins after they were brought to Anchorage by airplane, definitely threw out the theory that Francis had taken the lives of the others and then ended his own life. Dr. Walkowski found two bullet holes in the head of Francis, either one of which would have been fatal, and virtually precluded the self-infliction of the second.

The autopsy showed that neither Jenkins nor Brittell, whose bodies were found covered with leaves and grass on the trail, had been shot. They had been severely beaten with a blunt instrument and their throats cut with a sharp instrument.

The spectacular massacre was revealed yesterday when District Attorney J.W. Kehoe and Commissioner Mayfield went into the lonely mountain section to investigate the death of Francis. Francis was lying on the floor of his cabin, a pistol in his hand. A search of the trails in Ruby Gulch led to the discovery of a man's foot protruding from some grass and leaves. The officials, who were accompanied by a coroner's jury, uncovered the bodies of Brittell and Jenkins.

In a creek nearby was found a .30-.30 rifle with the stock broken. While this may have been the instrument used for beating the men, an axe could also have been used. An axe could inflict both the blows and the cuts, it was said.

Attempts were continuing to locate Mrs. Jenkins, who is known to have been absent from her cabin since September 10. Belief has been expressed that she, too, is dead and the body hidden. Had she attempted to flee from the section, she would have been seen by miners or stopped at Peters Creek Mining Company or at Talkeetna. Four inches of snow conceal the condition of the ground in the area of the search and it may be necessary to wait for the snow cover to melt, which may be before winter sets in.

A companion article, also on the front page of the newspaper, was entitled, "FINGERPRINTS ON WEAPONS TO BE CHECKED." This piece included a more personal profile of the victims:

Several theories in connection with the massacre in Ruby Gulch of the Cache Creek country, were being traced by law enforcement authorities today following the startling disclosures of the autopsy last night. Foremost among the theories was that the three men found dead were the victims of a murderer still at large. Facts to be learned when Mrs. F.W. Jenkins, wife of one of the victims, is found, are expected to shed considerable light on the situation. Fingerprints on a rifle and a pistol are also regarded as important clues that may lead to further discoveries. Officials saw the possibility that Mrs. Jenkins took the life of Dick Francis, but this theory was given scant consideration. It is considered most likely that she, too, is a victim of a murderer. Wounds on the bodies of Mr. Jenkins and Joy Brittell are such as to lead officials to believe that only a man could inflict them. The two men were apparently accosted on the trail, beaten and cut.

The fact that the bodies were concealed under grass and leaves leads to the conclusion that the murderer had no intention of taking his own life. Relationships among the residents of Ruby Gulch were known to have been tense for some time due to conflicting claims as to mining property and rights. Friends of Dick Francis, who was well known in Anchorage, said he was a man of sterling character, fair in all his dealings and definitely not a killer. They said he came here two or three times a year and frequently told of his troubles with Mr. and Mrs. Jenkins.

Francis was described as not vindictive. When the district court ruled against him in a court action with the Jenkins opposing him, Francis acceded to the court ruling. In response to reports that Francis carried a pistol while working in Ruby Gulch, friends said he was well acquainted with firearms but never carried one while in Anchorage.

Joy Brittell is the brother of Kenneth Brittell who

was teaching school at Squaw Harbor. Joy was single, came here from Nebraska and worked in the cannery last summer. He went to Cache Creek country last spring with Kenneth. The brother returned but Joy remained and was understood to be in the employ of Jenkins at the time of his death. Joy went to a university on the west coast at intervals and had plans for completing his college education.

Mr. Jenkins was described by acquaintances as a quiet man. His wife was said to have been eccentric. They said they had never seen any display of temper and knew little about him. The Jenkins came to Anchorage each fall for outfitting.

On Sunday, September 17, the search for Helen Jenkins entered its third day. In addition to the seven official searchers, several miners voluntarily joined the hunt. At various times anywhere from ten to fifteen men moved throughout the search area. While many worked in pairs or small groups, one man, the freighter Frank Lee, usually worked alone.

A lifetime of hard work and tough times had caused Lee to become stoical, extremely competent, and unusually perceptive. He had never enjoyed the benefits of much education and had once responded to a question about the extent of his schooling by saying, "I went one day to take my brother's place when he was sick." Frank Lee was quiet, serious, and dependable. He must have put a great deal of thought into what might have become of Helen Jenkins. He had always gotten along well with both the Jenkinses, and it was said by some that he was probably the closest thing to a friend that Frank Jenkins ever had. Today, as he tramped through the dying, snow-coated vegetation, he likely reflected that an entire week had passed without a sign of Helen.

At some point during the search, Ben Mayfield talked at length with John Clarke. He wanted more details about the day that Clarke had last seen Francis alive and a clearer idea of events on the day he discovered the dead miner.

Clarke told the commissioner that on Sunday morning, September 10, he had worked at one of his claims along Ramsdyke Creek, a site located about a twenty-minute walk from his cabin. Then, around eleven o'clock or so, he had gone over to see Dick Francis because he wanted to hear the latest news about the war in Europe and to get some tobacco that Dick had borrowed from him earlier. Dick wasn't at his cabin, but he had found him working at his mining pit, near Ruby Creek. He and Dick had then returned to Francis' cabin and had some cold coffee there, after which they returned to Dick's pit where Clarke helped him to set up some sluice boxes. It was sometime before one o'clock that he left Francis and returned to his Ramsdyke camp, he estimated. It was the last time he saw the miner alive.

The next morning he set out for Petersville to mail some letters, Clarke said. As he passed Francis' cabin, about 8:30 or so, he called out to him but got no answer. So, he approached the cabin, opened the door, and saw Dick lying on the floor with a revolver in his hand and a pool of blood around his head. He didn't touch the body, he said, but "watched it for a minute or so" to determine whether Dick was breathing. He then concluded that Dick was dead, and hurried off to report the news to officials.

He decided to go to the Bird Creek mine, Clarke said, because he thought there might be an airplane there that day. Along the way, he thought to stop at the Jenkins' camp to tell them about Francis. He went to Frank's mining pit where, ordinarily, Frank could be found at work, but no one was there. So he walked to the Jenkins' cabin, about a quarter mile distant, which he found to be locked. Thinking someone might show up, he waited around the camp for fifteen or twenty minutes. Then, he left for Bird Creek. Along the way, he passed by Rocky Cummins' cabin and told him that Francis had shot himself. Then, together, he and Rocky had proceeded on to the Bird Creek mining camp where Clarke told a camp supervisor about Francis' death. Finally, he said, the two decided that Rocky would walk to Petersville to report the death, while Clarke returned to Dick Francis' cabin to await the arrival of the U.S. commissioner.

When Mayfield finished his interview with Clarke, he pondered another matter. Upon his return to the Dutch Hills, he quickly realized that several of the miners were not shy about questioning Clarke for details about September tenth and eleventh. And now, the questioning had taken on a nasty, challenging tone. That wasn't all. Mayfield found himself increasingly frustrated as the miners "snooped around," and persisted in "digging into everything in an effort to uncover the identity of the killer." Later, he would characterize the men as "would-be detectives" and remark that he "had to call them down on several occasions." While he attempted to maintain a sense of law and order, he ruminated, these miners seemed determined to track down justice on their own. Mayfield reminded himself that he needed to monitor the situation carefully.

As the afternoon drew to a close, still no clue had been discovered as to where Helen Jenkins might be found. Then, after Mayfield and the men spent some time discussing the areas they had examined, the commissioner announced that the time had come to conduct a formal coroner's inquest into the deaths of Francis, Jenkins, and Brittell. The inquest would be held at Petersville this evening, he said, and the coroner's jury would be composed of the men who had served on the original search party.

Though little documentation is available that details this inquiry, it is reasonable to speculate that both search parties were in attendance at Petersville, along with the miners who had recently joined the effort. Ed Carlson had joined forces with this latter group and was also in the crowded room that evening when Commissioner Mayfield presided over the meeting. One of the few official records of the inquest that has survived the erosion of time is the testimony of Xan John Clarke.

COMMISSIONER MAYFIELD: What is your name?
CLARKE: Xan John Clarke.
Q. What is your occupation?
A. Miner.
Q. Where do you reside?
A. Anchorage, Alaska.
Q. Were you acquainted with the deceased persons?
A. Yes.
Q. When did you last see them alive?
A. I saw Mr. Jenkins and Mr. Brittell about a week ago.
Q. Where did you last see them alive?
A. At Mr. Jenkins camp on Little Willow. I had lunch with them.
Q. And when did you last see Mr. Francis alive?
A. Last Sunday, between 11 a.m. and 1 p.m.
Q. Where was Mr. Francis when you last saw him alive?
A. At his pit where he was fixing some sluice boxes. I had coffee with him at his camp and helped him set his boxes.
Q. How long did you stay there?
A. About half an hour.
Q. Where did you go after leaving Francis?
A. Back to my claims on Ramsdyke where I had been working.
Q. When did you next see the deceased?
A. About 8:30 a.m. the next morning, Monday.
Q. How did you find him at that time?
A. I hollered to him as I approached his tent and received no answer so I knocked then opened the door and saw him lying on the floor with a gun in his hand; I watched him for a minute to see if he moved and as he did not move I knew he was dead.

Q. What made you think he was dead?

A. Because there was no sign of life and I saw the blood on the floor.

A MEMBER OF THE JURY: Was Dick right or left-handed?

A. Right-handed.

MAYFIELD: What did you do next?

A. I went as fast as I could to Jenkins and could not find them at home or in their pit so I waited awhile for them to return.

Q. How long did you wait?

A. Fifteen or twenty minutes.

Q. Then where did you go?

A. I went from Willow Creek to Peters Creek and up Peters Creek to Cummings (sic) camp and told him all about finding Dick dead.

Q. Why did you go up Peters Creek instead of going down the creek to Petersville?

A. Because I thought there might be a plane landing at the Bird Creek field and it was nearer.

Q. Was Cummings surprised when you told him Dick was dead?

A. Yes.

Q. Where did you go from Cummings place?

A. Up to the Bird Creek camp to see if a plane was coming in so I could send word to Talkeetna.

Q. Did you go back home that night?

A. Yes, and on the way I waited at Dick's camp thinking you (Mayfield) might come that evening.

Q. Did you stop at Jenkins on your way back?

A. No. Rocky Cummings suggested that I had not better stop at Jenkins since Dick and Jenkins were enemies. Rocky also suggested that if Dick had committed suicide that he had probably done away with the Jenkins first.

(Witness excused)

It was probably a long, tense evening for everybody at Petersville that night. Later, Ed Carlson would insist to Mayfield that his partner, Dick, had been left-handed.

The coroner's jury soon prepared its official inquest verdict. It found that "Francis, Jenkins and Brittell died on or about the 10th day of September, and that Jenkins came to his death by having his head crushed by some heavy instrument and by having his throat cut by some sharp instrument while enroute from Clarke's cabin on Ramsdyke Creek to Wonder Gulch; that Brittell came to his death by having been struck on the head by some heavy instrument and having been stabbed in his throat by some sharp instrument; and that

Francis came to his death by having been shot twice through the head by a gun of some description and it would seem impossible that the wounds were self-inflicted; that Francis was killed in his tent on the mining claim on Ruby Creek; that these killings were executed by some person or persons unknown."

———

The first faint traces of light began to emerge the next morning at around seven o'clock. Though official sunrise would not occur until 7:30, the search party, now eighteen in number, could see that the day was cloudy and might even harbour some difficult weather. But the temperature was decent—above freezing—and would probably

Frank Lee, the respected chief freighter for the Talkeetna Trading Post, about 1936. His keen perception would lead to the resolution of a week-long search for the body of one of the murder victims. (courtesy Eleanor Trepte Martin)

rise as the day progressed. The absence of another snowstorm was an asset. Too, the snowfall sustained four days earlier had settled some now, and the process of evaporation had further reduced its effect. Ben Mayfield had recently told the *Anchorage Daily Times* that the search for Helen Jenkins would "continue until snow prevents the possibility of success." So, even though luck had eluded them, the men were grateful for the fair conditions that still prevailed, and anxious to take advantage of them.

When the light allowed, the men spread over the search area

once more. Though the day was overcast, the colors of fall were full-blown. Willow thickets, already brilliant with leaves turned yellow and gold, were enhanced by the fine clarity of the September air along Little Willow Creek. Frank Lee and Rocky Cummins worked together part of the morning in an area fairly close to the Jenkins' camp. Then, around noon, Rocky went off in another direction, and Lee resumed his solitary profile.

He was on the hill to the immediate north of the Jenkins' cabin, the same hill that Frank and Joy had ascended at the beginning of their journey. About 600 feet in height, the hillside held both the northbound trail and a small creek that trickled coldly down toward the camp. Though this area had already received a considerable amount of scrutiny during the search, Lee began to focus on the creek. The stream was a minor one but had worked itself deeply enough into the hill so that it left a creek bank topped by thick, tangled grass, now turned brown from frost and cold. The grass had collapsed in heavy overhangs up and down the creek, and it was along this threshold that Lee slowly moved.

He was still moving when he saw, or sensed, something almost indistinguishable from the matted, partially snow-covered grass that arched to the water. He had almost stepped on whatever it was that had caught his eye but moved quickly to correct himself. A second look at the area of distraction revealed only a slight variation in color, which Lee bent to study. Then, the rubber soles of footgear slowly began to emerge in his vision, and he moved the grass a bit to be sure. There, almost entirely concealed by vegetation, were two shoepacks, cream-tan in color.

Lee traveled down the length of the hillside to the cabin where Mayfield was supervising the search, and told him that he'd probably found Helen Jenkins. Later, Mayfield would describe the body as so well hidden along the creek bank that, even after Lee pointed to the spot where it was concealed, he had difficulty in seeing it. The men removed the body from beneath the grass overhang and observed that Helen wore a dark denim coat, dark pants, and an olive green wool sweater which bore blood stains. All of the pockets on her pants had been turned inside-out, and Mayfield took special notice of this.

The commissioner would later report that the right side of Mrs. Jenkins' head was "bashed in, the brain being exposed, and there was a long deep cut over the left eye." He added that "it appeared she had been hacked with an axe."

Now the slant of the light enabled Lee and Mayfield to observe that grass and brush seemed to be "smashed down" for about twenty feet in a diagonal direction from the creek to the hillside trail. Both theorized that the body had been dragged this distance and then hidden.

The activity near the creek caught the attention of nearby searchers, and soon word circulated that Helen Jenkins had been found. When several of the miners returned to the camp where the body had been transferred, they saw that Mrs. Jenkins' face was so brutally beaten as to be unrecognizable. But, they agreed, the coat was one she had often worn in the village of Talkeetna. One of the last searchers to arrive in camp was John Clarke, and when he appeared one of the miners said to him, "Don't this make you nervous?"

Mayfield directed that a search for evidence be made in the vicinity of where the body was discovered, and Frank Lee found what appeared to be a broken sliver of wood from a rifle stock. But, for some reason, both Mayfield and Lee believed that the sliver was one from the rifle recovered at Wonder Gulch, and that it had accidentally been dropped at this location. Regardless, the sliver was documented and retained as evidence. Though several men continued to look, nothing else of value was found.

The commissioner had procured the use of an old truck, probably from the Peters Creek mine, and now he directed that Helen's remains be wrapped and loaded on the vehicle for the drive to Petersville. Upon arrival there, the body was offloaded, and Mayfield told Mel Madson and two other searchers to drive the truck on to the landing at the Susitna River and make their way across to Talkeetna. Get to the telephone there, he said, and call Chris Christensen and tell him to come to Petersville to pick up the body. Madson and the men headed off down the road in the late afternoon light.

In Washington, D.C., an official in the Attorney General's Office of the Department of Justice sent a memorandum to the Director of the Federal Bureau of Investigation, J. Edgar Hoover. The official cited the request that had originated with Kehoe in the Territory of Alaska and advised, "Will you please comply with the U.S. Attorney's request and conduct whatever investigation is necessary in this matter."

a shameful indifference

The murders had a profound effect on Cache Creek country. Once part of a widespread network of independent people who enjoyed the comraderie and community of kindred souls, miners and prospectors now became bewildered and distrustful. For the most part, none had ever locked their doors and had taken comfort in that fact. A good deal of pride had also accompanied their doctrine that a man's word was his honor. But now one or more individuals had violated creek codes in the most wretched way.

Eleanor Trepte, a teenage girl working with her parents at their mine at Dutch Creek on the north side of the hills, recalled the reaction of everyone working at that camp.

> We were across the Dutch Hills from their (Jenkins') camp. We were at dinner in the cookhouse listening to the news on the radio, when the announcement came that three bodies had been found, and Mrs. Jenkins was missing. She was a very highstrung lady, and the thought came up that she may have gone berserk. Of course, they were still looking for her. Killer or killers were unknown. At our dinner table was absolute astonishment and fear of the unknown. We were all a little apprehensive until we packed up camp and moved on to town a few days later.

Frances Weatherell, nearing the end of her cooking job at Nugget Creek, heard about the alarm of miners all up and down Cache Creek.

> Now, when anybody approached another's camp they hollered their name and stood still until they were sure they were identified ('It's me, Joe, don't shoot!'). ... All we could think of was that somebody had gone nuts and was still roaming around half crazy. The whole atmosphere of our creek had changed. Men

carried guns wherever they went: to the (mining) pit, to their cabins, and some, even when they went to the outhouse. There (were) no clues. Cal (Reeve) came to camp and kept us posted on what was going on; his mine was just over the hills from us, and as he told us the news he had, it was passed on down Cache Creek to those worried ones there. So there I was, still cooking, and wondering if the killer would be discovered.

Phil Brandl, now a retired miner, was about 21 years old at this time and working at one of the mines along Cache Creek. He knew of the Jenkinses, describing them as loners "who kept to themselves. No one ever knew how successful or unsuccessful they were in their mining." After the murders, he says, "Everybody was up in arms. No one went up to a cabin without first calling ahead. No one traveled alone. Jim Beaver and I worked the same shift, and whenever the water or the equipment needed checking, we always went together."

On Thursday, September 19, pilot Christensen landed at the Petersville airfield, loaded the remains of Helen Jenkins into his plane and took off for Anchorage, where he was interviewed by local media. That afternoon the *Anchorage Daily Times* ran huge headlines that announced the discovery.

POCKETS INSIDE-OUT ON MRS. JENKINS' BODY
ROBBERY SEEN AS MOTIVE

Pockets of the clothing on Mrs. F.W. Jenkins, whose body was found last night ... were turned inside out and were taken as proof that robbery was the motive of four murders in the Cache Creek country September 10. News of the discovery was brought to Anchorage by pilot Haakon Christensen who arrived shortly after 3 o'clock this afternoon with the body of Mrs. Jenkins. Dr. A.S. Walkowski was conducting an autopsy this afternoon to ascertain the nature of the wounds that caused her death.

Searchers found the body of Mrs. Jenkins late yesterday afternoon, hidden in the growth of grass overhanging a gravel bank. It was only (450) feet from the Jenkins' cabin which is reported to have contained placer gold taken by Mrs. and Mrs. Jenkins from their claims over a period of years.

Pilot Christensen said a close examination of the body will be necessary to ascertain the exact nature of the wounds. The head was either beaten or shot, he said. He did not know whether there were knife wounds.

Belief was expressed that the murderer or murderers searched the clothing of Mrs. Jenkins for the keys to her cabin, turning the pockets inside out as they searched. Whether the cabin had been visited remained a matter of conjecture as no indications could be found. The coroner's jury is scheduled to have a session tonight at which a verdict may be reached. Speculation as to the motive of the murders has been rife ever since the discovery of the crime and it was said that the conditions of the pockets on the clothing of Mrs. Jenkins is the first evidence to substantiate the contention that Mr. and Mrs. Jenkins were murdered for their gold. Joy Brittell, who was with Mr. Jenkins, was also murdered and the life of Dick Francis was taken in an attempt to make the crime appear as a triple murder and suicide, according to one theory.

While Anchorage read about the discovery, Dr. Walkowski conducted his examination of Helen Jenkins' body. When he was finished, he indicated that her death had resulted from massive fractures to her head, one exposing the brain at the right forehead, together with several deep, jagged cuts to her head and neck. "This woman was evidently killed by someone other than herself," he reported.

The autopsy results were relayed to Talkeetna and then to Ben Mayfield at Petersville, where he was preparing to hold another coroner's inquest. That evening, the jury issued a verdict that "Mrs. Jenkins died on or about September 10, 1939, about 450 feet from her home on Little Willow Creek on a trail leading from her cabin to the top of the hill; that her body was placed to one side of the trail and covered with grass; that she came to her death by having her head cut and crushed by some heavy and sharp instrument; that some person or persons unknown is responsible for her death."

Commissioner Mayfield's investigative work loomed large on the horizon. At this point he was probably very tired, short on sleep, and rather overwhelmed. But he had received another communication earlier that day, this one from a man named R.C. Vogel, the sole agent for the Federal Bureau of Investigation in the entire Territory of Alaska. The wire had originated in Juneau and read, "Unable to proceed Petersville at this time. Please advise names parties involved, when and where offense occurred, whether any witnesses and result coroners inquest."

Mayfield must have felt some relief that there was a chance the FBI might share the burden of the investigation.

———

The Talkeetna commissioner stayed on at Petersville and Little Willow Creek for the next three days. Though he had released everybody that had served in the search parties, he said that he needed to "get things straightened up, do some more investigating, and appoint a caretaker for Jenkins' place."

He also had to sort out and document the many costs incurred by the search parties and for the use of the machinery made available by the Peters Creek Mining Company. Finally, he needed to prepare for the likelihood that the FBI would join the investigation, so he probably spent a substantial amount of time creating a record of events that covered the past several days.

On September 20, the *Anchorage Daily Times* ran a front page article that described the autopsy results of Helen Jenkins. Aside from the massive head injuries, the article reported that Dr. Walkowski had "found no other severe injuries on the body. There was a bruise on the front of the right shoulder, but otherwise there was no evidence of other injuries." The report went on to say that "the head wounds were apparently inflicted by blows with a blunt instrument such as an axe head."

Another article appeared in the *Seattle Post-Intelligencer* around this time, and featured the remarks of Maxine Brittell's brother, Tim Craig, then a student at the University of Washington. Some of its content reflected the magnitude of the rumor mill on the subject of the Jenkins' assets.

U. STUDENT LUCKY TO LEAVE ALASKA ALIVE

Tim Craig, twenty-three year-old University of Washington pre-medical student, doesn't know whether he wants to do any more placer mining in Alaska. He feels he was lucky to get "out" alive after his first summer there, he said yesterday. A week ago, just a few days after Craig left a camp near Mount McKinley, the mass murder in which three men and one woman were killed, took place nearby. Craig was acquainted with all of the victims, and one of them was his sister's brother-in-law, Joy Brittell. Craig ... said instead of returning to Seattle he almost remained to work, as Brittell did, for J.W. Jenkins. Both Jenkins and his wife were killed. The other victim of the unsolved tragedy was Dick Francis, sixty-year-old sourdough, with whom Jenkins had been feuding for fifteen years, Craig said.

Craig said according to one version he had heard, the $200,000 in gold which the Jenkins were supposed to have buried in their yard was the motive. "I don't think that's true," Craig said. "They might have had plenty of money in the bank, because we had occasion to borrow money from them this spring and they wrote a check for it. Then Mrs. Jenkins showed me some huge nuggets worth about $500 before I came back and she didn't go about it like a miser. I think they did have about $10,000 in gold around their place because they had had the best summer in fifteen years.

Craig said he had witnessed some of the bitter feuding between Jenkins and Francis. Francis, he said, had mining property above Jenkins' place and caused trouble by running tailings into Jenkins' ditches, cutting down water pressure and slowing operations. Jenkins, he said, had once obtained a court judgement against his enemy.

There is little reason to believe that the Jenkinses did not have something substantial to show for their many years of hard work. Both were very frugal people, and there is scant evidence that they spent money on much more than their mining operation. This is best illustrated by the number of claims they owned and Jenkins' ambitious expansion of the ground he mined. Talk continued to circulate that Frank and Helen had buried gold on their mining claims because they didn't trust banks. Estimates of this accumulated wealth seemed to be limited only by one's imagination.

Once tightly controlled against any kind of intrusion, the Jenkins' holdings were now at a level of vulnerability that did not escape Ben Mayfield's attention. Aside from the exotic lure of hidden wealth that local pundits placed there, the property seemed to be a magnet for the general scrutiny usually associated with dramatic events. Since no Jenkins relation had yet appeared to assume the responsibility for the estates of the deceased, Mayfield engaged Frank Huffman as a caretaker for the property. Huffman, who must have possessed a sense of responsibility that favorably impressed the lawman, was a likeable fellow and easy to get along with. Fifty-five years old, he was happy to have the work and settled in at Frank and Helen's cabin.

It was quieter in Cache Creek country now. Mayfield went about his work as the cries of distant ravens rang keenly on the cool air and the dense murmur of shallower creeks foreshadowed the great cold to come. The mining camps were all finally closing down for the season. Even Petersville had recently completed its work and terminated its employees; only a winter caretaker for the large complex remained.

On September 22, another wire made its way from Juneau to Mayfield at Little Willow Creek. It was from the FBI agent named Vogel, who advised: "Proceeding Fairbanks tomorrow morning. Advise me care of U.S. Attorney Fairbanks whether I can contact you at Talkeetna Sunday or first of week."

Sunday was two days away, and Mayfield certainly intended to be in Talkeetna to accommodate the federal bureau. He told Huffman that he would travel to Petersville the next day and wait there for George Weatherell, who was scheduled to pass the mine on his last freight and mail run of the season. Mayfield noted that he could travel the thirty-plus miles to Talkeetna with the freighter at a cost of $2.50 for the wagon trip to the river landing and another $2.50 for the boat ride across the river to the village. Compared with the expensive aircraft flights the investigation had necessarily incurred thus far, he believed it would be a prudent means of travel for a territorial court system operating on a frugal budget.

Since the arrival of the FBI appeared to be imminent, Mayfield let John Clarke know that it was advisable for him to accompany the commissioner to Talkeetna. Clarke had returned to his Ramsdyke cabin when the searchers had been released, but Mayfield got word to him now to meet him at Petersville in time to connect with Weatherell's freight wagon. Mayfield also told Clarke to bring Francis' malamutes with him. Until now, there had been some question about what would become of Amos and Andy, but the Petersville caretaker had indicated that he could use them for hauling coal and wood during the winter.

Cap Morgan's mine at Nugget Creek, though winding down, was still in operation. Only ice in his sluice boxes could force Cap to shut down, and that hadn't happened quite yet. Frances Weatherell was still cooking for what remained of the crew, and "wondering if the killer would be discovered." She, like many others, had not dismissed the possibility that a maniac still remained somewhere in the area with the potential to act again. While some of the men at Nugget tried to reassure Frances with the theory that the murderer had long since departed the area, she noticed they all had guns within reach, if not on their persons.

Then there was the matter of Clarke. His account of events had first been met with uncertainty, then skepticism, as people grappled with the suicide-versus-murder theories. By now though, Frances had matched the description of the Ramsdyke miner with the "empty eyes" of the man she'd seen walk off the train at Talkeetna in the spring. And Cal Reeve, who mined nearby and had been among those who had volunteered to search for Helen Jenkins, was absolutely convinced that the newcomer was responsible for the mayhem in Cache Creek country. Frances had made up her mind that she agreed with Cal.

Frances' new husband was fed up with the tension, rumors, and theories that were rampant along the creeks he traveled. When George Weatherell arrived at Nugget camp on his last trip for the season, he told Frances that he intended to "take her back to civilization." He also let her know that he was transporting $10,000 in gold clean-ups packed in U.S. mail sacks and would benefit from an extra pair of eyes as he traveled the rugged route out of Cache Creek country. The idea of performing as a "guard" on the trip appealed to Frances, but she insisted that George obtain Cap Morgan's permission for her to leave her job earlier than planned.

Having gained Cap's consent, Frances prepared to leave. She made certain her gun ("my trusty .250-3000") was loaded, and that George's .30-06 was readily accessible. After all, she reasoned, four people had presumably been murdered for gold, and caution was now in order.

"When we started out with the mail and some freight lashed to the go-devil that next day, I'll admit I had goosebumps and a sinking feeling in the pit of my stomach," Frances said. "I said farewell to the crew and heartily wished I would see them all again!" Frances rode on top of the canvas-covered go-devil with her guns, while George drove the tractor that hauled the load. They spent a couple of hours crossing a broad swamp, and then laboriously gained a ridge where they accessed the Cache Creek road. Somewhere in this area they transferred the mail and freight to a wagon George had positioned there and hooked it up to the tractor; then they moved along the road and on through the Peters Creek canyon. Along the way, George shouted over the noise of the tractor that he'd heard Ben Mayfield and John Clarke would be at Petersville today and might need transportation to Talkeetna.

Frances was leery as they approached the mine at Peters Creek.

Sure enough, as they pulled up at the complex, Mayfield emerged from the cookhouse.

"Ben Mayfield came out to greet us," Frances said. "No, Clarke had not showed up yet, and we would have to wait. I protested. I was, by that time, the least cooperative woman Ben Mayfield ever encountered. He seemed to assume he had the authority to make us wait."

Frances calculated that if she and George moved on without Mayfield and Clarke it would be a loss of $10 to the Weatherells, but she said she was "of the opinion that we could lose that $10 without breaking us."

Let Clarke walk, she said.

When Mayfield protested, Frances suggested another idea. After they got to Talkeetna, she proposed, she and George would send a plane out to get Clarke. The ensuing argument was recorded by Frances in her memoirs, years later:

"You act like you think this man is guilty of a crime," Ben said.

"I do think he is," I said.

"It could have been lots of others," Ben said.

"Except for Rocky and Ed," I said, "we know where everybody else was all the time!"

"Well, it could have been them or a stranger," Ben said.

"You're nuts," I said. "A stranger would have to find a plane to take him out of the country, and you know darn well neither Ed or Rocky could have done it!"

George finally moved in between us and said, "We will wait up at the (mine owner's) house on the hill. It's too late now to start for town and cross the river in the dark. If Clarke comes, you can be ready to start at the first daylight. That's when we will be moving out."

Ben had to settle for this, and we got the keys to the big house from the caretaker and drove on up there. We took the mail bags inside and fixed our meal, and settled down to wait and sleep. Late afternoon, Ben came walking up the hill and told us that Clarke had arrived with the dogs (and) that he was tired and glad to have a chance to rest overnight.

I said to Ben, "I want you to tell Clarke how I feel about him, and see for damn sure he doesn't have any kind of weapon on him—not even a knife. You're the law, and whether you think he is innocent or guilty, you're the one that is taking him in to be questioned ... so there must be some suspicion besides mine that he murdered those people!"

Ben looked at George. "Are you worried, George?" he asked.

"Well, (Frances) is going on that wagon too, you know, Ben, and if she thinks Clarke is dangerous I don't know any way to change her mind. So what's the harm in playing it safe for all of us? I got at least $10,000 in the mail sacks, which might be tempting, and Clarke is smart enough to know I carry the clean-ups. If he did away with us, he could still take the boat and get across the river, and who knows where we might be found, or when?"

Ben considered this a bit and then he said, "I don't think the man is crazy enough to try anything like that!"

I said, "He hasn't showed too much intelligence so far as I can see.... If any one of us out on the creeks had done this job and robbed those people, we would have known we would have a big problem trying to get away with the gold. This man evidently didn't know that. He just saw that gold and thought of it as money. He can't even claim he mined it and show where he worked his claim!"

"Well," said Ben, "a man is innocent until he is found guilty, and you have no proof of his guilt."

"That's right, Ben," I said, "but whoever killed Joy and the Jenkins tried to put it on Dick Francis as a grudge killing. And now this man has Dick's dogs—dogs that Dick loved and raised from pups. But left them tied up to die when he killed himself? You can't believe that!"

"Besides that," I went on to say, "Dick was a little guy; and as much as the Jenkins hated him, could you see him walking down the trail behind them, nobody paying any attention to him, while he swung that axe?"

Ben just shook his head and said he was going back to camp and would see us in the morning.

We did not sleep too well (since) we had a long trip ahead of us: thirty-six miles of it sitting on a wagon, or on a cat, and going about three and one-half miles an hour at the fastest. After ten hours it would still be dusk by the time we got to the river. And it was a good thing I did not know what a stupid thing George was going to pull on the way in.

We were lashing down the load when Ben and Clarke came up the hill the next morning. Everything went in under the canvas (and Francis') dogs were left behind with the watchman, who said he could use them in the winter to get fuel. George's gun went in the load and I kept mine under my arm. When we got on the load I told Clarke to get on the front of the load, and I guess Ben had warned him somewhat.

"Why do you want me to ride there?" he said.

"Because I am going to have this gun pointed at you all the way," I said. "Unless you want to walk, you'll have to put up with it!"

He protested, "I don't know why you're worried. This is the U.S. Commissioner with us (and) I wouldn't dare do anything with him along."

I thought of that woman with the crushed head and of all the people I knew on the creeks. Most of them hadn't heart enough to kill a parka squirrel, and surely none I knew felt they needed another man's gold....

His eyes were just as cold and expressionless as when I first saw him. I have always felt that women read more from eyes than men do.

I then said to him, "All you have to do is just sit still and ride along. I am not going to shoot you in front of the commissioner either, so we'll just say he is here to watch out for both of us."

I didn't tell him I figured Ben needed a back-up gun, because (Mayfield) did not have a gun on him in the first place. Don't ask me why, I guess he figured being with George was all he needed. But George was driving the cat and had his back turned, and even though he would not have "confessed man-like," I had a strong feeling he felt better with me on the load. Me and my trusty .250-3000.

And then, when we were partway down the road, a big bull moose came out and stood in the road, looking at us.

George said, "Shoot it!"

And I said, "No." And he turned around and said to me, "Bring me the gun!"

I protested, and that damn stupid moose just stood there as I climbed down off the load and gave him the gun. And he shot it! He gave me back the gun and got his knife from his belt and said to Clarke, "Come on, and cut its throat."

Afterwards, I asked him what the heck he had on his mind — if he had a mind at that time.

This time Clarke said, "No," in a loud voice.

George said, "Why not?"

Clarke said, "I don't want to get any blood on me. If I got to town and the people saw blood on me, they would probably lynch me right there."

Well, George had to get out the axe (and) cut the moose's throat.... He and Ben did a quick job of cutting the moose up; George was good at it, lots of practice. But then we had to load it on the wagon and cover it up ... with extra canvas, and I knew the darn meat should cool out, and so did George by that time.

However, he planned to take it across the river and divide it with the town people. I knew that, but we lost the meat before we got it across the river. It soured on the load—too hot....

As I said, it was a long trip, and not until we got in that boat did I take the gun off Clarke. By the time we got across the river I imagine he was a very confused man.... I was thoroughly fed up with the whole thing.

And, of course, the people in town had to "hear" all about it after George had turned the mail and its precious gold over to Mr. Nagley.... When I got to bed that night ... all I could think of was those useless killings, and why did it have to happen in a country where everybody was good to each other and tolerant of each others' failings?

———

On September 24, two weeks after the murders, Frank Huffman was feeding the wood stove in the Jenkinses' cabin. It was around noon, and he was probably preparing for lunch. Helen had made sure that a generous supply of kindling wood was always in reserve nearby, but continuous use of the stove during the searches and investigation had dramatically reduced the pile. As Huffman bent to pick up some of the remaining sticks, he noticed some dark leather bags near the floor, dusty with duff and debris from what had once been a dense covering of kindling. Curious, he picked one up and noted its heaviness. After loosening the bag's strings he pulled it open and looked at the raw gold within.

There were three more buckskin pokes in the last of the wood, and Huffman brushed them off and found that all contained gold. When measured later on a Troy weight scale in the cabin, one bag weighed out at just under seventy ounces. Another contained around forty ounces, and the remaining two about thirty ounces apiece. The gold, worth several thousand dollars, had been only roughly cleaned, and small quantities of black sand and other impurities were still mixed in with the glowing metal. Huffman thought to send word of his discovery to Ben Mayfield in Talkeetna.

On the same day, in Talkeetna, John Clarke walked into the commissioner's office and recorded two claim notices for ground on Poorman Creek. His declaration said that he had staked the claims on September 13. Recorder Mayfield noted that the ground was near the claims that Dick Francis had leased from the Anchorage bank in the early fall.

FBI agent R.C. Vogel must have arrived in Talkeetna on Sunday night. Vogel's arena of responsibility was vast, and he had traveled a great distance to comply with the order given him by the director of the FBI. His office was located in Juneau, around 900 miles from the Interior of Alaska, and he had flown that distance and more, on Pacific Alaska Airways, to reach Fairbanks. He soon departed for Talkeetna, probably on the Alaska Railroad.

Unaware of the agent's movements, the *Anchorage Daily Times* sent a Western Union wire to FBI Director, J. Edgar Hoover, the next day:

THREE MEN AND ONE WOMAN MURDERED BRUTALLY BEATEN TWO WEEKS AGO NEAR TALKEETNA STOP KILLER STILL LOOSE ALASKA AUTHORITIES UNABLE SOLVE STOP HUNDRED IN COMMUNITY TERRORIZED MANY PACKING FIREARMS PLEADING FOR EXPERT INVESTIGATION STOP HOW CAN YOUR DEPARTMENTS ASSISTANCE BE OBTAINED.

That afternoon the newspaper published a prominent editorial at the center of its front page. Framed with black bars for emphasis, the piece was entitled, "Shameful Indifference."

One of the most heinous crimes in the history of Alaska stunned residents of the territory two weeks ago, yet a most shameful indifference in bringing the murderer or murderers to justice has followed.

A woman was beaten to death with a blunt instrument. Two men were beaten to death and the heads almost severed from the bodies with a knife. Another man was shot twice through the brain, left lying in a pool of blood on the floor of his cabin. Never has Alaska been confronted with such ghastly crimes.

Two weeks have gone since the quadruple slayings came to light. About 150 persons in the Cache Creek country are living under most tense circumstances. Many are packing weapons for fear of attack. What is being done about the massacre? Where are the law enforcement agencies of the territory and of the United States?

B.H. Mayfield, U.S. Commissioner at Talkeetna, is apparently the only official showing concern. He has spent all his time in the hills seeking the solution of the crime. Mr. Mayfield is to be highly commended for seeing the need of action and for accepting undesirable responsibilities that are not a part of his office.

Reports indicate that there is not a single representative of the U.S. Marshal's office assigned to the Cache Creek massacre. The district attorney's office made a preliminary investigation and apparently withdrew from further action. Endeavors are reported to have been made by some officials to have the Federal Bureau of Investigation take over the case. But, to date there has been no sign of response. Meanwhile, evidence that would prove valuable in solving the crime is being lost through indifference.

What is the answer? Are the citizens of Alaska going to remain indifferent with four lying dead and an entire mining section terrorized? Are the law enforcement agencies going to admit they are baffled and make no attempt at solution? Does the Federal Bureau of Investigation contend that a quadruple murder is not worthy of precedence over investigations of automobile thefts, gambling rackets and vices in the states?

If so, we may as well quit "pretending" we are civilized and that we maintain law enforcement agencies for the protection of life, limb and property.

———

Commissioner Mayfield sat down in his office with Agent Vogel and proceeded to brief him on the particulars of the murders and the evidence he had gathered. He carefully described the bitter feud between the Jenkinses and Francis, and explained that his knowledge of that conflict had caused him to at first believe that Francis had committed murder and then taken his own life. But the autopsies had altered that theory, he said.

Mayfield went on to furnish a general background of the Jenkinses. They didn't have many friends and had a reputation for being difficult to work for, he said. He indicated that Frank Jenkins had been involved in several disputes over mining claims with a number of people and went on to name the individuals involved. Then he produced a list of the young men that Jenkins had employed that summer and told Vogel that Bob Meade had departed the Jenkins' mine on the morning of the killings.

The trail Meade had taken led to Rocky Cummins' cabin, Mayfield said. Meade estimated he had spent ten or fifteen minutes there before he continued on to Petersville and, eventually, the McDonalds' Peters Creek Roadhouse. Mayfield told Vogel that the roadhouse was twelve miles due south of Petersville, and that it would take the average person five to six hours to walk the distance. Since John Clarke had estimated that he last saw Francis alive between 11 a.m. and 1 p.m. that day, Mayfield said he didn't feel it was possible for Meade to have been in the vicinity of Francis' cabin and still make it to the McDonalds' roadhouse by three or four o'clock that afternoon.

Belle McDonald's husband, Mac, had verified Meade's arrival at the roadhouse about four that afternoon, Mayfield said. He had reported that the young mine worker was out of breath and had appeared nervous. He had also remarked that Meade was restless all during the night that he spent there, before departing for Talkeetna the following morning. Mayfield told Vogel that since Meade's path took him continually south, he would not have passed either the Jenkins or Francis camps, which were both much farther to the north.

Jenkins' other employees had been accounted for, he said. Don Sheldon was in Talkeetna on September 10, and Ira Diess was at the McDonalds' roadhouse around three o'clock that afternoon.

Mayfield went on to describe the area where the killings had taken place as "rather desolate, with only a few mining cabins sprinkled here and there." He put the distance between Francis' cabin and Jenkins' camp at about a mile and a half to two miles, and the distance between Francis and Clarke's cabin at about two miles. As far as he could determine, no one was in the general vicinity of where the killings took place that day, following the departure of Meade. No one at Petersville, about six or seven miles south of the Jenkins' cabin, had heard or observed anything that day—nor had anyone at Bird Creek, about five miles northwest of the Jenkins' camp. As far as he could establish, just John Clarke and Rocky Cummins had been closer to the scenes of the killing than anyone else. And both disclaimed any knowledge of them.

Mayfield concluded this part of his briefing by stating that it would appear that the killings took place around noon, or later, on September 10, if Clarke's statement was accurate with regard to the last time he saw Francis.

Next, Mayfield ventured the opinion that if this were not a case of murder and suicide, it might be murder with robbery as the motive. The Jenkinses were generally perceived as successful and "well-fixed," he said. The stories that circulated about the gold hoarded on their property may have caused one or more people to believe they could exploit the Francis-Jenkins feud by making it appear that the miners had killed each other. Too, the fact that the pockets on the trousers of Mrs. Jenkins were all turned inside-out could indicate that someone searched her clothing for the cabin keys, hoping to gain access to the structure and hidden gold.

The commissioner remarked that he felt it unlikely that Francis would have gone to the trouble of concealing the bodies so carefully, if he intended to take his own life.

Rocky Cummins (right), pictured here in the 1960s, mined near the area where the murders occurred, and traveled to Petersville to report the first news of Dick Francis' death. Next to him is Jim Beaver, another mine worker along Cache Creek at the time of the murders.

Mayfield now explained the logistics of the crime scene area. He observed that Francis had been found dead a mile southwest of the spot where the bodies of Jenkins and Brittell had been discovered. Mrs. Jenkins had been found close to two miles southwest of the Francis cabin. It would appear, he thought, that it would have taken one person a number of hours to have committed the killings.

He had interviewed Rocky Cummins, Mayfield said, who confirmed that Meade had stopped by his cabin on the morning of the tenth and remained there for about fifteen or twenty minutes. When Mayfield asked the miner if Meade had mentioned that Jenkins and Brittell were going to pick up the radio at Clarke's cabin that day, Rocky had answered "in the negative." Mayfield told Vogel that Cummins was around 60 years old and an old-time prospector who had been mining in the area for a long period of years. He hadn't made much money from his mining activities, but he had apparently recovered enough gold to get by. He didn't appear to be the type to have committed a crime of this kind, the commissioner ventured. "Still," he added, "there is no way to check his activities on that Sunday."

Now, Mayfield turned to the subject of John Clarke. He was the only other person in the area of the crime scenes who did not have anyone to verify his statements as to his whereabouts on September 10, he said. He told Vogel that he knew little about Clarke when he had first appeared in Talkeetna in the early spring. After about a month in town, the man had gone over to the Cache Creek area and then staked a number of claims on Wolf and Ramsdyke Creeks in the Dutch Hills. Mayfield gave a list of the recorded claim notices to Vogel and then commented on Clarke's name.

Though the Ramsdyke miner signed his name to claim locations as Xan J. Clarke, he had told Mayfield he preferred to be called John Clarke. He had explained that since there were other John Clarkes in the vicinity, he had assumed the name "Xan" so that his mail would not go to other people. Clarke was originally from Canada, it appeared, but had served in the U.S. Army for a number of years, Mayfield said. He had apparently applied for, and received, final citizenship papers sometime in recent months.

Mayfield told Vogel he had learned that Clarke had worked for some months at the Evan Jones Coal Company, had sustained an injury there, and had obtained a $2,000 settlement from the company. It was also Mayfield's understanding that Clarke had at some time associated with a man named Percy Pue, who appeared to have a shadowed past. Though he'd been an Anchorage resident for several years now, Pue was known to be a bank robber who once served time in the state penitentiary near Chicago. The commissioner said he thought it appropriate to identify Pue's whereabouts during the time of the Cache Creek crimes. He also informed Vogel that Pue was thought to be associated with the disappearance of a miner who had vanished from Anchorage the previous year.

Finally, Mayfield said, he'd learned that Clarke and two other men had gone prospecting somewhere in Alaska during the summer of

199

1938, and only Clarke and one of the men had subsequently returned to Anchorage. The third man, he said, had not been seen since.

Agent Vogel listened as the commissioner described his frustration with the vigilante-minded miners who suspected that Clarke was responsible for the killings. Despite his protests, Mayfield said, several of them had questioned Clarke on a number of occasions and "attempted to pin him down as to his whereabouts and activities" during the time of the killings. At one point some of the men had ransacked Clarke's cabin. Several had also managed to go through Helen Jenkins' diary at the time the murder-suicide theory prevailed. Consequently, he said, the contents of the journal were now familiar to "a great many people."

Mayfield spoke about the coroner's inquest and noted that Clarke had stated without hesitation that Dick Francis was right-handed. But, Francis' partner, Ed Carlson, had insisted that Dick was left-handed.

Next, Mayfield reviewed Clarke's description of events on both September 10, when he had visited with Dick, and the morning of September 11, when he discovered the body. One item that bothered him was the discrepancy in time estimates that Clarke and Cummins had reported. When questioned, Clarke told Mayfield that he found Francis dead about 8:30 the morning of the eleventh. But, Rocky Cummins had estimated Clarke's time of arrival at his cabin to be sometime between 8 and 9 a.m. Given the distance between Francis' and Cummins' cabins, an estimated two to three hour walk, the time frames were in conflict.

Clarke had also given varying descriptions of the route he had traveled to the Jenkins camp, following his discovery of Francis. For that reason, Mayfield recommended, it would probably be appropriate to question him in more detail on the subject.

Finally, Mayfield described Clarke's role in the discovery of the Jenkins and Brittell bodies in Wonder Gulch. While other searchers had been assigned to trails elsewhere, Clarke and a father-son team, Jack and Charles Francis, had approached Wonder Gulch and, at Clarke's direction, split up. Clarke told one of the men to search the ridge on one side of the gulch, and the other to inspect the opposite side. Clarke told them he would search down in the gulch itself. After the men separated and eight or ten minutes had passed, everyone in the area heard three shots from Clarke's .45 automatic pistol. It was the signal that everyone had agreed upon to alert the others of a discovery, Mayfield said.

The lawmen must have spent hours and hours—perhaps most of the day—going over the data and evidence. Outside the commissioner's office the skies are partly cloudy, and patchy carpets of fallen leaves lend a golden aura to the village. Inside the rustic building the FBI man is assimilating an enormous aggregate of information about the victims, their neighbors, and the mining community itself. Mayfield, probably smoking, is no doubt heartened that his once solitary burden is now shared, and cheered with the knowledge that the man he's working with has had advanced training in murder investigations.

Finally, Mayfield hands over the testimony taken at the coroner inquests, the autopsy reports, his own notes and reports, and last, the evidence itself.

Helen's diary is set out, along with the guns and ammunition. Vogel examines the .38 Colt (Army Special) revolver with the five-inch barrel that was found clasped in Francis' lifeless hand. Then he moves on to the .30 calibre Winchester (Model 94) rifle, thought to have been used as a ruthless bludgeon on Frank Jenkins and young Joy Brittell.

The battered Winchester barrel and stock, found together but joined only by the most tenuous of connections in Wonder Gulch, have finally separated. The stress of handling, the rough and unsparing journeys from the gulch to Little Willow Creek and Petersville, and the final unpacking in Talkeetna have all contributed to its condition. The stock, Vogel notes, is split in half itself (its condition when found), and held together only by the metal butt piece at its far end.

Mayfield also shows Vogel the sliver of wood that is believed to have broken from a rifle stock. Originally thought to have been recovered in Wonder Gulch, Mayfield says he has since determined that it was indeed a new discovery, located about a dozen feet from the place where Helen Jenkins' body was found.

Mayfield opens his safe and shows Vogel the fifty-four ounces of gold contained in the glass bottles found by Kehoe. Finally, he informs Vogel that he has received a letter from Frank Jenkins' brother in California. Ray Jenkins is unable to travel to Alaska until October, he says, but has asked that arrangements be made for Frank's body to be buried in Anchorage.

When Agent Vogel finally leaves Mayfield's office, the day's late light filters through breaks in high clouds, enhancing the gold of village trees. The scent of frost-touched woodland cranberries hangs in the cool, crisp air.

On September 26 the *Anchorage Daily Times* ran banner headlines again, and printed long-awaited details of the coroner jury investigations.

SAY 'FRIEND' KILLED FOUR,
HOOVER ORDERS INQUIRY
JURIES HOLD SLAYER KNEW HIS VICTIMS
Report All Were Slain, Could Have Been Done By One Man

A "friend" of the four victims of the Cache Creek massacre committed the wholesale slaughtering two weeks ago, it was indicated by two coroner's juries in their verdicts, according to reports arriving in Anchorage today. The juries, one fixing the cause of the deaths of Joy Brittell, F.W. Jenkins, and Dick Francis and the other considering the death of Mrs. F.W. Jenkins, held that all four were killed by a person or persons unknown. The verdicts officially recorded the massacre as a quadruple murder instead of a triple murder and suicide, as some theorists contended. The verdicts pointed out that the four deaths "could have been done by one man," and continued to say that they were "most likely done by someone acquainted with all parties and with local conditions."

Under the direction of U.S. Commissioner B.H. Mayfield of Talkeetna, the juries conducted extensive investigations in the Cache Creek country to learn of the circumstances of the deaths. One jury, considering the deaths of the three men, returned the verdicts September 17 and the other reached the decision September 19. The verdicts seemed to support the theory that a "friend" of Jenkins and Brittell was walking with them on the trail September 10, when the victims were carrying a radio set and batteries. It is considered possible that the "friend" walked in the rear carrying a rifle, with Brittell ahead of him and Jenkins in front. Without warning, the "friend" could have struck Brittell on the head with the butt of the rifle. Hearing the thud, Jenkins might have turned around just in time to see the rifle swinging for his head. Jenkins would then have raised his hand to ward off the blow. Supporting this theory are the facts that Brittell's head was struck on the right side and Jenkins' head on the left. Jenkins' left forefinger was also smashed. With the two men knocked out, the "friend" could then have finished them with more blows on the head and by slashing their throats.

Supporters of this theory also contend that the "friend" might then have gone to the Jenkins cabin and summoned Mrs. Jenkins to go to the aid of her husband who was "sick." A piece of buttered bread from which a few bites had been taken, was found in the Jenkins cabin as though Mrs. Jenkins had left hurriedly. The doors of the cabin were locked, as though she had planned to remain away some time. Outside the cabin, the "friend" might have struck Mrs. Jenkins on the head with the blows that took her life, searched her pockets for the keys to the cabin, hidden the body and then searched the cabin.

Belief has been expressed that the murderer wore gloves as the pockets of Mrs. Jenkins' slacks were found inside out. Had the murderer's hands been without gloves, he could have taken the keys without pulling the pockets out.

The theory continues, that after doing away with Mr. and Mrs. Jenkins and Brittell, the "friend" might then have gone to the Francis cabin and fatally shot him. The fact that there were no gunshots in doing away with the first three might indicate that the slayer did not want to put Francis on guard. Because of the tense situation in Cache Creek, gun shots would probably have aroused the attention of Francis.

Theorists also point out that if the murderer put one instead of two bullets through the head of Francis, it might have been the "perfect crime," and gone into the official territorial records as a triple murder and suicide.

Alongside the featured article, the newspaper ran a report about the entry of the FBI into the investigation.

G-MAN ON WAY TO CRIME SCENE
Citizens Pack Weapons In Fear
Slayer May Take More Lives

Federal investigation of the Cache Creek murders has been ordered by the Federal Bureau of Investigation, the Anchorage Times was told today in a radiogram from J. Edgar Hoover, chief of the bureau. Ralph C. Vogel, special agent for the FBI in Alaska, is either in Fairbanks or Talkeetna enroute to the scene of the massacre that took the lives of three men and a woman.

The radiogram was sent in response to a wire from the Times advising Mr. Hoover of the tense situation in the Cache Creek country, and inquiring whether federal aid would be forthcoming. Inquiries were made after it was learned that many of the more than 100 residents of the Cache Creek country are carrying weapons in fear of their lives.

It is feared that if the murderer or murderers are still at large in that section, there would be no hesitation in taking more lives should it be considered necessary to prevent a solution of the crimes. Miners in the section are reported to be staying home after dark because noises arouse suspicions and weapons are drawn. One woman cook in a mining camp was reported to have quit her job and to have left the section because she found it impossible to sleep nights. Others are reported to be making arrangements to leave.

Speculation about the murders had reached an almost fever pitch now, and the next day the *Times* ran a front-page article about Agent Vogel's arrival in Talkeetna, including these remarks: "Rumors had been circulated widely that federal investigation of the massacre was already under way and that Commissioner Mayfield and a federal agent had been seen 'crawling among the bushes in four feet of snow,' in a search for clues. However, the reports were denied by Mr. Mayfield when he told a times correspondent, 'I did not see a single G-man in the bushes or anywhere else.'"

While newspapers worked earnestly to keep Alaskans informed about the investigation, it is possible that public conjecture, together with news coverage of this sort, had combined to provoke the irritation of U.S. Attorney Joseph Kehoe. Later, in a letter to Ken Brittell, Kehoe expressed his displeasure at the indirect influence the public might have on the investigation.

"You must realize that there is a wealth of rumor and unfounded suspicion floating about which comes from people who have only an idle interest and who really know nothing of the facts, the people, or the country. These people make it more difficult to conduct an orderly investigation and the only result of their meddlesomeness is to keep the guilty informed of the progress of the case," he wrote.

———————

Along the slopes of the Dutch Hills the four-inch snowfall has now been reduced to a spare white carpet. No new snow has fallen throughout the searches and ongoing investigation. The singular wind and snowstorm, so volatile on the day of the discovery of the bodies of Jenkins and Brittell, seems now to have been eccentric, to have existed solely to lend dramatic emphasis to the end of their lives and to those of Dick Francis and Helen Jenkins.

The bodies of Francis, Jenkins, and Brittell are loaded into pilot Christensen's aricraft at the Petersville airstrip on September 15, 1939. The sledge used for their transport from the Dutch Hills to Petersville is in foreground. (Courtesy Diana Francis King)

13   the vogel investigation

A **serious criminal investigation** was now in process. The presence of an FBI agent in Talkeetna, or just the knowledge of that presence, seems to have tempered some of the anger among the miners, almost all of whom had now returned to Talkeetna from Cache Creek country. Agent Vogel was probably a conspicuous figure in the village, but he maintained as low a profile as he could while he worked to gain information about the case. He intended to visit the scenes of the killings but decided to first take advantage of those interviews that were available locally. His first inquiry was made with Frank Lee.

The village of Talkeetna in 1939. The Talkeetna and Susitna Rivers converge in the background. (courtesy June Scheele)

The trading post freighter gave Vogel details about his role in the search for Helen Jenkins and his subsequent discovery of her body. He didn't have much to say beyond this but did allow that he had put some thought into what might have happened to her. He had his own theory, he said. When Vogel encouraged him to continue, Lee said he thought Helen may have become alarmed when her husband and Brittell had not returned from Wolf Creek at a reasonable time. She may have climbed the path to the top of the hill to get a good view of the northbound trail, hoping to see the men somewhere in the distance. Lee thought Helen might have been killed "somewhere on the hill," and her body then concealed in the small creek nearby.

Lee also told Vogel that during the course of his freighting activities he had seen Helen with a pair of field glasses on a number of occasions, looking over the country in the vicinity of Peters Creek. He said that he'd searched both the Jenkins' cabin and the surrounding area for the glasses, but did so without success.

Ira Diess and Don Sheldon were still in Talkeetna, and Vogel met with the two young men. Diess said he had left his job at the Jenkins' mine due to a foot injury, but that during his two-month period of employment Frank Jenkins had cleaned out two pits. He estimated that $2,000 in gold had been removed from each location. He ventured the opinion that the Jenkinses would probably bury their gold, because Mrs. Jenkins was "always afraid of a fire in the cabin." He went on to tell Vogel about the ploys that Helen had talked about using for the purpose of hiding gold. When asked, Diess said that he hadn't noticed if the Jenkinses carried keys around, nor had he seen either of them with a pair of binoculars.

Ira Diess said it was his impression that the Jenkinses were not well liked, had few friends, and had been involved in law suits over their mining claims. He related statements made by Helen that she intended to prosecute both Dick Francis and John Clarke, the latter for breaking into an old cabin belonging to the Jenkinses.

Vogel asked if anyone had visited the Jenkins' operation during the time he worked there, and Diess said that John Clarke had been there on a couple of occasions. Joy and Ken Brittell, along with Maxine and Tim Craig, her brother, had also visited from time to time. Asked if Rocky Cummins had ever come by, Diess said that he had not. The reason for this, he thought, was because the Jenkinses did not like Cummins. They didn't like Dick Francis either, because Frank Jenkins claimed that Francis "maliciously" dumped tailings from his mine operations into the ditch from which Jenkins received his water supply, reducing the water pressure Jenkins needed.

Questioned about his location at the time of the killings, Diess said that on September 9 he and his brother were visiting with Al Stinson at his cabin about five miles south of the Jenkins' mine. They left there the next morning at about nine o'clock, he said, and proceeded to the McDonald's roadhouse. They were there when Bob Meade showed up, around four o'clock or so. He had talked to Meade a bit, who mentioned that he had stopped by Rocky Cummins' place on his way out.

Don Sheldon, now nearing his eighteenth birthday, gave a similar account of the visitors he had seen at Jenkins' camp. Since his term of employment had been longer than Diess', he put the number of John Clarke's visits to the camp at six or seven. He was of the opinion that the Jenkinses were financially well off, he said. Though it was rumored that the couple hated banks, he knew that they had an account at the Bank of Alaska in Anchorage, because his monthly salary of $150 was paid to him by checks drawn on that bank.

When the agent asked Sheldon if he had ever observed either of the Jenkinses carrying keys, he replied that on one occasion he had seen Frank Jenkins with a ring that held six or seven keys. He had also observed that the couple locked their cabin whenever they left it, even if only for a few minutes. Vogel asked about the gold Frank Jenkins had mined, and Sheldon said that when he worked there four different mining pits were cleaned up. His estimate of the gold recovered was somewhere around $10,000 or more in value. No, neither of the Jenkinses had ever discussed where they kept their gold.

Finally, Sheldon remarked that he had recently observed John Clarke in Talkeetna wearing a black raincoat that he was certain belonged to Frank Jenkins. Describing unique details of wear and tear on the coat, Sheldon said that it at least had the identical appearance as one that had belonged to Jenkins.

A day or two had now passed since his arrival in Talkeetna, and Agent Vogel was gaining a solid working knowledge of the case. Though the moon was in its full phase, his days here had been cloudy ones, with temperatures hovering near freezing at night and warming during the daytime. These were the last days of September, and when the agent periodically left the commissioner's office he moved along a backdrop of birch and cottonwood trees, now steadily discarding leaves that settled to the ground in thin, golden carpets. The pungent scent of highbush cranberries drifted in the air and mingled with the soft rushing sound of the pale green rivers that moved with diminished depth and flow along the western boundary of the village.

Vogel was staying at the Fairview Hotel and likely took his breakfast there too, well before the first traces of light emerged at around 7:30 in the morning. The commissioner's office was conveniently situated just next door to the hotel, and it was here that Vogel sat down for an interview with John Clarke. Ben Mayfield was also present in the room. Vogel began by asking Clarke to describe the last time he had seen Dick Francis alive.

Clarke said that his watch was always off from four to six hours, and it had only one hand, but he guessed that it must have been sometime between eleven in the morning and one in the afternoon on September 10. He said he had gone to the miner's camp to pick up some tobacco that Francis had borrowed from him the week before, and to hear the latest news of the European war.

That morning he had worked for a couple of hours at his Ramsdyke claims, Clarke recounted, and then gone over to Francis' camp where

The U.S. Commissioner's office and home in 1939. A murder suspect was questioned at length in this building. (courtesy June Scheele)

he found him working at his mining pit. They had gone to Dick's cabin where they drank cold coffee and Francis returned the Velvet tobacco to him. The older miner invited Clarke to stay for lunch, but he declined, making an excuse that he had to return to his own cabin. Both had then gone back to Francis' mining pit where Clarke helped him with his sluice boxes. Here, he reported, the two engaged in a conversation about the war; eventually, though, Dick Francis had gone into a "tirade" about Mr. and Mrs. Jenkins.

Clarke told Vogel that he was tired of listening to Francis rant about the Jenkinses. He had heard similar outbursts all summer when the miner would speak of Frank Jenkins as "rat face" and Mrs. Jenkins as "the old bitch." Francis spoke intelligently on other subjects, but whenever Clarke mentioned the Jenkins' name, Dick would become angry and raise his voice. To avoid any more such conversation he had departed. It was the last time he had seen Francis alive.

Vogel asked Clarke about his activities on September 11, and he responded that he had started out for Petersville that morning to mail some letters. When he passed Francis' cabin he had called out to him but received no answer, so he looked in the cabin and saw Dick lying on the floor with a pool of blood around his head. Though he didn't enter the cabin, he concluded that the miner was dead and immediately left to report his discovery. He headed in the direction of the Bird Creek mine, he said, because it was closer than Petersville, and he thought that an airplane might stop there sometime that day.

Clarke said that on the way to Bird Creek he decided to stop at the Jenkins' cabin on Little Willow to tell them about Francis, but he found the door padlocked. He looked in the window, but saw no one there. So, he proceeded to the Jenkins' mining pit, located about a quarter mile from the cabin. No one was there either, so he returned to the cabin where he sat outside and waited for fifteen or twenty minutes. Finally, he had continued on his way to the Bird Creek mine.

As he neared Bird Creek, he stopped at Rocky Cummins' camp, Clarke said. He told Rocky that he had found Francis dead and that it "looked like Dick shot it out with someone." He also told Cummins that he had gone by the Jenkins' cabin but was unable to find anyone there. Rocky then speculated that if Dick had shot himself, he must have done away with the Jenkinses first. Still, Rocky had wanted to go to the Jenkins' cabin "to find out what Frank might know about Dick's death." But Clarke told Rocky he wasn't a private investigator, and it might not be wise to go there.

Together, the two had gone on to the Bird Creek mine, Clarke said, and arrived there about eleven o'clock. He reported the matter to Ed Johanson, one of the mine's owners, after which he and Rocky had remained for lunch at the camp. They left the mine at about half past noon, and at some point decided that Rocky would go to Petersville to report the death, while Clarke would return to Francis' cabin to await the arrival of Commissioner Mayfield. He waited there all day, Clarke said, but when Mayfield hadn't appeared by dusk he returned to his own cabin for the night.

Vogel took notes, and then asked Clarke what else he had done on September 10, aside from visiting Francis and retrieving his tobacco.

He had spent the entire day working at his claims, Clarke said.

You didn't return to your cabin for lunch that day? Vogel asked.

No, he hadn't, Clarke said. He explained that earlier in the morning, when he had gone to his claims prior to the visit with Francis, he had taken several flapjacks along with him for his lunch. They were in his coat pocket, and since it was too warm to wear his coat, he had left them at his Ramsdyke claims when he went over to see Francis. When he returned to his work site, he ate the flapjacks and remained at work there until evening.

When asked, Clarke said that the claims he was working were about a mile from his cabin. He must have missed seeing Jenkins and Brittell when they picked up the radio and the battery, he said. It wasn't until he returned to his cabin that he noticed the items were no longer there.

No, he didn't hear any shots or commotion, Clarke said.

Vogel now instructed Clarke to draw a map that showed the relation of his own cabin to those of Francis, Jenkins, and Cummins, and the routes he had traveled to each on the day he had discovered Francis' body. When Clarke had done this, the agent told him to draw in the locations where the four bodies had been found. Clarke complied, and Vogel studied the diagram.

The agent observed that the trails Clarke had followed were a considerable distance from the spots where the bodies of Jenkins, Brittell, and Mrs. Jenkins had been recovered. Vogel also observed that Clarke had not gone back by the Jenkins' cabin when he had returned from the Bird Creek mine on September 11.

Why didn't you stop there to see whether the Jenkinses had returned? Vogel asked.

Because Rocky told him that whatever he did, he should stay away from the Jenkins' cabin, Clarke said.

Vogel now recalled that Ben Mayfield had been unable to reach the Dutch Hills until the late afternoon of September 13, so he asked Clarke if he had made any effort to determine if the Jenkinses had returned during the twelfth and thirteenth.

No, he hadn't, Clarke said.

Vogel turned to Clarke's map again, and studied it.

So, when you traveled to the Jenkins' camp to report Francis' death, you traveled down Ruby Creek to Willow Creek, and then around to Little Willow, and up that creek to the Jenkins' cabin? Vogel inquired.

Yes, said Clarke.

And you went from there to their mining pit? Vogel asked.

That's right, Clarke said.

The agent inquired about the letters Clarke had intended to mail at Petersville, and the miner replied that they had both been addressed to his wife at Pasco, Washington. He couldn't recall just when he had written them, he said. He would sometimes write a letter that he wouldn't mail for a week or two because the distance was so great between his cabin and Petersville.

Vogel made more notes, then asked Clarke to describe his activities on September 12.

He was up about daybreak, Clarke said, and had gone directly back to Francis' cabin to wait for Mayfield. Dick's dogs were howling and raising a fuss, so he'd gone into his cabin and cooked some food for them on Dick's stove. That's when he covered Francis' body with a blanket. After he had fed the dogs he sat just outside the door of the cabin, waiting for Mayfield.

When Vogel asked how he had passed the time, Clarke said he read Francis' magazines. Vogel asked for the names of the magazines, but Clarke said he didn't remember. The only thing he could recall was an article about the possibility of war between Mexico and the United States.

When the commissioner hadn't shown up by late afternoon, he returned to his own cabin on Ramsdyke Creek, Clarke said.

And on September 13? Vogel inquired.

Clarke responded that at daybreak that morning he had packed some of his clothes and gone over to a cabin on Poorman Creek that was owned by the First National Bank of Anchorage. He explained that Dick Francis had been negotiating with the bank for a group of placer claims along Poorman that included the on-site cabin. In fact, Dick had already taken some of his tools and things over there to prospect with. Clarke had taken his own things there on the thirteenth with the intention of staying for awhile because it was closer to Francis' cabin than his own on Ramsdyke. That's why he was near Poorman Creek, when Commissioner Mayfield flew over and airdropped the note directing him to go to Francis' cabin.

Continuing, Clarke said that Frank Jenkins had told him "confidentially" that he planned to take over this same group of claims on Poorman Creek. So, while Clarke was there on the thirteenth, he staked out two claims for himself, with the intention of later checking at the recorder's office to see if anyone else had already filed on them.

Outside the commissioner's office the sky was gray with ragged overcast, allowing only a somber light to enter the windows of the building. The golden leaves of the birch and cottonwood, so brilliant in the sunlight, now assumed the muted glow of raw, unwashed gold.

Vogel asked about Clarke's finances.

The Ramsdyke miner balked at the question and declined to answer. But the agent, now emerging as a consummate professional, is persistent.

Clarke said he had around $2,000. No, he didn't make any money from his claims this past season, but that was because he spent most of his time prospecting. He had about $700 invested in his ground and expected to make money next year. Also, Ken Brittell had paid him $500 for the right to mine on one of Clarke's claims.

Did you do any hunting this year? Vogel asked.

No, he'd been too busy prospecting all summer to have time for that, Clarke said. Besides, he didn't own a rifle and never had owned one.

The agent returned to the subject of Clarke's claims. Did you discover any gold on your ground this year? he inquired.

You know, Clarke said, if the motive behind these killings was robbery, the person who got the Jenkins' gold would not be able to dispose of it. Gold can be identified by the creek it comes from. Jenkins' gold could be identified if someone tried to pass it.

Vogel took note of the odd response, but made no comment.

The agent asked Clarke to estimate the time it took him to walk from his cabin to Francis' cabin, and from there to the Jenkins' camp and Cummins' place.

But the miner said he couldn't be sure and didn't feel right about making guesses. He said that he may have "already made too many guesses."

How did you know that Dick Francis was right-handed? Vogel asked.

I don't know for sure, Clarke said. I just assumed he was.

What would the approximate distance be between the Jenkins' and Cummins' camps? Vogel asked.

Clarke said he didn't want to venture a guess. He suggested that the agent could find that out from Bob Meade, because he had walked that route on the morning of September 10 after "quitting Jenkins."

Did you see Meade that day? Vogel asked.

No, he hadn't seen Meade then or since, Clarke said.

Without being asked, Clarke asserted that he hadn't told Rocky Cummins that Frank Jenkins had come to his cabin for a radio on the morning of September 10.

No one made any comment to that effect, Vogel said.

Clarke said he just thought he would mention it. It seemed odd, he said, that someone else would know that Jenkins and Brittell were going to get the radio that day.

When Vogel asked him to explain further, Clarke said that Cummins told him he had learned from Bob Meade about the trip to get the radio. Also, that Meade had departed Jenkins' camp about an hour before Jenkins and Brittell left for Ramsdyke Creek. Clarke said he thought it peculiar that Rocky would tell him this.

While they were discussing the killings, Clarke continued, Rocky had also told him that two or three years earlier Frank Jenkins had threatened to kill Cummins. Rocky seemed to think that if Dick had been shot and killed, then Jenkins was the one who had done it.

When Vogel inquired about Francis' body, Clarke said that it didn't look like a suicide to him. It looked like Francis had shot it out with someone. If someone committed suicide, he said, his feeling was that the person would "go limp and drop the gun."

The agent asked Clarke when he had last seen the Jenkinses and Brittell alive, and Clarke said it must have been September fifth or sixth, when he had lunch at the Jenkins' cabin. He'd stayed for the whole day, reading their newspapers. He had also remained for dinner, and then departed for his cabin. On his way there, he added, he stopped off briefly to visit with Dick Francis.

Why didn't you get the tobacco he had borrowed from you when you stopped there? Vogel asked.

It just hadn't occurred to him to do that until Sunday the tenth, Clarke replied. Actually, he wasn't in any hurry to get it back, he just wanted it "before the old boy smoked it all up."

How much tobacco did he borrow from you?

Eight cans.

The agent asked him if he remembered anything particular about the day he had eaten his meals at the Jenkins' cabin.

Yes, Clarke said. Mrs. Jenkins said she was going to demand a sanity hearing for Francis—that she had already communicated with the court about it. She also claimed that Francis had not made any money from his ground.

Did Francis appear to you to be sane? Vogel asked.

Yeah, he was fine, Clarke said, except when he talked about the Jenkinses.

The lunch hour had come and gone, and at some point Agent Vogel called for a break. The commissioner's office was located on the first floor of a double-story log and frame building where Mayfield and his family occupied living quarters on the upper floor. Possibly the two officials ate their lunch here, prepared by Mrs. Mayfield. John Clarke may have gone to the Fairview Hotel or a local roadhouse for his own meal, but before he left Mayfield's office the FBI agent told him to bring his .45 automatic pistol with him when he returned. Outside, the day remained somber and gave off an atmosphere of impending precipitation.

———

The three men met again and Agent Vogel resumed his question-

214

ing, this time focusing on the search efforts. He asked Clarke to describe the role he had played during the hunt for Jenkins and Brittell.

He was in charge of that search, Clarke said, and had assigned the men to examine three different trails between the Francis cabin and Ramsdyke Creek. The trail he decided to search himself was the one nearest Wonder Gulch, and he instructed Jack and Charles Francis to go with him. When they had gone beyond the summit, the plateau-like expanse between Wonder and Ruby Gulches, he directed the Francis men to split up and cover the ridges on either side of Wonder Gulch. He moved down the gulch itself, Clarke said, because it was the most difficult trail.

After ten minutes had elapsed, Clarke said, he saw a yellowish-colored boot just barely visible in the snow and grass, and called out to Jack Francis. At the same time, he signaled the rest of the search party by firing his .45 automatic three times. When the Francis men arrived, they looked around and pointed out what appeared to be a second body near the one Clarke had found. The men didn't touch or disturb the bodies, because Mayfield had given them strict instructions about this. They had, however, examined the immediate area and discovered a broken rifle barrel and stock in the gulch creek about fifteen or twenty feet from the bodies.

Who found the rifle? Vogel asked.

He couldn't remember if he had noticed it or if Jack or Charles Francis pointed it out, Clarke said. One of the Francis men also found four footprints in the soft dirt beside the creek bed. Charles Francis had commented that perhaps the impressions had been made by Mrs. Jenkins. They all examined these prints, and Clarke had measured them with his hands.

Clarke demonstrated to the agent and Ben Mayfield how the measurement from the outside of his one hand to that of the other was ten inches. By placing his hands together over the prints, he said, he was able to calculate the size. They were small, almost too small to have been made by a man.

What did you do while you waited for Commissioner Mayfield and Attorney Kehoe? the agent inquired.

He and Jack Francis had gone over to the cabin on Poorman Creek, Clarke replied. When Vogel asked him why he had done that, Clarke explained that he wanted to stage some food there because there would probably be an ongoing search for Mrs. Jenkins, and some of the searchers might want to use the place because it was closer to the search area. He also wanted to cook some food for Dick Francis' dogs. In fact, he had done so, and then he packed it back to the Francis camp and fed the animals.

Vogel paused, then asked Clarke if he had any theories about the killings.

When the bodies were first discovered, Clarke said, everybody thought it was a case of murder and suicide. When the autopsy report was released, however, showing that Francis had two bullet holes in his head, they began to wonder if it was possible for a man to shoot himself twice in the head.

Clarke went on to say that since he was a newcomer to the country, people seemed to suspect him. He'd been around this area only since the early part of March, he explained. For this reason people appeared to be suspicious of him.

Who else is mining in that general area? Vogel asked.

Rocky Cummins is over near Bird Creek, Clarke replied, and Ed Wagner lives alone at his cabin a couple of miles from Rocky's camp. Also, Ed Stronk and Max Kron were prospecting over at the Tokositna River area around that time, about six or seven miles north of his place on Ramsdyke.

Clarke told Vogel that he went back to his Ramsdyke cabin after Mrs. Jenkins' body was found, because he had heard that Rocky Cummins was going to travel over to the Tokositna River to check on the welfare of his sometime partner, Ed Stronk. Clarke had gone there, he said, because he was afraid that Rocky intended to "plant some evidence" in his cabin.

What made you fear that? Vogel asked.

Because several of the men in the search party suspected him of being involved in the killings, Clarke said. They questioned him constantly and had even searched his cabin and gone through all of his clothing, trying to find some evidence that would link him to the killings. So, he had offered to accompany Rocky as far as his Ramsdyke cabin. But Rocky had backed out, giving some excuse about not wanting to go at that particular time.

Agent Vogel paused again, and then asked to see Clarke's .45 pistol.

After Clarke handed it over, the agent studied it and observed that it was marked "U.S. Property."

Where did you obtain this firearm? Vogel inquired.

From a man named Thoeny, Clarke responded.

Tell me what you know about him, Vogel said.

Clarke said that he thought Thoeny had first traveled to Alaska about a year and a half earlier. From New Mexico.

Where is he now? Vogel asked.

He wasn't sure, Clarke said, but he was in Girdwood, Alaska, a year ago. He added that Thoeny had probably returned to the states.

The FBI agent examined the gun again, and then told Clarke that he'd have to keep it for awhile as part of the investigation. And, I'll need to take your fingerprints, Vogel said.

The agent also took down Clarke's personal history, making note of his Canadian birth, his army service, and his recent approval for U.S. citizenship. Finally, he told Clarke that they were finished questioning him for the time being, but to remain available should they need him.

When Clarke had gone, the two lawmen sat and talked in the late afternoon light.

Mayfield was still disturbed about Clarke's conflicting portrayals of the route he had traveled to the Jenkins' camp after his discovery of Francis' body. The route he described to Agent Vogel today was the longest route to Jenkins' cabin, the commissioner said. When questioned at the time of the searches, Clarke told Mayfield and others that he had taken a different and shorter trail; he said he'd gone down Ruby Creek and then traveled directly over the hill to Jenkins' mining pit because he thought Jenkins would be working there at that time. From there, Clarke told them, he'd gone to the Jenkins' cabin. The route itself may or may not be of significance, Mayfield said, but it was vexing that Clarke's stories about this detail were not consistent.

Mayfield also said he was positive that Rocky Cummins had told him that Clarke appeared at his camp around 9 o'clock in the morning on September 11. But Clarke said he had been at the Francis cabin at 8:30 that morning. The distance between the camps, he said, made that impossible.

Vogel asked about the letters that Clarke had given him to mail, and Mayfield said that when he had taken them to the post office in Talkeetna he noticed both were addressed to Mrs. Norma Clarke in Pasco, Washington. He mailed them on September 16, he said.

With regard to the .30 calibre Winchester rifle found in Wonder Gulch, Mayfield said he believed the rifle belonged to Dick Francis. He had checked with others too, and everyone who knew Dick agreed that he had owned one of the same make and caliber.

Speaking of guns, the commissioner said, it appeared that neither Jenkins nor Brittell had been carrying a rifle or revolver with them when they met their deaths. He thought this was unusual, since most everybody traveled armed in the mining district because of grizzly bears.

Finally, Ben Mayfield told the FBI agent that he had recently learned a little more about Clarke's activities during the summer of 1938. The man named Thoeny was Clarke's partner that particular summer, and the two had gone prospecting with a third man, somewhere in the Nelchina district. Shortly thereafter, Clarke and Thoeny had returned to Anchorage without the other man. He had not been seen since, and Clarke and Thoeny were suspected of having killed him. A body had never been found, however, and no evidence of foul play had been uncovered,

Vogel took note of the information.

The day was late, and Vogel asked Mayfield to lock the .45 automatic pistol in his safe. First though, he recorded the gun's serial number and remarked to the commissioner that he was going to check to determine if there was any record of it having been stolen. Vogel then returned to his room at the Fairview Hotel.

———

The next morning, before sunrise, John Clarke knocked on Agent Vogel's door at the hotel at half past seven. There were some things he wanted to tell him, he said.

Vogel listened while Clarke talked about Rocky Cummins. He had acted oddly a few days after Mrs. Jenkins' body had been found, Clarke said. He had pointed his rifle at Frank Jenkins' mailbox and made a strange remark. Ask Mayfield about it, he said.

Clarke went on to explain that it had been his intention to remain at his camp on Ramsdyke Creek for two or three more weeks after the bodies had been found. He had come to Talkeetna instead because Mayfield had asked him to be available for questioning and because he didn't feel particularly safe while Rocky Cummins remained in the Dutch Hills.

Clarke complained that Mayfield was prejudiced against him. The lawman's report had identified Clarke as the discoverer of the bodies of Jenkins and Brittell, but had not mentioned that Frank Lee had discovered the body of Mrs. Jenkins.

After Clarke left, Vogel went next door to resume his work. He asked Ben Mayfield about the incident that involved Rocky and the mailbox, and Mayfield said that Rocky had had "the jitters." The miner had been on his way to a coroner's inquest at Petersville on the evening of September 19, and had seen what he thought to be a man in the shadows near Jenkins' camp. Rocky had pulled his rifle to his shoulder and called out, "What are you doing here?" Then he realized that the figure was Jenkins' mailbox and not a man. It was an example of the uneasiness that everyone was feeling in the mining district at the time, Mayfield said.

The commissioner opened his safe and removed the ring of keys that he and Attorney Kehoe had found on the shelf at the Jenkins' Little Willow cabin. Together, he and Agent Vogel walked a short distance down the street to the group of buildings owned by the

Jenkinses in Talkeetna. Today the skies were only partly cloudy, and a breeze out of the north moved nervously in the trees, causing more golden leaves to break loose and drift in the air.

Recent hard frosts had crumpled the grasses and spent wildflowers that had flourished on the Jenkins' property throughout the summer and early fall. Mayfield and Vogel followed a well-worn path to the main cabin and gained entry with one of the keys.

The FBI agent would later report that "apparently the Jenkins were in the habit of preserving everything that has come into their possession, as it was observed that the cabin is filled with old clothing, trunks, suitcases, papers, letters, etc., which date some years back." The two lawmen were in the cabin to determine if any gold might be hidden there, so their work was cut out for them.

Several hours later, when no gold had been uncovered, the two gave up the search. Before they left the property, the men walked through the stiff, frost-covered vegetation to another cabin and some supply sheds nearby. Those that were padlocked were accessed with the keys on the ring, and a quick inspection was made of each. Nothing of importance was found, and the men returned to Mayfield's office.

Mayfield gave Vogel an affidavit and some correspondence that he considered pertinent to the case. The sworn affidavit was signed by a prospector who had heard Dick Francis make threatening remarks about the Jenkinses a year earlier. The correspondence, between Helen Jenkins, Judge Hellenthal, and Attorney Arthur Thompson, had been found in the Jenkins' Little Willow Creek cabin during the searches, he said, and discussed a court injunction and Francis' sanity.

Agent Vogel reviewed the material and then left the commissioner's office to circulate in the village. There were other men he wanted to interview, and the first one he located was an old-timer named John Muir, whose case of frostbite had placed him in the same hospital ward with John Clarke the previous winter.

The elderly prospector told Vogel that Clarke had left the hospital as soon as he'd received settlement money from the Evan Jones Coal Company. When Muir was released from the hospital, he said, he had returned to his home in Talkeetna. Sometime later, in late February or early March, Clarke had shown up in the village and come to visit him. Then, just prior to Clarke's departure for the Cache Creek area, he had visited again and asked Muir if he could borrow an oilskin raincoat from him. Muir told Vogel that he had loaned him a coat, but hadn't seen Clarke again until recently, when he'd returned to Talkeetna with Commissioner Mayfield.

When he asked for the return of his coat, Muir said, Clarke gave him a much better one than the coat he'd borrowed. But the following day, Clarke had returned and said he needed to take the coat back. Clarke had then taken Muir to Nagley's store and bought him a brand new raincoat. Later, he heard that the coat Clarke had originally given him was thought to have belonged to Frank Jenkins.

Vogel moved on and talked with another man named Frevik, who had been among the searchers on the day Helen Jenkins' body was discovered. The agent asked him if he had spent any time with Clarke during the search, and Frevik told him that after Mrs. Jenkins had been found, Clarke wanted to go to the Poorman Creek cabin to get his packsack. Mayfield had suggested that Frevik go with him, he said, so the two set out and arrived at Poorman in about an hour's time.

They were in the cabin only ten or fifteen minutes, Frevik recalled, and during that time Clarke complained that someone had gone through his packsack. Clarke also claimed that his telescope was missing, but, after he looked further, he found it in the packsack. There was a full carton of twelve cans of Velvet tobacco in the cabin, and Clarke removed four of them and asked Frevik if he wanted any. When he declined, Clarke remarked that he would leave the rest of the cans for anyone who might come by and want tobacco. They had then returned to the Jenkins' cabin, Frevik said.

Later that day, Vogel or Mayfield questioned Clarke about the raincoat, and he explained that it had indeed belonged to Frank Jenkins. He had stopped at the Jenkins' camp on his way to Petersville, he said, and because it was raining he'd asked the caretaker, Frank Huffman, if he could wear one of the three or four raincoats that were hanging in the bunkhouse. Huffman told him to help himself. He meant to eventually turn the coat over to Mayfield, Clarke said.

At day's end, the two lawmen talked about the trip they would make to Cache Creek country the next day. Mayfield found a sleeping bag for the FBI agent, and some extra field gear for both of them in case the weather and traveling conditions were bad in the mining district. A pilot from Cantwell would pick them up in the morning, Mayfield said.

The last day of September dawned at around eight o'clock, with partly cloudy skies and frosty temperatures throughout the area. Sometime later, Chris Christensen landed at the Talkeetna Village Airstrip, probably in his new Aeronca aircraft. He loaded the men and their gear into the plane, took off, and ascended to altitude over the Susitna River. As they headed west, Vogel could see the pale green rivers below, now low and slow and braided by the maze of sandbars that had formed from the rivers' silty deposits.

A dense carpet of birch, cottonwood, and spruce stretched before them and far into the distance, broken by sporadic ponds, lakes, and broad, brindled swamps. The vast forest of trees stood heavily stripped of leaves, but the remaining foliage displayed the brilliant yellow and gold of late fall that stood in striking contrast to the dark spruce. The aircraft continued to ascend as it traveled west, from 345 feet above sea level at Talkeetna, to around 3,000 feet in altitude as it approached the snow-laced hills ahead. As they passed the Peters Hills and entered Cache Creek country, scattered trees below were nearly barren, except for a few yellow leaves that held fast here and there, reluctant to bow to nature's cold will.

Mayfield asked Christensen to fly over the scenes of the killings and, as the pilot flew slow circles over Little Willow Creek, Ruby Gulch, and Wonder Gulch, Vogel took photographs of the cabins and trails. The FBI man would later write that "the cabins are some distance apart and the country is rugged and mountainous in parts, while creeks and swamps abound in other sections."

When Vogel had finished, Chris began a slow descent alongside the Dutch Hills and in minutes approached the Bird Creek mine. He made a low and noisy pass over the buildings there, to alert the men below to his arrival. Then he lined up with a short, crude airstrip and landed.

It was colder here at an altitude of about 2,400 feet, and a modest layer of snow covered the area. Scattered scrub brush still retained a few dull leaves that crackled dryly against one another—like a seasonal death rattle—in the breeze. The lawmen unloaded their gear and walked for forty-five minutes to the Bird Creek mine. When they arrived at the camp's cookshack, Mayfield introduced Vogel to John Johanson, a part-owner of the place who had remained to shut the mine down for the season.

Vogel got down to work and questioned Johanson about the day that John Clarke and Rocky Cummins had appeared at the mine with the news about Dick Francis' death. The miner responded that it had been about 10:45 in the morning on September 11 when the two showed up at the camp and told his brother, Ed, that Dick had shot himself. About fifteen minutes later, he had arrived at the cookshack and joined the conversation himself. At one point, he had advised Clarke to stay away from the Francis cabin to avoid disturbing any fingerprints that might be found there. But later, Clarke had remarked that though he "hated to go back" there, he felt that Dick's dogs needed some attention. As Clarke and Cummins left Bird Creek, Johanson said, Clarke said that he was going to return to the Francis camp.

Johanson had little more to add, so the two lawmen set out, on foot, to the east. Just below the area where Bird Creek emptied into Peters Creek, the men accessed a trail that paralleled Peters Creek on a southeasterly course. In about an hour they reached Rocky Cummins' camp. Rocky was there, along with Ed Wagner, another longtime prospector who was around 65 years old. Wagner, who usually lived alone in his cabin about a mile south of Rocky's camp, was now staying with Rocky because of the killings. Until the matter was resolved, they explained, they thought it a cautious thing to do.

Vogel asked Rocky to describe events as he remembered them, and Cummins said that John Clarke had appeared at his cabin on September 11 at about nine o'clock that morning. He said that he had met Clarke on only one other occasion, and that at first Clarke seemed not to recognize him. Then, Clarke told him about Francis' death, and Cummins had questioned him for more details. Clarke told Rocky about his journey to the Jenkins' camp, he said, and how that camp seemed to be deserted when he got there.

Rocky agreed to go with Clarke to the Bird Creek mine, he said, and along the way the two men had discussed Francis' death. Cummins said he told Clarke that he wondered if maybe Jenkins had killed Francis. He also asked Clarke why he hadn't gone into the cabin to see if Dick might still be alive. Clarke had replied that he "saw the blood and the gun and was afraid to touch him." During the journey, Clarke had also mentioned that Mrs. Jenkins was going to demand a sanity hearing for Francis. Clarke talked about the feud between the miners, and how he'd been warned by others not to take sides.

Vogel questioned Cummins about Bob Meade, and Rocky said that the young mine worker had appeared at his cabin early on the morning of September 10. He told Cummins that he had "quit Jenkins" and was on his way to Talkeetna. Then, he had let loose with a stream of curses against the Jenkinses. He was angry because the couple had not given him directions to the right trail, or offered him a sandwich for his long walk. Meade had remained at Rocky's for about twenty minutes, Cummins said, and then started out in the direction of Talkeetna.

Did Meade mention anything about Jenkins and Brittell going over to Clarke's camp to get a radio and battery that morning? Vogel asked.

No, Rocky said, furrowing his brow. He didn't recall that.

Did Meade say anything about Jenkins and Brittell going on a journey of some sort? Vogel inquired.

No, Rocky said.

So, you didn't tell Clarke that you had learned from Meade that Jenkins and Brittell were going to pick up a radio at Clarke's camp?

Rocky said no.

When Vogel asked Cummins about conversation at the Bird Creek mine, Rocky recalled that John Johanson told Clarke he didn't have to return to the Francis cabin. But Clarke had said he wanted to return there to feed Dick's dogs. Cummins also recalled that just before he and Clarke had parted after leaving Bird Creek, he told Clarke that if he did return to the Francis cabin he shouldn't touch anything, because fingerprints might be around. He told him to stay away from the Jenkins' cabin, too.

Vogel asked Cummins if he had a friend by the name of Ed Stronk, who prospected along the Tokositna River.

Yes, he did, Rocky said. In fact, a day or two after Mrs. Jenkins' body was found, he had planned to go to Ed's cabin, which was located about six or seven miles beyond Clarke's cabin on Ramsdyke. He wanted to go there to see whether Ed was all right. But Clarke had somehow heard about this and offered to accompany him part of the way. Rocky made an excuse that he could not go at that time, he said, because he was afraid of Clarke.

Ed Wagner was questioned about his activities on September 10, and the old prospector replied that he had spent the whole day with another couple named Wagner, who had a mining camp near the Bird Creek mine. When asked, Wagner said that he had not seen Rocky on September 10 nor had he seen Bob Meade.

The agent had no more questions and indicated to Mayfield that it was time to move on to Little Willow Creek. The two left Rocky's camp and headed in a northeast direction, tramping through two or three inches of snow on an almost lateral course along the slopes of the hills. The sky was cloudy with random, open breaks, and only the soft, crushing sound of the men's footsteps altered the utter quiet of that part of the Dutch Hills. The men continued in this way for a couple of hours, over subalpine vegetation and tussocks that crackled with frost and snow, until Mayfield paused and pointed out the lines of Little Willow.

The creek was not yet frozen but moved in a cold, languid path that bore faint resemblance to its summer force. Soon, the men could see bluish smoke rising from a smokestack and, in a short time, could make out the rustic camp that belonged to Frank and Helen Jenkins. Mayfield likely called out the customary "hallo!" Frank Huffman probably emerged from the Jenkins' cabin and waved in greeting as the lawmen approached.

How Huffman had gotten word to Mayfield about the gold pokes he'd found, remains unclear. Regardless, the two officials now had their first look at the buckskin bags filled with gold. Ben Mayfield located a Troy weight scale in the cabin and weighed out the 170 ounces of gold, and the two men marked each bag for identification, and as evidence.

Mayfield hadn't been able to transport all of the evidence back to

Talkeetna during the hectic time in the Dutch Hills, when the searches and recovery of the bodies had demanded all of his attention. He had instead secured certain items in the Jenkins' cabin, and brought them out now. Agent Vogel examined the homemade canvas packboard that Mayfield had found about a quarter mile from where Helen's body had later been recovered. He observed small blood flecks on a section of the canvas and, with a knife, cut out a three-inch by foot-long strip and marked it for identification. He would have it tested to determine if the blood was human, he told Mayfield.

The FBI agent now examined Frank Jenkins' guns: one .30-30 Winchester rifle, one .30 calibre standard rifle, a Winchester repeating shotgun, three .22 rifles, and one .45 automatic pistol. At this time Huffman told Vogel about a conversation he had with John Clarke about four days after the searches had ended. The two were sitting in the Jenkins' cabin drinking coffee and discussing the possibility of Francis shooting himself with the .38 revolver. Huffman said he remarked, "I wonder how Jenkins was fixed for such guns as that." Clarke, he said, got up from his chair and walked to the shelves just inside the cabin entrance, and looked up at the top shelf. Then, with no further comment, he had returned to his chair.

Huffman said that after Clarke departed, he inspected the top shelf and found a .45 pistol partially concealed behind some gold pans there. It occured to him, therefore, that Clarke had at some time seen the pistol on the shelf.

Vogel examined the box of .35 Remington soft point cartridges that had been found on the table in the cabin when Mayfield and Kehoe had forced entry. Six shells were missing. He took note of the fact that the cartridges were probably for use in a Remington automatic or a Remington slide action rifle, but that no rifle of that description had been found at the cabin.

Now the agent inspected the Fairbanks-Morse radio that Jenkins had carried in his pack, and the men connected it to a battery they found in the cabin. The unit was still in good operating condition, Vogel noted, but the same could not be said of the battery that Brittell had carried, because all of the acid and water had leaked out.

Frank Huffman told Vogel and Mayfield that on the day following his discovery of the gold pokes, he had gone over to both Francis' cabin and Wonder Gulch. While looking around he had found a .38 Remington special cartridge shell, about a half-mile north of Francis' cabin. He showed it to the men, and Vogel labeled it and added it to his store of possible evidence.

Huffman also said that he had inspected the Francis cabin for bullet holes, but hadn't found any. He noticed, however, that something appeared to have been burned almost directly in front of the cabin.

As the day grew late, Huffman eventually fixed dinner for everybody. It was probably over the meal that he told Agent Vogel that people in the area might suspect him of something because he was so new to Talkeetna. For this reason, he said, he would like to establish his whereabouts on September 10. He had been coming to Alaska off and on for many years, but it was only recently that he had come to this area for the first time. He had been in Anchorage on September 8, and left there on the ninth to walk to Matanuska (near Palmer), where he spent the night. The people there would remember him, because he had gotten into a dispute with a drunk at the hotel there. On the tenth he had caught a ride on a freight train to Talkeetna, arriving there in the early morning hours of September 11.

Vogel made note of Huffman's statement, and after the evening grew dark the men all turned in for the night.

————

The three arose before sunrise on October first, and Frank Huffman worked at kindling the reduced embers in the wood stove for both heat and a good cooking fire. The temperature had dropped to below freezing during the night, and a chill likely pervaded the one-room cabin while Huffman worked to coax a favorable fire to life. As the surrounding hills took form in the first morning light, the men could look out and see a blanket of heavy overcast that cast a sullen tone on the atmosphere.

Frank Huffman must have won Agent Vogel's confidence, because when breakfast was finished he accompanied the lawmen on their trek to the death scenes. The three climbed the hill above the camp and inspected the alcove along the little creek where Helen Jenkins' body had been discovered. The men looked around, and Mayfield found a blue wool stocking cap that he identified as one that Helen had owned. The only other thing that drew Vogel's interest was a safety pin that he found in the small creek, just beneath the place where Helen had lain.

The men moved on to the north, and in about an hour's time reached Dick Francis' tent-cabin, which Vogel observed to be neat and orderly. Ben Mayfield explained to the agent how Francis had been found with the revolver in his hand, leading everyone to believe that he had committed suicide. After Francis' body had been removed, his partner, Ed Carlson, had asked for permission to clean the place up. He had consented, he explained, not knowing that it might be considered a murder scene.

The FBI agent spent a long time examining the canvas and wooden supports of the tent, both inside and out, in an effort to locate the bullet holes that should have resulted from the shots that passed through Francis' head. He found none. An examination of the floor also produced no results. Vogel commented that the dampness and moisture in the structure did not allow him to process any fingerprint impressions.

Vogel could find no tobacco in the cabin, though he had learned that Francis had received three cartons of the Velvet brand with his supply order a few days prior to his death. While he looked around, a strip of moosehide caught the agent's attention. It was hanging from a nail, and measured about two inches wide and five feet in length. The hide contained bloodstains, and Vogel added it to his collection of evidence.

Outside, about a dozen feet from the cabin, Huffman pointed to the burned area that he had commented on earlier. Vogel took samples of the charred remnants, and then returned to the cabin to draw a sketch of the structure's interior. With Mayfield's help, he also made a diagram of the position in which Francis had been found, and the proximity of various objects in the room to the body

As the men moved farther north to Wonder Gulch, it began to snow. The new snowfall served to reinforce the crusted, four-inch snow cover still present in the gulch, causing Vogel to later report that it wasn't possible to properly examine the area. After a cursory inspection, the three continued moving north.

The men covered another mile through the snow and flattened vegetation and reached the end of the ridge that loomed above Ramsdyke Creek. Given the snow and angle of descent, it was probably slippery going as the three slowly made their way down the steep, rocky, and alder-tangled ridge face. When they finally reached the shallow creek, they crossed easily. The men worked their way downstream a short distance to Clarke's cabin, where they gained entry and remained for the next hour and a half.

The first thing Vogel noticed was a Little Ben alarm clock. He wound it to test its working condition, and the clock began to tick. He also saw a .22 Winchester rifle hanging on the wall, and took it down for examination; he paused to record its serial number. Vogel then began a thorough inspection of the cabin for any trace of burned or bloodstained clothing. While he and the men searched, he noted that the place was "arranged in a neat and orderly fashion, and contained a large quantity of supplies." Vogel found a large, one-pound can of Velvet tobacco, and observed that several other Velvet tobacco cans were utilized as containers for nails and screws.

For the next hour the men searched the cabin both inside and out, but could find no sign of suspicious clothing or other evidence of value. Outside, the snow continued to fall and, finally, the agent made the decision to end the effort. As the three prepared to depart, Vogel picked up the alarm clock. For the hour and a half they had spent here, he noted, the clock had kept perfect time.

Just where or when Agent Vogel injured his leg is not clear, but he did so, and it's possible that the damage occurred when the men climbed back up the ridge to Wonder Gulch. The injury seems not to have been serious enough to impair his ability to complete the long trek back to the Jenkins' cabin; nevertheless, it was troublesome enough to keep him from ascending another steep hill over to Poorman Creek and the cabin he wanted to inspect there. He asked Mayfield to make the inspection for him, and the commissioner did so, probably rejoining the men as they neared the Willow Creek area.

Mayfield reported that there was no evidence of bloodstained or burned clothing at the Poorman cabin site—just some food supplies and a carton containing eight small cans of Velvet tobacco.

The men probably returned to Little Willow Creek both tired and hungry after their rugged mountain travels. Vogel and Mayfield spent a second night at the Jenkins' cabin, which enabled the agent to rest his injured leg.

Unknown to the agent, the Washington, D.C. division of the FBI had sent a letter to his Juneau office that day. The letter quoted the *Anchorage Times*' telegraphed request for assistance, and ended with instructions for Vogel: "You are instructed to give this case preferred and expeditious attention...." It was signed by John Edgar Hoover.

———

Ben Mayfield may have requested that Charles and Jack Francis be available at Petersville at this time, because the two men were there when the lawmen arrived at the mining complex. Today was the day that Mayfield had arranged for a flight back to Talkeetna, and Vogel's interview with the father and his son would be his final inquiry in Cache Creek country.

Jack Francis confirmed Clarke's story that he had instructed the Francis men to search the opposite sides of Wonder Gulch, while Clarke traveled down the gulch itself. He said that after Clarke had walked about a hundred yards down the gulch, which took him about eight or ten minutes, he had called out and then fired three shots. When Francis had reached the death scene, Clarke said to him, "I see one body, do you see any more?" So he looked around, Francis said, and saw what appeared to be another body directly behind the one Clarke had discovered. The bodies were well camouflaged with tall grass and, due to the falling snow, it was fairly difficult to see them.

Jack Francis said that it was he who had discovered the rifle barrel and stock lying in the creek water, but that it was Clarke who pointed out the footprints along the creek bed, some twenty-five yards above the bodies. Clarke had "specifically called these prints to their attention," he said, and had asked the two men to examine them with him. Clarke then measured the prints with his hands.

They looked around some more, Jack recounted, then returned to Dick Francis' cabin to get out of the snowstorm while the discovery was reported to Ben Mayfield. While there, Clarke asked him to go with him to Poorman Creek. Clarke said he wanted to put in a supply of food at the Poorman cabin for the searchers, in case the place was used while the men looked for Mrs. Jenkins.

Clarke had then collected some supplies from Dick Francis' cabin and the two had trekked through the wind and snow to Poorman Creek, where Clarke decided to cook some food for Dick's dogs. While they were at Poorman, Jack said, they discussed the case and Clarke stated that it certainly looked like Dick Francis had shot Jenkins and Brittell. On the way back to Ruby Creek he and Clarke had spread out, looking for Mrs. Jenkins' body along the way.

Vogel questioned Charles Francis, who substantiated his son's account and added that Clarke had remarked that the footprints along the creek bed appeared to be those of a woman.

When Christensen flew over the Peters Creek cookshack, Vogel and Mayfield gathered up their things and walked down to the airfield. There, the smiling Dane greeted them, loaded the men and their gear, and took off. In twenty minutes the lawmen were back in Talkeetna.

Two men from Mt. Shasta, California, were in Talkeetna, talking to people in the village and waiting for Commissioner Mayfield to return. The older of the two was Dick Francis' brother, Isaac, and with him was his son-in-law, Roy Berg. The men had been in Anchorage where they had provided data for Francis' death certificate and assumed responsibility for the dead miner's estate. Now, they were in the town where everybody knew Dick, and Isaac was anxious to find out what he could about his brother's death.

The men likely turned up at the commissioner's office soon after word got around that Christensen had landed at the local airstrip. Eventually they sat down with both Mayfield and Vogel, and Isaac Francis told them that his brother had never returned to California after he had journeyed to Alaska, over two decades earlier. He hadn't seen Dick for twenty-five years, he said, but family members had kept track of him through the occasional letters that Dick had written to their mother in Mt. Shasta. He had brought some of those letters with him, because they spoke of the bitter conflicts his brother had been involved in with the Jenkinses. They might be of value to the investigation, Francis said, as he handed the letters to Agent Vogel.

While Ben Mayfield briefed Francis about the investigation, Vogel read the letters and took some notes. When he was finished, he asked to keep one of the letters that included a snapshot of Dick Francis. After the men left the office, the agent studied the handwriting and the photograph and observed in his notes that the letter appeared to have been written with the right hand. In the photograph, he noted, Dick Francis was posing with a rifle in a stance that would be taken by a right-handed person. Then Vogel filed his papers away and went looking for John Clarke.

Back at Mayfield's office, the FBI agent asked Clarke to explain why the Brittell radio had been stored at his Ramsdyke cabin. Curiously,

Clarke hesitated. Vogel waited. Finally, Clarke said that Ken Brittell had brought the radio to his cabin about two weeks before the killings and asked that he take care of it until Joy Brittell could pack it out.

Vogel moved to another subject. He reminded Clarke that he had denied ever owning a rifle. Yet, he said, a .22 Winchester rifle had been observed in his cabin at Ramsdyke Creek.

Clarke replied that he didn't consider a .22 to even be a rifle, and for that reason he hadn't mentioned it.

Where did you get the rifle? Vogel asked.

From Thoeny, Clarke said, referring to the man he'd spoken of in an earlier interview. At the same time that Thoeny had given him the .45 pistol, he said.

The two discussed the tobacco that was found at the Poorman Creek cabin, and Clarke denied that the carton was his. Dick Francis might have put the tobacco there before his death, he said. Ask Al Stinson and Ed Carlson. The three of them were negotiating for the claims and cabin at Poorman, and they might know if Francis had taken any supplies there.

Vogel asked Clarke about the footprints in Wonder Gulch, and Clarke insistently denied that he had been the first to discover them. Charles Francis had been the one that brought the prints to his attention, he said.

Vogel asked again about the route that Clarke had followed from Ruby Creek to the Jenkins' camp after his discovery of Francis' body. Clarke repeated his earlier statement; he had gone down Ruby Creek to Willow Creek and then up Little Willow to the Jenkins' cabin. When he found it locked, he had gone on to the Jenkins' mining pit.

Vogel ended the interview and left the office to look for Al Stinson. When located, the veteran miner said that he had known Francis for many years, and the two had formed a partnership to work the Poorman Creek claims. In early September, the last time he had seen Dick alive, Francis had suggested that Clarke be taken into the partnership but Stinson had argued against the proposal because he didn't trust Clarke. When Vogel asked if Francis had taken any supplies to the Poorman cabin, Stinson said that Dick had told him he had taken a few items there, in order to have them on hand for his prospecting activities. To another question, Stinson answered that Dick had definitely owned a .30-30 caliber Winchester rifle.

Now, Vogel returned to the Fairview Hotel, packed all his gear and papers together, and prepared to leave for Anchorage.

——

Enroute to Anchorage with Chris Christensen, Agent Vogel talked with him about the supply order that he had airdropped to Dick Francis before his death. Chris went through his log book and identified the delivery date as September 7. Sometime prior to that, he said, a prospector named John Hill had given him some gold along with Francis' supply order and asked that they be delivered to the owner of the Reliance Grocery in Anchorage. Vogel made a note to contact the grocer and inquire if he still had the order on file.

Located at the head of Cook Inlet and bordered by the Chugach Mountains along its eastern rim, Anchorage was now home to a population of 4,229 people. The town dated its origins to 1914 when Dick Francis had arrived in Alaska and had, through the years, acquired the basic accouterments of commerce. Vogel checked in at the Anchorage Hotel, located in the downtown core, and then walked over to the federal building which housed the office of Deputy U.S. Marshal Grover Triber. While in Talkeetna Vogel had received a telegram from Triber, informing him that a man named Lee at Indian, Alaska, had requested that a "G-man" be sent there immediately to investigate a suspicious person that might be connected to the "Talkeetna murder case." Vogel had asked Triber to look into the matter until he could leave Talkeetna.

The two lawmen met and Triber told Vogel that he had contacted Lee, who said that an individual from Talkeetna had arrived at Indian some time after the murders, and had behaved suspiciously. The man was 30 to 40 years of age and had little money and few supplies. He told people that he was there to hunt wolves and coyotes for bounty money, but he had stayed at Indian for only two or three days and then departed on the railroad for Anchorage. His general behavior had created an air of suspicion, enough for Lee and another man to notify Anchorage authorities. Triber said he was still working to gain more information.

The marshal told Vogel that he and Anchorage's police chief had discussed the Talkeetna murder case on various occasions and had concluded that it would be worthwhile to keep two Anchorage men in mind as suspects. The first was a man named Barick, who had returned to Anchorage from a prospecting trip—some said at Peters Creek—sometime after the killings in September. The second man was Percy Pue, an ex-convict from Chicago. Both men were friendly with Clarke, he said.

Triber said that an old prospector in Anchorage told him that Barick was a racketeer from Chicago. The marshal had also learned that Barick and Clarke had become acquainted with each other sometime in 1938. Barick was currently living in a cabin at the lower end of Anchorage. As for Pue, he was lodged in the local jail, charged with violation of the immigration laws because he was a Canadian subject and in the country illegally. Anchorage's Chief of Police Bob Huttle had more details about both men, Triber said.

Agent Vogel walked to the Anchorage police station and met with Chief Huttle. When he inquired about Percy Pue, Huttle said that the Canadian had come to Anchorage several years earlier, after having served time in the penitentiary at Chicago for involvement in a robbery there. There was also some suspicion that he was linked to the disappearance of a man named Bobby Packenbush, whom Pue had worked with at a gold mine near Palmer. It was rumored that Packenbush had angered Pue by insinuating that he had stolen gold at the mine. Sometime around the fall of 1937 Packenbush had disappeared, Huttle said, and one year later his body had washed up on an inlet beach, not far from Anchorage. While Pue was a definite suspect, sufficient evidence against him hadn't been obtained.

The subject turned to John Clarke, and Chief Huttle told Vogel what he knew about him and the man named Thoeny. Around July of 1938, he said, Clarke, J.G. Thoeny, and a man named John Dexter had departed Anchorage and gone prospecting somewhere in the Nelchina mining section, east of Palmer. Later, Clarke and Thoeny had returned to Anchorage without Dexter, who had not been seen or heard from since. At some point either Clarke or Thoeny had been questioned by U.S. Attorney Kehoe, who was told that the men last saw Dexter going down a hill toward a mining camp, along a well-established trail. Later, Huttle said, Dexter's pack was found on the trail, a short distance from where Clarke and Thoeny had left him.

Huttle gave Vogel a letter he had received from Dexter's sister just a few months earlier, which contained a photograph of her brother. Then he told Vogel that, to the best of his knowledge, J.G. Thoeny had left Anchorage a year ago and had probably returned to the states. He said that Thoeny had never been arrested for anything in Anchorage, and he had no information about his background. Though he suspected Clarke and Thoeny of being implicated in some way in the disappearance of John Dexter, there simply was no evidence against them.

Sometime later, probably at his hotel, Vogel was contacted and told that a man wanted to speak with him about Bobby Packenbush. The agent made arrangements to meet with the man, who turned out to be Packenbush's brother-in-law and the owner of a dairy in Anchorage.

In 1937, the man said, Packenbush was employed at the Lucky Shot mine near Palmer in a work crew that included Percy Pue. Sometime in September, Bobby came to Anchorage and told him that Pue was "out to get him" because he had accused Pue of "high-grading gold" from the Lucky Shot. The dairy owner told Vogel that he had insisted that Bobby stay at his home for protection but, shortly thereafter, Packenbush had left the house and was never seen again. At some point an Anchorage taxi driver had informed his wife, Bobby's sister, that it was futile to look for Bobby in Anchorage, because he was "in the bay at Spring Creek." When Attorney Kehoe attempted to question the taxi driver, the man had refused to talk.

A year after his disappearance, the man continued, Bobby's body had washed up on shore, three miles across the inlet from Anchorage. Both Bobby's hands were gone at the wrist and both feet were missing from his ankles. His front teeth had also been knocked out. Several people in Anchorage suspected Pue's involvement. In one instance, when Bobby's ex-wife had expressed her opinion that Pue was responsible for Packenbush's disappearance, Pue had threatened her.

When asked, the dairyman said he had no reason to believe that Pue was connected with the killings in the Talkeetna area, but he thought it might be helpful to mention this incident. He had also known Dick Francis for many years, he said, but didn't have any information about the Cache Creek killings.

As the afternoon wore on and Vogel made his rounds, that day's issue of the *Anchorage Times* was distributed throughout Anchorage. Once again banner headlines dominated the front page.

FIND JENKINS GOLD
G-MAN FLIES HERE TO CONTINUE PROBE

Theory that Mr. and Mrs. F.W. Jenkins were murdered at Cache Creek with robbery as the motive, was apparently blasted with the discovery of $5,000 in gold dust hidden in the Jenkins cabin, it was learned here late this afternoon.

Meanwhile, investigation of the massacre which took four lives, moved on to Anchorage with the arrival of R.C. Vogel, special agent for the Federal Bureau of Investigation.

U.S. Commissioner B.H. Mayfield, who has figured prominently in investigations of the slaughter, announced the discovery. Mr. Mayfield expressed the opinion that the $5,000 in gold must represent the summer's cleanup for Mr. and Mrs. Jenkins. An additional 53 ounces of gold, worth approximately $1,500, was found in the Jenkins' cabin when the deaths were first under investigation.

> Mr. Vogel came to Anchorage with Pilot Haakon Christensen and is stopping at the Anchorage Hotel while carrying forward his investigation of the deaths of Mr. and Mrs. Jenkins, Joy Brittell and Dick Francis. The investigator declined to comment on the case, giving no indication whether arrests were near. When advised that Commissioner Mayfield had announced the discovery of the gold in the Jenkins cabin, Mr. Vogel commented: "There's no better authority than Mr. Mayfield."

The next morning Agent Vogel was called to the desk phone at the Anchorage Hotel. The caller identified himself as the attorney for the Evan Jones Coal Company, and said he thought it might be of value for Vogel to know that the company was preparing to file charges against John Clarke for defrauding the company of the settlement money he'd received for his alleged back injury. The lawyer said he felt that the necessity for this action might indicate that aspects of Clarke's character and reputation were suspect. Vogel made notes and asked the attorney if he had any information about the killings. The lawyer replied that he hadn't; his concerns were based on the facts that Clarke had been in the vicinity of the killings and that certain people were suspicious of Clarke.

When Vogel had finished with the call, he set out on a circuit of the small hotels, boarding houses, and bars in downtown Anchorage. Though the temperature had dropped to several degrees below freezing during the night, the morning began to warm with the daylight as the sun emerged, now and then, through partly cloudy skies. Vogel met with a man who was said to have information about the man named Barick. The old-timer, who now lived on a pension, said that Steve Barick had come to Anchorage in June or July of 1938 from Seattle. Sometime that summer at one of the local bars, he had a conversation with Barick, who told him that he was "one of Al Capone's men," and that if the local authorities knew what he knew, it would be "curtains" for Barick. The old-timer knew little else about the man except that he was a "lone wolf" who lived in a cabin in Anchorage by himself and had returned from a prospecting trip around September 15.

Vogel moved on to the Northern Hotel and interviewed the manager there. She told him that John Clarke had stayed there on a number of occasions and hadn't caused any problems. In further response, she said that Clarke did not seem to have any friends in

234

particular, but that she had noticed that he and Steve Barick appeared to be friendly with each other.

Following the directions that Triber had given him, Vogel moved to the edge of town and found the cabin where Barick lived. He was in and agreed to talk with the agent. He was 32 years old and from Chicago, he said, and had been coming to the territory off and on since 1927. He had met John Clarke at the Northern Hotel in the fall of 1938, and had seen him again in the very early spring of 1939 while in Seattle. No, he hadn't seen him since.

When Vogel asked him how he had spent his summer, Barick said that during the first two months of the summer season he had prospected along the Knik River, about twenty miles east of Palmer. Around July, he and a friend named Joe did some prospecting in the same area, but Joe had departed because he didn't like the snow that still remained there. So, he prospected with a man named Tex until around the fifth of September, and then prospected alone until the fifteenth, at a place called Idaho Peak. The manager of the Gold Mint mine could verify this, he said, because he passed his cabin there every morning.

Vogel asked him if he had ever been in the vicinity of the Dutch Hills, and Barick said he hadn't. When asked, he said that Clarke was merely a casual acquaintance. No, he had never seen Clarke with a rifle, but on one occasion he saw him cleaning a .38 caliber blue steel revolver of the break-open type. He said he was positive that the revolver had not had a swing-out cylinder.

After the interview, Vogel walked back downtown to the federal jail. Percy Pue was in. He told Vogel that he had been in the territory for the last several years and had spent the past summer working on a fishing boat in Bristol Bay. He'd done that until early September, he said, and then had checked in at the 5th Avenue Hotel in Anchorage until the afternoon of September 11, when he had gone to Palmer. He had returned to Anchorage on the twelfth. No, he hadn't been near Talkeetna this past summer. Yes, four or five years ago he'd done some time in the Illinois State Penitentiary, but it was a "bum rap." No, he said, he didn't know John Clarke.

Vogel moved down the street to the 5th Avenue Hotel and talked to Patsy Miller, the proprietress. She opened her record book and told the agent that Percy Pue had registered at her hotel on September 6 and, to her knowledge, had been there until a few days ago, when he was picked up for violation of the immigration laws. Vogel noted that Pue's story checked out.

As he moved about Anchorage, the FBI man asked everyone he talked to if they knew a man named J.G. Thoeny. Despite numerous inquiries, he had met with no success. Next, he walked to the local post office and inquired if any records were on file that related to Thoeny, Clarke, or John Dexter. The postal clerk, Ralph Grover, produced three cards, one in the name of J.G. Thoeny, which carried instructions to "hold mail until fall." The card was dated July 7, 1938. The other two cards, bearing the same date and notation, were made out in the names of Dexter and Clarke. While Vogel waited, Grover talked with other postal workers and finally told the agent that he believed that Thoeny had left Anchorage for the states in the fall of 1938, without leaving a forwarding address.

The agent was back at the Anchorage police station late that afternoon. Chief Huttle was out, but Vogel got into a conversation with Walter Brewington, an officer on the force. Brewington had known Dick Francis for twenty years, he said, and had always found him to be "calm and easy-going." About a year ago, though, an elderly prospector in town told him that he had seen Dick and that it was his impression that Francis was "slipping." The two lawmen talked about Francis' guns, and the officer remarked that Dick had owned a fine single shot Colt .22 caliber revolver. Dick was really proud of it, he said. When Vogel asked him if he knew whether Dick was right or left-handed, Brewington replied that he was almost positive that Francis was right-handed. But he had heard too, some years back, that Francis was having trouble with his right eye and had reduced his hunting activities because he had to change his rifle from one shoulder to the other.

Vogel made a note that no Colt .22 caliber revolver had shown up among Dick Francis' things.

By now, the *Anchorage Times* had distributed its daily newspaper, and today it carried an article that focused on the investigation.

F.B.I. AGENT PROBES MURDER CASE LOCALLY
Robbery Theory In Cache Creek Killings
Holds Despite Gold Discovery

Investigation of four murders in the Cache Creek country was carried forward in Anchorage today by Special Agent Ralph C. Vogel of the Federal Bureau of Investigation with no new developments disclosed. Meanwhile, the theory that robbery was the motive for the slaying of Mr. and Mrs. Jenkins, Joy Brittell and Dick Francis persisted despite the fact that approximately $5,000 in gold dust was found in the Jenkins cabin.

Mr. Vogel declined to comment on his investigation, giving no indication whether an arrest was near or how he would proceed after completing his work in Anchorage.

The *Times* was advised that B.H. Mayfield, U.S. Commissioner at Talkeetna, had announced discovery of the gold. While the gold may have represented the seasons' clean-up for Mr. and Mrs. Jenkins, it was pointed out locally that other gold might have been found in the cabin by the murderer. The gold dust was found in buck-skin pokes hidden in a wood pile near the kitchen stove. Belief was expressed that the murderer might have overlooked that place as a cache for gold and might have found other hiding places in the cabin....

———

The next morning Vogel looked for the prospector who had talked with Officer Brewington. He found Charlie Harper, who said that the last time he'd seen Dick Francis was during the fall of 1938. At that time, he said, he looked a little more worn than he had in the past, but was rational in his conversation. Francis did mention that he was afraid that Mrs. Jenkins might come to his cabin and poison his food "in order to get rid of him." Vogel asked Harper about his familiarity with Francis' guns, and the prospector said he knew that Francis had a rifle and a .38 double action revolver with either a six or seven-inch barrel. Harper said that Francis had a good disposition, but sometimes had a hard time getting along with his partners. As far as he knew, though, Dick didn't have a quarrelsome nature.

The agent left Harper to keep an appointment with Dr. Asa Walkowski at the funeral home where the autopsies had been conducted on the bodies of the Jenkinses, Brittell, and Francis. After a general conversation about the circumstances of the deaths, Vogel told Walkowski that he was especially interested in knowing more about Dick Francis' examination. Had he noted any evidence of powder burns in the vicinity of Francis' head wounds? Had he been able to determine from which direction the bullets had penetrated Francis' head?

Dr. Walkowski told him that he hadn't seen any powder burns on either side of Francis' head. He added that there had been a considerable amount of hardened blood clotted around the wounds on both sides of the head, and that this had caused some difficulty. As for the direction of the bullets, he said, he had since revised his original findings. When he had initially received the bodies for autopsy, late in the day on September 15, he had felt a sense of urgency to report autopsy results to the coroner's jury at Petersville because the group was with-holding a verdict, pending his advice. For this reason he had, unfortu-nately, hurried through the examinations, and now believed that in doing so he had acted unwisely. He felt this way because his original conclusion was that the bullets had entered from the right side of Francis' head. He had based this on his hasty judgment about what appeared to be "burnt edges" around the head wounds.

Since that time, Walkowski said, he had reviewed his findings and spent some time in deeper reflection. Now he felt certain that what he had hastily identified as burnt edges, was only encrusted blood. For this reason, and after a closer examination, he now felt that the bullets had entered from the left side of Francis' head.

The doctor and the agent entered the room where the bodies re-mained in legal custody. Walkowski explained that all the bodies had been thoroughly treated with formaldehyde. In Francis' case, he said, the embalming fluid had caused the skin to contract around his head wounds; therefore, the wounds were not as large as they were when he had performed the autopsy. He went on to point out the wounds on either side of Francis' head, and gave Vogel the medical reasons that he felt supported bullet entry from the left side. One of these, he pointed out, was a narrow flap of skin that extended downward and backward on one of the wounds on the left side of the head.

As he detailed the trajectory of upper and lower wounds from left to right, Walkowski became specific and said that if the upper left wound had been made first, "it would not have been possible for Francis to have inflicted a second wound." And, even if the lower left wound had been made first, it was his opinion that "it would have been highly improbable that Francis could have again shot himself."

The two examined the bodies of Frank and Helen Jenkins and Joy Brittell, and the doctor told Vogel that none of the three had been shot. But, in addition to the damage done by bludgeoning to his head, Joy Brittell's face displayed facial and nose abrasions that ap-peared to indicate that he had been dragged for a distance on his face. No such marks had appeared on the Jenkinses, he said.

After Dr. Walkowski left the funeral parlor, Agent Vogel remained to take photographs and measurements of Dick Francis' head wounds. While so engaged, he talked with a man named Hugo, an employee of the funeral home. He had been present at the autop-sies, he said, and both he and Dr. Walkowski had looked for pow-der burns on Francis' head, especially as the impression had been given that the miner had committed suicide. But they could find nothing that appeared to be powder burns. Hugo commented that he would recognize such burns because he had seen five or six cases of suicide from gunshot wounds where definite indications of powder burns were present.

When the agent had finished with his photographs, he took samples of the hair that surrounded the bullet wounds on both sides of Francis' head. These would be analyzed, to determine if there was any evidence of the hair having been singed or burned. Next, he catalogued the clothing and personal effects of all the victims.

Helen Jenkins had been wearing brown pants, a denim coat, and an olive wool sweater over a red polka dot blouse. There were bloodstains on the front and back of the sweater and blouse, and a great deal of blood on both the right and left shoulders. Vogel also noted that her blouse and long underwear appeared to be torn around their collars, "as if the body had been dragged by grappling the clothing in this area."

Frank Jenkins had worn a denim coat, khaki pants, a brown shirt, suspenders, and white work gloves. Blood stains appeared on the shoulders of the upper garments, and on the front of the left side of the pants. Among the items found in Jenkins' pockets was a watch that had stopped at 9:46 o'clock. Other items included a .22 automatic bullet, one .22 long rifle bullet, a jackknife, and some nails and safety pins.

Vogel noted that Joy Brittell had worn khaki pants, a wool shirt, and long underwear. Bloodstains appeared on the right side of the pants, the right rear pocket, and around the waistline. More blood appeared around the shoulder areas of his shirt and long underwear, both front and back. In one pants pocket a ring containing ten keys had been found; the agent noted that these appeared to be identical to the keys recovered by Mayfield at the Jenkins' cabin on Little Willow Creek. The other pocket contained four miscellaneous rifle cartridges and a jackknife.

All of Dick Francis' clothing, Vogel recorded, was "badly worn." He noted that a quantity of blood appeared on the left leg of his trousers, particularly around the left thigh. In the left hip pocket, two gloves had been found; the right-handed glove was of rubber and canvas composition, with blood flecks appearing at the wrist line. The left-handed glove was made of white canvas only, and displayed "a quantity of blood on the left index finger." More blood was found on both straps of his suspenders, as well as on the right sleeve of his long underwear. In addition to the gloves, Francis' pockets had contained four miscellaneous rifle cartridges, a can of snuff, and a watch that had stopped at 4:06 o'clock.

When the FBI agent had finished for the day, he probably saw the October fifth issue of the *Anchorage Times* that carried an article on the front page entitled, "Brother Searches For Killer Of Francis." The article described Isaac Francis' quest for information about his brother's death and included remarks about the FBI investigation: "Meanwhile, the federal investigation of the heinous crimes continued in Anchorage with R.C. Vogel, special agent for the FBI, working quietly. Mr. Vogel declined to make any comment on the case."

————

While Vogel was busy in Anchorage, John Clarke had apparently made some decisions in Talkeetna. There is no way of knowing whether he actively offered his Ramsdyke mining ground for sale, or if he was approached with an offer, but on October 6 he signed a warranty deed that transferred ownership of his twelve Norma placer claims on Ramsdyke Creek to two men named Durand and Campbell. The deed listed each claim and included the Quartz Creek water right. It also included the cabin there, together with its contents, along with the pieces of mining equipment that Clarke had accumulated the previous summer. Clarke was paid $200 for the property covered in the deed, and at 4:30 on the afternoon of the sixth, Durand walked over to Ben Mayfield's office and recorded the document.

————

On the same day, Agent Vogel and Deputy U.S. Marshal Grover Triber boarded the Alaska Railroad in Anchorage and left town, bound for Seward. It was probably a restful ride that provided both men with the time to talk. Although Vogel hoped to spend some time conferring with the U.S. Attorney in Seward, the men learned upon their arrival that Kehoe had been called to Valdez for a court hearing. While Vogel weighed his next move, he was contacted in Seward by L.V. Ray, the attorney who had represented Frank Jenkins during one of his court disputes. The agent agreed to meet with him.

Ray told Vogel that he had represented Frank Jenkins in a mining case during the early 1930s, and had met Mrs. Jenkins at that time. She seemed "somewhat demented," he said. He thought it probable that Helen Jenkins was the one really responsible for all the trouble that existed between Jenkins and Dick Francis. Ray also told the agent about the episode that had resulted in Frank Jenkins' conviction for unlawful possession of beaver pelts.

The elderly attorney told Vogel that he had discussed the recent killings with a judge from Fairbanks, and both had agreed that it might be worthwhile to investigate the activities of two men, one of whom currently resided somewhere in the Talkeetna area. These two individuals had once been suspected of involvement in a triple murder case in Alaska around 1915, Ray said, but no evidence was ever obtained against them and the bodies of the victims had never been recovered. He had also talked with a deputy marshal in Anchorage who had advised Ray that if he were investigating the Talkeetna case, he would immediately arrest two particular individuals. Unfortunately, Ray could not recall their names.

It's not clear just how long the FBI agent had intended to spend with Kehoe in Seward, or if he even intended to wait there for his return. His next move, however, determined that decision for him. He was down at the steamship docks and studying the passenger records for arrivals and departures, when he learned that John Clarke had purchased a first class ticket on the *SS ALASKA* that was scheduled to sail for Seattle from Seward on October 7. That was tomorrow. Vogel booked passage for himself on the same boat.

Vogel immediately put together a wire that he sent to Attorney Kehoe in Valdez. He included comments about the investigation he had conducted thus far and advised Kehoe that he felt suspicion pointed to John Clarke because several discrepancies had surfaced in his statements. He ended it by inquiring if Kehoe wanted Vogel to detain Clarke at Seward, pending further investigation. He also advised that he had booked passage south on the next day's boat.

Attorney Kehoe responded by telegraph and said that he would meet Vogel's boat when it stopped at Valdez. They could discuss the matter at that time, he said. For now, he did not desire anyone to be held at Seward.

Late the next day, Vogel boarded the Alaska Steamship Company's *SS ALASKA*, a 350-foot steamer that could accommodate over 300 passengers. The boat was probably crowded on this particular day, because now was the time of year when a great many miners, fishermen, and other seasonal workers left the country because their months of opportunity had ended, and winter would soon arrive in the north. Several hours later, the steamship made its way through Prince William Sound to Valdez, a port surrounded by the stunning, rugged beauty of the Chugach Mountains and nearby glaciers. When the ship docked, Vogel stepped into the cold ocean air and left the boat to find Kehoe.

How much time the men had to talk while the boat paused at Valdez is vague, but the two met and discussed the case. Kehoe gave Vogel a lengthy report he had written about his trip to Cache Creek country, the searches, and the delivery of the bodies to Anchorage. He also turned over fingerprint impressions he had made of Jenkins, Brittell, and Francis, along with notes he had compiled about the killings. The subject then turned to John Clarke, and Agent Vogel

241

recounted details of his investigation, and the discrepancies he had encountered while interviewing Clarke.

Attorney Kehoe told the agent about his own experience with Clarke. In the early winter of 1938, he said, he had learned from certain sources that a man by the name of Dexter had accompanied Clarke and Thoeny into the Nelchina region that summer and had disappeared. Though Clarke did not report the disappearance, other prospectors in the area had eventually expressed concern. However, by the time he was finally notified, heavy snows and inclement weather had prevented any possibility of sending out a search party, or of otherwise investigating the matter. But he had gone to the hospital in Anchorage in January of 1939, when he learned that Clarke was hospitalized for an injury received at the Evan Jones Coal Company. When interviewed, Clarke had professed that he had no knowledge about what might have happened to the man. Since that time, Kehoe said, nothing further had been discovered about the missing man.

The two lawmen talked about Clarke and the nature of the evidence that might link him to the killings in Cache Creek country. In the end, Kehoe said he was of the opinion that there was not sufficient evidence to hold Clarke. The investigation would have to continue.

As the *SS ALASKA* made its way down the rugged coast of Alaska in a southeasterly direction, Agent Vogel probably spent the next two days dividing his time between his cabin and paperwork, and occasionally making his way around the ship. On the third day at sea, as the steamer neared the agent's home base at Juneau, Vogel heard an unexpected knock at his cabin door and opened it to find John Clarke standing in the passageway. He wanted to talk some more about the case, Clarke said.

Vogel listened as Clarke explained why he was leaving Alaska. Talkeetna was a very small village, he said, and some of the people there acted as though they suspected him of involvement in the killings. They wouldn't talk to him or otherwise associate with him. For this reason, he had decided to leave.

Clarke went on to discuss aspects of the case that were on his mind. He wanted to repeat his earlier statement that on September 11 Rocky Cummins had told him that Jenkins and Brittell had gone to Clarke's cabin for the radio the previous morning. But, he added, he wasn't telling Vogel this to throw suspicion on Rocky.

It had also occurred to him that the agent might think it odd that he had cooked food for Dick Francis' dogs in Francis' cabin. He had done this, Clarke said, because he was very fond of dogs and didn't want to see them go hungry.

Clarke talked about Francis' body, and its position when he had discovered it. There was a lot of blood on the floor around Francis' head, he said. But he had heard that several members of the search party believed that Francis had been shot somewhere outside of his cabin, and then dragged in. That couldn't be possible, he said, especially in view of the amount of blood on the floor. No bloodstains appeared anywhere else in the cabin, not even around the entrance to the cabin.

Clarke looked at Vogel and said, "Do you think that if I had anything to do with the killings that I would have said that I had seen Dick Francis on Sunday, September 10?" He went on to insist that if he had had anything to hide, or had in any way been involved with Francis' death, he certainly wouldn't have gone back to Francis' cabin like he did. And he certainly wouldn't have reported finding the body.

Agent Vogel asked Clarke about his family background, but Clarke didn't want to discuss the subject. Finally, though, he said that his parents were dead and that his brothers and sisters lived on both the East and West Coasts. No, he didn't know their addresses. When Vogel asked him where he might be contacted should it become necessary, Clarke said he would be living with his wife in Seattle. He gave the agent an address.

Sometime later, the resonant whistle of the *SS ALASKA* sounded, announcing the ship's approach to Juneau. Vogel packed his things together and made his way to the deck. He had completed his part of the field investigation and would now return to his office to prepare a lengthy report for FBI headquarters in Washington, D.C. But there was something that he needed to do right away. After the steamship was secured at the Juneau dock, Vogel stepped onto the pier in the cool, moist air of Southeastern Alaska and headed directly for the naval communications facility.

Vogel sent a telegram to the FBI office in Seattle in which he briefed agents there about his investigation. A suspect in the case, he said, was due to arrive on the *SS ALASKA* in Seattle on the morning of October 13. Prior to that time, an agent should interview Clarke's wife about the contents of two letters that Clarke had written to her in September. The interview should also inquire about the man's background, including his relatives. Vogel gave the address where Mrs. Clarke could be located, then briefly mentioned something else he'd learned about John Clarke. Mrs. Clarke, he advised, might not know about Clarke's two previous marriages.

Soon after Vogel's wire arrived in Seattle, a special agent knocked on the door of the house he'd been directed to. The record shows

243

that Mrs. Clarke was at home and agreed to talk with the agent. She had met John in late 1934, she said, when she worked as a stenographer for the Northern Pacific Railway in Pasco, Washington. At that time he was in the army and stationed in Hawaii, but he had gone to Pasco on a furlough to look at some land he wanted to buy there. In the spring of 1935, he had been granted a military transfer to Spokane and had visited her again in Pasco. They began to see each other regularly and were married in December, 1935, at Spokane.

In response to the agent's inquiries, Mrs. Clarke said that she wasn't very familiar with her husband's past life. She knew that he was born in New Brunswick, Canada, in 1903, and had migrated to the United States with his parents, who were now dead. He was an only child, but she had heard him mention that he had an uncle in New York City. No, he had never mentioned being arrested for violating any law. He certainly had never impressed her as being of the criminal type.

When asked, Mrs. Clarke told the agent that she was positive that her husband had never been married to anyone but her. He was a confirmed bachelor until he met her, she said.

She further responded that when her husband had been discharged from the army in the spring of 1938, they had moved to Seattle. That summer her husband had gone to Alaska and worked at the Evan Jones Coal Company, near Anchorage. He had been injured there in the winter and was hospitalized at Anchorage until February 9, 1939, when he had returned to Seattle.

What had he done then? the agent asked.

He had some correspondence with a man about staking some gold claims in Alaska, she said, and in March he had returned there. Sometime later, her husband had written and informed her that the arrangement with the man hadn't worked out, so he had decided to stake some claims of his own in the vicinity of Talkeetna, Alaska.

The FBI agent asked to see the two letters that Clarke had sent to her in September. She produced these, and the agent studied them. Both were postmarked at Talkeetna on the same date in September, and bore the return address of "Xan J. Clarke, Northern Hotel, Anchorage, Alaska." The first letter included birthday greetings for Norma and informed her that Clarke would be home "next month." He advised her not to write to him anymore, because the letters would miss him; he would telegram when he got to Ketchikan. He could hardly wait to see her, he said.

The record shows that the second letter was longer.

Dearest Norma,
    Received your letters, honey. I expect to be home next month.

Darling, a fellow committed suicide and evidently murdered his neighbors and I had passed by his cabin on the way to the mail station and happened to (unintelligible). (Unintelligible) investigating the whole thing. When this whole thing is over, Honey, I'll be going home and will wire you from Ketchikan to meet me at the boat. Hope you are feeling well, Honey. I'm feeling fine and do love you an awful lot Sweetheart, and I'm so anxious to see you again. Now don't you worry your pretty head about a ship strike as I'll fly out if I can't come any other way.

Love,

John.

When the Seattle agent told Mrs. Clarke that he would like to take the letters for further review, she responded that she preferred to keep them. But, she said, if it was important for the government to examine them, she would allow it. The agent left with the letters.

Three days later John Clarke appeared at the FBI office in Seattle. He said he had arrived by steamship from Alaska that same day and wanted to provide the FBI with some information about the Talkeetna investigation. He had been appointed as the supervisor of the searches conducted there and had signed certain employment expense vouchers at the request of U.S. Commissioner Ben Mayfield. These vouchers listed the time each searcher had put in and contained other statements that he could not swear were true, Clarke said.

He had also paid out $175 of his own money in connection with the searches, Clarke said, and the commissioner had told him that he had to submit a voucher to obtain reimbursement from the Territory of Alaska. He felt confident that he would eventually get his money back, but he didn't want to ever be accused of any kind of graft or of "padding the payroll" because he had signed the expense vouchers.

Clarke complained that members of the search parties had accused him of being responsible for the mass murder. He also complained that the commissioner at Talkeetna had not arrived at the scene of the killings until three days had passed after he, Clarke, had reported the death of one of the victims.

The agents listened to Clarke and took notes about his concerns but informed him that the FBI had no jurisdiction over the search parties or the procedures that had been used. Any complaints, they told him, should be communicated to the governor of the Territory of Alaska.

Agent Vogel's days in Juneau were dominated by components of the Cache Creek country investigation. He drew up statistical profiles of the victims, and those of the two men that he felt bore scrutiny. After recording John Clarke's age, weight, height, and known background, he noted that he was married and had been divorced from two other marriages. Identifying marks included a four-inch scar that ran along his right jaw, from the ear to the chin; another four-inch scar traveled the left jaw in the same manner. A one-inch scar lay under his right eye, and another above. His left index finger was amputated.

The other possible suspect was Larry "Rocky" Cummins, a miner who was around 55 to 60 years of age, 6 feet, 6 inches in height, and weighed 150 pounds. He was single, an American citizen, and his hair was gray. He added that Cummins was "an ex-Army man, and at one time is believed to have been engaged in bootlegging around Ketchikan, Alaska."

The agent communicated with other FBI divisions, instructing them to trace the ownership of the revolver found in Francis' hand, the broken rifle found in Wonder Gulch, and the .22 rifle observed in Clarke's cabin. He wanted all of the armed forces to be queried to determine if Clarke's .45 pistol, marked "U.S. Property," had been stolen.

Vogel compiled a reference list of all the evidence that he had sent off to Washington, D.C. for analysis. Another record was made of the discrepancies observed in Clarke's testimony, including his denial that he had ever owned a rifle; his denial that he had been the first one to point out the footprints in Wonder Gulch; the different routes he said he had traveled to the Jenkins' camp following his discovery of Francis; and his statements that conflicted with those made by Cummins.

As a part of this record, Vogel also commented that he found it odd that Dick Francis would borrow up to eight cans of tobacco from Clarke, all at one time. And that Clarke had declined Francis' lunch invitation on September 10 and had instead eaten flapjacks at the claims he said he was working that day. Vogel added that Clarke had been the one to discover the bodies of all three men.

He began to assemble a report that incorporated the massive amount of information, details, and observations he had collected, and its composition probably consumed the major part of his work days. Updates and newly emerging data demanded his attention, too. Ben Mayfield had written to advise the agent that he had located Bob Meade in Fairbanks. He also indicated that J.G. Thoeny had left Anchorage for the states sometime in 1938. Further, Frank Huffman had found another piece of gun stock near the place where Jenkins and Brittell had been found in Wonder Gulch. He would forward it to Vogel as soon as it reached him from Little Willow Creek, Mayfield advised.

Deputy U.S. Marshal Triber advised Vogel that he had interviewed

Ed Carlson, who told Triber that he had burned some of Francis' old clothing, and had removed certain things from the cabin. In Juneau, the agent added new data to old, and began a long list of investigative chores that needed to be tackled.

Vogel wanted to locate Ken Brittell to see if he had information of value, particularly about Frank Jenkins' firearms. He wanted to know if Jenkins had owned a .35 Remington automatic or slide action rifle that would accommodate the Remington cartridges found on the table in his cabin. Might the rifle stock sliver found near Mrs. Jenkins' body have originated from a still-missing rifle of this description?

The agent wanted interviews with as many members of the two search parties as possible, and in-depth interviews with Bob Meade, John Hill, and Ed Carlson, among others. He wanted to follow up on the suspicious character observed at Indian, Alaska, and the men suspected of involvement in the triple murder case so many years before. The list went on and on, and included the necessity for more information about J.G. Thoeny, who had allegedly given Clarke two firearms and accompanied him to the Nelchina area in 1938.

But Vogel's major focus centered on his report, which would serve as an important blueprint for any subsequent investigation performed by the FBI.

———

Around the time that Agent Vogel had departed Anchorage for Seward, the *Anchorage Daily Times* had printed a small article on its front page entitled, "Silence Surrounds G-Man Move." It reported that Vogel "continued his silence on the investigations, but unofficial reports from Cache Creek and other points indicate that many new and untold angles to the case have been uncovered...." The article ended with a statement that might indicate that law enforcement officers had pressed the newspaper to temper its coverage of the multiple killings:

In the interest of solving the mystery surrounding the four deaths, the Anchorage Times has pledged its cooperation with law enforcement agencies and will refrain from publicizing (details) of the crimes that might impede the investigations. This stand was taken in the belief that readers would prefer to have investigators operate with a free hand.

Now, while Vogel labored at his report in Juneau, the newspaper printed a notice that Dick Francis would be buried in Anchorage's cemetery on October 18. Situated at the center of the front page of the newspaper, the small article noted that services would be held at the Carlquist-Menzel funeral parlor at two o'clock. It went on to report that Mr. and Mrs. F.W. Jenkins would be buried in Anchorage later on in the week, and that Joy Brittell's body would remain interred in Anchorage until the spring, when Ken Brittell could accompany his brother's remains to the family's place of residence Outside.

The next day the paper reported that Francis' funeral arrangements had been canceled because a Masonic lodge in Oroville, California, had wired its affiliate in Anchorage, requesting that Masonic rites and burial be performed for Francis. New funeral plans for the miner were pending, the newspaper said.

On October 20, at two o'clock, funeral services arranged by Ben Mayfield were performed for Frank and Helen Jenkins at the Carlquist funeral chapel. Burial services, also arranged by Mayfield, were carried out at Anchorage's only cemetery. There, forty days after their brutal murders, the loyal couple was quietly laid to rest in the cold, still earth of the peaceful cemetery.

The following day an eloquent statement, composed by an anonymous author, appeared on the front page of the *Anchorage Daily Times*. Expressing both lament and allegation, the piece probably spoke for all Alaskans who cared about law and order in the north.

AN OPEN LETTER

Every evening from our local broadcasting station we hear announced the number of days that have passed since the Cache Creek murders were committed and are reminded that no arrests have been made. The announcer could just as well recall to our attention the killings near Moose Point, in the upper Talkeetna section, here in or near our own city, in the Upper Chickaloon district and too many other places to mention where murders have been committed and practically no investigations made by our officials.

Gone is the time when the miner can safely live in the hills and work his ground and leave his poke of gold or platinum dust on the shelf in his tent or cabin, or the operators of the larger camps send their cleanups down river, over the hills, or across the tundra to the nearest post office unguarded. Petty stealing of food supplies has been replaced by wholesale murder, and unless some drastic action is taken,

Alaska will no longer be a place where men will dare to go out into the hills to prospect, trap and mine, as, of all places within the confines of the United States, Alaska has become the safest place in which to commit murder. Why is such a thing possible?

The system, or rather, lack of system, of our present law enforcement setup is such that outside of our incorporated towns and cities there are no trained criminal investigators whose work it is to immediately undertake the investigations of reported crimes excepting that the Federal Bureau of Investigation has stationed an agent at Juneau and the Alaska Game Commission has its Wild Life Agents, a very fine body of capable men, handle the violations of the Game Laws. It is beyond all comprehension, but nevertheless true that were John Doe to come to Anchorage, or any of our other Alaskan cities, and report that Bill Smith has killed a spruce hen, a mink or a moose, illegally, three hundred miles away, within a few short hours some 15 well-trained, equipped and capable men, could, without waiting to receive authority from anyone, descend upon Bill Smith in planes kept waiting during the open season, or dog teams kept the year around and the chances are about 10 to one that Bill Smith would answer to one of our courts for his crime.

But should John Doe's report be to the effect that Bill Smith had killed 10 men the story is startlingly different. There is not one single officer within the whole Territory of Alaska whose duty it would be to undertake an investigation.

We are all more or less acquainted with the history of the recent Cache Creek murders. Many wonder why and how such bungling could take place. The United States Commissioner is a lesser U.S. judge and not an investigating officer. The Commissioner at Talkeetna, a capable man, knew the above stated facts and therefore did all within his power to investigate the reported crimes and I would in no way criticize him for his efforts to solve these awful crimes, but he is not a trained criminal investigator and even should he have found evidence which led him to strongly suspect that some party

> there was guilty of the crimes, there was little, if anything, he could do about it.

The letter went on to review the authority and duties of other law enforcement officers in Alaska, and observed that U.S. marshals were just "service officers" that couldn't investigate remote murders without consent from their superiors. More important, they needed the authority to spend any money that the investigation might require. The author asserted that by the time evidence could be transmitted to officials in Washington, D.C., to convince them that expenditures were necessary, "the snow would have covered Smith's 10 victims." The letter argued that U.S. marshals were not trained criminal investigators either, and had, for the most part, acquired their jobs "as rewards for being in good standing with the political party then in power...."

As for the district attorney, the author said, here again the position required no criminal investigation skills, and provided no funds with which to investigate reported crimes. Even if the attorney should spend his own money in such an endeavor, the officer stood "a good chance of not being reimbursed, unless he has previously received authorization covering the same."

The statement then made an impassioned tribute to Dick Francis.

> Those of us who knew Dick Francis over a long period of years, knew, from the first, that he could not have been capable of committing such horrible crimes. He was a quiet, honorable, peaceful, kind, hard-working miner. When the facts of these crimes became known it was proved, beyond a question of a doubt, that Dick's otherwise spotless good name had been outrageously and unjustly defamed. Ignorance, inefficiency, indifference, cowardice, or a combination of all of these weaknesses, is damnable and unforgivable.

The statement concluded that:

> All of the above stated facts plainly show us that if Alaska is to enjoy its rightful share of peace and safety, we must have trained criminal investigators whose duty it will be to immediately investigate reported crimes. At the present time there is no provision for such a force.

250

the o'donnell interviews

On Sunday, October 22, six weeks to the day after
his life had been ended by two gunshots to the head, Dick Francis
was memorialized at the Masonic Temple in Anchorage. Known for
its creed, "Love your fellow man—Lend a helping hand," the Masonic organization had arranged for six of its members to serve as
pall bearers. Other members performed the burial service at the cemetery on that cold day. The miner's final resting place was in the
Territory of Alaska, the country he loved.

Soon, snow fell on his grave.

The day before, the *Anchorage Times* had wired the Director of
the FBI once more:

RESIDENTS HERE AND CACHE CREEK DISTRICT FEAR
INVESTIGATION FOUR MURDERS ABANDONED STOP
TENSION STILL HIGH MANY CARRYING ARMS STOP FBI
AGENT VOGEL INVESTIGATED DEPARTED MADE NO
STATEMENT STOP APPRECIATE ANYTHING YOU CAN
SAY ON PROGRESS OR PROBLEMS INVOLVED THANKS.

J. Edgar Hoover replied the same day: "FBI has not completed its
investigation four murders mentioned and Mister Vogel is continuing
this investigation but no statement concerning this matter will be
made until investigation completed."

On the same day Agent Vogel finished his report in Juneau and
prepared for its distribution to Washington, D.C. and other divisions
of the FBI. It was sixty-seven single-spaced pages in length.

On October 26, Agent Vogel shipped two more pieces of evidence to Washington, D.C. for analysis. They were two rifle stock
slivers, eight inches and two inches in length, one of which had
recently been discovered in Wonder Gulch by Frank Huffman.

As October slipped away, winter settled fully on the north country. Absent the dynamic of rushing creeks and rivers and the calls of summer songbirds and waterfowl, an aura of quiet fell on the Susitna River Valley. Waterways not shallow enough to have already frozen, moved leadenly and with a hushed tenor, burdened with a heavy skim of slush ice. As the thick, glinting ice clusters moved languidly along northern gravelbars, sandbars and riverbanks, they produced a soft, whispery hiss, a lulling prelude to the months of darkness ahead. Great stands of birch stood barren, and dark, sinewy spruce stood frosted with light snow. Only the raucous cry of a magpie, the bold call of a night-black raven, or busy tracks in the snow gave random and distinct indications that life went on.

In Talkeetna it was a pleasant time. A season's hard work was completed and sore muscles could rest. News and stories from various parts of the mining district were passed around, and at local roadhouses there was new gold dust for drinks and a good meal that you didn't have to cook yourself. But the reality of the terrible killings in Cache Creek country hovered pervasively about the community and remained an inescapable topic of conversation.

On November 2, Agent Vogel wrote a report that contained updated information. He noted that he had shipped the two Wonder Gulch rifle stock slivers to Washington, D.C. for fingerprint analysis and tests for the presence of blood. He had received a communication from Ben Mayfield indicating that John Clarke had been seen in Girdwood, Alaska, during the summer of 1938. He had also been seen in Anchorage the following winter, at which time he had been observed in possession of a .45 Colt pistol and a .38 calibre weapon.

Vogel reported that he had sent Helen Jenkins' diary to Washington, D.C. to see if the handwriting was consistent throughout the journal. He asked that all bureau records be searched to determine if J.G. Thoeny had a criminal record. He noted that someone in Lincoln, Nebraska, had phoned the FBI's Omaha office to report that a teacher named McClanahan, in a town called Otoe, "knew who the killer was."

Vogel wanted to know the amount of gold that Frank Jenkins had disposed of at the U.S. Assay Office in 1938, and whether he had sold any there in 1939. He wanted to know if, true to rumor, Jenkins' gold could be distinguished from that taken from other creeks. He wanted Clarke to be interviewed about the .38 calibre revolver seen in his possession in 1938.

Along with his report, the agent sent a letter to J. Edgar Hoover, requesting that all bureau records be searched for any trace of information about J.G. Thoeny. He remarked that the current data he had to work with was scant: the man was said to be about 55 years of age and was allegedly from New Mexico or Arizona.

In early November, J. Edgar Hoover sent a laboratory report to Vogel that contained the results of the examinations conducted on the evidence submitted earlier. The hair samples taken near Francis' head wounds showed no indication of having been burned, singed, or charred. No gun powder particles had been detected either, but the laboratory technician remarked that the embalming and other treatment of the body may have had some affect on the test results.

No blood was found on the broken rifle stock found in Wonder Gulch, the rifle stock sliver found near Mrs. Jenkins, or the jack-knives found in the pockets of Frank Jenkins and Joy Brittell. But human blood was found on the revolver found in Francis' hand, and the moosehide strip found in Francis' cabin. The strip of canvas taken from the homemade packboard had "given a reaction indicating the presence of blood," and, though the test results weren't conclusive, the technician noted that it was reasonable to assume that the specimen was stained with human blood.

The report noted that a powder residue was found in the barrel of the .38 revolver found in Francis' hand. The rifle stock sliver found near Mrs. Jenkins' body had been compared with those found in Wonder Gulch and was positively identified as having originated from a different rifle altogether, possibly a Remington of some sort.

On November 4, Agent Vogel wrote to U.S. Attorney Kehoe and requested the list of items removed from the pockets of Jenkins and Brittell. It had occurred to him, he said, that the keys reported to have been removed from Brittell's pocket may instead have come from Jenkins' pocket.

On November 10, Director Hoover advised Vogel that no record of Thoeny's prints appeared in the FBI's fingerprint files. Vogel also received an official statement that Kehoe had taken from John Clarke in January, 1939, when the attorney had interviewed him about the disappearance of John Dexter in 1938.

In the meantime, Frank Huffman was emerging as a talented sleuth. On November 13, Commissioner Mayfield forwarded a badly broken gun stock to Vogel in Juneau. Huffman, he reported, had recently found it about 135 feet below the spot where Mrs. Jenkins' body had been recovered. Vogel examined the stock and observed that it bore the trade mark "Remington." A metal piece for a rifle sling remained attached, just below the trade name.

Frank Huffman's tenure as caretaker for the Jenkins' camp now came to an end. In Talkeetna, on November 13, Raymond Jenkins was appointed as the administrator of the estate of his brother, Frank Jenkins.

———

Agent R.C. Vogel was likely overwhelmed with duties. His ability to operate the FBI's single office for the great Territory of Alaska and to simultaneously conduct a full-blown investigation of the infamous Cache Creek murders, must have been taxed to the limit.

Enter Special Agent E.M. O'Donnell—recently assigned to the case by Director Hoover. After some time spent with Vogel in Juneau, O'Donnell repeated the first leg of Vogel's own journey to the Interior by flying from Juneau to Fairbanks on November 15. Winter had settled in at the northern city, and the temperature there was 10 below zero when the agent emerged from the aircraft and walked to the small airport building.

On November 16, O'Donnell located Robert Meade at a boarding house called the DeLuxe Rooms and began his interview by asking Meade to provide him with some background information. He was 23 years of age and a native of Syracuse, New York, Meade responded, and had gone to the West Coast the previous March—first to Long Beach, California, and then to Tacoma, Washington. He stayed there for three weeks with his sister, then boarded the *SS ALASKA* for Seward in April. He had worked in Anchorage for a time and then obtained employment with the Alaska Railroad in Talkeetna until August, when the company had discharged several men. Meade described how he had obtained work at the Jenkins' camp and gave a general review of the work he had done for the month he had been employed there.

Agent O'Donnell asked him if he had observed any strangers at the camp, and Meade replied that he hadn't. The only visitor he had seen was another miner named John Clarke. The last time he had seen him there was around September 6 when the man had visited the camp at lunchtime and then stayed through the day. He was still there when Meade, Jenkins, and Brittell had returned for dinner at the end of their shift. Clarke had remained for dinner as well, he said.

O'Donnell wanted to know if the amount of gold that the Jenkinses were taking from their claims was ever discussed in Meade's presence, and he replied that the couple was "very close-mouthed" about the subject. However, on one occasion Frank Jenkins had mentioned that one of his mining pits had once yielded $9,000 in gold value. But Helen Jenkins had immediately corrected him, saying that the amount taken out had been only $6,000 worth. Other than this, Meade said, he could relate very little, as the Jenkinses didn't talk to him much and, as a consequence, he had little to say to them. The end result was that he spent most of his off-time in the bunkhouse.

When asked, Meade explained that he had left the job because Jenkins had completed his last gold clean-up on September 9, and no longer needed him. He described his last morning at the camp and his departure there at about 8 a.m. Jenkins and Brittell were just about ready to leave for the radio at that time, he said. Meade had ended up at Rocky Cummins' place and stayed there for ten or fifteen minutes, during which time he and Cummins had talked about activity at the Jenkins' camp. Yes, he had mentioned that Jenkins and Brittell were on their way to get the radio at Clarke's cabin. And yes, he admitted, he had told Cummins that he didn't like Frank Jenkins. The reason for this, he explained, was that the miner was "a very hard and difficult man to work for, and attempted to get all he could out of his men." No, he had not told Cummins that the Jenkinses had refused to give him any food for the trail, or furnish him with directions to Talkeetna.

O'Donnell asked Meade to describe the route he had then taken, and he replied that he had proceeded on a trail to the Peters Creek mining camp at Petersville, where he stopped for a few minutes to smoke some cigarettes. He then moved on down Peters Creek, and after several hours had arrived at McDonald's roadhouse, sometime between 2:45 and 3:15 in the afternoon. He remembered seeing Ira Diess there. He had remained at the roadhouse for the night, Meade said, and was up at six the next morning. He then headed on in to Talkeetna, arriving there at about two o'clock in the afternoon on September 11.

When the agent asked Meade why he hadn't remained in Talkeetna for further questioning when Mayfield had asked that he do so, he replied that he was anxious to get a permanent job for the winter. He was worried that if he waited too long he wouldn't be able to find one. Also, he had seen John Clarke on two separate occasions in Talkeetna and had heard the talk that he might have committed the killings. It made him feel afraid of Clarke, Meade said, and anxious to get out of Talkeetna.

Did Jenkins or Brittell seem to be apprehensive about their safety at any time? the agent asked. No, Meade said, but Mrs. Jenkins was always very suspicious of everyone, and on several occasions had voiced her dislike for Dick Francis.

As Agent O'Donnell neared the end of his interview, he noted that Meade was 5 feet, 9 inches tall, weighed 175 pounds, and had black hair and brown eyes. He also asked for Meade's permission to take his fingerprints, and Meade complied. Later, when O'Donnell composed his report for the case file, he noted that "Meade appeared to be a straightforward young man who answered all inquiries promptly and truthfully."

On November 21, O'Donnell talked to a deputy marshal in Fairbanks who told him that an Alaska Railroad conductor was suspicious of some men who had traveled on the train in September. They were very drunk when they boarded at Talkeetna, he said, and had left the train at Cantwell. But later, the conductor heard that Haakon Christensen had flown them back to Talkeetna on September 9. He wasn't sure just what had aroused the conductor's suspicions, the deputy said.

Someone else told O'Donnell that two University of Alaska students had been questioned about Frank Jenkins by an agent with the Internal Revenue Department. The students had worked at a mine in the Cache Creek district during the summer just past, and the agent had apparently asked if they knew how much gold Jenkins had taken out of the ground. The informant said the agency apparently suspected that the Jenkinses weren't reporting the actual amounts of gold they were mining, in order to avoid income taxes.

On November 24, O'Donnell was in Talkeetna, now a snowcovered village bordered on the west by gelid, slush-choked rivers that were heavily rimmed with ice. Smoke from wood and coal fires rose from log cabins and frame buildings, and random howls of restless malamutes and huskies carried on the air. The agent met with Ben Mayfield at his office, and the two reviewed aspects of the Cache Creek case. Mayfield told the agent that Ray Jenkins had been appointed to administer his brother's estate and was in Talkeetna, making plans to start work on the Jenkins' claims in the spring. The commissioner also said that in addition to the approximate $6,500 in gold found at the Little Willow Creek camp, the Jenkinses had about $1,500 in an account at the Bank of Alaska in Anchorage.

Mayfield was still vexed as he reported that he couldn't locate anyone who had heard Clarke's original description of his path of travel to the Jenkins' camp on September 11. At this point, he said, he was beginning to think he was the only one who had heard Clarke describe a route that differed substantially from the one he later described to Vogel.

Agent O'Donnell followed Mayfield's directions to the cabin where Ray Jenkins was staying, probably Frank and Helen's home on Talkeetna's Main Street. There, Jenkins told the agent that he had spent about three years working with his brother on claims in the Dutch Hills but had returned to California in early 1932, when an argument developed between them over seasonal profits and how they would be divided. Earlier, he said, they had drawn up a contract that gave one-half of the proceeds to him and the other half to Frank and Helen, after all the expenses were paid. When Frank and Helen had disputed this, he left Alaska because they weren't dealing fairly with him.

Later, Jenkins said, when he was sorting through his belongings in California, he couldn't find the contract that he was certain he had packed among his things. Then recently, when he was going through some of Helen's personal effects that Mayfield had collected, he found the missing contract. Now he was convinced that he had not been dealt with fairly.

But Ray Jenkins' attitude softened when the agent turned to the subject of the crimes. Yes, he had heard about the rumored wealth of his brother and sister-in-law; he had heard the stories that were circulating, but he believed them to be exaggerated or untrue. He personally knew that Frank and Helen had lost about $30,000 to bank failures in Seattle in 1933, he said. Jenkins went on to explain that whatever Frank and Helen had accumulated since that time "was the result of hard work and being very frugal." When the agent asked about other accounts the Jenkinses held, Ray Jenkins named a bank in Oregon and two in Seattle.

The two men discussed the dispute between the Jenkinses and Dick Francis, and Ray Jenkins said that he was "very much surprised" when he returned to Talkeetna to learn that a feud had arisen among the three of them. When he had worked with his brother in the early '30s neither of them had had any problems with other miners in the area. Helen was "rather quarrelsome," he said, "but no one paid much attention to her." He and his brother had always gotten along very well with Dick Francis, and it was his opinion that Dick would not bother anyone. Furthermore, he did not believe that Francis was responsible for the killings.

Did Jenkins have any opinion about who might have been involved? the agent asked. No, Ray responded, he knew of no one who might have become an enemy to Frank or Helen. He had written numerous letters to them from California for seven years, but they had never written back.

O'Donnell left the Jenkins' property and walked down the road, looking for Frank Huffman. He found him at the Talkeetna Trading Post, among the old-timers who gathered there to drink and swap stories. Recently relieved of his solitary duties as caretaker at Little Willow Creek, Huffman was probably enjoying the friendly company. The agent sat down with him and the two reviewed the information that Huffman had already reported about the case. Huffman acknowledged that he had found some important items of evidence during his term as caretaker, including his most recent discovery of the Remington gun stock. The snow must have slowly flattened the grass around the stock, he speculated, causing it to eventually become exposed. Other than that, he couldn't offer much more than the information he'd already given Mayfield.

O'Donnell asked Huffman if he had heard any of the searchers question Clarke about his activities on the day of the murders, and Huffman replied that the only one he could think of was Cal Reeve. But he had heard two other men—Ole Dahl and a man named Hanson—mention that Clarke might have had something to do with the crime.

The agent moved on to Frank Lee, who was probably enjoying some semblance of rest after another long mining season. The quiet freighter acknowledged that he had been a part of the second search party and had been the one to find Helen's body. He said that he had known Frank, Helen, and Dick Francis very well, since he had freighted supplies to all three miners for many years. He went on to describe the day of the successful search, and how he had happened to see a small part of Helen's boot in the grass.

O'Donnell asked Lee if he had any opinions about the crime. Did he have reason to suspect anyone in particular? No, Lee replied, no one other than John Clarke. When O'Donnell asked him to explain, Lee talked about the part of the day when Jenkins and Brittell had to travel past Ruby Creek on their way to get the radio at Ramsdyke. He seemed to think that the two men had probably passed Francis' camp at about the time that Clarke said he was there visiting with Dick. If that were the case, he couldn't understand how Clarke could have failed to have seen the two men in the distance. The grass is so short in that area, Lee said.

November 25 found Agent O'Donnell at the Anchorage Police Station, where he spent some time with Chief Huttle. Asked for his opinion of the case, the officer said he felt that Clarke was likely responsible for the crimes. He based this on the fact that Clarke appeared to have been involved with the disappearance of John Dexter, who had accompanied Clarke and Thoeny to the Nelchina area in 1938. Huttle indicated that Clarke's proximity to the Cache Creek killings had influenced his opinion as well.

O'Donnell looked around town for Cal Reeve. When the two met, the agent asked the miner to describe his part in the searches in the Dutch Hills. Reeve told the agent that on September 12 he had been mining near Nugget Creek, several miles from the Jenkins' camp, when he heard about Dick Francis' death from the freighter, George Weatherell. Then he heard about the search on a radio news broadcast a couple of days later and decided to go over to the Jenkins' camp to see if he could help. On his way there, Reeve said, he met up with the search party that was transporting the bodies of Jenkins, Brittell, and Francis to Petersville. He talked with the men and then went over to Rocky Cummins' camp, where he talked to Rocky and a miner named Wagner. After some discussion, Wagner decided to go to Peters Creek and tell Mayfield that he suspected Clarke of the killings; shortly thereafter, Reeve and Cummins had gone over to Dick Francis' cabin. The two had made a thorough search of the tent walls there but couldn't find any bullet holes.

The next day, Reeve recounted, he, his father, and Rocky Cummins had gone over to the Jenkins' camp where they encountered Ed Carlson and some other men. They all talked for awhile and decided to walk over to Ramsdyke Creek and search Clarke's cabin for evidence. They spent some time there, but couldn't find anything that was suspicious.

On September 18, he returned to the Jenkins' camp, Reeve said, and arrived there just about the time that Frank Lee found Helen Jenkins' body. He noticed that Clarke was standing on the top of the hill, well above the spot where the body was located. While everyone else left their positions to gather near the body, he observed, Clarke had remained on the hill. Only after the men had transferred the body to an area just outside the Jenkins' cabin had he finally come down and joined the others. At that time he had walked up to Clarke and asked, "Don't this make you nervous?" Clarke had replied, "Yes."

He continued to question Clarke, Reeve said, and asked him about his activities on September 11. Because Clarke's replies were much the same as those he had given at the coroner's inquest, Reeve said he decided to challenge him on a few points. He asked him if he didn't think it odd that the Jenkins' camp was empty when he had arrived there after finding Francis dead. Clarke had replied that he didn't. When Reeve asked him why he hadn't gone past the Jenkins' camp when returning to Francis' cabin after reporting the death at Bird Creek, Clarke had replied, "No one could hire me to go that way."

He had also questioned Clarke about the day of the killings, Reeve said, and Clarke told him that when he returned to his cabin that day he noticed that someone had been there and taken the radio. He also said that whoever it was had used his stove to make some coffee. At this point, he hadn't asked any more questions.

When O'Donnell asked if there was anything else he might want to add, Reeve said that Rocky Cummins told him that when Clarke showed up at his cabin on September 11, Rocky had wanted to report the news to Peters Creek. But Clarke had insisted on going to Bird Creek. The only other observation he had made, he said, was that Clarke had appeared to be "very nervous and disturbed" during the search for Mrs. Jenkins.

———

While Agent O'Donnell was making his rounds in Fairbanks, Talkeetna, and Anchorage, Agent Vogel was receiving more test results in Juneau. He learned that the rifle stock slivers discovered in Wonder Gulch were conclusively found to be parts of the broken Winchester stock recovered near the bodies of Jenkins and Brittell; no blood or fingerprints had been detected on either. Tests on Helen Jenkins' diary had established that all entries were made by the same person. Vogel had also received a copy of a long letter that Ken Brittell, in Squaw Harbor, had written to U.S. Attorney Kehoe, in which he gave information he thought might be helpful to the investigation.

Brittell stated that when he and his wife left Wolf Creek at the end of the season and had stopped at the Jenkins' camp, Frank told him that he had taken an estimated $5,000 to $6,000 worth of gold from his ground that summer. Brittell also related his knowledge of Jenkins' guns, saying that he knew he had two .30-30 calibre rifles— one a Winchester and the other a slide action repeater. But most of Ken Brittell's letter focused on John Clarke.

Brittell told Kehoe that he had not learned about the murders in remote Squaw Harbor until September 21, when the news was brought via a steamship that stopped there. Since that day, he said, he was "of the belief that in some manner Mr. Clarke was involved." He recounted events of the past summer, when Clarke had staked claims in such a manner as to acquire both money and other concessions from Brittell and his brother at Wolf Creek. He also said he believed that Clarke had misrepresented John Hill and Frank Sandstrom when he attempted to secure some of the concessions. Throughout this time, he said, Clarke made various statements that caused Brittell to feel that "the truth might have been carelessly handled."

Clarke had admitted to him that he had swindled the Evan Jones Coal Company out of $2,000, Brittell said. Clarke had also asked him several times if he knew how much gold Frank Jenkins was taking out of his ground. He wanted to know where the claims were located and what values had been found there. Brittell then described Clarke's strange behavior on the day that the Brittells left Wolf Creek, when he had surreptitiously followed them up Wonder Gulch.

Brittell told Kehoe about Joy's arrangement to store the radio at Clarke's cabin, until he could pack it over to the Jenkins' camp. He continued: "I want to mention at this point that Mr. Clarke is supposed to have stated that the radio was "taken from the cabin," and I know

260

that he kept his cabin securely locked at all times during his absence and it is extremely unlikely that either Mr. Jenkins or Joy would break the lock to enter as that is one point upon which they were both very particular. Yet Mr. Clarke says he was not at home on that date. Neither is Clarke one who would leave his cabin open for *anyone*."

During the summer Clarke would visit both the Jenkins and Francis camps, Brittell said. He knew of one occasion when Clarke told Francis that the Jenkinses were going to seek a permanent injunction against him. At this, Francis had allegedly made various threats against the Jenkinses. Clarke, he believed, "was one of the few people in a position to use the threats of Mr. Francis to an advantage in connection with a crime of this kind."

"Has Mr. Clarke proved that he was not at home on the day my brother and Mr. Jenkins were over after the radio and battery?" Brittell inquired.

Ken Brittell said he had heard a rumor that the Jenkinses may have withheld gold from the U.S. Mint. He doubted this. He had worked for the couple for three summers, and each of those years he had helped them to review their statements from the mint and to assist them in determining how much value per ounce they had received for their gold.

John Clarke always carried a hunting knife wherever he went this summer, Brittell told Kehoe.

During the past summer, Clarke had talked about discovering a pay streak of gold on his ground that held very good values, Brittell wrote. "Yet he sold this in Talkeetna for an extremely low price for what he purported to have found," he observed.

Agent Vogel sent off a request to the Seattle FBI office asking that John Clarke be questioned about his ownership of a hunting knife during the past summer. If he still has the knife, Vogel instructed, it "should be obtained for examination for bloodstains."

———

In Anchorage during this time, the local chamber of commerce passed a resolution that sought an increased FBI presence in Alaska. The president of the chamber sent a copy of it to the Attorney General of the United States, and remarked that "the four crimes recently committed have aroused great comment in this section and while the Chamber of Commerce in no way wishes to criticize the present law enforcement officers, it is the honest belief of this body that with the rapid expansion of the Territory and the (increased) influx of transients from the states, crimes (occur more) frequently than they did in days past."

The resolution identified the Cache Creek killings as "the most terrible and revolting crime in the history of the Territory" and characterized the nature of the killings as so brutal "that the entire mining district is shocked and disturbed, and the people of this division are horrified." One section decried the lack of a proper criminal investigation. Had an investigation by the FBI commenced immediately, the resolution asserted, "the crimes would have been solved and the guilty brought to justice."

The statement cited other "violent deaths and mysterious disappearances" in the past fifteen years, which had not received appropriate attention. Among these were the disappearance of a prospector from his mining claim after his cabin was blown to bits; the disappearance of another prospector who had vanished while prospecting; the disappearance, under suspicious circumstances, of John Dexter; the death of an Indian in a trapping dispute; and another death believed to be related to the same dispute. The resolution added that "these are only a few of the crimes that come readily to mind."

The chamber concluded by urging "that in the interest of justice and better law enforcement, an agent representing the FBI be stationed in this division with authority, in cooperation with the District Attorney and the Marshal, to make immediate investigations of reported capital crimes."

The group formed a committee that would urge other Alaska chambers of commerce to follow suit. As the days passed, the Pioneers of Alaska, the townspeople of Talkeetna, the American Legion, and other groups pledged to join in the campaign with petitions of support. Eventually, the widespread effort asked that an FBI agent and office be established in each of the territory's four judicial districts.

A local newspaper printed an article about the campaign, and FBI Agent O'Donnell, who was still in Anchorage, probably clipped it out and sent it to Vogel in Juneau. Then he met with Steve Barick at the Northern Hotel. When asked if he knew J.G. Thoeny, Barick said that he did. He got to know him in Anchorage, prior to his departure for the Nelchina area with Dexter and Clarke. Actually, he'd spent a considerable amount of time with him around town, because he and Thoeny both played the accordion. Thoeny had a really nice accordion, he said.

O'Donnell asked Barick if he knew where Thoeny might be, and Barick responded that he did not; the last time he'd seen him was in August of 1938. When asked to describe Thoeny, Barick said that he was about 50 years old, stood about 5 feet, 7 inches tall, and weighed about 150 pounds. He had dark brown hair, a wrinkled face, and a tanned complexion. He was of Italian nationality, he thought.

Anything else? O'Donnell asked. Anything unusual?

Barick said that Thoeny played the accordion extremely well, and was "slow-talking" in speech. When the agent prodded him some more, Barick said that a friend of his had once talked with Clarke when both were inebriated. Clarke had told his friend, he said, that Thoeny was the one who had killed Dexter.

The next day O'Donnell went to the Bank of Alaska and inquired about accounts held by the Cache Creek victims. The cashier there said that Mrs. Jenkins had maintained a checking account at the bank for the past sixteen years. When he reviewed the records, the agent observed that all the checks written on the account had been in payment for labor at the Jenkins' mine.

At the First National Bank of Anchorage, the cashier advised O'Donnell that they had no account registered to the Jenkinses, but that Dick Francis had done business there and was still indebted to the bank. He also said that the bank had sent a lease agreement to Francis that covered property located on Poorman Creek, sometime before the killings. He suggested that the agent see the bank's attorney, Warren Cuddy, for more detail. In a subsequent conversation, Cuddy told O'Donnell that he had drawn up the lease and then sent it out to Francis with Haakon Christensen in late August. But, he said, it had never been signed or returned to the bank.

On November 29, Agent O'Donnell walked the cold, snowy streets of Anchorage in search of Ed Carlson. When he found the longtime Alaskan, the two sat down for a lengthy interview. Francis' ex-partner said he had known Dick for about eighteen years and had financed the cabin at Ruby Creek. He had also loaned money to Francis from time to time and Dick had always repaid it. But Dick had borrowed about $350 from him when he was involved in the last lawsuit with Frank Jenkins, and that had not been repaid. He still had a note for the debt, Carlson said.

Francis had finally decided that the Ruby Creek claims were just not profitable, Carlson said, and had made arrangements to lease the claims at Poorman Creek. In fact, he had been in the process of preparing the ground there shortly before the killings. Carlson recounted how he had walked over and inspected the Poorman property and seen Francis' recent work for himself. For this reason, he said, he just didn't believe John Clarke's story that Francis had been working at the claims on Ruby Creek on September 10. He had checked the sluice boxes there himself, and they looked to him as though they'd been in place for a long time. He was positive that Clarke was lying about helping Dick with the boxes at Ruby Creek on that day.

O'Donnell asked him about his other activities after Francis' death, and Carlson said that he was there with Mayfield and Kehoe when the gun was removed from Dick's hand. The next day, after Francis' body had been taken away, he wanted to clean the place up. Since it was widely believed that Dick had committed suicide, Mayfield told him to go ahead. He had then burned some of Dick's old, ragged clothing in a pile outside of the cabin, and hauled water from the creek with a bucket to wash the blood from the floor of the cabin. No, he hadn't seen blood anywhere but on the floor, where Dick had lain.

Later, Mayfield had asked him to make a thorough search of the cabin and cartons there for bullet holes and bullets, Carlson said. He had done so, but couldn't find any. By that time, there was suspicion that Dick had been murdered, and for this reason he had examined the sluice boxes at Ruby and then gone over to inspect the several days of work that Dick had performed at Poorman. Everything there had the appearance of fresh operations, he said. It made no sense to him that Francis would waste any more of his time and work on the Ruby ground.

Ed Carlson seemed to have formed some strong opinions about Clarke. He told O'Donnell that he had learned that Jenkins and Brittell had staked ground at the mouth of Poorman Creek. There was a good possibility that Clarke knew that and had reasoned that Francis would be enraged by it and cause trouble. Clarke could then dispose of all three of them, making it appear to be murder and suicide, he said.

When he had finished questioning Carlson, O'Donnell asked him if he knew of any members of the search parties that might be found in Anchorage. Carlson named three, and the agent set out to find them.

He located Rudolph Bensil, who said that he had been working at the Peters Creek mine on the day that Rocky Cummins had appeared at the camp and reported Francis' death. Bensil said that Rocky appeared to be very nervous. He had that impression because Rocky, while relating the facts about the death, had torn up one of the egg cartons that was being used as a base for the coffee pot at the mine's cookshack. He tore the carton without seeming to know that he was doing so.

In response to other questions, Bensil told the agent that he had worked with John Clarke one day during the search for Helen Jenkins. He appeared to be very cool about the whole thing, Bensil said. At one point, Clarke told him that he didn't think it was of much use to look for her because the body might look like any one of the many alpine mounds of earth scattered around the hills in that area. Clarke had even suggested that they sit down instead of continuing to look for Mrs. Jenkins.

The whole time he worked with Clarke he had continually "run Jenkins down," Bensil recalled. Clarke also said he thought that Francis had murdered the Jenkinses and then committed suicide. And it was good riddance, Clarke had added, because Jenkins was the only man who could afford to keep all the claims that he had staked. Clarke had gone on to identify the number of claims that Jenkins held and to calculate the several thousand dollars it would cost to hold them. He told Bensil he found it hard to understand how such a small outfit could hold so many claims.

Bensil had one more incident to relate. He had been among the men who had brought the bodies of Jenkins and Brittell out of Wonder Gulch on Dick Francis' sled. They had eventually made their way to Francis' camp, where they were instructed to add Francis' body to the sled. They were on the trail above Dick's cabin, he said, and when they started to leave the sled to go down to the cabin, Clarke announced that he wouldn't stay alone with the dogs. He told them he was afraid that they would run away. So, a member of the search party had to stay with him, Bensil said. He remembered this incident because he thought it was unusual; it seemed to him that Clarke appeared to be afraid to stay alone with the bodies.

The agent also located James Connors and James Bishop, partners who had been working on claims near Peters Creek when Ben Mayfield asked them for help with the first search. They had searched in an area to the west of Clarke, Connors said, but the weather had turned so bad that they couldn't see and were forced to go to a lower level. It was here that they learned that Clarke had discovered the bodies of Jenkins and Brittell. They hadn't even heard Clarke's gun shots.

O'Donnell asked the men if they had noticed anything out of the ordinary during the search, and Connors said that the only thing he thought unusual was that Francis' Ruby Creek ground looked as though it hadn't been worked for some time; the diggings there did not appear to be fresh and the sluice boxes looked as though they had been in place for a considerable length of time. Connors also said that he spent some time searching for bullets and bullet holes in Francis' cabin. He examined all of the boxes and cartons there too, but could find no signs of either.

Agent O'Donnell kept on the move that day, and next talked to Deputy U.S. Marshal Triber, who reported that he had been unable to learn anything more about the man who had acted suspiciously in Indian, Alaska. The agent then visited John Hill's home in Anchorage, but his wife told O'Donnell that Hill was working at a mine north of Anchorage and wouldn't return until after Christmas.

The agent did locate the retired deputy marshal who told Seward attorney L.V. Ray that he suspected two individuals of involvement in the crime. The elderly man confirmed that he had discussed the case with Ray, but said that he suspected only one person. When he gave the name, O'Donnell told him that the man had positively been identified as having been in Talkeetna at the time of the killings.

The next day the agent followed up on a suggestion made by Cal Reeve and visited Ed Johanson at his home in Anchorage. The co-owner of the Bird Creek mine said he remembered that Clarke and Cummins had shown up at the mine about 10:30 in the morning. He hadn't talked to them as much as his brother had, but he remembered that Clarke was wearing a holster with a .45 pistol in it. The two men stayed for lunch, and while they were eating Clarke mentioned that he was going to Seattle. Johanson had asked him where he stayed there, and Clarke had replied, "I would hate to tell you." There was little more he could add to what his brother had told Vogel, he said.

At some point O'Donnell talked to a prospector who had been on the same steamship that Clarke, Thoeny, and Dexter had traveled on to Alaska in July, 1938. They had all traveled steerage, he said, and that's where he'd met them. Clarke appeared to be the leader of the group because he did most of the talking. He was telling the other two "just what the situation and the prospects were" in Alaska. Thoeny had talked about being a miner somewhere in the Southwest. He had "a very excellent accordion" and played it well, the prospector recalled. No, they hadn't had any firearms that he had seen.

When the ship arrived at Seward they had parted company, the prospector said. But, about three days later, he met Thoeny on the street in Anchorage. Thoeny told him then that he, Clarke, and Dexter were all set to go mining. Somewhere else he heard that Dexter was financing their prospecting trip. He didn't see Thoeny again until middle or late August, when he met him on the street again in Anchorage. This time Thoeny told him that the mining venture had not been successful. When the prospector asked him about Clarke and Dexter, Thoeny told him that he and Clarke had returned to Anchorage, but that Dexter had remained in the Nelchina area to look for work.

Thoeny seemed to be very nervous, the prospector recalled. He had indicated that he was very anxious to leave Alaska but was having financial problems. Clarke had promised to pay Thoeny's bill at the Northern Hotel but had left Anchorage without doing so. Later, the prospector heard that Thoeny had sent a wire to someone in the states, asking for funds to pay his bills and for boat passage back Outside. There was little else he could tell the agent, he said.

December arrived, dark and cold and snowy. The heart of winter beat sluggishly now. Even the dull glint of icicles seemed to pale in the reduced periods of daylight, as the landscape assumed profiles in black and white. On the eastern boundary of Anchorage the Chugach Mountains sprawled in cold, massive dignity, a stately backdrop for the activity in the growing town along the banks of Cook Inlet, where the temperature now averaged about 15 degrees.

On December 8, the U.S. Marshal's office advised Agent O'Donnell that a miner named Al Dreese had been found dead in a cabin located several miles northeast of Chickaloon, in the Nelchina mining district. The circumstances of his death were as yet undetermined, the official said, but he thought it worthy of mention because Dreese was the individual who had first reported the disappearance of John Dexter in 1938. The official also provided O'Donnell with a physical description for Dexter, recently obtained from the California Driver's License Bureau. He was 26 years of age in 1938, 5 feet, 8 inches tall, weighed 160 pounds, and had blue eyes and light brown hair. Dexter also had tattoo marks of a skull and the number thirteen located above one elbow, the report said.

On December 11, O'Donnell tracked down a man in Anchorage who prospected and mined in the Nelchina mining district each season. His name was George Belanger, and he said that he had a well established camp there, including a cabin, equipment, and a small tractor. The miner told the agent that he remembered Clarke, Thoeny, and Dexter, and their trip to the area in 1938. Around the eighth of July that year, he and his partners had heard an airplane land on a lake about three miles from their camp; he had gone over and consequently met Clarke and the other two men. Since it was raining at the time, he had invited all three to spend the night at his camp. They took him up on his invitation, spent the night there, and left early the next morning to set up their own camp at the lake. Before they left, he said, they asked about prospecting chances in that part of the country, and he gave them some advice about where to go. They had also borrowed two pair of rubber boots from him and his partners.

Belanger said that he didn't see them again until August 10, when he took his tractor to the lake to pick up some supplies a plane had dropped off for him. He met Clarke and Thoeny on the trail near the lake and invited them to spend another night at his camp. When he inquired about Dexter, the two men told him that the younger man had "gone down Alfred Creek" to see a miner about work.

That evening, the miner continued, the men told him they wanted to sell him what was left of their grub, so they would have a few dollars cash when they arrived in Anchorage. The next morning the men returned to their own camp, and that afternoon Belanger went over to look at the grub they had to sell. He paid them $11 for it, he said, and also told them that they should go down the Alfred Creek trail to make sure that Dexter had arrived at the miner's camp okay. Clarke had indicated that they would do that.

But, on August 13, he returned to the lake again, Belanger said, and "noticed they had taken the trail in the opposite direction from Alfred Creek." Dexter's bedding and duffle bag were still at the place where they had camped.

Several days later Al Dreese came to his place to find out when a plane might be coming in at the lake, Belanger said. While he was there they had talked, and Dreese told him that Dexter had not been seen on Alfred Creek. So, Belanger had gone over to the lake and collected Dexter's duffle and bedding to keep for him. Eventually, he said, he looked through both for an address, but could find nothing but Dexter's name in the duffle.

————

In Otoe, Nebraska, an agent interviewed Bob McClanahan, who was teaching high school there. He had gone to school with Joy Brittell in Kimball, Nebraska, McClanahan said, and they had formed a close friendship. He had worked for Frank Jenkins for a season in 1933 and knew both Frank and Helen pretty well. He went on to describe Helen's eccentricity and Frank's difficulty in getting along with people. "He antagonized people," McClanahan said. He said he didn't know John Clarke, but went on to name four or five miners that Jenkins had disputes with, Francis among them.

When the agent told McClanahan that the Omaha office had received a phone call from someone who claimed that McClanahan knew who the killer was, the school teacher shook his head. He had discussed the murder case with friends on several occasions, he said, but he had never made a statement to anyone in which he claimed to know who the killer was.

In Washington, D.C., J. Edgar Hoover wrote a letter to the Anchorage Chamber of Commerce acknowledging the group's resolution that urged an increased FBI force in Alaska. He advised the organization that he had recently assigned an additional agent to Alaska and remarked that "At such time as additional personnel is available for assignment to Alaska you may be assured that this matter will receive most careful attention."

In Juneau, Agent Vogel received word from an agent in Washington, D.C., that all of the United States armed forces had been surveyed for any record linked to the background of the .45 automatic pistol that Vogel had appropriated from Clarke. No record of loss, theft, or legal disposition had been located for that particular gun, he was informed. Furthermore, a firearm of this type had never been sold by the government as surplus property, because sales were strictly limited to officers of the services, the National Guard, and the Reserve Corps. Any firearm sold in that manner also required a signed agreement that the officer would not transfer possession to any other individual, the agent said.

Another letter, from the United States Mint, advised Vogel that "it would be impossible to determine the region from which gold was mined by examination of the gold."

Vogel also learned that a search of the FBI fingerprint files had failed to turn up any information about Clarke.

A report filed by Agent O'Donnell around this time recommended that a search be made for the rifle barrel that matched the broken Remington rifle stock found by Huffman at Little Willow Creek. Mayfield should be alerted to watch for it too, he said. Another examination of Dick Francis' cabin should be made for bullets and bullet holes, including a search beneath the floor boards of the cabin. O'Donnell also noted he had learned that J.G. Thoeny had once claimed to be from Albuquerque, New Mexico.

Around this time, Frank Huffman appeared at the FBI's Juneau office and sat down for a visit with Vogel. He was on his way to Seattle on the *SS ALASKA*, he said, and thought he'd let the agent know that his position as caretaker for the Jenkins' property had ended. When Vogel asked him for details about his discovery of the Remington rifle stock, Huffman told him that it hadn't been concealed but instead had the appearance of being tossed into the long grass by someone going down the trail toward the Jenkins' cabin.

Huffman informed Vogel that he had gone over to the Francis cabin again and had spent two days examining the place for bullets. He was unsuccessful, he said, and couldn't even find marks that might indicate a bullet had passed. He had also put more thought into what he could recall about the search for Helen Jenkins. He was now of the opinion that Clarke's actions were suspicious on the day Mrs. Jenkins had been found. When her body had been taken down to the Jenkins' cabin and placed on a small platform nearby, everyone had gone there to view the body except John Clarke. He had remained in the background, Huffman said, and "his eyes would travel back and forth from the platform to the spot where Mrs. Jenkins was found."

The year was now 1940, and Ray Jenkins began to perform his duties as administrator for his brother's estate. His first act was to officially record the contract agreement that he, Frank, and Helen had drawn up in 1929, when the three had agreed to act as partners on certain claims.

Jenkins was also presented with the first creditor claim to be filed against the estate and learned that Frank and Helen had indeed prepared for a permanent injunction against Dick Francis and Ed Carlson. Arthur Thompson, the Anchorage attorney who had filed the claim, testified that he had prepared a draft of an injunction on July 25, 1939. On August 29, he said, he had secured three affidavits from witnesses willing to testify that Jenkins' dam and ditch had been filled with tailings that summer. Thompson's claim for his work amounted to $75 and was approved by Ben Mayfield, now also acting as probate judge.

On January 18, 1940, Ray Jenkins filed an Inventory and Appraisement for Frank's estate which included five lots in the Talkeetna townsite valued at a total of $800, and gold dust valued at $6,500. Forty-five mining claims were listed and valued at a total of $17,000.

Deposits made by the Jenkinses in four different Seattle financial institutions totaled more than $12,000, and hydraulic equipment on the mining claims was assessed at $2,000. A 40 Diesel Caterpillar, Fordson tractor, portable saw mill, sleds, oil drums, planer, drill press, vise, anvil, forge, chains, and miscellaneous tools rounded out the inventory. Significantly, perhaps even poignantly, Frank and Helen's personal belongings and household goods were valued at $100. Among these was a phonograph, perhaps a special luxury in Helen's spare life. The total appraised value of the estate came to $41,209.26.

———

Special Agent O'Donnell had resumed his investigation in Anchorage on January 15, at which time the temperature there registered at 6 below zero. Because January temperatures in Southcentral Alaska were more commonly expected to drop to much lower levels, this particular temperance gave some ease to Alaskans who had braced themselves for the coldest and bleakest month of the year. Daylight graced the land for only half a day now, but soon that would begin to change, and everyone knew it.

Birch trees, graceful but taut in the cold, mingled with black spruce throughout the town, casting pale shadows on the snow, while chickadees and tiny redpoll finches flitted among them to forage for seeds. Smoke and vapor from heated structures in Anchorage's more populated area moved visibly upward, and exhaust fumes from chunky, ponderous automobiles trailed in ethereal paths along narrow, icy roads.

As his wife had predicted, John Hill was back in Anchorage after the holidays. O'Donnell inquired about his past season in the Dutch Hills, and Hill told him about working Belle McDonald's ground at the higher reaches of Willow Creek, as well as working with John Clarke at Ramsdyke Creek. The upper Willow Creek claims were just a quarter mile from Dick Francis' Ruby Creek camp, he said, and he and his stepson had seen Dick on several occasions, even visiting each other's camp now and then. The agent asked if he was aware of the bad feelings between Francis and Jenkins, and Hill said he was. But, he added, he was of the opinion that those feelings were not so severe as to result in either of them causing the other any bodily harm.

Hill went on to describe his experience with Clarke, when he and his stepson had spent two weeks digging the mile-long ditch, only to be deceived by Clarke's misrepresentation of their agreement. At that point, he said, he "did not want to have anything more to do with him," and he and Frank Sandstrom had returned to upper Willow Creek.

Among other things, Hill told O'Donnell that during the summer Clarke had asked him, "Do you suppose the Jenkins have their gold cached in the old camp?" Curiously, the prospector did not mention that after leaving Clarke's camp he and Sandstrom had discovered that both their guns were packed with mud and rocks. But he did mention that on the day he and Sandstrom prepared to leave the Dutch Hills for Talkeetna, Clarke had invited him to spend the rest of the season at his Ramsdyke camp because "he had plenty of food" there. Hill said he told Clarke he didn't care to, but now told O'Donnell that his real reason for declining was that he was afraid of Clarke.

No, he hadn't seen any other strangers in that part of the Dutch Hills during his time there; he had seen only the Jenkinses, Joy Brittell,

Dick Francis, and Clarke. He'd stopped at Dick's camp when they departed the Dutch Hills, and collected Francis' grocery order and some gold dust to pay for it. At that time, he said, he'd told Dick to be "very careful of his dealings with Clarke," because he didn't think Clarke was a man to be trusted.

On January 20, the agent was contacted by Dr. Walkowski, who wanted to discuss Dick Francis' autopsy once more. When the two met and reviewed the report, the doctor told O'Donnell he had definitely determined that "the bullets transversed two sections of the brain, either one of which could cause instant death." It was his opinion, he said, that "it would be impossible for both wounds to have been inflicted by Francis himself." He stood by his opinion that the shots had entered the left side of Francis' head and exited the right side.

On the same day, O'Donnell contacted the U.S. Signal Corps to find out if it had had any success in locating a telegram sent by J.G. Thoeny during August, 1938. An agency representative responded that they had made a search of their records for that month but had found no evidence of a wire sent to or received by Thoeny.

On February 2, John Clarke wrote a letter to Commissioner Ben Mayfield. He wanted to know what had become of his .45 caliber pistol. This particular firearm was not a stolen weapon, Clarke declared, but was sold by the U.S. Army because it was unserviceable. He wanted to know when he would recover his gun.

On February 5, FBI Director Hoover sent a laboratory report to Agent Vogel in Juneau. The report focused on the photographs of Dick Francis' head wounds the agent had taken at the undertaker's parlor in Anchorage. It had not been possible to determine which of the bullet holes were entrance or exit holes from the photos, the advisory said, because the wounds portrayed there were "not consistent in the detail upon which such determinations are made." The inconsistencies did not allow for a reliable conclusion, Vogel was told.

In the meantime, Agent O'Donnell continued with his work. In mid-February, he turned up in Fairbanks, where the temperature registered at 8 below zero. He visited the U.S. marshal's office to inquire about the men who had been suspected of involvement in a triple murder case around 1915. But he eliminated the individuals from any possible connection with the Cache Creek case when he learned that one of them had been dead for several years, and another was very old and living in Juneau.

On February 25, O'Donnell visited the University of Alaska in Fairbanks, where he located the two students who had worked for wages in the Dutch Hills during the summer of 1939. One told the agent that he had worked at Mike Trepte's mine at Dutch Creek, on the north side of the hills, and had seen Dick Francis on only one occasion—when he had traveled in to the Trepte camp in the spring. The other told a similar story. Both, however, stated that they were unaware of the feud between Francis and Jenkins. Neither had seen any strangers in the Dutch Hills during their time there.

As the days passed into March, Vogel's Juneau office continued to receive information. Commissioner Mayfield reported that while he was engaged in taking the census for his district, he had encountered a woman who had related an incident to him involving John Clarke. She had been working in Anchorage in early 1939, while living at the Inlet Hotel. Clarke was staying at the same hotel, and he was dating a girl who lived in the room next to hers. One night, the young woman had come to her room "in a very frightened condition," and told her that Clarke was threatening her. The woman had spent the rest of the night with her in her room, she said, and after that would not go anywhere alone.

Mayfield also informed Vogel that someone had told him that Clarke intended to return to the Cache Creek area when spring arrived and was bringing someone else along with him. However, the commissioner said, he'd also learned that someone in Talkeetna had written to Clarke and told him he shouldn't come back to the village because he was not wanted there.

On March 5, Ben Mayfield responded to Clarke's inquiry about his pistol. Among other things, he told Clarke that his .45 automatic would be returned to him "if and when the FBI authorized (Mayfield) to do so." Mayfield sent a copy of his letter along to Vogel.

On March 12, Agent Vogel informed Mayfield that there was no record of the legal disposition of the .45 pistol, or any record of it having been stolen. He suggested that if Clarke could not show legal title to the firearm, it should be forwarded to an army arsenal in Benecia, California.

Sometime in March a special agent appeared at John Clarke's residence in Seattle and said he'd like to ask him some questions. The agent noted that Clarke was not at all happy about this and "gave vent to his feelings concerning the injustice of being suspected of this crime after he had attempted to act throughout as an honest man." Eventually, though, Clarke had settled down and gone over the case again, repeating the same story he had given Vogel in Alaska. At one point he complained bitterly about Commissioner Mayfield and told the agent he was convinced the lawman suspected him because Clarke was a stranger to Talkeetna.

Clarke expressed his opinion that Francis had not committed suicide, but had been murdered. His reasoning was based on the fact that Francis' body had looked as though it had been arranged in the position he had found it. In his opinion, someone who had been shot like Francis was would have sprawled out when he fell and then dropped his weapon. But Francis was on his back, he said, with the hand-held pistol lying across his stomach.

During the interview Clarke said he felt that Rocky Cummins' actions were suspect, but added that he didn't want to make any accusations or cause any trouble. He had reasons for suspecting Rocky, one of them being that on September 11 the miner had immediately speculated to him that Francis had killed the Jenkinses and then committed suicide. Cummins had also been very jumpy and nervous after the bodies were found, Clarke said. Further, Cummins was not on good terms with Frank Jenkins because of a claim dispute between them that had occurred in the past. Finally, Rocky was the only person he knew of who was in the vicinity of the crimes at the time they occurred and who could have been able to commit the murders and get back to his cabin undetected. He didn't mean to accuse Cummins, Clarke repeated, but he did seem to be the most logical suspect in the case.

Now Clarke spoke in his own defense. He had no possible motive for killing the victims. He had never had any hard feelings toward any of them; in fact, he was on good terms with them all. He couldn't have had a robbery motive, because it was common knowledge that gold could be identified by the creek it had come from. If he was the killer, he would never have been able to dispose of any gold that had come from Jenkins' creek.

The agent asked Clarke about the hunting knife he had carried during the mining season, and Clarke became defiant. He wouldn't discuss it, he said.

The agent wouldn't let go of the subject. Finally, Clarke said he had no idea where the knife was. It could still be at his cabin at Ramsdyke Creek, or it could be lost. He told the agent that the knife didn't fit its sheath well and was always slipping out and being lost. He'd lost it so many times, he said, that he became disgusted with the effort it took to keep track of it. So he'd put it away somewhere or misplaced it or lost it. In fact, he hadn't even had the knife for several weeks prior to the killings.

When the agent continued to dwell on the subject of the hunting knife, Clarke refused to discuss it any further. Eventually, the agent noted, Clarke "resumed a hostile attitude, saying that he was being unjustly suspected and accused, and that he would not discuss this case any further."

The Seattle agent asked Clarke about the disappearance of John Dexter in the Nelchina region, and Clarke refused to discuss it as well. He had already been interviewed about that matter by the U.S. Attorney in Alaska, he said, and the facts were on file with his office. He did not want to discuss the subject again.

Toward the end of the interview, the subject turned once again to Ben Mayfield. Clarke complained that the Talkeetna commissioner had mishandled the investigation of the killings; Mayfield had conducted it so poorly, he said, that he had written a letter to the U.S. District Judge at Valdez, Alaska, in which he had detailed all of Mayfield's shortcomings. Clarke rummaged around, found a copy of his letter, and gave it to the agent.

After his interview with Clarke, the agent moved on to the U.S. Mint Service in Seattle, where he talked to the assayer in charge. He inquired about Clarke's assertion that gold could be identified by the creek where it had originated. The assayer responded that although gold characteristics varied greatly over a large area, they ran very much the same in specific areas. He went on to say that "all the gold taken out of the vicinity of Talkeetna, even though taken from different creek systems, was similar in a general way, and characteristics did not vary a great deal." It would be difficult, if not impossible, to definitely identify gold taken from the Jenkins' claims. In fact, he was familiar with the Jenkins' gold, and in his opinion it had no distinguishing characteristics.

Before he left, the agent asked that his office be contacted if any unusual gold deposits were made from the Talkeetna area.

In April, Ken and Maxine Brittell had completed the school term in the Aleutians and were in Seattle to await the birth of their first child. Sometime that month Maxine appeared at the agent's office and was interviewed. She described her summer season at Wolf Creek, and the various experiences she and the others had had with Clarke, relating much of the same information that her husband had in his letter to Attorney Kehoe. She said that no one in the vicinity of the Dutch Hills knew very much about Clarke, but he had impressed her as being "rather hot-tempered and potentially violent." Clarke was on friendly terms with Dick Francis, she said, and seemed to visit there often. He had also gone by the Jenkins' camp on occasion, and it was her impression that Clarke would later repeat what he had heard there to Francis. Mrs. Jenkins would often talk about "running Francis out of the country," she said, and it was quite possible that Clarke had repeated this "to stir Francis up."

When the subject turned to the day of the killings, Maxine said she couldn't understand how Clarke had missed seeing Frank Jenkins and Joy when they had gone for the radio. Clarke always padlocked his door when he was gone, Maxine said, and she believed that Mr. Jenkins and her brother-in-law would never have broken into the cabin if they had found it locked.

Sometime after this interview, when Maxine was visiting with her family, she learned that John Clarke had visited her mother's home in Seattle, looking for her brother, Tim Craig. Craig was not in at the time, she was told, but Clarke had asked her mother if she knew whether Tim had taken any photographs of him in the Dutch Hills the previous summer. He had left without an answer but later again tried to contact Craig. Now, she learned, her brother was uneasy about the possibility of his coming back.

The spring of 1940 was an early one in the Susitna River Valley, and for the first time in more than twenty-five years, Dick Francis and Frank and Helen Jenkins were not among the miners and prospectors who moved to Cache Creek country. As ice began to break up in the rivers, allowing random leads to open up, the soft ripple of shallow water over riverbed stones signaled an end to winter's quiet dominance. Now, the sun was high and hot and dazzling as it struck the heavy April snow pack and rebounded in skittish rays that darted about the landscape. Northbound migrations of waterfowl passed through the valley for days on end, their wild calls broadcasting an urgent excitement that carried through the air to the people below as they labored to reach their camps.

Ray Jenkins was already in at Little Willow Creek, having traveled there in late March. He wanted to put the cabin in order for the coming season and become familiar with the equipment and the general layout Frank had made of the camp. While he was organizing the cabin, he found a bank book in the name of Xan John Clarke. It had been issued by the Bank of Alaska in Anchorage and reflected deposits made during the summer of 1939. Jenkins studied the book for awhile, then set it aside to give to Ben Mayfield.

A month earlier, he had worked with Mayfield to assemble the necessary paperwork that would enable him to work the Jenkins' claims. It was urgent that the annual labor be performed on the property, or the claims would return to "open ground," resulting in a great loss to the estate. Acting as probate judge, the commissioner had issued an Order To Do Assessment Work and Operation that authorized Ray to "work the claims to the best advantage" to satisfy assessment requirements and to produce revenue for the estate.

Jenkins was also authorized to hire a work crew of four people after the first of May and to pay each person $5 per day, plus board. He was instructed to employ the crew only when mining conditions permitted and to lay off workers when the lack of water, or a similar condition, warranted such action. Jenkins himself was authorized to draw a monthly salary of $250 as supervisor of the work, and to purchase equipment and supplies "subject to the approval of the court."

Ray Jenkins was probably glad to be in the hills, removed from the immediate burden of legal paperwork that accompanied his role as estate administrator. In February another attorney, L.V. Ray of Seward, had filed a creditor's claim for $750 against Frank's estate. He had worked hard, the lawyer said, to represent Frank Jenkins during his protracted conflicts with Dick Francis in 1934, 1935, and 1936. Jenkins, however, hadn't paid him for his work during all that time. The miner had claimed that he was "hard pressed for cash," and that his mining operations had not been successful during that period. The attorney had spent his own money for travel to Anchorage for court appearances, lodging, meals, secretarial services, and court filings, he testified. Attached to Ray's claim was extensive documentation to back it up.

Ray Jenkins did what preliminary work he could at Little Willow, and in late April the third Jenkins brother, Charles, arrived from California with a friend of his named Blodgett. The two men went to work with Ray to get the equipment running, so that the snow pack could be pushed around to hasten the clearing of the ground in strategic locations. The men also worked on the water ditches, probably spreading stove ashes over some portions to encourage thawing, and clearing other areas of winter debris. Mostly they worked on the snow, scraping and plowing and moving it into big hills along the boundaries of where they would mine. The sun, direct and intense now, warmed the cleared spaces and quickened evaporation.

Soon, a couple named Stahler arrived at the camp. Ray Jenkins had hired Mrs. Stahler to cook for the crew and her husband to work in the mining pits until sometime in July.

On April 30, in Talkeetna, Ben Mayfield was in his office when a man entered and said he wanted to examine the mining claim notices and records on file there. He told the commissioner that he was especially interested in claims near those that Francis and Jenkins had held, and this led to a discussion between the two men about the killings the previous fall. The man, named Kinnett, seemed especially well informed about the killings, Mayfield noted, and went on to explain that he was a miner who represented "big-money interests."

As Mayfield chatted with Kinnett, he noticed that the man seemed unfamiliar with the different phases of mining. Nevertheless, he spent the next several days poring over the records. Sometime later, Mayfield heard that the man had left the village and made his way to Petersville.

Now the days moved into May and grew even warmer. Parka squirrels emerged from their dens, and small songbirds reappeared in the hills, their music mingling with the soft murmur of melting creeks. Now and then an eagle or a hawk patrolled the area, while winter-thin bears rooted around in the remote areas of the hills for anything they could find.

On May 20, Charles Jenkins and his friend, Blodgett, set off on foot for Petersville, probably to mail some letters. About a mile and a half from their destination, they came upon a tent near the road, and three men who sat beside it. All looked up as they approached. Various pieces of mining equipment were strewn about, along with gasoline, food, and other supplies. Two of the men were brothers, they said, and a third man gave his name as Mitchell. A talkative sort in his mid-thirties, Mitchell told Jenkins and Blodgett that he and the others intended to do some prospecting in the area.

While he talked, a fourth man emerged from the tent, whom Mitchell identified as someone named Christiansen. The tall, thin man had a scowl on his face and a rifle slung across his arm, the barrel of which he kept pointed at Jenkins and Blodgett. The two men must have shown some uneasiness, because Mitchell remarked that Christiansen was "cleaning the gun." He and the others had just arrived the day before, he added, and were organizing their outfit. Christiansen, glowering, stood silently with the rifle pointed at the men and remained that way until they continued on their way to Petersville.

By the first of June the snow was almost gone, and new leaves began to sprout from willow bushes and scattered stands of alder. Vegetation also began to send tentative shoots through the brown matted tangle that covered the hills, testing for warmth and sun and space. During this time, both the Jenkins brothers and Blodgett searched the Jenkins' camp area and Wonder Gulch for any evidence of the killings that might be visible at this time of the year—before the inevitable wild growth of foliage made that impossible. They searched several times but found nothing.

By June 11 the snow was all gone, and the men prepared to mine. Blodgett, apparently working alone, was repairing a water dam in an area about 200 feet south and 40 feet east of where Helen Jenkins had been found, when he saw the .35 caliber rifle barrel in the grass. No stock was attached to it. Mindful of Commissioner Mayfield's instructions not to disturb any evidence that might be discovered, Blodgett didn't even touch the grass that cradled the weapon.

He located a wooden stake and drove it solidly into the ground to mark the spot where the barrel rested, and went to tell the others. Ray Jenkins sent word of the find to Mayfield in Talkeetna.

Some days later, Mr. Stahler was working in the same general area and came across a two-celled flashlight containing longlife, heavy-duty batteries. Unsure of its significance, he picked it up and took it to show to the Jenkins brothers. Later, they calculated that its position had been about 150 feet south and 75 feet east of the spot where Helen had been found. The men all agreed that Mayfield should probably see it, too.

Still later, when the men were moving an outhouse to a new site, they found a small leather purse that appeared to have been thrown beneath the structure at its old location. It was soaking wet, so the men relocated it to a sheltered spot to dry out. Ray Jenkins sent another message to Talkeetna.

The commissioner was apparently tied up with matters that demanded his attention, because he did not travel to Little Willow Creek until July 12. Once there, he followed Blodgett to where the gun barrel lay and finally removed it from the plant life that had screened it until now. Old, dried grass stuck to the metal in places, and Mayfield carefully scraped it away. Upon examination, he found one cartridge in the chamber and two in the magazine, bullets which matched those found on the table in the Jenkins' cabin. He felt confident that it was Mrs. Jenkins' rifle, he told the others.

After Mayfield had wrapped the rifle barrel in newspaper and canvas, he asked the Jenkins brothers and Blodgett to join him in a thorough search of the area. The four men spent a long time there, but turned up nothing more. Finally, Mayfield gathered up the barrel, flashlight, and purse, and went back to Talkeetna.

A special FBI agent, J.D. Noble, arrived in Talkeetna on July 23, and introduced himself to Ben Mayfield as the new investigator on the case. Summer was now in full force, and wildflowers sprinkled the village with color, while the adjacent rivers flowed a strong, silty gray along dirt banks lush with greenery. With most of the population gone to Cache Creek country, Talkeetna had assumed a quiet serenity that was stirred only by the activity of local merchants and frequent transients, who moved to and from the mines to conduct business or arrange for supplies.

The two lawmen sat down in the commissioner's office, and Mayfield brought Noble up to date on the more recent developments connected with the case. The most important discovery was the rifle barrel that had been found in the area where Helen Jenkins had been murdered, he said. He told Noble it was "undoubtedly the gun which had been used in killing Mrs. Jenkins." The cartridges it contained were the same as those found in her cabin. He had recently sent the barrel to Vogel in Juneau, so that he could send it, along with the stock, to Washington, D.C. for examination.

Mayfield brought out the flashlight Stahler had found, and showed it to Noble. He was certain it belonged to Mrs. Jenkins, because it contained batteries of the type sold by Sears, Roebuck and Company, and he knew that Helen always ordered supplies of this kind from the Sears company in Seattle. It appeared to him, he said, that whoever had murdered Mrs. Jenkins had thrown it off into the brush while proceeding down the hill to the Jenkins' property.

The commissioner also mentioned that Ed Carlson had recently stopped by his office to tell him he had thought some more about the day he had cleaned the Ruby Creek cabin. Carlson now recalled a spot around the door entry area that appeared to have been scrubbed, with fresh dirt thrown over it, Mayfield said. Agent Noble took note of this and said he would talk to the miner when he went to the Dutch Hills to conduct another investigation of the death scenes.

Next, Mayfield spoke about Kinnett, who had appeared in Talkeetna in the early spring and shown an interest in the Francis and Jenkins claims. He'd aroused Mayfield's suspicions because he represented himself as a miner but didn't seem very knowledgeable about mining. Mayfield had since learned that Kinnett had gone to Ruby Creek and taken up residence in the tent-cabin where Francis' body had been found. This caused Mayfield to wonder if he might be a contact of Clarke's, and if his real purpose was to travel to the area to pick something up for him. When Ed Carlson had traveled to Ruby Creek he found the man there, Mayfield said. Kinnett departed shortly after that and returned to Talkeetna. At present, he was working as a laborer on the new federal airport project at the east side of town.

The commissioner offered a theory about one aspect of the case. Since both Jenkins and Brittell appeared to have been beaten with Francis' rifle, he thought it likely that a third party would have had to kill Francis first, to take his gun. He knew Francis well enough, Mayfield said, to know that he would never let his rifle out of his sight.

Agent Nobel went to the airport site to interview Kinnet, who said that he had been at Indian, Alaska, and had talked with one of the members of the Dutch Hills search party who told him that the Francis and Jenkins claims contained rich deposits of gold. He had also learned about details of the murders from the same man, he said. When the agent asked him if he had personally known any of the victims or John Clarke, Kinnett responded that he did not. The sole source of his knowledge had been the man who had served with the search party.

When Agent Nobel asked about his activity at Ruby Creek, Kinnett explained that he had gone there to determine the value of the ground. But the snow had not yet melted when he was there in April, he said, and it had been difficult for him to accomplish anything. When he learned that he couldn't obtain the claims he was interested in for less than $4,000, he had returned to Talkeetna.

Kinnett was asked why he had portrayed himself as someone who represented others that could finance the purchase of claims in the area, and he showed Noble a letter from a general contractor in Seattle. The agent observed that the letter asked Kinnett to acquire eight claims at Poorman Creek, near Petersville. Kinnett explained that he had notified the contractor about the $4,000 cost, at which point the man had become discouraged about making the investment. He had taken the job at the Talkeetna airport while he waited for the snow to melt in the Dutch Hills.

Agent Noble questioned the man in great detail, but finally decided he wasn't knowledgeable enough about the killings to warrant further suspicion.

The next day, the agent was approached by a longtime Talkeetna resident and prospector named Harry Berg. A hard-working individual who was well respected in the area, Berg told Noble that he hoped the Cache Creek investigation wouldn't be finalized on the theory that it had been murder and suicide. He had known both Jenkins and Francis for many years and was well acquainted with the feud between them. But Dick Francis got along well with just about everybody else, Berg said. Knowing Dick as he did, he had arrived at some conclusions about the deaths of Frank Jenkins and Joy Brittell.

Francis was an excellent marksman, Berg said, and always carried a gun. If he'd killed the two men, he would surely have committed the act by shooting them. He was positive that Francis could never have been near enough to the men to strike them with a gun or with any other instrument.

Berg insisted that Dick Francis would never have killed an innocent third party like Joy Brittell, if he had intended to commit suicide following the act. And, even if he had, he knew Dick well enough to believe that he would have left a note admitting his guilt, so that no innocent party would suffer suspicion. Dick got along well with most people, Berg repeated, and he was the kind of man who wouldn't want to cause anyone else any hardship.

Finally, Harry Berg said it was his theory that if Dick had intended to kill himself, he wouldn't have made any attempt to conceal the bodies of Jenkins and Brittell.

On July 25, Agent Noble and Ben Mayfield traveled to Petersville and from there to Little Willow Creek, arriving at about two o'clock in the afternoon in pouring rain. Noble talked to Charles Jenkins and Blodgett, and they showed him where the rifle barrel, flashlight, and purse had been discovered. Although they hadn't been able to determine absolutely that the purse had belonged to Helen, Charles Jenkins said he was convinced it was hers. When found, the purse had the appearance of having been ransacked and then thrown beneath the privy.

Later, in diminishing rain, Noble hiked over to Ruby Creek and introduced himself to Ed Carlson, who was tending to his mining affairs. The elderly man confirmed that he had recalled more details about the day he had cleaned the cabin floor. It had been a real chore to scrub the interior of the room, he said, but as he swept the debris toward the door he noticed that the dirt near the doorway was easily removed. He hadn't given it much thought at the time, Carlson said, because he believed his partner had committed suicide.

When Carlson explained that he had also swept the blood from the rear of the cabin toward the door, the agent knew it would probably be futile to try to determine if any blood had existed around the doorway, prior to the time Carlson had cleaned up.

The agent told Carlson there was a possibility that the bullets that had penetrated Francis' head had washed down through the cracks between the cabin's floor boards, when Carlson had drenched the floor with water. He wanted to pull up the boards, and conduct a thorough search for the bullets. Saying that the same possibility had crossed his mind, Carlson readily agreed.

The two men went to work and began to transfer the entire contents of the cabin to the outside. As each carton or item was removed, Noble carefully examined it for signs of a bullet or bullet hole. None were found. Now, the agent took some of Carlson's tools and, with Carlson's help, began to pull up floor boards, inspecting each for unusual signs.

The Dutch Hills were in the full flush of summer, and the creaking sound of rusty nails separating from wood mingled with the murmur of Ruby Creek and the occasional calls of songbirds. In the distance to the south, the Peters Hills were partly visible under mostly cloudy skies. To the west, sloping in tundra-covered contours to more than 3,000 feet, rose the south-side flanks of the Dutch Hills. More great adjuncts of the mountain group rose gradually to the north and east, covered with thick green foliage and random, late-blooming wildflowers.

The agent spent a long time examining the dirt beneath the structure. When his initial search was not successful, Noble told Carlson he was going to sift the dirt. Probably making use of some screen he found at the camp, Noble began another long process of thoroughly filtering the soil within the confines of the floor area. When he had finally finished with this tedious procedure, no trace of a bullet had been found.

As so many had done before him, the agent examined every inch of the now empty structure, both inside and out. In the end, despite what was probably the most meticulous search ever conducted for evidence of the discharge of a firearm in Francis' cabin, he found no trace of a bullet or bullet hole. After he helped Carlson put everything back together, Noble called it a day.

The next day Noble and Mayfield made yet another search of the death scenes. Characterizing these searches as "extensive," Noble moved from Little Willow, where Helen had died, to Wonder Gulch, where wildflowers and new grasses graced the area. After a substantial amount of time there, the two men gained the long ridge that paralleled the gulch, and hiked its length until they reached the end and could look at Ramsdyke Creek below. They then worked their way down the rugged bluff through thick, wet brush until they were on the creek bank, surrounded by the wild, remote country of the eastern part of the Dutch Hills.

The men entered Clarke's former cabin and began to search. Noble was looking for Clarke's hunting knife and a .38 caliber pistol. He was also looking for bloody clothing, cash, gold, and any other possible evidence of the killings. Noble and Mayfield spent a long time at it, but the results were, as Noble later reported, negative.

The men moved through the wet brush and back up the steep ridge face to open country, then covered the miles back to Little Willow Creek.

———

While Noble was working in the Susitna Valley, R.C. Vogel was coordinating other facets of the investigation in Juneau. In July, he learned that the .38 Colt revolver found in Dick Francis' lifeless hand had originally been sold by its manufacturer to the U.S. Army Post Exchange in Anchorage, more than a decade earlier. But efforts to locate that agency were ended when Vogel was advised that the exchange no longer existed. The agency's records had possibly been transferred to an army agency in Vancouver, Washington, he was told, so Vogel sent instructions to his Seattle associates to try to locate the facility.

The agent had received quick results on his request for an analysis of the .35 Remington rifle barrel and stock that he had shipped to

Washington, D.C. In early August, J. Edgar Hoover sent him a laboratory report which stated that the stock and barrel were two parts of the same rifle: "A piece of wood which was in the frame of the rifle was found to fit perfectly with the broken surface of the stock." Technicians had tested the parts for blood, but none was found. Two dark brown hairs had been found, one on the left side of the barrel's trigger guard, the other near the bolt. Tests on these showed only that the hairs had come from a white person.

Vogel informed Ben Mayfield of the test results and told him that the rifle had unquestionably been used "by the unknown suspect" in the murder of Mrs. Jenkins. He added that he also felt certain that the gun had belonged to the Jenkinses. In this respect, he sent inquiries to the Remington manufacturing plant in Connecticut to initiate a process that would trace the weapon's chain of ownership.

By August of 1940, Agent Vogel must have been uncomfortably aware that almost a year had passed since the grisly killings in Cache Creek country. And because John Clarke could be placed at the scenes of both the disappearance of John Dexter and the killings in the Dutch Hills, the agent found himself inexorably drawn to focus on this man who angrily denied any involvement—and to the mysterious J.G. Thoeny, about whom so little was known. Vogel remembered Agent O'Donnell's report of the previous December, which included a statement made by Steve Barick. A friend of his had had a drunken conversation with Clarke in late 1938, at which time Clarke had allegedly claimed that Thoeny was the one who had killed Dexter.

Vogel had tried to track Barick's friend, a man named Wise, who was first reported to be at the U.S. Marine Hospital in Seattle. Inquiries had, however, revealed that he had left there for an unknown location. Recently, Vogel had learned that the man had been seen in Anchorage, where he was said to be working for the Alaska Railroad. Vogel dispatched a new agent, H.F. Dodge, to Anchorage.

On August 20, the agent finally found Wise and interviewed him in his room at the Anchorage Hotel. Asked to describe his relationship with John Clarke, Wise said that he'd met him in the early winter of 1938, when they were both staying at the Northern Hotel in Anchorage. He didn't know much about the man, but he had gone out on drinking parties with him on several occasions. Whenever he had a few drinks, Wise said, Clarke would bring up the subject of the prospecting trip to the Nelchina area that summer. Clarke had rarely spoken of Thoeny by name and had instead referred to him as his partner.

On one occasion, Wise said, Clarke told him that his partner and Dexter had made the trip together but that the two had separated and "Dexter never showed up again." Another time, Clarke told him that he, his partner, and Dexter had gone prospecting but that "Dexter left the party and went away by himself." Yes, he had thought it odd that Clarke would tell two different stories about the same trip, but he didn't think that much about it, because Clarke "was always telling disconnected stories." When he was sober, he was close-mouthed and never mentioned the trip, Wise said. When he'd had a few drinks, he became talkative and always brought the subject up. The prospecting trip, he said, seemed to always be on Clarke's mind.

Did Clarke tell you that his partner, Thoeny, had killed Dexter? Dodge asked.

No, said Wise. One night he, Clarke, and several others were at the Ambassador Club in Anchorage where they all had several drinks. When the conversation drifted to the subject of the prospecting trip, Clarke had said that he guessed there was some talk around Anchorage that Dexter had been killed. He had gone on to say that if Dexter had been killed, it must have been his partner who had done it, because he, Clarke, hadn't had anything to do with it. He hadn't said that Dexter had been killed or that Thoeny had done it, Wise said. He added that a man named Joe, who worked at a local laundry, had heard Clarke make the same statement.

Agent Dodge asked Wise if he could recall anything else about Clarke and Thoeny, and Wise remembered hearing that someone named Ben had claimed that Clarke and Thoeny had returned to Anchorage from the Nelchina trip with some of Dexter's equipment, including a camera. The lady who ran the Alaska House Hotel in Anchorage might know more about that, he said. He'd also heard that when Clarke and Thoeny had originally arrived in Alaska, they had overnighted at some rooming house in Girdwood, south of Anchorage. A woman who worked there, named Kay, had told someone that the two had left some of their personal belongings with her and asked that she keep them until they sent her shipping instructions.

Wise told Dodge that he didn't believe that Clarke was John Clarke's real name. He didn't, however, have proof of that. Clarke claimed to be a U.S. Army Reserve officer, he remembered, and he thought that Thoeny was known as "the Arizona prospector." He'd never met or known Thoeny, he added. No, he hadn't ever seen Clarke after the Cache Creek murders were committed.

Dodge left the Anchorage Hotel and walked over to the New Method Laundry, where he asked for Joe. Joe didn't remember the night at the Ambassador Club that the agent described. No, he didn't remember ever hearing Clarke make any statement about Dexter being killed, or Thoeny having killed him. He did remember that Clarke would always talk about the prospecting trip when he got drunk. To the best of his recollection, he said, Clarke merely stated that Dexter had left him and Thoeny to go to work for some miner in the area. Dodge pressed Joe for anything else he might recall, and he said that on at least two occasions Clarke had told him that Dexter "had $1,000 or better on him" when he had left the men. When asked about Thoeny, Joe said he didn't know him well, just enough to speak to. No, he didn't know where he came from or anything else about him.

At the Alaska House Hotel, the proprietress said she knew Ben and he was "a great talker." The kind of person, she said, who would "hear a rumor and repeat it as a fact." No, she had never heard anyone mention that Clarke and Thoeny had returned from their prospecting trip with any of Dexter's equipment.

Dodge went looking for the woman who had felt threatened by Clarke at the Inlet Hotel in early 1939. At that hotel the clerk told the agent that the woman he was looking for was named Barbara and that she was now married and living in downtown Anchorage. He gave the agent directions.

Barbara agreed to talk to Dodge. She had met John Clarke at the Idle Hour Night Club in July or August of 1938, she said, and after that had occasionally gone out with him. Later that fall, though, Clarke came to her room at the Inlet Hotel and became quite angry with her because she wouldn't drink with him. No, he didn't threaten her then, she said. During the winter, however, Clarke had taken her home from a dance and had come into her hotel room and attempted to "get fresh" with her. When she would have nothing to do with him, he became very angry and grabbed her by the throat and started to choke her. At the same time he told her that if she screamed he would "finish her off." She finally persuaded him to let her go, Barbara said, and she went to the woman's room next to hers and spent the rest of the night there.

To the best of her recollection, Clarke had gone Outside after his stay at the hospital in Anchorage. When he'd returned in early 1939, he had tried to persuade her to go out with him again, but she had refused. She had never talked to him again.

In response to other inquiries, Barbara said that she actually knew very little about Clarke since he seldom talked about himself. No, he had never mentioned a trip he took with Dexter and Thoeny, nor had she ever heard him mention their names. She did recall that he often talked about owning several guns, but she'd never seen him carry one.

In mid-August, two men stopped at the Jenkins brothers' mining camp at Little Willow Creek. One had a familiar face that Charles Jenkins soon realized belonged to Mitchell, the man he had encountered along the road to Petersville in the spring. His scowling, gun-cleaning acquaintance wasn't with him this time; the man who accompanied him now said that he was an ex-sailor from California. They were on vacation, Mitchell said, because they had "struck it rich." That day they were headed for Poorman Creek to visit with some miners there.

Over coffee, Mitchell showed the men his new watch chain that held twenty gold nuggets. The leading jeweler in Anchorage had made it for him, Mitchell said, with gold he had found when he worked for two weeks in July on a Petersville mining company claim. Then he brought out another two and a half ounces of gold and passed it around. He'd sold a large quantity of gold to the Anchorage jeweler at $35 an ounce, he said. When Jenkins asked him what kind of royalty he'd paid the Petersville company, Mitchell told him 30 percent.

The two men had flown from Anchorage to Talkeetna by airplane, Mitchell boasted, and had paid for their groceries at Nagley's store with gold. Charles Jenkins noted that both men wore brand-new clothes. One carried a new 30.06 bolt action rifle, and the other wore a new Colt revolver in a shoulder holster.

The men stayed an hour at the Jenkins' camp and then left in the direction of Poorman Creek. Several days later, Charles Jenkins talked to the foreman of the Petersville operation, who said he knew nothing about Mitchell having mined a company claim. Someone else present at this conversation said he thought the man might have worked for a month at the Bird Creek mine. Jenkins later remarked to Blodgett that he doubted the truth of Mitchell's stories and that the source of the man's gold might be suspect.

―――――

In Juneau, Agent Vogel continued to focus on Thoeny. In September, he wrote to special agents at Phoenix, Arizona, and El Paso, Texas, informing them that "it is highly important that a man named J.G. Thoeny be located." He went on to describe the 1938 Nelchina prospecting trip, Thoeny's departure from Alaska, and the possibility that he had returned to the southwestern United States. The man was sometimes known as the "Arizona Prospector," but information about him was otherwise vague. It was believed he had been a miner in the Southwest, and was possibly from Albuquerque, New Mexico. The agent provided Thoeny's physical description and noted that he spoke slowly and played the accordion exceptionally well. He didn't appear in any of the FBI's records.

In late September, an agent in El Paso advised Vogel that local credit bureau records, directories, mining company records, and files of the El Paso Chamber of Commerce had yielded no information about Thoeny. An inquiry at the El Paso sheriff's office had turned up no criminal record on the man. The agent said he would continue to check other sources.

In October, an agent in San Antonio, Texas, reported that fingerprint files and arrest records in Austin had revealed nothing about Thoeny.

In late October, the El Paso agent contacted Vogel again to report that records had been searched at Albuquerque's post office, police department, mining equipment stores, credit organizations, and chamber of commerce, with no results. The Bureau of Information in Santa Fe had likewise revealed no record of Thoeny.

Other information continued to filter in as well, including a report on the attempt to trace the ownership of the Remington rifle found near Helen Jenkins' death scene. An agent in St. Paul, Minnesota, told Vogel that a Remington official had reported that company records no longer existed for the time frame in question and that he felt "it would be impossible to trace this rifle."

In Fairbanks, one of Vogel's agents interviewed Don Sheldon, who was now attending the University of Alaska and resided at the dormitory there. Sheldon said that Frank and Helen Jenkins had owned a .35 caliber Remington rifle when he'd worked for them, and to his knowledge no one else in the area had owned a similar rifle. He wasn't certain that he could positively identify the weapon found near Helen Jenkins' body, but he could verify that the Jenkinses had owned one like it.

The search continued for the army post exchange records that might reveal a chain of ownership for the .38 caliber revolver found in Dick Francis' hand. In December, Vogel's Seattle contact told him the records had been stored for a time at the Army's Vancouver barracks, but at some point they had been transferred to another post exchange at Haines, Alaska. Vogel sent an inquiry there.

In mid-December, Vogel dispatched another agent to Anchorage for more interviews. There, a U.S. marshal told the agent that a man named Louis Anderson had gotten drunk in a local bar and claimed that he knew something about the killings in Cache Creek country. When the agent found Anderson, he asked him if he'd ever worked in the Ruby Creek area.

He had, Anderson said, but he hadn't been near Ruby Creek since 1925. Willing enough to talk, he told the agent he'd lived in or near Anchorage for more than forty years and had prospected all over the territory, including the Dutch Hills. He had known Dick Francis for fifteen years, because the Ruby Creek miner had taken to spending some time each winter in Anchorage. Francis was very quiet and reserved, Anderson recalled; he just couldn't believe that anyone could be an enemy of someone as inoffensive as Dick. No, he couldn't remember ever making any particular statements about the murders. He had only joined in the frequent conversations about the matter with the other local miners. They talked about it all the time, he said.

The agent listened to Anderson and finally decided that he had nothing of significance to add to the investigation. As he prepared to leave, Anderson suggested that the agent talk to a man named Pete Peterson, who lived at the Northern Hotel where Francis had often stayed. Pete knows everyone, he said.

When the agent found Pete, the two talked about Dick Francis and John Clarke. Peterson had met Clarke at the Northern Hotel sometime in the fall of 1938. He noticed that Clarke was drunk on many occasions, at which times he would talk freely. But when he was sober, he was close-mouthed and seemed not to want to talk about himself. Once, Peterson said, he had gotten into a conversation with another local named Joe Burke, and Clarke's name had come up. Burke had advised him that he "would do well to have nothing whatever to do with Clarke." Burke seemed to know Clarke, Peterson said, and when he asked why he should avoid the man, Burke told him, "This fellow Clarke is not really what he claims to be, and he should be left strictly alone."

Pete Peterson remembered that when Clarke moved in and out of Anchorage in 1938 he seemed to have "plenty of time," which he spent "loafing around Anchorage, and drinking with his friends." But when he arrived in Anchorage on his way to Cache Creek country in the early spring of 1939, he appeared to be in a great hurry. Clarke seemed to have definite plans about what he intended to do, he recalled, and even enlisted Peterson in helping him to pack his gear and supplies for a hurried departure north. As soon as the supplies were acquired and packed up, Clarke had left immediately for Talkeetna.

Peterson also told the agent he had recently heard that Rocky Cummins, who mined near Jenkins in the Dutch Hills, had told someone he knew more about the killings than he had reported.

Peterson had known Dick Francis for many years. He just couldn't believe that a man of Francis' temperament could become involved in serious trouble with anyone, he said.

As the agent moved around Anchorage in the cold and snow, he encountered others who had known Dick Francis, one of them an engineer who worked with the town's water system. He had known Francis for about five years, and had encountered him on Anchorage streets on many occasions. Francis had seemed to be a very reserved individual, the engineer recalled, and spoke very little about his personal affairs. He had never known him to take a drink.

On December 18, the agent tried to find Burke, but had no luck. That same day he spent a good deal of time talking with Police Chief Bob Huttle, who had talked with several old-timers in Anchorage, but couldn't come up with anything significant to the case. Huttle repeated his suspicions about Clarke. Francis just wasn't the type of person who would commit murder and then take his own life, he said.

Now, as the holidays drew near, and winter and darkness strengthened their holds on the north country, the agent concluded his interviews and returned to Juneau to compile his report.

———

In Talkeetna, Ray Jenkins was back in his brother's cabin for the winter. When he had returned in the late fall, he had gone to Commissioner Mayfield's office to file the important documents required of all claim holders. He attested to the work that Frank and Helen had done during the 1939 season and to the work he and his crew had performed that summer. He listed all forty-five claims, with the addition of two properties on Peters Creek called the Lost Chord claims. Discovered at some point to have been registered to Helen Jenkins, Ray had added the claims to the work list. Jenkins declared that Frank's estate had paid out $3,927 to satisfy assessment obligations and for "general hydraulic mining."

Shortly thereafter, Ray Jenkins obtained Frank's will from Mayfield (who had found it in the Little Willow cabin) and submitted it to the court. When it was established that Helen Jenkins was Frank's sole heir, the circumstances of the couple's deaths triggered some legal discussion about the will's effectiveness. Since it was not known if Frank or Helen had died first, the court remarked, the matter needed to be addressed.

About this time Ray Jenkins either asked for, or was compelled by the court to engage, the assistance of an attorney to help him with his estate duties. An Anchorage attorney named Roach now took on that role.

In November, Probate Judge Mayfield approved payment of estate claims to Carlquist and Company, the Collector of the Internal Revenue, the Alaska Rehabilitation Corporation, Attorneys L.V. Ray and Arthur Thompson, Albert Stinson, the Helen Jenkins estate, Attorney Roach, and Ray Jenkins.

By now, Mayfield was also exchanging correspondence with a California attorney named Hahn, who identified himself as the legal representative for Frank Jenkins' three sisters and brother, Charles, in Monrovia and Chico. Had Ray Jenkins listed his sisters and brother as heirs? Hahn asked. Had he claimed a partnership interest in the Jenkins' claims? Had he made any claims on the estate? What, approximately, was the value of the estate?

In December, Ben Mayfield responded to the California attorney and assured him that when Ray Jenkins had petitioned the court to appoint him administrator, he had named all his siblings as heirs. He had also claimed a one-third interest in all the estate property, Mayfield said, but the claim was still under consideration by the court. Mayfield concluded his letter with the appraised value of Frank Jenkins' estate, and added that Helen's estate had been valued at $2,294.35.

Left to right: Marjorie, Jack, and Charles Francis at the Peters Creek Mining Company operations in 1939. The Francis men were a notable part of the search party that located the bodies of victims Frank Jenkins and Joy Brittell. (courtesy Diana Francis King)

———

As 1940 drew to a close in Juneau, R.C. Vogel prepared to review and ponder the files of over fifteen months of investigation.

291

In Seattle on January 14, 1941, a federal agent called on John Clarke at his residence and asked for more information about the deaths in Cache Creek country. Clarke was reluctant to talk about the subject, the agent noted, and protested that he had already been questioned on many occasions and had no more information to offer.

The agent said he wanted to know about the .38 calibre revolver that Clarke had been seen with in Alaska.

He had no idea where the gun was, Clarke said. The last time he had seen it was during the early part of the summer in 1939, when he and a neighboring miner, Ken Brittell, had used the .38 to shoot birds. But, he said, it was likely that his gun had been stolen by the search party that had ransacked his Ramsdyke Creek cabin following the deaths of Francis, Brittell, and the Jenkinses. Clarke went on to complain that a .22 calibre rifle had also turned up missing from his cabin, together with several articles of his clothing.

When asked to describe it, Clarke said that the revolver was of the break-open type with a short barrel and hammerless configuration. It used special ammunition, and if the agent wanted more details he could question a man named Pete, who lived at the Northern Hotel in Anchorage. He had shown the gun to Pete in 1938, and he would remember it.

The interview was not a lengthy one, and at the end, the agent asked Clarke to cooperate by providing a sample of his hair for examination. Clarke complied, and the agent left with the hair in an envelope.

On January 16, an agent named Rogers reported to Vogel from Arizona that he'd turned up some information about J.G. Thoeny. Examination in Phoenix of a publication called the Mining Journal revealed that Thoeny had leased a property called the Comstock Phoenix Mine in early November of 1938. The mine, once operated by the Comstock Phoenix Mining Company, was located in a canyon near Virginia City, Nevada. Little else was known at present, the agent advised, but the editors of the journal had provided him with names of people in Silver City, New Mexico, who might know something about the man. The editors had also reviewed their own records and noted that Thoeny had once subscribed to the Mining Journal but ceased doing so in October, 1932.

Rogers said that he had contacted the Arizona State Criminal Identification Division for information, but a review of their files had not divulged any criminal record for Thoeny. The agent told Vogel that he would conduct additional inquiries in Provo, Utah, and Virginia City and Reno, Nevada.

The temperature hovered at zero as one of Vogel's agents trekked through the snow in Palmer, Alaska, searching for two longtime miners that had prospected in the Nelchina mining district in 1938. Though he was able to locate only one of them, a man named Gallivan, the old-timer was happy to talk to him.

He and Cameron, his partner, had been prospecting in the Nelchina area near Crooked Creek, Gallivan said. It was here, in July, 1938, that they had encountered Clarke, Thoeny, and Dexter for the first time. He and Cameron saw the three men on several occasions, so had spent some time in conversation. Gallivan noted that Thoeny and Clarke appeared to be much older than Dexter and seemed to be in charge of their venture. Dexter appeared almost to be under their influence, he said, though the younger man didn't seem to be of the same type as the other two. Dexter's speech indicated that he was pretty well educated, Gallivan recalled, and he seemed out of place in such company as Clarke and Thoeny.

He had last seen the three men together on August 6, the miner said. On or about August 10, when he was moving down a trail to a lake where aircraft delivered supplies, he saw Clarke and Thoeny approaching on another, nearby trail. When they met they stopped to talk, and Gallivan asked them where Dexter was. Clarke told him that Dexter had gone across the lake to check out some prospecting site there.

No, neither of the men had appeared to be nervous, Gallivan said. But he noticed that Clarke did practically all of the talking. Shortly after this encounter, Clarke and Thoeny had "quit the vicinity," and he had never seen Dexter or the other two again. Later, when word began to circulate among some of the local prospectors that Dexter had not shown up at the locations he was said to have headed for, several of them began to search for him. Gallivan was among them, and they looked several times for some trace of the man. But they hadn't had any success.

Now Gallivan confided his personal thoughts to the agent. It was his theory, he said, that Clarke and Thoeny had "undoubtedly murdered Dexter for his money, then dug a grave under the water at the shallow edge of the lake, and buried his body." He and the others had searched in that area for signs of a body but without success.

When asked if he could recall anything else about Clarke and Thoeny, the prospector said that both men had appeared to be of foreign birth or extraction. And Thoeny had talked frequently about El Paso, Texas, as though he had spent a lot of time there. He had also talked about prospecting in southern New Mexico and Arizona, and had once mentioned that he was a member of the International Order of Odd Fellows, which he had joined in California—Fresno or Bakersfield, Gallivan thought. Thoeny had also mentioned visiting the Odd Fellows lodge in Anchorage on several occasions.

The agent thanked the elderly prospector, left Palmer and made his way to Anchorage. In early February he visited the Odd Fellows lodge there and spoke with an official named Grover. He remembered Thoeny, and said he'd seen him at the lodge several times in the early summer of 1938. He had produced his membership card, Grover said, and had told him he was a member of the organization in some southwestern state like Arizona, Nevada, or New Mexico. The Anchorage lodge didn't keep detailed records of visiting members—just required proof of membership to enter the premises. He remembered little else about Thoeny.

———

On February 13, 1941, Xan John Clarke must have been an angry man. Perhaps the interview with the Seattle agent just weeks earlier had provoked him, or maybe he was disturbed by the request for a sample of his hair. At any rate, his agitation was directed toward the Federal Bureau of Investigation. Not, however, to an agent, field office, or regional division of the agency. On this day Clarke completed an angry letter to the Director of the FBI.

> Dear Mr. Hoover:
> This will refer to your investigation of the Jenkins case, Peters Creek, Alaska, in the fall of 1939.
> About a year ago I made a complaint concerning my working clothes and shirts which disappeared from my trunk in Seward and on the boat while enroute to Seattle, and also that my trunk was repeatedly searched. An FBI agent followed me from An-

chorage to Seward and got on the boat with me, bound to Juneau, and as I pointed out before, this search and the subsequent theft of my clothes, without due process of the law, is quite highhanded, even for an FBI agent.

Mr. Vogel, an FBI agent, asked me while I was at Talkeetna to let him have my 45-cal revolver for checking up purposes, which I did. When I left Talkeetna, Mr. Vogel was in Anchorage, and the U.S. Commissioner at Talkeetna would not return my gun nor give me a receipt for it, but told me to see Mr. Vogel about it.

I would like to get a statement from you concerning this 45-cal revolver which is in the possession of the U.S. Commissioner at Talkeetna. Is he, or is he not, holding this revolver at the express wish of the FBI?

Regarding the 38-cal revolver: this is an old style, revolving turret, hammerless type of revolver, with 5 chambers, shooting short cartridges. I assume this revolver was taken from my cabin by the U.S. Commissioner or members of the search party. Kindly notify me in whose possession it was found and I will prefer charges against him.

Your high-handed methods and utter disregard of my (unintelligible). If this letter is also disregarded, I shall make a complaint through my congressman, and take any legal action he may advise. As a citizen and taxpayer, I would like to believe that I still have some rights.

Very truly yours, John Clarke

cc: Seattle Office, FBI

The next day Clarke went to the FBI's Seattle office and presented a copy of the letter to an agent there. He repeated his catalog of complaints to the agent and indicated that he was tired of waiting for the return of his possessions. He had made numerous requests, he said, but had gotten no response. He went on to explain that he had written the letter for the sole purpose of obtaining his revolver and any information about his missing clothing. Then Clarke left.

At this time in his career, John Edgar Hoover was a rather beleaguered man. Though he had periodically been in personal contact with Agent Vogel in Juneau—mostly to do with his supervision of evidence and laboratory reports—the FBI director was pressured by growing national uneasiness. As German aggression escalated in Europe, apprehensions increased in America that the United States might become involved in the expanding conflict.

Indeed, the FBI had been dealing with the threat of German Nazi espionage at a national level for some time now and had investigated

250 espionage cases in 1938 alone. Worse, Hoover's agents had actually uncovered the activities of thirty-three German spies in America in 1940, some of whom had posed as inspectors in American defense plants. An American spy for the Japanese had also been apprehended, and German, Italian, and Japanese consular offices in the United States were found to be centers for propaganda and espionage.

Hoover's agency had also been working on war contingency plans and had taken on security inspections of Army and Navy arsenals, aircraft factories, and more than 2,000 key industrial plants in the United States. Foreigners who had not complied with America's new Alien Registration Act were also investigated. In addition to domestic responsibilities, the FBI formed a new branch of the bureau called the Special Intelligence Service to monitor and infiltrate German spy rings in South America.

Though the Director was burdened with national security concerns, he sent a letter to John Clarke on March 1, 1941.

> Dear Mr. Clarke:
> Reference is made to your letter of February 13, 1941, containing an inquiry concerning a .45 calibre Colt Automatic pistol which was obtained from you by a representative of this Bureau during an official investigation conducted at Alaska in September and October, 1939, which gun is presently in the custody of the U.S. Commissioner at Talkeetna. For your information, firearms of this type bearing the stamp "U.S. Property" are confiscatable under a federal statute unless the possessor can exhibit proof of the legal purchase thereof from an authorized governmental agency. Therefore, any question you may have relative to this weapon should be directed to the U.S. Attorney, Seward, Alaska.
> It is further suggested that you also direct to the mentioned U.S. Attorney any other inquiries in connection with this matter.
> Very truly yours, John Edgar Hoover
> cc: Seattle, Juneau

One week later, in Juneau, Agent R.C. Vogel reacted to the letter written to Director Hoover by the man he no doubt felt was his prime suspect. On March 7, he sent a firm letter to Hoover.

> Dear Sir:
> It is observed from the letter of Clarke dated 2-13-41, addressed to the Director, that Clarke refers to an unlawful search of his trunk by an FBI agent, as well as the seizure of certain clothing. This is to advise that there is absolutely nothing to this accusation.

With reference to Clarke's comments concerning the .45 calibre automatic pistol, it is stated that upon examination of this pistol at Talkeetna, during the latter part of September, 1939, I noticed that it was marked "U.S. Property." Clarke could not show
title to this pistol, although he claimed that he obtained it as a gift
from an individual named Thoeny during the summer of 1938. He
voluntarily turned this weapon over to the writer when informed
that I desired to have it examined in connection with this case. It
was my intention to determine whether this .45 calibre automatic
pistol fired the fatal bullets resulting in the death of Dick Francis.
However, the fatal bullets have never been found. Investigation
has likewise failed to reflect that the .45 calibre automatic pistol
in question has been stolen and thus far Thoeny has not been located. It is stated, however, that Clarke and Thoeny are suspected
of being in some way involved in the disappearance of John Dexter, who disappeared under mysterious circumstances in July, 1938.
Dexter was last seen in the company of Thoeny and Clarke.

Agent Vogel went on to detail Clarke's written requests for the
return of his pistol from Mayfield, and Vogel's own suggestion that
Mayfield forward the gun to the commanding officer of the U.S. Army
Arsenal in Benecia, California, if Clarke could not show title to it.
His letter continued:

With reference to the .38 calibre revolver mentioned in Clarke's
letter, this is to advise that it was learned that Clarke had a revolver of this description in his possession when he was in Anchorage, in the spring of 1939. The Seattle office was thereafter
requested to ascertain from Clarke what disposition was made
of his weapon. Clarke states he last saw this weapon during the
summer of 1939, and when in the Seattle office recently Clarke
suggested that the U.S. Commissioner or some member of the
search party had taken this revolver. However, it is known that
Clarke is careless with the truth, and his statements, therefore,
should be viewed with this fact in mind.

Agent Vogel also documented correspondence from Clarke to
federal Judge Simon Hellenthal of Anchorage, and to Commissioner
Ben Mayfield at Talkeetna. The letters to the judge had accused
Mayfield of misconduct in connection with the search parties, Vogel
advised, and of deliberately withholding certain information pertaining to the case from the FBI. Vogel informed Hoover that "These
accusations of Clarke are likewise without foundation."

Vogel's letter concluded with the statement: "Clarke is a vicious and hostile character, as is borne out by the information concerning him contained in this file, and it is the opinion of the writer that he is a logical suspect."

Investigation leads and results continued to arrive at the Juneau office. At the end of March an agent reported to Vogel that a search at the Chilkoot Army barracks at Haines, Alaska, had not turned up any records of the Army post exchange that had originally taken shipment of the gun found in Dick Francis' hand. He added that Army regulations provided for the transfer of any retired post exchange records to Washington, D.C., and for the destruction of records that were over eight years old. He would make an inquiry at Washington, D.C., he said.

In April, Vogel received a laboratory report from Director Hoover that reviewed the results of microscopic examination of the hair specimen taken from John Clarke—along with those found near the trigger guard and bolt of the .35 Remington rifle. The specimens had been compared and were found to be dissimilar. The hairs found on the rifle were not John Clarke's.

An El Paso agent reported that no prospecting license had ever been issued to J.G. Thoeny in Santa Fe, New Mexico, nor was there any record of his having been a member of the Odd Fellows organization there, or in Albuquerque.

In May, an agent in Salt Lake City reported that he had gone to Virginia City, Nevada, and made inquiries about Thoeny. He had learned from a man named Lazarri that Thoeny had leased the Comstock Phoenix Mine for three months in late 1938 and early 1939. Lazarri said he didn't have a copy of the lease but he did remember Thoeny. He had been interested in some kind of promotion scheme, Lazarri recalled, but he didn't know any details about it. He did remember that Thoeny "spent most of his time drinking and gambling in Virginia City and talking about his experiences in New Mexico, Arizona, and Alaska."

The agent reported that he had located a man named Fred, who had worked on the Comstock property during the term of Thoeny's lease. Fred told the agent that Thoeny wanted to promote the property so that he could interest the Eastman Kodak company in it. Thoeny had tried to persuade him to plant some gold around the mine, Fred said, to make it appear to be a good producer. He had refused to do it. To the best of his recall Thoeny had left Virginia City after about four months there.

The Virginia City postmaster had no record of Thoeny receiving mail there, the agent said, and the local sheriff knew nothing about the man. At Reno, a check with three Nevada mining associations had turned up nothing.

Agent Vogel also received a report from Washington, D.C., that seemed to end the search for a history of the .38 revolver found in Francis' hand. Unless the gun had been used in the shooting of an officer, or some activity that would trigger an official communication between an army post exchange and Washington, D.C., no record would be on file, Vogel learned. Nevertheless, his correspondent had searched the records, but no information about the gun had been found. A check with the Small Arms Divison of the War Department had revealed nothing either.

In late May, a Los Angeles agent named Cook visited Charles Jenkins and his friend, Blodgett, in Monrovia, California. Jenkins told Cook that he'd talked to several people during his season at the mine in 1940 but hadn't learned anything of importance to the case. He did think it was strange that Clarke had chosen to go to the Bird Creek mine to report Francis' death, instead of Petersville. There was no trail to Bird Creek, he explained, and it was a stiff, uphill trek to get there. It would have been much easier to follow the well-traveled trail to Petersville.

They had talked to several people who were suspicious of John Clarke, the men told Cook. They had also learned that the new owner of Clarke's Ramsdyke property had received a letter from Clarke, in which he stated that he intended to return to the Cache Creek area to prospect. The owner had apparently written back and advised Clarke that he shouldn't return because he was not wanted there.

Jenkins spoke of his suspicions about the men named Mitchell and Christiansen. The gold that Mitchell had carried and bragged about just couldn't have been so easily and quickly acquired, he insisted. He then spoke about some of the Jenkins' gold he'd heard about from the few people who had seen it. One woman, a miner's wife named Mrs. Skies, had told him about an incident that had occurred in the spring of 1939, when she had stopped to visit Helen Jenkins. Skies said that another woman who was new to the country also happened to be there. When this woman mentioned that she had never seen gold nuggets, Helen had brought out a large black purse which contained six pokes of nuggets, sorted according to size. Skies said that most of the nuggets were extra-large.

None of these large nuggets were ever found after the murders, Jenkins continued. Just the gold dust recovered by the investigators had ever turned up. Jenkins said he also knew that his brother Frank had owned an unusual piece of quartz that was about six inches long, four inches wide, and an inch in thickness. A strip of pure gold, approximately an eighth of an inch wide, had seamed through the quartz. The rock had also been all black on one side, and pure white on the other. This unique piece of quartz was never found either, he groused.

During this time an agent named Falkner was in Anchorage making inquiries when he received a call from Ben Mayfield, who happened to be in town and was calling to pay his respects. The two men met, and Mayfield said that although he had no new information about the investigation, he couldn't help but feel that John Clarke had played some part in the deaths of the victims. He didn't have any more evidence against Clarke than he'd ever had, he said, but he had given a great deal of thought to the circumstances of the case and could "never get very far away from the conclusion that Clarke must be involved in it."

In June, a Salt Lake City agent reported that he had traveled to the little town of Tonopah, Nevada, to talk to the owner of the Desert Gem Shop there, a man said to have known Thoeny. The shop owner, named Art, had acknowledged that he had known Thoeny off and on for several years and that Thoeny had stayed with him at his place for two or three months, beginning in November, 1938. When asked to describe Thoeny, Art said that he was an odd person, who mostly liked to play his accordion. He was quite a prospector, he added, and seemed to know a good deal about mining properties. Thoeny never talked much about his past, but did say that he had been to Alaska and that he had a mine in New Mexico. He had left an old pickup truck in Tonopah with a miner named McNamara, Art said. He might know where he went.

The agent looked around the town and found McNamara, who said that he had become acquainted with Thoeny during his stay in Tonopah. To the best of his recollection, Thoeny was from New Mexico, but had mining interests in Colorado. Yes, he had left an old truck on his property, but Thoeny had never returned for it. This, he said, led him to believe that the vehicle was stolen. When the agent asked if he knew where Thoeny might have gone, McNamara said that he thought he had headed for Colorado to do the annual work on his mining property, near Denver.

The Salt Lake City agent reported that after he left McNamara he had made inquiries at the Tonopah post office and with the local sheriff. Neither had any knowledge about Thoeny.

In July, a Seattle agent reported that he had contacted the secretary of the Washington headquarters for the Odd Fellows and asked him to check the group's membership lists for Thoeny's name. The secretary had responded that a search of the entire records of his office had revealed nothing about J.G. Thoeny.

Later in July, a Juneau agent reported that he had responded to two reports of suspicious activity that might be of value to the investigation. He had researched these in Palmer and Cordova, Alaska, but concluded that neither were relevant, so dismissed them from further consideration.

In early August, an El Paso agent related that the Silver City and Santa Rita chapters of the New Mexico Miners and Prospectors Association had no information about Thoeny. A review of the records and payrolls of a major mine in Silver City had produced no results. He had interviewed a mine assayer who traveled extensively throughout New Mexico, but the man said that he had never heard of Thoeny. The agent had also learned that a post office box in Belen, New Mexico, was listed to a name similar to Thoeny's. He would see that it was checked out.

Later in August, another El Paso agent reported that Thoeny had once held a post office box at Belen but had changed his address to a box at El Paso in April, 1938. This postal box was currently held by two assayers with the American Smelting and Refining Corporation, one of whom acknowledged that he had known Thoeny but hadn't seen him since 1939. He and his partner had, as a courtesy, allowed their mailing address to be used by Thoeny, he said, and had agreed to hold his mail for him. Thoeny had checked in with them once, in the spring of 1939, but had never returned after that.

The El Paso agent noted that the mail addressed to Thoeny bore postmark dates in 1940, and included items from the Albuquerque National Trust and Savings Bank; the Freeland Mining Company in Denver; and an Odd Fellows lodge in Bakersfield, California. He recommended that the organizations be contacted.

In September, a federal agent in Denver reported on his efforts to track Thoeny. He had interviewed an official with the Freeland Mining Company in Denver who was not familiar with the name, but had conjectured that Thoeny may have been placed on a general mailing list sent out by Freeland to many miners in the area.

The agent had visited the U.S. Land Office in Denver to determine if Thoeny had registered any mining claims in the area, but a search through the records there had produced nothing. Another records search at the post office in Idaho Springs had also proved fruitless. At the mining assayer's office in the same town a supervisor had advised that no metals had ever been assayed there for anyone named Thoeny. A state highway patrolman named Rosette, who knew many miners in the Idaho Springs area, had never heard of Thoeny. The town marshal there hadn't either.

In October, an El Paso agent named Corbett filed a report detailing his inquiries in New Mexico. He had visited the Albuquerque Trust and Savings Bank in that town, and the head cashier there had accessed records indicating that J.G. Thoeny had originally opened an account at the bank in 1936. Thoeny had last visited the bank in February of 1941, the cashier said, to obtain a copy of his statement. His account record showed no financial activity had taken place since that time, and that his address was listed only as general delivery in Albuquerque.

When Agent Corbett checked with the superintendent of the Albuquerque post office, he was informed that no mail had been sent to or received by a J.G. Thoeny there, nor did they have any record of an address for the man. Additional inquiries at the Albuquerque Gas and Electric Company, the Albuquerque Police Department, and the county sheriff's office had produced nothing.

In November, Corbett traveled to Santa Fe where he went to the State Driver's License Bureau. A search through the records there disclosed that a license had been issued to a John George Thoeny of Belen, New Mexico, in 1938. No license had been issued in 1939, 1940, or 1941.

After Corbett moved on to the State Motor Vehicle Bureau in Santa Fe and turned up nothing there, he headed back to El Paso.

———

Ray Jenkins put in another season on the Jenkins' claims in 1941, but there is little indication that he had much of a crew for assistance. Since Charles Jenkins and his friend, Blodgett, had been interviewed by the FBI in California in late May, they must not have returned to help Ray as they had the previous year; certainly, if they were part of a 1941 crew, they should have been in place at Little Willow and ready to mine at that particular time.

One possible indication that Ray Jenkins may have reduced the scope of his operation is contained in a letter that he wrote to Ben Mayfield from Little Willow Creek on July 21 of that year. After some discussion about a grocery bill and a few other estate matters, Jenkins closed the letter with the comment: "I have been working on Rubby (Ruby Creek), but I am getting awfully low on water. Things are quiet out this way this summer. Ed Carlson is the only one I have seen so far up here."

In early August, as the frenzied growth of summer began to pall, Commissioner Mayfield received more correspondence from Alvin Hahn, the California attorney. Was the estate ready for distribution? he asked. Mayfield replied that the final report had not been filed.

Later that month, in response to a request from the federal Social

Security Board, Mayfield consulted Helen's diary and compiled a report on the number of days that Joy Brittell had worked for Frank
and Helen Jenkins in 1939. Thirteen days in June, and the first nine
days of September were logged, he advised.

On September 26, when the last of fall's golden leaves still held to
the cottonwood and birch, and the rivers began to slowly clear of silt
during frosty nights, Ray Jenkins filed his Proof of Labor claim for the
year's assessment work. While he didn't declare the amount charged
to Frank Jenkins' estate, he identified the work performed as "hydraulic mining on Little Willow and Ruby Creeks, and general prospecting
on all claims, repairs to camp and cabins, and repairs to ditches."

A week later, Ray Jenkins received a letter from Anchorage attorney Roach, who subtly chastised him for submitting estate checks for
payment without first receiving court authorization for the expenditures. "This, of course, is what you agreed to when you applied for
the bond, and I thought was understood by this time," Roach said. At
the end of the letter he remarked, "Sorry to hear that the season was
not successful."

Was Ray Jenkins having some difficulty in coaxing the claims to
produce the healthy returns that his brother had always managed?

Then, in late October, with snow on the ground outside his office
in Talkeetna, Ben Mayfield received a letter from an attorney that
addressed the deaths of Frank and Helen Jenkins and the issue of
inheritance. Since it was impossible to determine which individual
had survived the other, Mayfield read, estate distributions would be
made as if the deaths had been simultaneous. In that case, the letter
advised, "the heirs of each person would inherit the same as if they
had never been married...."

Apparently some effort had been made to learn if Helen Jenkins
had any heirs, but without positive results. On November 27, the first
evidence that Ray Jenkins had become the administrator of Helen's
estate emerged when he filed a petition to address matters of her
estate. Included in the document was his statement that "... said deceased left no heir surviving her and the administrator, after due and
diligent search, has been unable to find any...."

Finally, on December 1, Ray Jenkins filed an Amended Inventory
and Appraisal for the estate of Frank Jenkins. Now, almost a year
after the submission of the first inventory, the estate valuation had
been revised to reflect the apparent determination that Frank's interest in many of the claims and certain properties had been reduced to
a one-third interest as a result of the co-partnership agreement introduced by his brother. Another significant devaluation had emerged
when it was discovered that some of the Seattle banks Frank and

Helen had deposited in were still in receivership as a result of the great stock market crash of 1929. The persistent rumors that the Jenkinses hated banks because of bank failures in 1933, resonated in revised figures procured from four savings and loan associations that still remained under court supervision almost a decade later. How much of that could ever be recovered, remained unclear.

Those had been tough times for a hard-working miner.

———

On December 7, 1941, Japan bombed Pearl Harbor and galvanized a stunned America to action. On December 8, President Roosevelt asked Congress to declare war on Japan, and in less than an hour both the Senate and House had done so. Three days later, Germany and Italy declared war on the United States, and Congress reciprocated in kind.

unprecedented times

A **review of the effect** of World War II on the Federal Bureau of Investigation is worthwhile, to explore the possibility of any subsequent influence on the investigation of the Cache Creek country murders.

Our first hint lies in the fact that, following El Paso Agent Corbett's report in October, 1941, no more entries or reports were filed for the investigation until May 14, 1942.

J. Edgar Hoover had learned about the bombing of Pearl Harbor when his special agent in charge at Honolulu had telephoned him in New York. The agent held the phone to his open window which enabled Hoover to hear the explosions of the bombs for himself. The Director immediately returned to Washington, D.C., where he ordered the FBI on a 24-hour schedule. He canceled all annual leaves and instructed all FBI offices to warn industries with war contracts to be vigilant against espionage or sabotage.

Tremendous security responsibilities were now placed on the FBI, and Hoover and his agents proceeded to round up foreigners that had failed to register as aliens in America. Now considered to be anti-American and a threat to national security, 770 Japanese and over 3,000 German and Italian people were detained within 72 hours.

When the United States went to war, the FBI employed 2,602 agents. When it became clear to Hoover that the demands on his agency would require rapid and unprecedented response, he sent out orders to his field offices to begin interviews for hundreds of new agents. He also instructed his people to relax the qualification standards, in order to expedite the process. The director needed more agents fast, because FBI offices all over America were deluged with rumors and reports of suspected espionage and sabotage. Though most of the rumors would eventually prove to be false, each required a vast amount of manpower to investigate.

The responsibility also fell to Hoover's agency to organize and conduct security training programs for police forces throughout America. The rationale that educated law enforcement officers could strengthen the effort against espionage and sabotage proved very effective as the war progressed.

Everyone else wanted to help too, and this consumed even more agent hours. Various citizens and groups, like the American Legion, wanted to form their own investigative divisions to help combat subversive activity. Though Hoover felt that these proposals smacked of vigilantism and so declined to support such ventures, the director finally worked out an arrangement that enabled patriotic groups to report suspicious activity to FBI field offices.

Director Hoover and his associates also became involved with the development of double agents in order to cope with persistent attempts by German forces to commit espionage in the United States. Top German officials were said to be bitter about the capture of their thirty-three spies in America in 1940, and the Nazis appeared now to be going to great lengths to replace them. Thwarting the German effort to cripple American industrial production through sabotage was a top priority with the FBI.

The turmoil of war reached the FBI's Alaskan field office at Juneau, where agents were caught up in security responsibilities of grave importance. U.S. military planners had realized the strategic importance of Alaska well before the onset of World War II, especially with regard to the close proximity of Japan to Alaska's stormy and mercurial Aleutian Islands. Such circumspection had generated the construction of the Fort Richardson Army base at Anchorage in 1940; military defense bases on the Aleutian islands of Unalaska/Dutch Harbor and Umnak in 1941; and another base at Cold Bay, on the Alaska Peninsula, in 1941. Security clearances and readiness now became critical throughout Alaska.

It is significant to note that after September, 1940, Juneau Agent R.C. Vogel had placed a priority on finding J.G. Thoeny. The concentrated search for the man throughout the West and Southwest in 1941 seems to indicate that Vogel regarded Thoeny's apprehension as perhaps the last remaining opportunity to gain important information about his prime suspect. This supposition is strengthened by the fact that by 1942 no Cache Creek case activity of any significance had been conducted in Alaska for well over a year.

Probably because FBI headquarters in Washington, D.C. required that all cases be reviewed on a periodic but frequent basis, a Juneau agent named McDonnell filed a seven-page report on the Cache Creek investigation in May, 1942.

The agent presented a substantial review of the information that had been gathered about the Dexter-Clarke-Thoeny prospecting trip to Nelchina in 1938. He also noted that the two older men had overnighted at Girdwood, following their arrival on the boat at Seward that summer. A woman named Kay Kennedy had worked at a rooming house there, he observed, and was said to have become acquainted with the men. Attempts to locate Kennedy had been unsuccessful, he said, but should be renewed.

McDonnell also noted a report that miner Larry "Rocky" Cummins was heard to have stated that he knew more about the case than he had divulged to the FBI. Though another agent had earlier recommended that Cummins be interviewed again, it hadn't been done. Cummins should be contacted, he advised.

The Juneau agent summarized the ongoing search for Thoeny, noting that his only known address was thought to be a post office box at Belen, New Mexico. He was also believed to be a member in good standing of the Odd Fellows organization in Bakersfield, California. McDonnell recommended that contact be made with these locations, as well as the Albuquerque Trust and Savings bank, where Thoeny had an account—though it appeared to be an inactive one.

Certain individuals had occasionally reported suspicions about others, McDonnell said, but further investigation of these had not produced anything of particular value for the case. One example he cited in this category was suspicion directed toward a man described as a "moody, mysterious sort of individual" who had been present at a general conversation among workers at Jonesville, where all were employed by the Evan Jones Coal Company. The talk had turned to the Cache Creek murders, and someone had insisted that, despite wartime, the FBI was still working on the case. The suspicious man had suddenly turned on the speaker, it was reported, and said, "To hell with the FBI. They won't find who killed the people." The man then left the room abruptly. Sometime later, McDonnell noted, the man committed suicide.

McDonnell concluded his review with a list of eight individuals and organizations that should be contacted for more information and sent the report off to Washington, D.C.

On June 3 and 4, 1942, Japanese aircraft bombed the American defense base at Dutch Harbor on Unalaska Island in the Aleutian Chain.

On June 7, a Japanese force of 3,000 landed on and occupied Attu, the westernmost island of the Aleutian Chain.

On June 10, more than 1,000 Japanese soldiers invaded a small

American weather installation on the Aleutian island of Kiska, and established a strong entrenchment there.

On June 12, eight German spies landed on the eastern shores of the United States in darkness and fog. Hitler had ordered this new covert assault on America, with instructions that the group destroy or disable strategic bridges, railways, and factories. On the night the men landed, they experienced a startling, unexpected encounter with a young Coast Guardsman who was on routine patrol. Efforts to downplay their presence there did not ease the patrolman's suspicions, but he took no action and continued on his rounds. Fearing that the guard would report them (and rightly so), one spy soon turned himself in to the FBI. Though the other saboteurs scattered along the East Coast, the FBI tracked them down and arrested them within two weeks. All were convicted of sabotage at trial.

The FBI entered a challenging world of intrigue: spy activity that made use of espionage tools such as codes transmitted by tiny pinpricks through certain letters in magazine articles; fountain pens that contained messages retrievable only by pen breakage; and "micro-dots" that contained a full-page message on a dot no bigger than a period at the end of a sentence.

Espionage activity was insidious and unending. A German-American automobile executive in Detroit was discovered passing data to Germany about American aircraft and diesel engines, after U.S. factories had converted to war production.

The FBI agent force had now doubled in number and responsibilities.

———

In June, a Los Angeles agent, H.C. Cook, filed an investigative report that focused on J.G. Thoeny. Cook had recently contacted the Odd Fellows at Bakersfield and learned that Thoeny had been suspended for failure to pay his dues. He hadn't been a member for three years, the recording secretary told Cook. Thoeny had been a member of the Bakersfield lodge for many years and had usually sent his membership dues by mail from a place called High Rolls, New Mexico. The secretary remembered that Thoeny would occasionally include a letter with his dues, and from these he had formed the impression that Thoeny was engaged in mining or prospecting work located some distance from High Rolls. At one time, Thoeny had written that he was able to get into High Rolls only once every two months or so, because of the distance and difficulty in traveling the rough terrain.

Sometime later, Cook reported, the recording secretary had located one of the letters and sent it to him. From Thoeny at Belen,

New Mexico, it was dated December 23, 1937, and read: "Herewith find enclosed check for $6.00 to be applied as payment for lodge dues. Also want to express to you and the lodge my best wishes for a happy 1938. With best regards, I am, Fraternally yours, J.G. Thoeny."

At the same time the secretary reported that Thoeny had last renewed his membership by mail from Belen in June, 1938. A further search of the records had shown that the miner had been a member of the Odd Fellows since 1911, at which time Thoeny had listed his age as 25 years. On the member registry, Thoeny had stated that he was a surveyor by trade.

Agent Cook reported that he had sent Thoeny's letter to the Juneau office so that Vogel would have an example of Thoeny's handwriting and signature. He added that he would make inquiries at other Odd Fellows lodges in New Mexico.

On July 13, an El Paso agent visited the Albuquerque Trust and Savings bank and talked to its cashier. A quick review of J.G. Thoeny's account revealed that a balance of $202.68 remained there. But there had been no activity in the account since February, 1941, the cashier said, despite attempts the bank had made to locate him.

The cashier also told the agent that account information included a notation that Thoeny had been recommended to the bank by a man named Woods.

When the agent located Woods, he said he couldn't remember ever meeting a man named Thoeny. When the account notation was read to him, he said he just couldn't recall the man. He went on to say that he made a practice of never making such recommendations, especially in connection with banking matters. He could only conclude that Thoeny had used his name without authorization.

Back at the bank, the cashier speculated that though Thoeny had given Wood's name as a reference, it was possible that the bank had not contacted Woods for verification.

The El Paso agent ended his report with the statement that he intended to make further inquiries in Belen and High Rolls.

———

In Talkeetna that summer, Commissioner Mayfield approved an order for the payment of the wages that Joy Brittell had earned at the Jenkins' mine in 1939. Noting that the money was needed for funeral expenses and other costs, he ordered it paid to Brittell's estate from the Jenkinses' estates.

Around this time, major news arrived in Alaska. Congress had recently passed an act that ordered the closure of all nonessential industries nationwide, including the Territory of Alaska. Gold mines were among these, and the impact of the new measure would soon be reflected in the dramatically reduced number of mining declarations filed in 1942.

At the same time, another congressional act provided for the suspension or exemption of the annual labor formerly required of all claim holders—provided that the owner file a declaration of his intention to continue to hold the claims. Ray Jenkins did just that on June 6, 1942, when he filed to hold the forty plus claims owned by the estates of Frank and Helen Jenkins.

A month and a half later, Helen Jenkins' estate was escheated to the Territory of Alaska. Because she had left no will and no heirs were known to exist, Ben Mayfield carried out the process that, in cases of this sort, required a transfer—or reversion—of her one-third interest in the Jenkins' holdings to the territory. This included her interest in the mining equipment and thirty-eight of the claims listed in Frank's estate. Mayfield signed the necessary decree, and Ray Jenkins was released as estate administrator. Helen Jenkins' estate was closed.

———

In August, 1942, six of the Nazi spies that the FBI had apprehended along the East Coast in June were electrocuted to death in the United States.

In September, construction was begun on two major American military defense bases at Adak and Atka in the Aleutian Islands.

———

In November, an El Paso agent visited High Rolls, New Mexico, and talked to Mrs. Hill, the assistant postmaster there. She knew who Thoeny was, but estimated that he hadn't been in High Rolls for around six years. She remembered, however, that Thoeny had passed through there on a bus three or four years earlier. Her niece had boarded the same bus at High Rolls, she said, and had talked for a short time with Thoeny; he had told her that he was going to El Paso to pick up his car, and that he intended to move on to either Arizona or Colorado to do some prospecting.

At nearby Alamogordo, the agent talked to the secretary for the Odd Fellows lodge there. He said that Thoeny had lived in High Rolls for many years, but that he doubted if he had ever been a member of the Alamogordo lodge. While the agent waited, Mr. Thomas searched his records, which showed no mention of Thoeny.

The El Paso agent talked to another man at Alamogordo who told him that it was his guess that Thoeny hadn't been in that vicinity for the past six or seven years. But he knew all the prospectors in the area, and would ask if any of them knew where Thoeny might be.

When the agent filed his report, he advised that he would attempt to locate Mrs. Hill's niece to determine if she could remember anything more specific about her bus conversation with Thoeny.

On December 14, in Juneau, Agent McDonnell reported that while in Anchorage the previous summer he had met with Jack O'Connor, a wildlife agent with the Alaska Game Commission. When McDonnell told O'Connor that he was trying to locate George Belanger, the miner who had become acquainted with Clarke, Thoeny, and Dexter at Nelchina in 1938, O'Connor said he knew George well and that he was working for the Alaska Road Commission at a remote camp called Little John.

When McDonnell asked if Belanger had mentioned any new information about Dexter's disappearance, the wildlife agent said there was nothing he could recall. Asked if he knew whether Belanger still had Dexter's personal belongings, O'Connor replied that the last time he'd spoken with him, George had mentioned that he was still holding them.

A few days later, McDonnell met with the superintendent of the Alaska Road Commission in Anchorage, and learned that George Belanger was employed as a bulldozer operator with the agency; Little John was a remote camp that had no airstrip, railway, or access of any kind, the official said. Belanger's work locations were changed frequently, he added, so if the agent wanted to interview him it would be necessary to first determine exactly where Belanger was and to make advance arrangements with the Road Commission for transportation.

There is no evidence that McDonnell ever attempted to travel to Belanger's work site, but in September he returned to the Alaska Game Commission to talk to O'Connor. This time he asked about Kay Kennedy, the woman who had met Clarke and Thoeny in Girdwood shortly after their initial arrival in Alaska in 1938. The wildlife agent said he'd heard that she had married a man named Donahue and was living in San Francisco.

In Juneau, McDonnell concluded his report with a request that a San Francisco agent locate and interview Kennedy.

When the agent left his office that day, snow lay upon the streets of Juneau, and darkness had descended. The holidays were at hand, and Christmas decorations downtown added a cheerful tone to the dark, wintry landscape. In a couple of weeks the new year would emerge. America was still at war. The Cache Creek country murders remained unsolved.

———

As 1943 arrived, the United States intensified its war efforts, and the FBI continued to grapple with the pervasive threat of national sabotage. A San Francisco agent named Magee, however, managed to find the time to track down Kay Kennedy's place of residence in the city. There he learned from new occupants of the house that Mrs. Kennedy's husband, a sergeant in the U.S. Army, had been transferred to Florida. He was provided with Kennedy's new address.

On January 15, 1943, Magee sent a summary of the Nelchina prospecting trip, including the involvement of Thoeny and Clarke, to the FBI field office in Miami. It was important to contact Kay Kennedy, he advised, to learn what she might know about Thoeny.

On January 30, an El Paso agent named Roberson reported that Assistant Postmaster Hill's niece had been located in El Paso. When interviewed about her conversation with Thoeny on the bus in 1938 or 1939, she said that her memory of the bus ride was vague. So vague, Roberson advised, that she could provide no information of value about Thoeny.

One example of how burdened with wartime duties the FBI may have become, might lie in the fact that two Miami agents, named Armitage and Skidmore, weren't able to interview Kay Kennedy until three months had passed after the request for contact with her had been filed.

In late April the woman told the two agents that she had worked at the Girdwood Trading Post in Alaska for several years and she did remember Clarke and Thoeny—but no one named Dexter had been with them. Sometime in the summer of 1938, the two had appeared in Girdwood and stopped at the trading post to spend the night, Kennedy said. They had asked her what the cost was for a night's lodging, and when she told them it would be fifty cents each, they decided to sleep in a railroad box car that was parked on the siding at Girdwood.

Clarke and Thoeny were dressed like prospectors, Kennedy recalled, but they looked "phony" to her. When they had sorted through their duffle bags she had seen what they had packed, and their gear wasn't the equipment ordinarily carried by prospectors who knew their business.

The two men spent a lot of time at the trading post, Kennedy continued, and told her that it was their plan to do some hunting. When she told them they would need a license, they had responded that they didn't need licenses and had no intention of getting them. They spent the evening at the trading post, she said, and sat around and talked. The older man, Thoeny, had also played the accordion. No, neither man had mentioned anyone named Dexter.

The men had spent the night in the rail car, she said, and around

312

noon the next day had set off for Anchorage on foot. Before departing, though, they had left certain parts of their duffle with her at Girdwood and asked her to ship the items to them in Anchorage on the next train.

When the agents asked Kennedy if she knew anything about Dexter's disappearance, she replied that she was not familiar with the details, but she had been "suspicious about the two men at the outset." She felt this way primarily because the men intended to hunt without a license. After their departure she had immediately written a letter to Jack O'Connor, the game warden at Anchorage, informing him about the statements the men had made.

She hadn't seen nor heard of either man after that, until late that year when she heard that Clarke had injured his back while working at the Evan Jones Coal Mine, near Palmer. He was in the railroad hospital in Anchorage, Kennedy said, and when she was in town she had gone by to visit with him.

During these visits Clarke had been very reluctant to talk about himself or any of his activities, Kennedy recalled. But he did say that he had been born in Rumania. Later, she heard the rumors that he'd faked the work injury.

Asked by the agents if she recalled anything else about the men, Kennedy said that she had the impression that Thoeny had spent some time in Arizona. And when the men had been together at Girdwood, Clarke had acted as though he "was undoubtedly the leader and made all decisions." He had a long, narrow scar on the right side of his face, she remembered, and carried himself in a very erect manner, as though he had had military training. Thoeny had a sharp, "beaky" nose, and was obviously Italian.

The Miami agents concluded their interview, and filed their report on May 6.

Later, in Juneau, an agent made note of his intention to contact Jack O'Connor and obtain the letter Kay Kennedy had written to him about her encounter with Clarke and Thoeny.

———

The FBI faced a multitude of demands during the summer of 1943. The most serious threat continued to be that of foreign infiltration and sabotage, and the agency focused on the cultivation of employees in American war defense plants, for service as confidential sources and informants. Security in the most major plants was further enhanced when the FBI placed its own undercover agents there.

The defense factories also required attention for another reason; members of the Communist party in America began to agitate the

American labor force to demand higher wages or to go on strike. Director J. Edgar Hoover was particularly incensed at the thought that such strikes might jeopardize vital defense-related production, and directed his agents to rigorously monitor the activity of the unions and the communist agitators.

More distractions emerged when some American war-supply companies committed fraud by selling defective war materials to the government. Impaired electrical wire that caused fire and communications failures in the war zones and faulty grenades that misfired or didn't perform at all were discovered among the materials distributed to American forces overseas. The FBI was charged with identifying the sources of the corrupt manufacture, and exposing the fraud involved.

During this time the number of prisoners of war incarcerated in the United States mushroomed to 400,000. Of these, up to seventy-five a month escaped, and it became the FBI's responsibility to track them down. This mission was especially urgent because authorities worried that escapees might be recruited by American Nazi sympathizers to commit espionage in the United States.

More agent hours were expended in tracking down draft dodgers.

While all of these domestic matters demanded constant attention, the need for secret agents increased. South America was now a hot bed of spy activity where German and Japanese operatives traded intelligence and military secrets. The FBI became effective at infiltrating this activity and was successful at planting misinformation through foreign spy channels and creating other forms of subterfuge.

In Alaska, the construction of a major airfield on Amchitka Island in the Aleutians was completed, and the base grew to accommodate thousands of troops. American bombers were launched from here to drop 640 tons of bombs on the Japanese forces entrenched at nearby Kiska Island.

On May 11, an American force of more than 10,000 men, backed up by battleships, cruisers, destroyers, submarines, and other vessels, proceeded to land at the Japanese-occupied island of Attu. A terrible battle fought for over two weeks in wretched conditions— Aleutian wind, snow, cold, and dense fog—resulted in the deaths of more than 2,500 Japanese soldiers and more than 500 Americans. An additional 1,000 Americans were wounded, and more suffered from frostbite, but the United States now occupied the island.

A new airfield was constructed on Attu, and another at the adjacent island of Shemya—to the east, in the turbulent Bering Sea.

It was at this time, while war raged in Europe, the Pacific, and along the far western reach of the stormy Aleutian Islands, that an FBI agent in Juneau filed the final report on the Cache Creek country murder investigation:

At Juneau, Alaska, July 7, 1943: A review of the file reflects that in all probability Richard A. Francis, carried as one of the victims, murdered the other three victims and then committed suicide. The file reflects there had been a long-standing feud between Francis and Jenkins over gold claims in the vicinity where they resided. Shortly prior to these crimes, victim Jenkins sought to have Francis brought before the Federal Court for a hearing as to his sanity. It appears likely that as a result Francis became more bitter toward the Jenkins. The file reflects that Francis had been of unsound mind for some time and on one occasion had left his tent at night and had fired a number of shots in the dark, believing that someone had tried to harm him.

It will be recalled that victims Frank Jenkins and Joy Brittell had proceeded to the cabin of John Clarke to secure a radio. In all probability Francis observed them returning with the radio and being of unsound mind clubbed them to death. Victim Mrs. Jenkins then became alarmed at their delay in returning home, loaded her Remington auto-loading rifle and started out to look for them. Francis then probably confronted her and wrested the gun from her grasp and used it as a club to kill her. Francis then probably returned to his own cabin and in remorse or a fit of despondence committed suicide. It will be recalled that two shots were fired in his head from a .38 cal. revolver, which gun was found in his right hand after his death. One of the bullets had entered the head above the right ear and had made its exit above the left eyebrow. The second bullet went through the brain. The latter would have been fatal whereas the former probably was not. It is likely that the bullet which emerged through the left eyebrow was the first shot fired and that Francis was then able to get off the second shot before losing consciousness.

It will be recalled that Dr. Walkowski of Anchorage, Alaska, performed the autopsy upon the victims' bodies and at first concluded that the two bullets which passed through Francis' head entered through the right side. Afterwards he expressed the probability that the bullets may have entered Francis' head from the left side.

The Bureau was subsequently furnished photographs of Francis with the request that it express an opinion as to whether the bullets entered or emerged from the left side of Francis' head. It opined that no definite conclusion could be reached but that

315

there was some evidence of powder marks on the right side indicating that the bullets may have entered on that side.

A memorandum appears in the file reflecting that on May 14, 1941, Dr. Walkowski called at the Juneau office. He stated that he had given a great deal of consideration from time to time to his autopsy report on Francis. He said that he is now definitely of the opinion that Francis was shot from the right side rather than the left. He said he had been influenced in his decision by the recent examination by him of a gunshot wound. The file also reflects that John Clarke has been considered as a suspect from the inception of this investigation. However, no definite evidence has ever been developed indicating his guilt. He has been interviewed on several occasions without obtaining any admissions or definite information linking him with the commission of these murders.

The new status of the case was contained in one word at the conclusion of the report: *CLOSED.*

The new status of the case was never made public.

epilogue

In 1943, soon after the FBI quietly closed the Cache Creek country murders case, Ray Jenkins filed another affidavit that declared his intention to hold the multiple placer claims in the Jenkins estate, thereby receiving the annual labor exemption for the ground.

Evidence that Ed Carlson had never budged from Ruby Creek appeared in mining records that same year, when he filed his own affidavit to exempt Sure Thing Nos. 1, 2, and 3 on Ruby Gulch from annual labor. He did the same for the Little Wonder No. 1 claim on Wonder Gulch.

In 1944, Ray Jenkins filed for the exemption again.

On June 15, 1945, the *Anchorage Daily Times* ran an article on its front page entitled, "Territory To Sell Claims Of Talkeetna Murder Victim." Readers were informed that: "Talkeetna's famous unsolved murders of 1939 gave the Territory of Alaska a one-third interest in 37 gold mining claims in the Dutch Hills about 80 (sic) miles northwest of Talkeetna, it was learned today from Ralph Rivers, territorial attorney general."

The article recounted how Helen Jenkins' one-third interest had been escheated to the territory and went on to describe the victims and the circumstances of their deaths. Though two years had passed since the FBI had closed the case, the newspaper innocently declared:

> Murder of the first three by Francis and his subsequent suicide were at first suspected until investigators concluded from the nature of Francis' wounds he could not have inflicted them himself. Robbery of placer gold said to have been kept in the Jenkins' cabin was suspected and mining claim feuds were mentioned, but the murderer has never been found and the four deaths still remain an unsolved mystery.

The article listed the creek locations of the Jenkinses' claims and reported that the property interest would be put up for sale at public auction in about a month's time.

In September, a newspaper Notice of Sale advertised Helen's interest in thirty-eight claims, three tractors, a shed and tools, sleds, and hydraulic equipment and supplies that would be sold at auction in Talkeetna on September 21, 1945. On September 22, Talkeetna Commissioner Theta Musgrove wrote to Alaska's attorney general and told him that "Three bids were made, the highest bid being for $700 made by Paul L. Gagnon."

Ray Jenkins entered into an alliance of sorts with Gagnon that same fall, when the two men staked out twelve new claims near the junction of Cottonwood and Willow Creeks.

In February of 1946, Jenkins signed a warranty deed granting his major interest in all of Frank's estate claims and property to Paul Gagnon. The amount paid Ray Jenkins is unknown.

In March, Gagnon filed for a claims labor exemption and then proceeded with an ambitious effort to improve and mine the Dutch Hills property. He purchased an expensive drill, a light plant, pump, and freighting sleds, and spent $2,000 on equipment repairs. Another $2,000 went for supplies and the cost of freighting them in to the claims from Talkeetna. Salaries totaling $25,000 were paid to a driller, four workmen (including himself and Ray Jenkins), and a camp cook for the 1946 mining season. When his costs were totaled, Gagnon had spent $33,950 on his mining venture that season.

In September, 1946, Gagnon served notice on Frank Jenkins' three sisters and brother, Charles, in California, advising them of the amount he had invested in the claims, and demanding that they, as fractional heir/owners, pay their share of the costs. There is no evidence that any of them responded, and in November Gagnon filed an affidavit with the court to establish forfeiture of their interests.

In 1947, Gagnon deeded a half-interest in his holdings to his wife, Maxine, and the two mined the claims for many years.

In 1984, longtime Alaskan, Nola Campbell, published a book called *Talkeetna Echoes,* a charming collage of stories, photos, and letters from old-timers who had spent time in Talkeetna and Cache Creek country. The publication included a letter from a man named Floyd Jaeger, written in 1974. Among other remembrances, Jaeger recalled a journey he once took with Rocky Cummins, excerpted here:

> Rocky and I almost perished together, 1946. I was with him when he decided to look after his claim ... in the Tokositna district, which he didn't see since 1939. We did not take much grub along, (because) there was beans, lard and flour stored away and

sleeping bags and tools in his cabin. It took us three days from Peters Creek, to work ourself through high water, mud and willows, up where his cabin was. It was gone, the flood what washed us out in Petersville also took Rocky's cabin.

He said to me, Floyd, this is the biggest calamity what hit me since 1922—and I ask, well Rocky what happened then. He answered that was the time when they took a $60,000 rum-boat away from me. It must have been around Vancouver, Canada.

We ate porkepine without salt for nearly 2 weeks, to get our strength back. On the way in, we slept in the cabin the murder suspect Taylor occupied during or before the murder of the Jenkins. Rocky sniffed around and found a letter written by a waitress from Seward to urge him on to take a job somewhere and forgett prospecting. This letter and a pair of bloody working gloves were hidden behind the door frame. If the F.B.I. would have found those items the murder would have been solved, right then in 1939.

Though it is curious that Jaeger identified the murder suspect as someone named Taylor, it is possible—if the story is true—that the two men slept in the Ramsdyke Creek cabin that Clarke had occupied in 1939, because it was situated along one of the main routes that prospectors traveled to access the Tokositna area.

However, it does strain credulity that, despite the meticulous searches by Agent Vogel, Agent Noble, Commissioner Mayfield, and the angry search party, a pair of bloody work gloves would have escaped their concentrated and thorough examinations of the cabin. Nor can other sources for the bloody gloves be discounted. It is altogether possible that transient hunters or trappers had taken up temporary refuge or occupancy in the remote cabin sometime between 1939 and 1946, and at some point had dressed out bloody game or pelts with the gloves.

Joy Brittell was buried in Anchorage's Memorial Park Cemetery; his unmarked gravesite is situated in the same tract as those of the Jenkinses.

Ken Brittell died in June, 1994, in Soldotna, Alaska, at the age of 85.

Maxine Brittell, now in her eighth decade, leads an active life in Alaska.

Ernie Bull passed away in Oroville, Washington, on November 19, 1997.

Wes Harriman retired to farming in New Hampshire, where he passed away in March, 1989, at the age of 75.

Ray Jenkins is believed to have died sometime in his seventh decade in Palmer, Alaska.

Frank Lee sold his Talkeetna property in 1946. He may have retired to Bellingham, Washington.

Ben Mayfield, after 29 years in Alaska, retired to Rainier, Oregon, where he passed away in December, 1984, at the age of 95.

Belle Lee McDonald died at the Sitka Pioneer Home at the age of 97, in April, 1975.

H.W. Nagley retired from his business and mining interests in the early 1950s and passed away in June, 1966. He was interred in Anchorage's Memorial Park Cemetery.

Frank Sandstrom is alive and well in Southcentral Alaska.

Frances Weatherell Sandvik left Talkeetna in 1953 and spent her last years in Why, Arizona, where she died at the age of 74.

Don Sheldon passed away in January, 1975. His biography, *Wager With the Wind*, was published in 1974.

Many efforts to locate biographical information for Special Agents R.C. Vogel, E.M. O'Donnell, and J.D. Noble were unsuccessful.

Dick Francis' gravesite in the Masonic tract of the neatly kept Anchorage Memorial Park Cemetery is overgrown with six decades of grass. No marker survives to designate his final resting place.

The gravesites of Frank and Helen Jenkins have likewise experienced the effects of time, and no markers survive.

A death certificate believed to be that of John Clarke indicates that he died of heart disease at the age of 68.

Though much of Cache Creek country is mined out today, certain parts of the region are still actively worked.

The Talkeetna River still flows past Talkeetna. In September the birch and cottonwood turn to gold and, in October, slush ice still moves southward with a whispery hiss.

The murder victims' gravesites in the Anchorage Memorial Park Cemetery.

Frank and Helen Jenkins are buried in unmarked gravesites at this location in the Anchorage cemetery.

MASONIC TR 9

Dick Francis is buried in this tract in Anchorage's Memorial Park Cemetery.

Joy Brittell is buried in an unmarked gravesite—at the lower part of this photo—in the Anchorage cemetery.

Frank Jenkins and Dick Francis were in their early thirties when they made their way up the Susitna River by boat to Susitna Station in 1911 and 1914. Dennis Garrett was 21 years old and fresh out of the army when, in 1984, he first ventured to the Petersville area to look at some mining claims he had heard were for sale there.

While Francis and Jenkins moved into the Cache Creek area on foot through raw wilderness with their belongings on their backs, Garrett drove on a paved highway from Anchorage to its juncture with the road that had evolved from the primitive trail traveled by freighter Frank Lee to the gold camps. Another thirty miles down this road put Garrett at the gateway to Cache Creek country.

Originally from Oklahoma, Garrett had grown up there with an enduring passion for geology. Along with dreams of Alaska and a penchant for adventure, everything seemed to come together for the young man when he saw the area around Petersville and heard about the big mining country beyond.

Dennis had some things in common with both Francis and Jenkins when they had arrived in the area: little money and a consuming desire to find gold. In contrast, however, his quest was made easier by a superior road system, methods of communication, and access to supplies. But Garrett lacked one important advantage enjoyed by the two veteran Dutch Hills miners. In the early 1900s they had prospected over miles and miles of untouched wilderness and unclaimed ground (albeit under harsh conditions), while Dennis would discover that any worthwhile ground in Cache Creek country was already staked, claimed, or spoken for. Any claims that might occasionally become available did so only at a price decidedly beyond Garrett's means.

Nobody called the region Cache Creek country anymore.

After a summer spent as an assistant with a jade prospecting crew in the rugged Brooks Range of northern Alaska, Dennis returned to Anchorage where he took any work he could find. His visit to the Petersville area never left his mind. In his spare time that winter, he visited the University of Alaska's research library to look for information on the geological history of the Dutch Hills and the Cache Creek system. His research led to mining claim histories and even to a copy of Nola Campbell's book, *Talkeetna Cronies*, which included a couple of pages about the Cache Creek murders. He happened upon a newspaper clipping that provided more details, and Garrett became fascinated with the mystery that accompanied the terrible events of September 1939. He was equally intrigued with the rumors that the Jenkinses had buried gold on their property.

Of medium height and build, Dennis Garrett was young, strong, and quick on his feet, and he possessed an iron will and uncommon determination. He willingly describes himself in those days as aggressive, "hungry," and bold. "Like a wolf," he says. His eyes, intelligent and blue, grow excited when he talks about geology—his conversation is laced with terms like *tertiary conglomerate, quartz stringers,* and *granitic intrusive rock.* During the winter of 1984-85 he moved around Anchorage trying to think of ways to realize his dreams of becoming rich by mining gold placer claims in Alaska.

When spring arrived, Garrett began to spend time at the federal Bureau of Land Management (BLM) building in Anchorage, where he sat down at the public computers to research mining claim ownership in Cache Creek country. A part-time sales job with an Anchorage baseball team left him enough time for the project, and he spent long hours trying to locate any ground that might be available for filing. However, these sessions became an exercise in frustration when, after several days had passed, Dennis encountered only interminable registers of claims held by others.

Then, on May 15, Garrett happened upon a record of a group of claims that had just been designated by the BLM as "abandoned." The tracts were located in the Dutch Hills on upper Willow Creek, Ruby Creek, lower Gopher Gulch, and Lucky and Puzzle Gulches. Dennis was electrified, and took just enough time to gather the data he needed to locate and file on the property. Then, he says, "I cleared the screen and ran out of the federal building."

Later, Garrett says, he would learn that the group of abandoned claims were central in a heated dispute between mining factions and that, incredibly, a lawyer for one of the conflicting parties had forgotten to file the annual paperwork required to hold the claims.

Garrett's excited enthusiasm spread among his friends, and after gathering food and gear, the group headed up the highway from

Anchorage, north to the Petersville Road. After turning onto the well-maintained early part of the road, they managed adequate traveling conditions for about twenty miles or so. Before long, however, the age-old throes of Alaska's spring breakup season appeared, and the road deteriorated to a hopeless condition. Finally, everyone set up camp in an abandoned cabin at Deep Creek, and Dennis and a friend set out on foot with 70-pound packs on their backs, dragging sleds behind them. The remaining eleven miles to the site of the abandoned claims loomed in the distance.

Elements of the Jenkins-Francis era now came alive as the two encountered mud, muck, and vast lakes of slush where dips and swales occurred along this primitive northern section of the narrow, half-frozen road. Finding no way to circumvent the huge slush basins, they pushed on through them, becoming soaked and causing Dennis to strip to his underwear and boots. "We almost drowned crossing Peters Creek," he says, but the young men eventually made it all the way to an old, forlorn camp along Willow Creek.

"When I got there I could tell that nobody had been back there for a long time," Dennis says. "The equipment was rusted and abandoned, junk was strewn about, there were no tracks, no corners, no poles, no flagging, no nothing. So, I said, 'Cool —this is truly abandoned.'"

It took them two days to stake twenty-five claims. "The snow was still pretty deep," Garrett says, "but I got on the high points and stacked up rocks and spray-painted them orange; then I stuck my (claim) notices in the rock piles in plastic bags." The two then made their way back through the miles of muck and slush to Deep Creek, where Dennis completed the paperwork that was required for filing on the ground. Some of his friends drove the hundred miles to the Palmer Recorder's Office with the documents and officially recorded the tracts.

In this way, the 22-year-old Garrett was introduced to Frank Jenkins' and Dick Francis' old diggings. He was about the same age Joy Brittell had been when he arrived in the Dutch Hills in 1935.

Eventually, most of Dennis's friends left, but two spunky young women remained and, with Dennis, set up a ten-man army tent at the confluence of Ruby and Willow Creeks. Garrett had a little floating suction dredge that he and the girls worked, and the three found some "pretty good color," he recalls. At other times, Garrett explored the area.

One day he headed over a ridge to the south, in the direction of Little Willow Creek. "I got into Little Willow Creek valley, and saw this really old trail," Garrett says. But before he could really examine the path, something gave him pause. "There was something about the place—it caused a feeling I can't describe, like a wave or something that started in my feet and moved up. My hair prickled, and I thought, Whoa—what's going on here. I had a shotgun with me and brought it up because I felt threatened. I can still feel the hackles rising again, just thinking about it."

Just weeks later, Dennis and the two girls explored the area again and stumbled upon an old cabin in severely deteriorated condition, barely visible in a jungle of choked willows, alder, and thick under- brush. "We discovered the cabin by accident, because the brush was so overgrown," Dennis says. "You would have practically had to fall out of an airplane to find it." The three discussed their growing dis- satisfaction with the damp and dank army tent, and decided to move into what was left of the old structure.

They patched the most damaged parts of the moldering place with visqueen and tarps and set up a small wood stove that Dennis had hauled in. During this process it occurred to Garrett that the place might be a remnant of the Jenkinses' Little Willow Creek camp, and he told the girls about the murders. The two, also in their early twenties, were intrigued with the idea that they might be at a site once occupied by the murder victims and proposed a seance to com- municate with the Jenkinses.

"I'm a very science-oriented person," Dennis says, "and I have a real hard time dealing with spiritual stuff. But some things temper my cynicism—like we were never aware of microwaves until we discov- ered them." He also recalled the powerful, unexplained feeling he had experienced upon entering the valley of Little Willow Creek on the old, faded trail. Garrett went along with the seance.

"We sat on the floor in a circle, around these candles the girls had lit. They asked questions like, 'Who was the murderer?' and 'Where did you bury your gold?'" Dennis recalls.

No one responded.

Garrett's introduction to the more recent history of the aban- doned claims began in early July, 1985. A letter from an Anchorage law firm warned him not to fool around with the equipment on the property and made it clear that the mining group that had held the claims was unhappy that he had staked the ground. Made equally clear was the group's intention to retain its rightful ownership of the place. Later, Garrett says, he learned that the mining group had gone to state offices and "paper-staked" the property.

To further complicate matters, Garrett explains, he learned that these particular claims were in the process of being conveyed from federal (BLM) ownership to the State of Alaska. Jurisdiction with re- gard to mining regulation had assumed complex dimensions.

Then two men, one dragging a trailer behind his pickup truck and the other on a backhoe, arrived on the property. They offered Dennis and the girls a drink of peppermint schnapps and said they had come to mine ground along Willow Creek. As the men chatted, Garrett realized that they were talking about some of the abandoned claims he had filed on. The two seemed knowledgeable about the property and talked about drilling reports and production records they had with them that documented the history of the ground. Though the men alluded to a connection with the "owners of the property," their affiliation was never made clear. Intrigued, Garrett said nothing about his own link.

After a month of "roughing it" in the hills, the girls finally left. Dennis, alone at his camp along Little Willow, pondered his circumstances and decided that opportunity was at his doorstep. He sensed that he could learn a lot from these men and their records; he could also observe the particular mining techniques that the claims required. When the men mentioned that they needed a bulldozer operator and would pay ten dollars an hour for the work, Dennis took the job.

After all, he reasoned, these claims were his. He would be working on his own claims!

In the evenings the men would sit around and talk, spinning tales of mining skulduggery that Dennis listened to with rapt attention. There was plenty of peppermint schnapps at the camp, Dennis observed. And beer. "These guys were fabulous drunks," Garrett comments dryly. "We wasted two days at a time going to the Forks Roadhouse to buy a case of beer." Traveling the seventeen rough miles from the Willow Creek camp to the roadhouse was slow going, he says, and once the men arrived at the old building they liked to sit, talk, and drink beer. It's not likely that any of the men knew that the place they were in was Belle McDonald's old Peters Creek Roadhouse; that a half century earlier an incensed Helen Jenkins had, in the same room, done her best to belt Christ N. Hansen with a stick of firewood and then a quart bottle; that the men in the roadhouse had been hard put to keep her and Frank under control.

The ancient logs of the building reposed silently, while the men talked about mining at Willow Creek.

"They'd pay $52 for a case of beer to take back to the camp," Dennis says of the men, "because the roadhouse had lost its package beverage license and sold beer only by the singles. This is not counting the money they spent on beer in the roadhouse."

They found "plenty of gold" that summer, Dennis recounts, and the two miners would leave for stretches at a time to cash it in. Soon, Garrett began to hear stories about the men paying for their fuel and equipment rentals with hot checks which, he thought, indicated that the gold wasn't making its way to any bank. "These guys were taking the gold to town, they were pissing it away, they were stashing it, drinking it up, whatever," he says.

As summer progressed to fall, Garrett grew uneasy over the fact that he had not yet been paid his wages. Despite assurances that they would settle up with him, the men instead spent longer and longer periods of time away from camp. The willow and alder leaves turned golden, the nights grew cooler, and September moved into October.

Radio messages from Anchorage to Dennis at the camp assured him that the men would return soon with food. Still, as the evenings grew even colder and the days of October slipped by, no one showed up.

Not even Frank Jenkins or Dick Francis had remained this long in the Dutch Hills.

Finally, Dennis got mad.

"I went to work," he says. Making use of the bulldozer, the backhoe, and the wash plant, he moved and washed gravel until he had collected a large amount of concentrates (pay dirt), which he placed in a 55-gallon oil drum. He remembers working sixteen hours a day.

Then everything in the camp froze solid, and snow began to fall. It snowed hard.

"I was in a metal cabin there at Willow Creek," Garrett says. "I had a Yukon stove in there and was gathering what was left of the diesel in the camp. I'd get up in the morning and turn the stove on— the diesel dripping into it—and I'd let it run until the place got warm. I had two tubs there, and I'd bust the ice out and put the ice to the side, and I started panning the concentrates. By the time I was finished, I had a one-pound coffee can almost full of extremely high-grade concentrates."

"I was running out of food," he continues. "I was down to my last can of green beans. I'd open both ends of the green beans and this frozen chunk of beans would fall out, and I'd heat it up and eat it. I was hungry. I was starving. I was freezing. The sun hadn't shone down in that valley for weeks. It was bitterly, miserably cold. One day I got up and thought: *This is the end.* I'm going to start walking out right now."

Garrett waded for four miles through snow that he describes as almost waist-high. "I was in my weakest state," he says, "and I was thinking—I'm not going to make it." Then, at a frequently used crossing along Peters Creek, he came across some snowmachine trails that he could walk on. "Once I was on that packed trail I knew that I was going to make it to the Forks Roadhouse." His relief was such that he found he could even appreciate the night. "It was real cold, but it was very beautiful—the moon and stars were out."

Dennis finally arrived at the old roadhouse that had been built by Belle McDonald so many decades earlier; just his sleeping bag and the heavy coffee can of gold concentrates were in his rucksack. The proprietors of the place "couldn't believe that anyone was still back on mining claims so late in the year," Garrett says. "I told them, 'Listen, I'm dying. Sell me some food and a room. I have gold to pay for it.' They weighed out my gold on a little scale behind the counter. I ate a bowl of something. I had been so poor all my life and was so disoriented that despite all of the gold I carried, I asked for the cheapest bunk they had."

The lowest-priced bunk was upstairs in the loft over the road-house, a large, open room full of cots that Dennis ended up having all to himself. This was undoubtedly the room where Bob Meade had spent his restless night of September 10, 1939, following his long and convoluted trek from Frank and Helen's Little Willow Creek camp. Dennis slept the exhausted sleep of other miners that had preceded him through the years.

Garrett says he ended up with a lot of gold that he squandered away in thirty days. "Tuxedos, parties, women, fancy hotels—what can I say? I was young. I'd been poor and hungry. And also, it seemed so easy to get. In the end I had five dollars in my pocket."

After the gold and fun ran out, Garrett did more research on the abandoned claims. He learned that mining interests previously connected to the property had filed an appeal with the BLM, contesting its decision to declare the claims abandoned; the appeal was pending. He learned that one faction had even been in the process of filing for a patented title to the property. These facts, combined with the maddening complexity of the pending transfer of the claims from the Federal Government to the State of Alaska held Garrett's attention. He suddenly found himself dealing with what he calls a "vertical learning curve."

But he was a player, he told himself. He had legally filed on the claims!

During 1986 and 1987 Garrett just performed maintenance on his claim stakes in the Dutch Hills. "Both the BLM and the State of Alaska wouldn't allow any mining until the property had been transferred from one agency to the other," he says. "It was a crazy time. It was difficult to determine just who held absolute jurisdiction, and whether federal or state mining regulations had a priority."

Garrett admits that by the end of the 1987 season he almost gave up. He couldn't mine, but he felt he needed to be on-site to protect his interests. By the end of the season he had spent a lot of time on the property with little to show for it. Was it worth it? he wondered.

That winter he resumed his research. This time he reviewed court databases and came across a lawsuit that had been filed by one of the mining factions connected to the claims. He noticed that it cited a reference to another case. "Each lawsuit led to another," he says he discovered, as he followed a trail of escalating contention over the ground. When he was finished, he had learned that two groups linked to the claims had been involved in a total of thirteen lawsuits over them. The full impact of what he was peripherally involved with hit home: he had staked into a virtual snake pit of mining dissension and intrigue!

A feud in the Dutch Hills.

During the winters, Garrett worked at various jobs to support himself. Stints in Anchorage as a barroom bouncer, maintenance man for a walk-in medical clinic, and janitor kept him going for a time. At one point he opened a detective agency that he called "The Company." (His business motto: "We can do it.") Later, he would invest in a bar, but eventually sold his interest in it to finance his mining endeavors. Another winter was spent as the manager of a trailer court.

In 1988, things looked up. Garrett managed to obtain a temporary permit to mine from the State of Alaska, and that season some miners approached him with a proposal to work some of the Willow Creek property. An agreement was reached, and the season was spent with preparations for mining. The focus was on equipment, which was located, repaired, modified, and hauled in to Willow Creek. It was a laborious, time-consuming effort, but everything was in place by fall.

"The banditos" showed up in 1989. When Garrett, now joined by his father, brother, and a friend he describes as his "girlfriend's first ex-husband," arrived at the claims in late spring, Dennis noticed that Willow Creek was muddy. While the others set up camp, one of the group investigated and found that people were dredging on the claims farther up the creek.

"Pretty soon," Dennis says, "here comes this simian-looking individual. He looks like his brother is the missing link. He comes thumping over in his pickup truck and says, 'What're you doin' here?'"

"We're here to mine our gold," Dennis responded.

"Who're you?" the man demanded.

"We're the guys who've owned these claims since 1985."

"You don't own these claims," the man insisted. "They're owned by a different company. We're working for them, and we're here to protect them."

The "companies" interested in the claims seemed endless, Garrett noted. Dennis dug through his duffel and pulled out his claim forms and related documents and showed them to the men. "They were scratching their heads and seemed ignorant about the papers," he says. "The biggest man quickly grew frustrated, and told his partner, 'We'll just have to bang some heads.'"

Dennis and his dad steeled themselves for a fight while the second man attempted to cool down the first. But when Dennis remarked that he was the rightful owner of the claims and there could be no resolution between them, the man's demeanor changed and he said, "Well, I guess I'll just have to bring our bulldozer down here and run it through your camp and knock all this stuff out."

The men argued some more before the two finally got in their truck and headed back up the creek.

As time passed and transients moved in and out of the area, Garrett says he learned that the two men had a reputation for "terrorizing" the mining district around Wiseman and Nolan Creek, far to the north. Garrett began to refer to them as *the banditos* in conversation.

Then an 86-year-old man showed up in an old truck, hauling a small trailer. When he told Dennis that he hoped to do a little dredging along Willow Creek, Garrett explained the status of the claims and told him to do whatever he liked. The old-timer set up his dredge and camp and settled in for a time, but at some point, someone chopped his dredge to pieces. The act set Dennis on edge. A few more verbal conflicts with the banditos raised the tension level.

Matters came to a head late one afternoon near the end of the mining season. Dennis says his small group had explored Gopher Gulch all that day, become lost in dense fog, and returned soaking wet to Little Willow Creek and their camp—the old, dilapidated shack thought to have once belonged to Frank and Helen Jenkins. Dennis went to work, chopping wood for a fire so that they could begin to dry their clothes.

Suddenly, he says, one of the banditos emerged from the brush with his rifle pointed directly at Dennis's stomach.

"Your permit's been revoked," the man said.

Dennis stared at the man's weapon and told him, "Fine, we're leaving."

Garrett's group packed up its gear, drove down the road to the state highway, and stopped at the Alaska State Troopers station. Dennis says he spent a long time writing out a seven-page statement that documented the provocations committed by the men that summer. In an exercised state now, Garrett told the troopers that he took the threat with the rifle very seriously and wasn't going to tolerate the intimidation. He would return alone to Little Willow Creek, he said, and if the men threatened him at his camp again, he would kill them. "You guys are so far away," he told the lawmen, "that this is all I can do."

The on-duty troopers conferred privately, Dennis says, and finally told Garrett he was within his rights. They decided to follow Dennis back to the Willow Creek area, doing so with their flak vests and shotguns. Nervous now, Garrett pointed out the group, and the troopers talked with the men, warning them that Garrett had testified he would kill them if they returned to his camp with firearms. Then they arrested the man who had pointed the rifle at Dennis.

Aside from these interruptions, Garrett and his associates had managed to put their equipment to work and make some progress. But the next year, 1990, BLM agents showed up and told them to leave. Until the property had been conveyed from federal to state government, they declared, no one could mine there. Dennis and his new partners protested by filing a suit against the agency, he says, but they moved off the property.

Miner Dennis Garrett's experiences and adventures in the Dutch Hills suggest he has been dealing with an eerie legacy. (courtesy Dennis Garrett)

Now Garrett researched the history of Gopher Gulch, high above the abandoned claims, and learned that it hadn't been mined since the 1930s. He even came across the agreement that Frank Jenkins had signed in 1933 with the Hatch brothers and Rice, and noted that the Gopher Gulch property had been Jenkins' first real start in the area. Other than Jenkins' documented activity at the gulch, only a long series of "Notice of Intent to Hold" declarations appeared, but even those eventually ceased.

Dennis and his fellow miners inspected what had once been Frank

Jenkins' "No. 1 and 2 Above Discovery" on Gopher Gulch. "It was confusing and frustrating," Dennis says. "It was so jumbled up, and the degree of thermal metamorphism had been so intense that you couldn't see any geologic structure. There were big chunks of angular quartz that I knew came from veins, and chunks of gold that were very angular and crystalline. I knew I was very near the source, but it was frustrating me because I couldn't find where the source was at."

But the men filed on the claims, and moved their equipment up the hillside. That summer, despite the lengthy and rigorous climb to the higher reaches, veteran Alaskan miners would periodically show up at their camp. Some said they were looking for "the potato patch." An old-timer from the Forty-Mile mining district appeared and said, "So, you're reopening the potato patch. Do you think it's worth it?"

Curious about the name attached to the site, Dennis began to ask how it had originated. Some told him it was said that nuggets were lying in neat rows there when a covering of moss was sluiced away. Another speculated that the nuggets found there had been "as big as potatoes," a theory Garrett laughs at. When he asked one visiting old-timer with a long, flowing beard why the site had been abandoned, the man replied, "It's because its cursed."

In the early 1990s Garrett and his partners made some progress at the potato patch but success was only sporadic, and the partners left. He remembers 1993, when his father and brother worked with him, as a particularly rough time. "We had harsh times. The screen wouldn't break up the clay. That clay really beat us up."

In 1994, Garrett says he was approached by a man he describes as "right out of central casting—a cross between Daniel Boone and Colonel Saunders." He was accompanied by two longtime friends who had spent their whole lives prospecting for the pay streak; the two had always dreamed of actually mining some day, and they now had money to invest in equipment. The four struck a deal and drew up an agreement. A backhoe, a couple of cat tractors, and a bigger wash plant were hauled up to the property, and the men set to work constructing settling ponds.

At some point "Daniel Boone" departed, and the two friends began to argue with each other. "We were actually starting to process placer ore," Dennis says, when the friendship fell apart and the venture ended.

Despite a drop in the price of gold in ensuing years, Garrett has persevered. The status of the abandoned claims remains complex and uncertain. Certain of these claims continue to be involved in litigation.

A legacy?

bibliography

BOOKS

Alaska Geographic, Volume 22, Number 4, *World War II in Alaska*, Alaska Geographic Society, Anchorage, 1995

Campbell, Nola. *Talkeetna Cronies*, 1974

Campbell, Nola. *Talkeetna Echoes*, 1984

Kari, James, and Fall, James. *Shem Pete's Alaska: the Territory of the Upper Cook Inlet Dena'ina*, Alaska Native Language Center, University of Alaska/Anchorage, 1987

Laurence, Jeanne. *My Life with Sydney Laurence*, Salisbury Press, Superior Publishing Co., Seattle, Washington, 1974

Whitehead, Don, *The FBI Story*, Random House, New York, 1956

NEWSPAPERS AND PERIODICALS

The Alaska Railroad Record

The Alaska Weekly

The Anchorage Daily Times

The Seattle Post-Intelligencer

GOVERNMENT SOURCES

Estate of F.W. Jenkins, Probate Case File, U.S. Probate Court for the Territory of Alaska, Third Division, Talkeetna Precinct, Case Numbers 1-45 1912-1939, Record Group 508, Alaska State Archives, Juneau, Alaska

United States of America vs F.W. Jenkins, U.S. Commissioner's Court for the Territory of Alaska, Third Division, Talkeetna Precinct, Criminal Case Files 1917-1931, Record Group 508, Alaska State Archives, Juneau, Alaska

R.A. Francis vs J.A. Wilkinson, Case File A-151, Civil Case Files, 1915-1960; U.S. District Court, District of Alaska, Third Judicial Division (Anchorage); Records of District Courts of the United States, Record Group 21; National Archives-Pacific Alaska Region, Anchorage, Alaska.

C.N. Hansen vs F.W. Jenkins and Raymond Jenkins, Co-partners, Case File A-719, Civil Case Files, 1915-1960; U.S. District Court, District of Alaska, Third Judicial Division (Anchorage); Records of District Courts of the United States, Record Group 21; National Archives-Pacific Alaska Region, Anchorage, Alaska.

United States of America vs F.W. Jenkins, Case File No. 1235, Criminal Case Files, 1902-1960; U.S. District Court, Third Judicial Division (Anchorage, Alaska); Records of District Courts of the United States, Record Group 21; National Archives-Pacific Alaska Region, Anchorage, Alaska

Frank Jenkins vs Dick Francis, Case File No. S-352, Civil, Criminal, and Bankruptcy Cases, 1911-1941, U.S. District Court, District of Alaska, Third Judicial Division (Seward, Alaska); Records of District Courts of the United States, Record Group 21; National Archives-Pacific Alaska Region, Anchorage, Alaska.

R.A. Francis vs F.W. Jenkins, Case File No. A-930, Civil Case Files, 1915-1960, U.S. District Court, District of Alaska, Third Judicial Division (Anchorage, Alaska); Records of District Courts of the United States, Record Group 21; National Archives-Pacific Alaska Region, Anchorage, Alaska.

Cache Creek Murder Investigation, FBI Freedom of Information and Privacy Acts Release, Federal Bureau of Investigation, U.S. Department of Justice, Washington, D.C.

Mining claim records, 1911-1947, Talkeetna Recording District Book Numbers 8-15; Alaska Department of Natural Resources, Palmer Recorder's Office, Palmer, Alaska.

OTHER SOURCES

Alaska Department of Natural Resources, Office of History and Archaeology, Anchorage, Alaska

Anchorage Municipal Loussac Library, The Alaska Collection, Anchorage, Alaska

Talkeetna Historical Society archives: U.S. Commissioner Affidavit for Search Warrant and Search Warrant, United States of America vs Belle Lee, December, 1922

Vital Statistics, Seattle-King County Department of Public Health, Seattle, Washington.

PERSONAL INTERVIEWS
June Berg
Phil Brandl
Maxine Brittell
Ernie Bull
Dan Cuddy
Dennis Garrett
Wes Harriman
Eleanor Trepte Martin
H. Willard Nagley II
Frank Sandstrom
Gale Weatherell
Ron Wendt

UNPUBLISHED SOURCES

Alaska Engineering Commission, "Report of the Resident Engineer," Ward Hall, 1916

Author unknown, miner's journal, 1935.

Brittell, Kenneth, letter to U.S. District Attorney Joseph Kehoe, November 3, 1939, Brittell collection

Kehoe, Joseph, U.S. District Attorney, letter to Kenneth Brittell, November 21, 1939, Brittell collection

Mayfield, Benjamin, U.S. Commissioner, letter to Kenneth Brittell, October 8, 1939, Brittell collection

Sandvik, Frances Weatherell, personal memoirs, Gale Weatherell collection

Wolfe, Dorothy, "Cache Creek Mines: Then and Now"; "Freighting in Early Day Supplies"; "Mining on the Old Stampede Grounds (as told to Dorothy Wolfe by Albert Stinson)", Talkeetna Historical Society archives, Talkeetna, Alaska

A lifelong Alaskan and longtime Talkeetna resident, Roberta Sheldon, shown here in the Dutch Hills, is the author of *The Heritage of Talkeetna*. She served for several years on the boards of Talkeetna's community council and historical society, and has been active on committees in many area land-use issues, including Talkeetna's comprehensive land plan. She and her husband, the late Don Sheldon, operated Talkeetna Air Service and raised three children in the village during the 1960s and 1970s.